Better Red

BETTER RED

The Writing and Resistance of Tillie Olsen and Meridel Le Sueur

CONSTANCE COINER

New York   Oxford
OXFORD UNIVERSITY PRESS
1995

OXFORD UNIVERSITY PRESS

Oxford   New York
Athens   Auckland   Bangkok   Bombay
Calcutta   Cape Town   Dar es Salaam   Delhi
Florence   Hong Kong   Istanbul   Karachi
Kuala Lumpur   Madras   Madrid   Melbourne
Mexico City   Nairobi   Paris   Singapore
Taipei   Tokyo   Toronto

and associated companies in
Berlin   Ibadan

Library of Congress Cataloging-in-Publication Data
Coiner, Constance.
Better red : the writing and resistance of Tillie Olsen
and Meridel Le Sueur / Constance Coiner.
p. cm.   Includes bibliographical references (p.) and index.
ISBN 0-19-505695-7
1. Olsen, Tillie—Political and social views.
2. Le Sueur, Meridel—Political and social views.
3. Working class writings, American —Women authors—History and criticism.
4. Communism and literature—United States—History—20th century.
5. Feminism and literature—United States—History—20th century.
6. Women and literature—United States—History—20th century.
7. Women authors, American—20th century—Biography.
8. Women communists—United States—Biography.
I. Title. PS3563.L82Z613   1995
813'.54—dc20   94-13045

1 3 5 7 9 8 6 4 2

Printed in the United States of America
on acid-free paper

For Virginia Coiner Classick and Mary Coiner

for Alexander Saxton—member of the Old Left, beloved teacher of the New

and, especially,
for Stephen Duarte and Ana Duarte-Coiner

PREFACE

In a dictionary of slogans and political usage, William Safire identifies the origin of "Better Red than Dead," a slogan of England's nuclear disarmament movement. He also explains the origin of the slogan's more widely known spinoff, "Better Dead than Red," popularized during the McCarthy period:

> English philosopher Bertrand Russell wrote in 1958 that if "no alternative remains except communist domination or the extinction of the human race, the former alternative is the lesser of the two evils." This was sloganized into 'Better Red than Dead' and became part of the 'Ban the Bomb' demonstrations. . . .
>
> An obvious turnaround was used by British author Stanley Reynolds in 1964, in a book urging an anticommunist crusade entitled *Better Dead Than Red*. This effectively sabotaged the slogan; after a while, most people did not know which slogan came first or who was for what. (34)

It's likely evident to most readers that my title expresses opposition to the virulent anticommunism suggested by a slogan such as "Better Dead than Red," an anticommunism that smeared progressive causes of any stripe with its "Stalinist" brush.

I hope it's also apparent that I intend "red" as a pun on "read." This is the first book-length study to explore Tillie Olsen's and Meridel Le Sueur's relationships to the American Communist Party, and their writing is more fully understood— better read—with some knowledge of those important, complex political and cultural ties. I also intend the title and subtitle to imply a third·meaning: In the context of this study, "resistance" means writing that subverts not only the dominant culture but also at times restrictive elements within a leftist subculture. In asserting the importance of their own concrete experiences as women, Tillie Olsen, Meridel Le Sueur, and other Party women struggled toward an engendered radicalism, a better Red.

With the collapse in 1989 of the Soviet Union and the Eastern Bloc, the

American media has embraced capitalism's global ascendancy and gleefully consigned Communism to history's dustbin. Historians of the American Left may have to work harder than ever to insist that the American Communist Party represented something far more complicated than the brutal authoritarianism of Stalin and post-Stalin regimes. On the other hand, because Cold War mythologies of Communist monolithism will now lose some of their currency in American culture, we may now find less resistance to the complicated legacy of the American Communist Party. Le Sueur and Olsen hold a special place in that complicated legacy.

Better Red began as a dissertation culminating an interdisciplinary (American literature, U.S. history) Ph.D. program at the University of California, Los Angeles. I'm grateful to David Peck for encouraging me in the fledgling stages of my interdisciplinary program. I'm indebted to my doctoral committee members—Daniel Howe, Robert Maniquis (Chair), Raymund Paredes, Karen Rowe, and Alexander Saxton—and to Carolyn Porter and John Carlos Rowe, who traveled from other University of California campuses to participate in evaluating my dissertation defense. Bob Maniquis, usually a demanding advisor, sympathized when I found my newborn more compelling than beginning a dissertation. "No book is more important than a child," he acknowledged, adding with a smirk, "unless, maybe, *Das Kapital*." My debt to Karen Rowe for her steadfast support, affection, and meticulous attention to detail throughout my graduate training is enormous. I hope the dedication adequately expresses my regard for Alexander Saxton, who in *The Great Midland* (1948), a working-class novel, created Stephanie Koviak, one of the strongest female characters in American literature. She got me started on the whole thing.

John Crawford, Meridel Le Sueur's editor and publisher at West End Press, commented on most of the dissertation, with especially close readings of the Le Sueur chapters. John's encouragement was especially important in the dissertation's early stages; through lively debates, often at the San Francisco Saloon in West Los Angeles, he alleviated the dread and isolation that seem common at the beginning of dissertations. Alexander Saxton and Trudy Saxton tested the dissertation against their own experiences in the Old Left. As readers and friends at the dissertation stage, Billy Smith and Jon Klancher belong in a special category; they provided editorial and emotional support, sometimes long-distance, often when facing their own pressing deadlines.

I'm deeply indebted to Paul Lauter, a pioneer in treating working-class writing as a legitimate category of literary analysis. A lifelong commitment to matters of concern to a number of progressive scholars, including issues *Better Red* addresses, has driven Paul to "educate, organize and agitate," to borrow one of Tillie Olsen's favorite slogans. I value Paul all the more because as a recipient of his encouragement I am only one of many he empowers and sustains.

And like many undertaking work concerning the literary Left in the United States, I've benefited richly from Alan Wald's scholarship, counsel, correspondence, and careful reading of the manuscript. Alan's scholarship, teaching, and activism constitute an unparalleled response to Tillie Olsen's caution to radicals (a caution to which my Introduction refers): "Don't let them take your history from you."

I'm grateful to Annette Rubinstein, A. B. Magil, Harriet Magil, and Dorothy Healey for responding to drafts of Chapters 1 and 2 and to Geoff Goshgarian for reading the entire manuscript. Deborah Rosenfelt, who has generously encouraged my work for years, read drafts of the Le Sueur chapters at the dissertation stage; shared tapes of her Tillie Olsen interview; and, as an editor of *Feminist Studies*, responded enthusiastically to my essay, "'No One's Private Ground': A Bakhtinian Reading of Tillie Olsen's *Tell Me A Riddle*," which now constitutes a portion of Chapter 7. As referees for *Feminist Studies*, Judith Kegan Gardiner, Paul Lauter, and an anonymous reader also commented valuably on the essay; Sidonie Smith responded thoughtfully to the essay, as well. As editors of *Left Politics and the Literary Profession* (Columbia University Press, 1990), Lennard J. Davis and M. Bella Mirabella commented helpfully on "Literature of Resistance: The Intersection of Feminism and the Communist Left in Meridel Le Sueur and Tillie Olsen," an essay that includes some material also contained in *Better Red*. Tillie Olsen, after reading an early draft of the portion of this study that addresses her life and literary texts, raised important questions and corrected inaccuracies, although any errors in fact or interpretation in *Better Red* are my responsibility.

Bill Bailey and other members of the Fort Point Gang helped me test some of *Better Red*'s working assumptions. Reeva Olson (Tillie Olsen's sister-in-law) and Nicole Sault were hospitable on my second trip to San Francisco to interview Olsen and some of her associates. Rachel Tilsen (one of Meridel Le Sueur's daughters) welcomed me into her home when I interviewed Le Sueur a second time in August 1989, and for years patiently fielded numerous questions by letter and phone. I also appreciate the gracious hospitality of Rick and Kay Bendel during my 1989 Twin Cities trip.

I've also profited, at different junctures over the years, from discussions with and encouragement from Barbara Abou-El-Haj, Rifaat Abou-El-Haj, Karen Alter Adams, David Brundage, Norah Chase, Julie Olsen Edwards, Marjorie Feld, Barbara Foley, Diana Hume George, Elaine Hedges, Karyn Hollis, Maurice Isserman, Katherine King, Mary Ellen Lennon, Daniel Manny Lund, Geraldine Moyle, Gary Nash, Trudy Palmer, Cheryl Pfoff, Mike Rose, Clare Spark, Nicole Stein, Peg Strobel, Chris Suggs, Linda Wagner-Martin, and Sandy Zickefoose. Lillian Robinson's scholarship and support have been important to this project, especially one lengthy handwritten letter of encouragement that remained a talisman. As a team and as individuals, Tom Dublin and Kitty Sklar have inspired, energized, counseled. Janet Zandy's special wisdom about our common work has been illuminating and comforting. My thanks to Liz Rosenberg for teaching me, under Binghamton's relentless cloud cover, the term for—and meaning of—horizontal light. And radical hats on to Billy Smith for over twenty years of fellow traveling.

The *Radical Teacher* editorial board, chaired by Susan O'Malley, has been an emotional and political home since I joined the board in 1979, but especially since 1989, when I began commuting from Binghamton to meetings in Middletown, Connecticut. My relationship to board members became especially important during the Gulf War, when Binghamton, like most of America, was bedecked with yellow ribbons. The board members' abiding commitment to progressive causes inside and outside the academy sustains me. I am also rejuvenated by their humor; the Left's peculiarities and inflexibilities are often the butt of their self-deprecating irony, which often rivals that of Jessica Mitford in *A Fine Old Conflict*.

I've been privileged to teach and learn from the serious, skilled, and vocal SUNY-Binghamton students, especially those who enrolled in "Multicultural Women Writers of the U.S." For research assistance and for what seemed like endless audio tape transcribing, I'm indebted to Diane Allen, Mary Bendel, Elizabeth Berliner, Judy Emerson, Marjorie Feld, Jennifer Glennon, Heather Gonzales, Sari Halper, Susan Lee, and—most especially—Amy Amoon. I also appreciate Roey Thorpe's compiling the index and proofreading. For assisting with photographs and other sources, I'm grateful to the staff at SUNY-Binghamton's Bartle Library Interlibrary Loan Department; Tom Carey of the San Francisco State University Labor Archives; Peter Filardo at the Tamiment Institute Library at New York University; Chris Focht; Jerome Liebling; Dallas Lindgren at the Minnesota Historical Society; Eugene Dennis Vrana, archivist/librarian at the International Longshoremen's and Warehousemen's Union; and especially Phiz Mezey, a champ in the eleventh hour. My thanks to Nora Roberts for helping Rachel Tilsen select the Le Sueur family photographs and for sharing her taped interviews of Annette Rubinstein and Myra Page. My warm-line to Lisa Fegley, SUNY-Binghamton's Word Perfect Wizard (and perhaps the University's most gifted teacher), took care of my word-processing anxiety and snafus. Gently, reassuringly, Lisa walked me through correcting any problem I encountered, sometimes even after business hours and on weekends.

My greatest debt in completing *Better Red* is to David Bartine, a colleague in SUNY-Binghamton's English Department who read every draft and for years provided unflagging support. David's loyalty to this project can be explained as much by his memories of the couple who raised him—his grandparents, "ordinary" working people of Olsen and Le Sueur's generation—as by our shared interest in canon reform and pragmatic reading theory.

I am deeply grateful for the essential financial support I received while writing my dissertation and manuscript, and I look forward to the day when I can contribute at least a widow's mite to the organizations that helped me. A Woodrow Wilson Foundation Charlotte W. Newcombe Fellowship, an American Association of University Women Fellowship, a UCLA Alumni Association Distinguished Scholar Award, and a Jean Nidetch dissertation fellowship supported work on my dissertation. I would like to thank the UCLA Center for the Study of Women, and especially Ruth Bloch and Anne Mellor, for awarding my dissertation the Center's first Mary Wollstonecraft Prize, funded by Barbara ("Penny") Kanner. An American Council of Learned Societies Research Fellowship for Recent Recipients of the Ph.D., a Dean's Research Semester Grant, a United University Professions Nuala McGann Drescher Affirmative Action Leave, a SUNY-Binghamton Summer Research Grant, and a United University Professions New Faculty Award provided financial support for completing the book manuscript. In applying for these grants, I have appreciated the ongoing support for my work from the administrations of my Department and University, especially from Bernard Rosenthal, Alvin Vos, and Dean Sharon Brehm. And over the years I've enjoyed the friendly help of administrators and office staff, including Mary Earl, Allan Eller, Carol Fischler, Gene Flood, Deanna France, Anne McCarthy, Arlene Nowalk, Peg Petcosky, Chris Storrs, Joseph Walker, and Barbara Walling.

I would like to thank the editors and other staff members associated with *Better Red* at Oxford University Press—William Sisler (formerly at Oxford), Elizabeth Maguire, Elda Rotor, Beth Hanlon, Rosemary Wellner, Ellen Fuchs, and Mike Groseth.

I've been sustained by the love and loyalty of my sisters and nieces and nephews. In countless practical and immeasurable emotional ways, Virginia Coiner Classick and Mary Coiner have been my chief advocates. And I'm indebted to my mother, who, like Eva in Olsen's "Tell Me a Riddle," experienced many 18-hour days, performing domestic tasks with the "ingenuity of poverty." Small wonder that she once missed a connecting flight from Los Angeles to Washington, D.C. because she was engrossed in Olsen's story. She read to me many hours, sang lullabies and hymns—I can still hear her quiet but expressive voice—and, because buying books was out of the question, encouraged multiple trips to the Maplewood Public Library.

When I was a graduate student and my daughter, Ana, was a newborn, I received a note from Tillie Olsen on one of those scraps of paper that are her trademark: "Thieve all the time you can for Ana" was all it said, but I hung on to that scrap of permission to love my child while working my way into a profession that is often incompatible with the needs of children and parents. I feel a special sense of gratitude toward those who cared for Ana during the hours I devoted to *Better Red*: Barbara Snyder, a virtuoso among child-care providers, for whom I stubbornly searched for over a year; the extraordinary staff at the Hill an' Dale Family Learning Center in Santa Monica, California; Virginia, John, and Anne Classick; magical Andrea Spolidoro ("Godspeople"), John Marshall, Nicole Sault, Kevin Fitzsimmons, and Enia Vidaurre. Ana has tried, at various points, to get into the spirit of this project, once by naming a new Barbie doll Dorothy Healey. Ana, I'll send a message into your future in your own voice, with your own current favorite expression: "You go, girl."

My greatest personal debt is to Stephen Duarte, who takes for granted—without my organizing, educating, and agitating—that participating equally in domestic labor is his obligation; more important, he also assumes that participating equally in child care is not only a father's obligation but his right. Born into the working class, the grandson of immigrants, Stephen is impatient with much in academia. When I asked him why he seemed instantly comfortable with Olsen, whom he met when we visited her at the MacDowell Colony, he reflected, " I think it was her hands. They were so familiar to me. Those are the hands I grew up with—workers' hands, the hands of my father, uncles, grandparents."

And, finally, I want to thank Tillie Olsen and Meridel Le Sueur for their permission to quote from the taped interviews and, in Le Sueur's case, from her unpublished journals; for their warmth, inspiration, and humor when we met; and, above all, for their legacy of courageous resistance.

Binghamton, New York   C. C.
May 1994

CONTENTS

Better Red

"You ain't been doin' nothin' if you ain't been called a Red."
Eliot Kenin, 1983[1]

Introduction

I was never a little lady—and never wanted to be a lady—wanted to be a woman and a Mensch in Rosa Luxemburg's terms.

Josephine Herbst: The Story She Could Never Tell

In late April 1975, as Lillian Robinson reports in a review essay titled "The Vietnam Syndrome," Tillie Olsen read *Tell Me a Riddle* at the State University of New York at Buffalo. As she and Robinson headed over to the reception after the reading, someone ran up to tell Robinson that the United States had begun the final evacuation of Saigon, and she passed the news on to Olsen. "A few minutes later, when we were gathered around her with our hors d'oeuvres and drinks," Robinson continues, "she [Olsen] made the announcement. 'You did this,' she added portentously to the group of students and young faculty, the kind of people who embodied the antiwar movement. 'You must never forget that you did this. You must not let them take your history from you, the way they did with my generation, the generation of the thirties'" (60). Meridel Le Sueur's life and work has embodied the same declaration—"You must not let them take your history from you"—to the working class and unemployed, especially women. In the afterword to *The Girl*, for example, Le Sueur describes the novel as a "memorial" to working-class women of the Depression whose voices she wanted to preserve and says the novel "was really written by them." This study, a response to Olsen and Le Sueur's cautionary declaration, contributes to a retrieving and revisioning of the '30s American Left[1] as well as to efforts to promote working-class writing as a legitimate category of literary analysis.[2]

This book examines two American working-class writers, Meridel Le Sueur (1900–) and Tillie Olsen (1912 or 1913–), in a contemporary context, addressing the complex intersection of feminism and the political Left as refracted in their lives and literary texts. This interdisciplinary study resides simultaneously in the provinces of history, literary theory, practical criticism, feminist theory, lan-

3

guage theory, and reading theory and requires that I employ tools from each of these intersecting areas of investigation.

Le Sueur and Olsen's lives and literary texts span two generations of radical women, those affiliated with the Old Left and those who came of age with the New Left and feminism's "second wave." One of the salient features of the 1930s was the failure of any leftist organization to consider developing women's militancy into a self-conscious feminism, yet in more or less covert ways, Le Sueur and Olsen's writing from the late '20s and '30s anticipates the concerns of feminists a generation later. We see in their texts a prescient if latent consciousness, a "knowledge, however unborn."[3]

But when '30s leftist critics mined literature for its "revolutionary social content," their critical apparatus sometimes did not allow for the complicated mediation of social reality operating within these texts. I am not carping anachronistically that these critics should have known better. They were limited partly because many major theoretical texts were not yet translated, including many of Marx's works on ideology; M. M. Bakhtin's and V. N. Volosinov's language and literary theory; the debates on Marxist aesthetics among Georg Lukacs, Walter Benjamin, and Bertolt Brecht; and Antonio Gramsci's pathbreaking work on hegemony, undertaken in a Fascist prison between 1927 and 1935. Moreover, since the '60s we have seen a proliferation of theory, including feminist theory, that was, of course, unavailable to '30s Marxists. Thus evaluations of Le Sueur and Olsen's work need to be modified.

The misperception of what Le Sueur and Olsen's texts have recorded has been further perpetuated by the generic label within which they were confined during the '30s. Their writing was identified as "proletarian," a term generally reserved for working-class discourse produced during the Depression decade. Le Sueur and Olsen's writing is "working class," but not in the limited and isolated sense conveyed by the label "proletarian literature." In a letter in which '30s novelist Josephine Herbst declined to contribute an essay to David Madden's *Proletarian Writers of the Thirties* (1968), she commented that her work "has been considerably damaged by the category ['proletarian'], and that the term since the Second World War has been used more as blackmail than as a definitive term with any valid meaning" (cited in Madden xv). Paul Lauter's more current and expansive conception of "working-class literature" better characterizes Le Sueur and Olsen's work. Lauter has identified "working-class literature" as texts by *and* about working people, at points coinciding with other literary categories (literature by women and people of color, for example, may also qualify as that of the working class). Lauter designates as members of the working class "those who sell their labor for wages"; have "relatively little control over the nature or products of their work"; and are not professionals or managers. He includes not only factory workers but also slaves, farm laborers, and those who work in the home ("Working-Class" 110).[4]

Although many '30s intellectuals mistakenly subordinated all social issues to those of class, at this historical juncture class is not a fashionable category of analysis among literary scholars, including feminists. Despite its place on the now-familiar list of race, gender, class, ethnicity, and sexual orientation, class is often the least addressed of these issues. There may be several explanations for this more specific than the nature of American academic liberalism. One may be that few people of working-class origin make it into the ranks of the professoriat, so few people with an "insider's" sensitivity to this issue are undertaking scholarship and shaping curricula.[5] Another explanation may be that many faculty and students have imbibed, at least to a certain degree, the myth of classlessness in the United States. Dispelling that myth is complicated by the fact that class origin—like sexual orientation but unlike race, gender, and some forms of ethnicity—is not always apparent, remaining hidden unless it is disclosed. While many university students of color proudly identify themselves with their particular cultural groups, few students of working-class origin readily announce—or, in some cases, even recognize—themselves as such.

This lack of class identification among working-class students provides a third explanation for the diminished status of class as a category of analysis among literary scholars. While many students rightly exert pressure on literature departments to consider gender, race, and sexual orientation as interpretive categories and to include texts by women, people of color, and gays and lesbians in college courses, few protest exclusions based on class. Indeed, few students seem even to *see* class markers, typically identifying Rita Mae Brown's *Rubyfruit Jungle* (1973), for example, as a "lesbian," but not as also a "working-class" novel; Sandra Cisneros's *Woman Hollering Creek* (1991) as both "Chicana literature" and "women's literature" but not as, additionally, a "working-class" text; Ann Petry's *The Street* (1946) as both "African-American literature" and "women's literature" but not as a "working-class" novel as well.

Therefore, by employing the term "working-class writing," I am attempting to foreground—but not privilege—the category of class and class consciousness in Le Sueur and Olsen, although other terms, such as Paula Rabinowitz's use of "revolutionary" and Deborah Rosenfelt's use of "socialist feminist," also effectively characterize their writing.[6] Le Sueur's and Olsen's writing, of course, cannot be reduced to a single category. As Rabinowitz has ably demonstrated, "Red" women's writing of the '30s "narrates class as a fundamentally gendered construct and gender as a fundamentally classed one" (*Labor* 8). Radical women's working-class writing should be viewed not as confined by a single class, party, gender, race, or cause, but as something undertaken within a kaleidoscopic social field.

In examining Le Sueur's and Olsen's texts, I proceed from the premise that what many critics might find to be moments of textual "inferiority" or "weakness" may be historically resonant, sometimes suggesting more about a given historical period than those moments that formalist critics might consider evidence of aesthetic excellence. A piece of working-class writing, as any form of discourse, displays conflicting and contradictory meanings. Pierre Macherey has observed that the "necessity" of a "writer's work" is founded on the multiplicity of its meanings. Discussing the conflict inherent in multiple meanings, Macherey argues that critics must not balk at the prospect of revealing "imperfection" in a text as long as that word is "not taken in a negative and pejorative sense" (78–79).

The purpose of identifying "imperfections" in the work of Le Sueur and Olsen is, then, not to point to errors they should have recognized and corrected. I work with the principle that history precedes form, and tears in the textual fabric indicate pressure that historical content brings to bear on form. Such points in Le Sueur's and Olsen's texts illuminate complex webs of historical forces at work in the 1930s. I also recognize the limited political utility of what I term "compensatory criticism," which ignores or glosses over weaknesses and contradictions in writing by women, people of color, and members of the working class as a way partly to compensate for its exclusion. Our task is not simply to promote, but to understand the undervalued. Failing to engage the problems of working-class writing leads us away from its historical complexity.

The critic's task, I believe, is not to repair or complete the text but to identify the *principle* of its silences, flaws, conflicted meanings, as Eagleton, discussing Macherey, indicates (*Marxism* 35). In Le Sueur's and Olsen's '30s writing, this principle lies partly in these writers' complex responses to the sexism of the American Communist Party (CPUSA), an organization to which they were deeply committed. For many on the Communist Left, "proletarian" and "manly" were nearly synonymous; the worker-protagonist in proletarian writing "almost by definition was male"; and "proletarian prose and criticism tended to flex their muscles with a particularly masculinist pride" (Rosenfelt, "Thirties" 395). The androcentrism of Communist literary policy reflected the androcentrism of the CP as a whole and that of the larger society. Party organizing during the early '30s, for example, focused on the workplace, when only about 20 percent of women worked outside the home, and throughout the decade Party union activity centered on the mining, steel, maritime, and auto industries, in which few women were employed. The Party at least tacitly endorsed the traditional sexual division of labor, and domestic issues, when they counted at all, were not a priority.

Le Sueur and Olsen were at once loyal CP members and emerging feminists, and their work refracts that tension, variously straining toward and away from Party tenets and attitudes. Their texts address the physiological and sexual experiences that shape women's lives—sexual initiation, pregnancy, childbirth, miscarriage, sterilization, battery, rape—at a time when these topics seldom appeared in literature, including working-class writing. Despite some Party critics' dislike of literary texts they considered introspective, self-indulgent, privatized, and bourgeois, Le Sueur and Olsen made emotional deformation, familial relations, and the developing consciousness of children the central subjects of their writing. At points their texts burst their own formal and political limitations, momentarily overcoming the restraints of the very revolutionary organization that fostered them.

Because Le Sueur and Olsen consciously and unconsciously subvert not only bourgeois but also orthodox Marxist literary categories, in the context of this study "resistance" means writing that opposes not only the dominant culture but also at times restrictive elements within a leftist subculture. In other words, by producing working-class discourse, these two writers challenge the bourgeois assumptions—often masked as classless and universal—of much canonical literature; and by creating working-class *women's* writing, they problematize the patriarchal nature of the Left and the masculinist assumptions of much proletarian literature.

Since this study applies elements of feminist criticism, I should locate my position within that now broad and richly varied field of investigation. This book, committed as much to historic and economic concerns as to gender relations, lies within the province of materialist-feminism, opposing the flight from history evident in much literary theory, including much feminist criticism. Eagleton rightly identifies "the *extremism*" of much literary theory as "its obstinate, perverse, endlessly resourceful refusal to countenance social and historical realities," even though "'extremism' is a term more commonly used" to dismiss those who "call attention to literature's role in actual life" (*Literary* 196).

In taking up issues of class in this book, I implicitly question, with other materialist-feminists, how we can constitute women as a distinct literary or cultural category without minimizing important differences among women in race, class, and cultural experience. As the splits along economic and cultural lines in the American women's movement have demonstrated, we need to understand and respect diversity. Rather than defeating sexism, a romantic, monolithic vision of a universally shared female nature or experience will "blind us to our varied and immediate needs and to the specific struggles we must coordinate in order to meet them" (Jones 371).

Moreover, I reject any categorical opposition between male domination and female virtue, subscribing instead to Julia Kristeva's view that "'woman' . . . represents not so much a sex as an attitude" of resistance to conventional culture and language; men, too, can oppose phallogocentrism (quoted by Jones 363). So long as male privilege is treated as a ubiquitous, undifferentiated force unmediated by factors such as class origin and political consciousness, our challenge to it will be blunted and strategies for resistance—and for alliance—difficult to devise. These mystifications about "feminine" and "masculine" are dispelled, however, when critics ground their work in history, examining the particular circumstances of a given text's production. And, finally, I have intended my approach to be dialectical—embracing contradictions and locating "in the same situation," as Newton and Rosenfelt have put it, both "the forces of oppression and the seeds of resistance" (xxii).[7]

I recognize that the feminist views I embrace must be exercised carefully in discussing the Communist Party's assessment of "the woman question." To that end I have tried to adopt a double consciousness that guards against imposing anachronistic, "hindsight" standards but nevertheless confronts the Party's limitations regarding women's issues and literary theory. Through this double vision I analyze, on one hand, the CP's position on issues raised by the "second wave" of feminism and, on the other hand, take into account how '30s Party women perceived the issues then and how these women *actually functioned* within the movement. Annette Rubinstein rightly cautions socialist-feminists of my generation about the dangers of ahistoricity and "hindsight" vision concerning the '30s and feminist issues:

> It is apparently very difficult for anyone who did not live through it to realize the emergency atmosphere of the early '30s and to understand how irrelevant, almost

impertinent, other issues seem when one is literally fighting hunger and homelessness for oneself and one's family. When the lifeboat is swamped, the only relevant
question about your partner is whether he or she can and will go on bailing. It is
absurd to ask whether he promises to wash half the dishes when you get back to dry
land.[8]

My attempt to "see double" has been supported by interviews of women active in
the Party during the '30s, including Le Sueur, Olsen, Reeva Olson, Angela Ward,
Dorothy Healey, Lucy Kendall, Ruth Maguire, Edna Whitehouse, Annette Rubinstein, Myra Page, and Harriet Magil;[9] publications such as *The Working
Woman* and *Woman Today*, in which the evident Party line does not obliterate
working women's voices; and testimonies of women activists in documentaries
such as *Union Maids*, *With Babies and Banners*, and *Seeing Red*.

I have also tried in this study to appreciate the Old Left's gut feeling about
Party life, which one member described to me as analogous to "a Christian mystery": in the case of many members, it hinged on faith. Peggy Dennis, widow of
former Party leader Eugene Dennis and herself an active member for 50 years,
speaks of that faith as a "lifetime commitment of Self not to oneself but to a collective activism governed and controlled by a structured organization that
commanded total allegiance" ("A Response" 454). One need not subscribe to such
"total allegiance" to appreciate its significance in the American radical tradition.

As I have already begun to suggest, work of current concern in literary theory,
practical criticism, language theory, and reading theory provides some useful tools
for exploring Le Sueur's and Olsen's writing. Some feminist literary theory has
taken the lead in exposing ways in which the dominant culture's modes of discourse move to silence the voices of women and other marginalized groups. Multiple forms of "indirection" and modes of "incorrectness" have drawn the attention
of theorists examining the discourse of resistance. As Mary Jacobus has noted, "the
culturally imposed or assumed 'lapses' of women's writing are turned against the
system that brings them into being—a system women writers necessarily inhabit"
("Question" 43). Many of the "flaws" or "lapses" in the work of Le Sueur and Olsen
display moments of resistance in which these writers turn against "the system."

Categorical boundaries, including those dividing genres and academic disciplines, have long been under scrutiny in feminist theory. In "History as Usual?:
Feminism and the 'New Historicism,'" Judith Newton has suggested for academics
an enlarged collectivity: "I can see it now—a materialist feminist literary/historical
critic working with a 'New Women Historian' and, in a brave move beyond the
dyadic bond, with a cultural materialist too, and perhaps with others as well"
(120). In "Literature as Women's History" Nancy Armstrong similarly attacks disci-
plinary boundaries and outlines "an antidisciplinary notion of culture." I intend
my study of Le Sueur and Olsen to support such efforts toward multidisciplinary
and collective scholarship. The hierarchies Armstrong seeks to overturn, those
"that subordinate fiction to history, intellectual labor to productive labor, and
female knowledge to that of the male" (367, 357), strikingly resemble those of the
'30s. Armstrong also climbs the formidable barricade separating "literary" and
"nonliterary" discourse. As I have indicated, more than one version of this sacro-

sanct boundary is pertinent to the perception of Le Sueur's and Olsen's work: canonical literature versus proletarian writing; male canonical literature versus women's writing; belles-lettres versus reportage; and manly proletarian literature versus writing about working-class women's experiences. In showing ways in which Le Sueur's and Olsen's work challenges such boundaries, my aim is not to elevate their texts to canonical status; rather it is—like the aim of Le Sueur, Olsen, Newton, Armstrong, and others—to problematize such boundaries.

However, as some recent work has indicated, if we are to promote reading strategies such as those suggested by Jacobus, and challenge traditional boundaries as Newton and Armstrong would have us do, we must carefully examine and rework longstanding cultural assumptions about what it means "to read." Armstrong expresses this concern in a reference to figurational reading of some "nonliterary" texts by women. She notes that these texts must be

> read with all the attention to technical detail that a literary text alone has formerly deserved. The point is not simply to identify the figurative behavior of nonliterary materials, but rather to explain the demonstrable political force of writing in all of its manifestations—the metaphors and metonymies that organize at once the object world regulated by the state and the subject's state of mind. (356)

As Armstrong recognizes, reading methods that reserve complex analysis, such as figurational scrutiny, for "literary" texts blind readers to many of the rhetorical and cultural complexities marking much "nonliterary" discourse.

In "Toward a Feminist Theory of Reading" Patrocinio P. Schweickart has noted the promoting of a similar blindness in what she terms the "utopian" impulses in reading theory, by which she means the attention on the (variously problematized) relationship between text and reader to the exclusion of considering the text's and reader's historical situations. Such bracketing has produced many reading theories that overlook "issues of race, class, and sex, and give no hint of the conflicts, sufferings and passions that attend these realities" (35). Reading theory's movement away from utopian disregard for gender issues, for example, would include consideration of how gender is inscribed in texts and the roles played by the reader's gender in the reading process. Recognizing that "literature acts on the world by acting on its readers," Schweickart calls for reading theory and pedagogy that generate active readers who will scrutinize a text for "the nature of the choices proffered by the text and, equally important, what the text precludes" (39, 50). Schweickart argues that dialogue between feminist theory and reader-response theory provides the best possibilities for replacing utopian theory. I would add that materialist-feminism—which, as I have said, counters the flight from history—is crucial to that dialogue.

David Bartine has traced the 250-year history of a dominant utopianism (what he calls "romantic reading theory") in American education and culture and the long-eclipsed "pragmatic" alternatives to romantic theory. Bartine argues that attempts to dismantle cultural myths and canons provide an "incomplete solution to the problem without reconstructing, according to a radically different plan, the reading activity and the reader" (*Reading, Criticism* 55). Using Jacobus's "The Question of Language: Men of Maxims and *The Mill on the Floss*" as one prominent model, Bartine, like Armstrong, argues for employing reading methods such as complex figurational analysis in a multiplicity of "literary" and "nonliterary" texts, and he believes that the rudiments of such analysis can be introduced to students at an early age and systematically developed throughout their education. Armstrong, Schweickart, and Bartine recognize the need to reteach readers to see what they have been systematically taught to overlook.

The desire to legitimate multiple silenced voices links some feminist theory and reading theory with M. M. Bakhtin's and V. N. Volosinov's theories of discourse.[10] Bakhtin's concept of "heteroglossia"—a "multiplicity of social voices and a wide variety of their links and interrelationships" (*Dialogic* 263), a concept closely related to Macherey's interest in the multiplicity and conflict of meanings—will provide one tool for examining the work of Le Sueur and Olsen, much of which is heteroglossic. Of course, Le Sueur and Olsen are not the only writers to experiment with heteroglossia. Many others have experimented with versions of the multivocality Bakhtin has identified as characteristic of the novel's form. I am interested here in the ways in which Le Sueur's and Olsen's formal explorations derived from their desire to dismantle traditional views of bourgeois individualism and move toward collective social change.

A second tool I draw from Bakhtin and Volosinov is their concept of the "dialogic" nature of all discourse. Volosinov finds that all "verbal performance in print" engages in "ideological colloquy of large scale: it responds to something, objects to something, affirms something, anticipates possible responses and objections, seeks support, and so on" (*Marxism* 95). Heteroglossia and the dialogic provide critical lenses for viewing the resistance embodied in Le Sueur's and Olsen's texts. In my readings of their work, I will employ some methods that may aid in the large task of displaying ways of seeing/reading what people have been trained to ignore.

Moreover, Bakhtin and Volosinov's version of pragmatics provides several additional tools that have aided my reading of the texts explored here. Volosinov suggests "little behavioral genres" as subdivisions of heteroglossia and discourse's dialogic structure. Examples of "rhetorical" or "little behavioral genres" include "the full-fledged question, exclamation, command, request" (*Marxism* 96).[11] Some of these rhetorical genres have been contemplated extensively within speech-act theory. In addition to traditional thematic, character, and image analysis, I will draw on a few insights of speech-act analysis to examine structures of commands, urgings, and pleas as those structures contribute to the dialogic character of Le Sueur's and Olsen's discourse of resistance.

Like any critical study, my discussion contains many reading techniques, but I want to point to one set I believe particularly appropriate to the previously mentioned calls for retraining readers. Many texts by Le Sueur and Olsen implicitly reject passive/receptive reading—the kind of reading so often promoted in training readers to "appreciate literature"—and invite, if not demand, active reading alert to multivocality. Many tools and forms of reading besides those I employ can meet such demands, but I want to call attention to the readings interspersed in Chapters 3 through 7 in which I examine relationships among specific speech acts (e.g., questions, commands), figurational structures, and heteroglossic effects. Some of the basic tools employed (extended command, request, affirmation structures, antithesis, metaphor, etc.) could be introduced early in children's reading and systematically built upon throughout reading education. However, it is important that they be introduced as rhetorical tools for readers to decipher the "cultural work"[12] done by texts rather than as some of them are now treated in reading instruction, as solely "aesthetic" devices peculiar to the realm of literature. Years of practice with the rhetorical as well as aesthetic effects of these structures would cultivate readers less likely to lapse into receptive passivity.

I will have much to say about Le Sueur's and Olsen's attempts to disrupt passive reading and draw readers into active collaboration. Stylistic experiments to draw readers into collaboration are, of course, as old as the activities of reading and writing for readers—such experiments probably date from the writer who first consciously used ellipsis for the purpose of forcing a reader to fill in the gap. Many of those experiments have arisen from a recognition, at least as old as Plato's *Phaedrus* (with its own experiments with disrupting passive reading), that reading tends to be a privatized, individual—rather than communal—activity. J. Paul Hunter comments on one genre, the novel, in relation to reading's solitariness. Hunter, who is aware that Bakhtinian theory struggles against the phenomenon he describes,[13] is concerned with ways in which the reading process and the central subject of the modern novel "seem to have a common meeting ground in their attention to isolation. . . . the act of reading a novel is, like the act of contemplating one's own consciousness, an anti-social (or at least asocial) act—very different from the sociality involved in hearing a story or attending the performance of a play" (42). It is certainly the case that many writers, for a variety of political and aesthetic reasons, have exploited the individualistic tendencies of the act of reading, while other writers—again, for a variety of political and aesthetic reasons—have attempted to disrupt this isolation. As I said about Le Sueur's and Olsen's uses of heteroglossia, I am concerned with their formal experiments as they attempt to subvert traditional notions of bourgeois individualism and promote collective social change.

While some reading theorists have called for crossing boundaries between "literary" and "nonliterary" texts, historian Joan Scott has transgressed traditional boundaries between history and literary theory. She argues that historians should borrow tools from poststructuralist thought about language theory. While not abandoning attention to structures and institutions, this interdisciplinary method "suggests a study of processes, not of origins, of multiple rather than single causes, of rhetoric or discourse" (*Gender* 4). Scott argues that history and literature are both "forms of knowledge, whether we take them as disciplines or as bodies of cultural information" (*Gender* 8). While I am aware of differences among various forms of historical evidence, I proceed from a similar assumption—that an examination of Le Sueur's and Olsen's "literary" texts provides a wedge into history, "an image, a unique and privileged glimpse" (Macherey 113) of the Communist Left not otherwise available to us.

I have not attempted an exhaustive study of the Party and "the woman question" during the '30s or of the literary Left during that period. Readers acquainted with the Left's literary history will find much that is familiar in Chapter 1. Al-

though Chapters 1 and 2 provide historical information as background for the remaining chapters, this study, which focuses largely on the lives and literary texts
of two writers, is necessarily circumscribed as a contribution to Party history. Even
so, this book is in some senses allied with the new social history that has sought to
augment institutional histories of the CP by focusing on its rank-and-file members and on factors such as race, ethnicity, and local circumstances.[14] Some of
this new social history was the subject of Theodore Draper's by now well-known
attack in *The New York Review of Books*. According to Draper, out of a post-New
Left nostalgia for a radical past, these "new historians" use their "bottom-up" find-
ings to distort evidence of the CPUSA's puppet-like response to Comintern
directives. "Social history that neglects leaders is like the proverbial *Hamlet* without the Prince," says Draper (46, 47).

Although I do not ignore Soviet influence or the dicta of the CPUSA leadership, "I am not Prince Hamlet, nor was meant to be," as J. Alfred Prufrock put it.
Because so few women were Party leaders, we cannot learn how women maneuvered within the Communist movement by taking the elevator to Party
headquarters on the ninth floor, despite Draper's concern that new social history
gets us stuck in the basement. That the CP's leadership was overwhelmingly male
and that its bureaucracy functioned undemocratically "from the top down" is a
matter of record, but the Party was not a monolith. Democratic centralism notwithstanding, the views and daily experience of rank-and-file women often varied
from those of male Party bureaucrats, as Olsen and Le Sueur insist.

David Montgomery reminds us that one central task of historical analysis is
"to trace the interaction between the ways people have lived and the ways they
have thought—between social being and social consciousness" (497). The literary
texts of Le Sueur and Olsen, as well as their lived experience as activist women,
will tell us at least as much about their political/social views—and, by extension,
that of other Party women—as would Party directives. Although Le Sueur's and
Olsen's texts do not refer explicitly to Party policies on literature and on the
"woman question," they enrich and complicate our understanding of women's experience within the Party.

This study is partly oral history, and my richest sources have been the writers
themselves, whom I interviewed extensively. I indicate use of material taken from
my interviews by a parenthetical "interview" in the text itself; I indicate use of material taken from interviews others conducted by the name of the interviewer
followed by "interview," also inserted parenthetically into the text. Entries in the
Works Cited pages, under the interviewee's name, supply date and place of interview. Since I cite portions of the experiences Le Sueur and Olsen (and other
interviewees) report, and analyze the two writers' experiences as refracted in their
literary works, I should comment on my view of "experience" as "evidence." Although I value reported experience in the study I have undertaken, Scott has
usefully raised questions about historians' tendencies to treat "experience" unprob-
lematically as the "bedrock" of evidence for building an historical case. Because
subjects and their experiences are constituted discursively, Scott argues for recog-

nizing the inseparability of "experience" and language and for examining the "conflicts among discursive systems, contradictions within any one of them," and the "multiple meanings possible for the concepts they deploy" ("Experience" 34).

Scott's emphasis on the collective, multivalent, discursive character of experience is in keeping with concerns of Le Sueur and Olsen—and of Bakhtin and Volosinov, on whom, as I have indicated, I rely heavily for analysis of their texts. Where I use interview and biographical material in this study (especially that which involves my main subjects, Le Sueur and Olsen), I do not offer it as the most authentic kind of truth, and I urge readers to consider that material not in isolation, but in relation to other voices, including each writer's *own* complicating multiple voices (e.g., Le Sueur's journal entries) and those rendered in their literary texts.[15] Together, the rendered and the "real" voices speak the "experience" of oppressed people in ways that historical analysis or literary analysis, as separable interpretive categories, have not equipped us to hear.

Writing about living subjects, especially those with whom one feels political and personal solidarity, is a touchy, even painful, business. Attempting to be at once sensitive and critical, I resemble a character in Joanna Russ's *The Female Man* who thinks of herself as standing in a puddle of water, holding two alternating electrical currents (138).[16] Many in the women's movement have made archetypes of Le Sueur and Olsen, who have become emblematic figures as much as historical ones, and yet I have more patience now than I did at the beginning of this project with interviews that tend to be honorific rather than penetrating. "Many people find their way to the *general* through the *personal*," Trotsky observed, and his following comment about biographies applies to the biographical and interview material included in this book: " . . . biographies have their right. And, that being so, better they should be written without great distortions (small ones are quite unavoidable)."[17] I beg my subjects' forbearance while claiming that their rightful place is in history, not myth.

I have organized this book as follows. Chapter 1 outlines the major debates of the '30s literary Left and defines proletarian realism and reportage, related genres that the CP promoted between 1930 and 1935. Chapter 2 sketches the Party's positions on "women's issues" during the Depression decade. These chapters draw attention to an important gap in American literary and social history. Scholarship on the history of Party women and Red women writers is still relatively sparse, although some valuable work has been undertaken.[18]

Chapter 3 sketches Le Sueur's biography and focuses on Le Sueur's "Women on the Breadlines" (1932) and "I Was Marching" (1934), which number among the best-known pieces of '30s reportage (and I briefly discuss "Evening in a Lumber Town," a lesser-known piece of Le Sueur's reportage published in 1926). Chapter 3 also addresses Le Sueur's position, first publicly expressed in "The Fetish of Being Outside" (1935), on how radicals create a literature of resistance. Written in the twilight of the CP's proletarian period, this essay adopts the Party line that it is not only possible but requisite for enlightened middle-class writers wholly to leave their own class and become ex officio members of the revolutionary working class;

"The Fetish" does not allow for oscillation between complicity and critique with regard to class sympathies. Chapter 4 discusses Le Sueur's novel, *The Girl* (written in 1939, revised from 1977–78, and published in 1978), and three of her short stories, "Our Fathers" (1937), "Annunciation" (1935), and "Corn Village" (1931). These texts, which I consider Le Sueur's most subversive work, to an extent elude what I loosely term the Party aesthetic and contradict the position articulated in "The Fetish of Being Outside." Although I have thus created two categories for discussing Le Sueur's work, I do not want to imply what would be a false opposition. Both orthodox and heterodox tendencies are at play in all her texts.

Chapters 5, 6, and 7 address Olsen's life and work, moving from her more to her less rhetorically conventional texts. Chapter 5 sketches Olsen's biography and discusses her '30s publications (except for "The Iron Throat," which later became part of *Yonnondio*), all of which appeared in 1934. As one might expect from a writer involved in open class warfare, Olsen's 1934 publications are more polemical and didactic than her later writing. Like Le Sueur's "Women on the Breadlines" and "I Was Marching," these texts are at times marked by an uncontested authorial voice and a completion and closure of meaning. Although the "message" in these polemical pieces is culturally and politically oppositional, the rhetorical model is that of the dominant culture: The writer directly addresses the readers, anticipating their responses and deflecting their objections; meanings are seen as delivered, unchanged, from source to recipient. Bakhtin terms this discursive model "monological." Olsen's *Yonnondio*, begun in the '30s and published in 1974, which I discuss in Chapter 6, and *Tell Me a Riddle* (1962) and *Silences* (1978), which I treat in Chapter 7, resist this conventional, monologic rhetorical/philosophical/political model.

Le Sueur's and Olsen's texts implicitly questioned orthodox Marxism's primacy-of-production theory and its concomitant privileging of the workplace and the industrial worker as the loci of struggle. These writers also legitimated the point of *re*production—work not limited to mothers but including all who in myriad ways attend to caring for others, work that Olsen terms "the maintenance of life" (*Silences* 34). Le Sueur's and Olsen's texts complicate oppositions between domestic and workplace labor and between private and public, personal and political, and individual and collective spheres, making women as worthy of our attention as the brawny "new Communist man."

Le Sueur's and Olsen's heterodox texts strain toward the decentered, postindividual, multivocal cultural forms of a different social order and in a sense foreshadow recent calls within the academy by scholars such as Scott, Newton, and Armstrong for collective, multidisciplinary efforts "to overcome the divisions of knowledge that prevent us from understanding who we are and what we do" (Armstrong 368). Le Sueur and Olsen's most subversive, heteroglossic texts embody what Raymond Williams terms a "*pre-emergence*, active and pressing but not yet fully articulated" (*Marxism* 126). Far from portraying a unified, robust revolutionary hero(ine) or political organization, their writing and their lives suggest that it is the contradictions within individuals and social movements that constitute the starting point and terrain for resistance.

ONE

The Thirties'
Literary Left

He confuses me about writing, for one thing.

Josephine Herbst, about her reluctance to get emotionally involved with Michael Gold

This chapter and the following one describe the historical parameters in which Le Sueur and Olsen fluctuated, consciously and unconsciously, between a full-volumed accord with and a muted dissent from the Party's positions on literature and "the woman question." This chapter deals with the American Left literary milieu in the late '20s and '30s by identifying the major debates within the Left, especially those between proponents of a new proletarian literature and writers influenced by Trotsky's *Literature and Revolution*. Although Le Sueur and Olsen were not major participants in these discussions, they were aware of and affected by their central issues. For the most part, Le Sueur, Olsen, and other women are absent from this chapter. Indeed, as much as anything I have written in this book, their noticeable absence comments on the patriarchal character of the literary Left.

I have organized this chapter in ways that will be familiar to those acquainted with the history of '30s literary radicalism: Drawing on primary sources as well as the valuable work of Daniel Aaron, James Burkhart Gilbert, Richard H. Pells, Walter B. Rideout, and Alan M. Wald, I discuss the CPUSA's shifting political and literary policies as well as literary debates between Party regulars and the anti-Stalinist Left. But I do so in order to provide, for those unfamiliar with '30s literary radicalism, the background necessary to understand how Le Sueur and Olsen, oscillating between versions of literary orthodoxy and heterodoxy, complicate the schema that have generally been used to map the literary Left during this period.

Because Meridel Le Sueur and Tillie Olsen embodied, during the '30s, both a deep commitment to the Communist Party and an emerging feminist critique of its androcentrism, their writing and Party experience constitute what Elaine Showalter terms an "object/field problem" in which we must keep two alternative

15

impulses simultaneously in view (34). While publishing in the Party press in 1934, Olsen was also at work on *Yonnondio*, in which the emphasis on domestic labor implicitly questions orthodox Marxism's primacy-of-production theory and the Third Period's privileging of the workplace and the industrial worker as the loci of struggle. Le Sueur, while producing "the agit-prop work that was needed,"[1] wrote a novel (*The Girl*, 1978) which would have raised Party eyebrows—if not caused a minor scandal—had it been published when completed in 1939. And neither shifting Party policy nor Left literary debates had much effect on the subjects of the three Le Sueur short stories discussed in Chapter 4—pregnancy, familial relations, and emotional and sexual repression. Paula Rabinowitz has significantly advanced the history of '30s literary radicalism by "engendering" it: "When gender is registered as a category," she argues, "differences other than those between the Third Period and the Popular Front or between the Communist and anti-Stalinist Left appear. The differently gendered political subjects of women's revolutionary fiction have other stories to tell" (*Labor* 62). The following will set the stage for Le Sueur and Olsen's "other stories."

The Left literary milieu of the United States engaged in a range of intense dialogues about the nature of art, about relationships between art and the working class, and about the appropriateness of various techniques for art from and for the working class. While many artists associated with the CPUSA engaged in those debates, the CPUSA dictated no official "aesthetic." At the 1935 American Writers' Congress Waldo Frank observed: "There is as yet no definite orthodox set of literary doctrines and dogmas to direct us as writers. We have to create our philosophy of revolutionary writing as we live our lives" (cited in Hart 189). Lawrence Schwartz notes that "there was little dictatorship by the primary literary spokesmen for the Party, and except for Browder's speech at the First Writers' Congress [the same Congress at which Frank spoke], virtual silence from the Party leadership" (84). Further, as Aaron observes, [CP general secretary Earl] Browder's speech was designed to assure writers that "there was no fixed 'Party line' about a good or bad work of art" (285). However, to say that there was no official Party policy about art is not to suggest the absence of "aesthetics" that vied for the attention of Left writers.

To put matters simply, Left literary dialogues were shaped out of two distinct sets of assumptions about the possibility of "proletarian art," which was promoted mainly from 1928 to 1935. Although there were many differences about the particulars of their views of art, one group of writers, many of them associated with *New Masses*, worked from the assumption that proletarian art was not only possible, but imminently realizable. Some, but by no means all, *New Masses* contributors argued that would-be proletarian writers must reject modern bourgeois experiments with form and develop new, unborrowed forms for proletarian literature. Such a belief led them to propose techniques that would clearly distinguish proletarian art from bourgeois art. Another group of writers, many of whom clustered around *The Partisan Review*, were variously influenced by Trotsky's argument in *Literature and Revolution* that purely proletarian literature and culture were an impossibility. These people considered it necessary to explore those techniques of bourgeois literature that could most productively be borrowed and adapted to the purposes of a working-class literature. Thus, fundamental tensions existed even within the literary Left.

For many writers and literary critics prominent during the '30s—Michael Gold, Granville Hicks, V. F. Calverton, Joseph Freeman, and Malcolm Cowley, among them—Marx's predictions seemed, in Edmund Wilson's words, "in the process of coming true" ("Case" 297). After visiting the Soviet Union in 1935, Wilson wrote that he had felt at the "moral top of the world where the light never really goes out," and after his own pilgrimage, Lincoln Steffens proclaimed: "I have seen the future, and it works" (cited in Gilbert 101; cited in Justin Kaplan 250). Descriptions in the American press of the construction of socialism invited comparisons to an America wracked by the Great Depression. While industrial production in the United States declined and unemployment soared, the Soviet Union was completing its first Five-Year Plan with apparent success and demanding ever more workers and technicians. Even an intellectual as cautious as George Soule, a liberal who was affiliated with the *New Republic* and who disapproved of the current tendency to speak apocalyptically, felt compelled by the course of events to acknowledge about Soviet Communism:

> If it goes on in the course of time to produce at least as high a standard of living as ours without our insecurity, to demonstrate the possibility of planning and control over a complex industrial system and to offer a full measure of the more intangible satisfactions, the effect will be as momentous in history as was the discovery of America at the end of the Middle Ages. Not only shall we know that capitalism as we have experienced it is undesirable, but that a different and better order is actually possible. (265)

To many writers and critics the Soviet successes demanded emulation.

Some writers interested in the Soviet view of relationships between social and literary revolution turned to Leon Trotsky, and his *Literature and Revolution* (1924) contributed to Left literary debates during the '30s. Trotsky aimed to purge revolutionary art of excessive vestiges of "individualism, of symbolism, of mysticism" (46–47). Trotsky called for a literature of "realism," an "artistic affirmation of the real world with its flesh and blood and also with its will and consciousness," and he stressed that this realism "may be of many kinds" (74). However, as we will see, Trotsky's view of relationships between the new revolutionary art, and various traditions and trends preceding and contemporary to it, was far more subtle than many '30s proposals for realism in a new-born proletarian literature. For Trotsky, proclamations of the birth of a new proletarian literature were as naive as Futurism's announcement of its break with the past: "In the advance guard of literature, Futurism is no less a product of the poetic past than any other literary school of the present day," Trotsky argued, and he underscored the point by adding, "we Marxists live in traditions, and we have not stopped being revolutionists on account of it" (130, 131).

In his analysis of the historic succession of generations of culture, Trotsky noted that "each new generation must pass through a stage of apprenticeship" in which the new generation "appropriates existing culture and transforms it in its own way, making it more or less different from that of the older generation" (194). This, he observed, is a long process requiring time the proletariat does not have. During the "years of social revolution" the proletariat will be involved in "fierce class struggles in which destruction will occupy more room than new construction." When the struggle is over, the proletariat will be "dissolved into a Socialist community and will free itself from its class characteristics and thus cease to be a proletariat" (185). It will have spent its time fighting to "do away with class culture . . . to make way for human culture" (186). Trotsky was not suggesting that the proletariat would be without influence on culture. He argued that "during the time of its dictatorship [the proletariat] will put its stamp upon culture." But, he added, "this is a far cry from a proletarian culture in the sense of a developed and completely harmonious system of knowledge and of art" (192). Thus Trotsky rejected simple calls for proletarian culture and literature.

When he turned his attention to formalism, Trotsky outlined a position consistent with his view of the relationship between revolutionary literature and the traditions before it. He maintained that "in spite of the superficiality and reactionary character of the Formalist theory of art, a certain part of the research work of the Formalists is useful" (163). The close analytic reading engaged in by Formalists is "necessary and useful, but one must understand its partial, scrappy, subsidiary and preparatory character" (163). Trotsky found the techniques of formalist analysis to be useful because he recognized form to be an essential characteristic of art. Far from dismissing bourgeois literature's experiments with form, Trotsky encouraged would-be revolutionary writers to study contemporary as well as past experiments with form: "One has to learn regardless of the fact that learning carries within itself certain dangers because out of necessity one has to learn from one's enemies" (205). Some American Marxist writers found in Trotsky a rationale for learning from the "modernist enemy."

In "America Needs a Critic" (*New Masses*, October 1926) Gold effusively praised *Literature and Revolution*, calling it "an amazing performance" and labeling Trotsky the revolution's Leonardo da Vinci. "Trotsky comes to literature, as to other social phenomena," Gold wrote, "with the scientific tools of the Marxian methodology" and gives us "what no American critic has yet fully given us, a sense of the social changes which precede each new school of art, and which determine the individual psychology of the artist, however 'free' he thinks he is" (7). In all this praise, however, Gold disagrees with Trotsky on one major point—his belief that proletarian art is an impossibility. Gold's departure from Trotsky on this important point launched a major debate on the literary Left.

Working-class writing thrived during the early '30s, when many leftists envisioned art's immediate task as helping to build an American working-class movement. During this period, despite Trotsky's argument against the possibility of proletarian art and culture, the American CP promoted what it referred to as "proletarian culture," with Gold—and to a lesser extent, Joshua Kunitz and Joseph Freeman—at the helm. (James Bloom reminds us that "gossip columnist Walter Winchell dubbed Freeman 'the Reditor of the New Masses'" [83].) However, even among these and other contributors to *New Masses* there were lively debates about the nature and function of proletarian art.

As Gold's 1926 review of *Literature and Revolution* indicates, his views of proletarian art in relation to bourgeois art are more complicated than his polemics and the disheveled, "manly" style he cultivated suggest. Michael Brewster Folsom (especially in "The Education of Michael Gold") and Marcus Klein are among those who have addressed Gold's complexity. In a recent study that furthers their work, James Bloom convincingly demonstrates that despite Gold's antagonism toward high culture, his "traditionalist nostalgia" reveals an identification "with the cultural heritage labeled the American Renaissance as much as it censures products of that heritage" (44–45). Bloom discusses Gold's "overreaching and venerable *intellectual* ambition," his "canonic appropriations, allusions, and commentaries," his "complicit mastery of the high culture he so often reviled" (67, 44). Gold's borrowing from high culture contradicts his dogmatic critical assertions about proletarian realism's essential independence from bourgeois art. But, as Bloom indicates, Gold's programmatic pronouncements about proletarian realism contributed to a "reductive view of Gold as a bully and a vulgarian," an image "which Gold himself helped foster" (14). I agree with Bloom that a full appreciation of Gold's work requires examining his contradictory impulses, and I consider the work of Bloom, as that of Klein and Folsom, to be a necessary complement to my own. However, my concern in this book is with Gold's influential pronouncements on ("manly") proletarian literature versus ("effeminate") bourgeois art, their relation to other positions held at the time, and their relation to what I have referred to as Le Sueur and Olsen's "other stories," their discourse of resistance.

From the beginnings of *New Masses* Gold had been at the center of the controversy over proletarian art. The second issue of the *New Masses* (June 1926) published a debate between John Dos Passos ("The New Masses I'd Like") and Gold ("Let It Be Really New!") on how the search for proletarian literature should be conducted. "The other night," Dos Passos begins, "he [Gold] made off into the underbrush after calling me a bourgeois intellectual before I had a chance to argue with him." Dos Passos resists Gold's categorical assertions: "I don't think it's any time for any group of spellbinders to lay down the law on any subject whatsoever. Particularly, I don't think there should be any more phrases, badges, opinions, banners, imported from Russia or anywhere else." Dos Passos advocated disavowing "imported systems" and "develop[ing] our own brand" of literature. In the search for proletarian literature Dos Passos argued for what he called "a highly flexible receiving station." But, he added, "the receiver has got to be tuned to a fairly limited range. That range has been vaguely laid down to be the masses, the people who work themselves rather than the people who work others." Dos Passos endorsed an expedition for proletarian literature that neither presupposes nor limits what it will discover:

Why shouldn't the *New Masses* be setting out on a prospecting trip, drilling in un-expected places, following unsuspected veins, bringing home specimens as yet unclassified? I think that there's much more to be gained by rigorous exploration than by sitting on the side lines of the labor movement with a red rosette in your buttonhole and cheering for the home team.

Dos Passos advocates a skepticism that Gold, apparently sporting a red rosette, views as "merely the flower of decay": Dos Passos wants a *New Masses* that is "full of introspection and doubt" (20).

Gold does not truck with "introspection and doubt." With characteristic certainty he declares in his debate with Dos Passos that America has a "world of revolutionary labor" to draw upon in creating a proletarian literature. This world, for which John Reed had "poured out his rich manhood," has its own "esthetic." He asserts, "I want the *New Masses* to explore in this world, not the other [that of bourgeois art]. Both worlds exist in America, but one is dying while the other is being born." Writers should take up residence in this "world of revolutionary labor. . . . live in it fully, burning all bridges behind them" ("Really New" 26). Writers should also "forget the past," including Shakespeare, Dante, Shelley, Bernard Shaw, and "the dead horses of Bible mysticism, Greek fatalism, Roman decadence, and British snobbery." Gold denounces the "pessimism, defeatism, despair, the fundamental chaos" of Dos Passos's work as antithetical to "a new world" ("Really New" 20, 26). Moreover, the expedition for proletarian literature must carry with it some presuppositions, Gold maintains: "I want a conscious exploration—with a compass" ("Really New" 26).

Robert Wolf, a contributing editor of *New Masses*, responded indirectly to Gold's distrust of all bourgeois literature in a lecture delivered at the Communist Academy in Moscow (printed in *New Masses*, February 1928). Writers not "closely connected organizationally with the workers' movement have often produced excellent agitational poems," Wolf argues. He cites as examples "Tom Mooney," a poem about the political prisoner written by William Ellery Leonard, a University of Wisconsin English professor, and James Rorty's memoriam to Sacco and Vanzetti. Wolf also appreciates T. S. Eliot, whom he terms a fascist, but one who "hates capitalist civilization for exactly the same things for which a good Communist poet should hate it." Wolf notes that Eliot has influenced poets with proletarian revolutionary sympathies (he identifies Freeman and Charles Recht) and encourages other proletarian writers to learn from Eliot as well (20–21).

About Gold's mistrust of bourgeois literature, Joshua Kunitz (writing under the name J. Q. Neets) was more direct. In the May 1930 issue of *New Masses* he published a review of Upton Sinclair's *The Mountain City* and Thornton Wilder's *The Woman of Andros*. Referring to Gold's notorious attack on Wilder, which began in *New Masses* (April 1930) and to which I will return, Kunitz argues that we can dismiss Wilder's ideology as reactionary while nevertheless "admiring his superb structure, his economy of means, his crystalline style." Kunitz insists that "we too need literary craftsmanship, technique" and "cannot agree with Mike

Gold's sneering remarks about Wilder's 'flawless rhetoric' and 'perfect English.'" With Gold in mind he concludes, "A wise proletarian does not pooh-pooh the very real technical achievement of the bourgeois writer. He attempts first to master it, and then to transcend it" (18).

In a letter in the July 1930 issue of New Masses, Kunitz (again writing as Neets) replies to Gold's response to Kunitz's reviews. Here the attack on Gold becomes more pointed and personal:

> Mike, I suspect, has not the faintest notion of the dialectic of the historical process. His is a childish nihilism, a blind, impetuous, irrational, almost mystical revolt against anything that savors of the past, of "old" culture. . . . revolution does not mean indiscriminate negation and wholesale rejection . . . on the contrary, it means . . . a new synthesis.
>
> A new life and a new art? Certainly! But not without a very definite utilization of those elements of the old culture that have vitality, dynamism, and a promise for the future. (23)

Kunitz, who terms it "foolish" to "sneer at 'dead splendors,'" cites Lenin on the subject:

> "We are much too much 'iconoclasts.' We must retain the beautiful, take it as an example, hold on to it, even though it is 'old.' Why turn away from real beauty just because it is old? Why discard it for good, *instead of using it as a starting point for further development*? That is nonsense, sheer nonsense." (23)

Among New Masses writers on literature and literary theory, Gold was not the only one to indulge in harsh reductionism, especially on the subject of bourgeois literature. In "The Literary Class War" (*New Masses*, August 1932) Philip Rahv published a new plan for Marxist literary theory. Rahv was more willing than Gold to borrow from the old culture. Indeed, Rahv proposed returning to and modifying Aristotle's notion of catharsis for the purposes of proletarian literature (although he insisted that no catharsis "can be effected by a writer who is not consciously up in arms against capitalism, who does not visualize the free, rational society of the future" [8]).

However, on the subject of modern bourgeois literature and why proletarian writers should reject its experiments with form, Rahv took a stance in this essay quite different from positions he would later assume in the *Partisan Review*. In "The Literary Class War" Rahv was no less unforgiving than Gold of modern bourgeois literature, characterizing it as "a rancid hotchpotch of mystic subjective introvert speculation, arbitrary and hallucinatory" (8). He described modern formal experiments as "word-game[s]" that provide the "ludicrous spectacle of grown-up people indulging in the most fatuous and infantile delusions." He compared these "word-dismembering" experiments, which the "bourgeois illuminati take . . . quite seriously," with "the well-known experiments of children with flies" (8). The vehemence of the young Rahv did not go unanswered.

A firm and sage response to Rahv appeared in the December 1932 issue of New Masses in A. B. Magil's "Pity and Terror." Magil, a participant with Gold,

Fred Ellis, William Gropper, Josephine Herbst, John Herrmann, Joshua Kunitz, and Harry Alan Potamkin in the November 1930 Kharkov Conference of Revolutionary Writers,[7] identified Rahv's version of reductionism as a substituting of "abstract schematism" for "the living dialectics of Marxism" (18). Such an approach had made Rahv, in his attempt to revive catharsis, fall victim to "obvious eclecticism" that stands "the entire method of dialectical materialism (not to mention Aristotle's *Poetics*) on its head" (16). Magil's response to Rahv's view of modern bourgeois literature's experiments sounds much like the responses of Wolf and Kunitz to Gold. Magil insists that "one cannot simply sweep away all these new experimental forms as so much chaff" (18). What Rahv "fails to understand is that some of these florid outbursts are the expression of a genuine protest (a confused, petty-bourgeois anarchist protest, it is true) against the existing order" (18). Magil cites Anatoli Lunacharsky as having "pointed out that even in the period of its decline the art of a dying social class is still capable of making significant contributions in the field of form." With the observation that such contributions can be accepted to "enrich the arsenal of proletarian art," Magil tempers both Rahv's and Gold's impatience with modern bourgeois art's formal experiments (18).

Magil, who is best known for his Party journalism, was also a poet, and some of his experiences shed light on Party literary debates. Magil reports that while he later supported the Party's renunciation of Trotskyism, his admiration for *Literature and Revolution* influenced his decision to join the CP. In keeping with his response to Rahv on the point of modernist experimentation in literature, Magil recalls that some contemporary modernist poets, including T. S. Eliot, W. B. Yeats, Thomas Hardy, H. D. (Hilda Doolittle), and Robinson Jeffers, helped shape his early interest in poetry (Buhle interview). Thus, in writing against reductionism in response to Rahv, Magil was working from the position of one who had studied the modernist techniques condemned by Gold and Rahv.

However, Magil points to another form of reductionism within the Party when he speaks about his decision to devote his efforts primarily to journalism rather than poetry. Joseph Freeman, who was instrumental in Magil's moving to New York (Buhle interview), had found, as Pells reports, that literary skills were less prized by the Party than journalistic and public speaking abilities (165). Accounts of the leadership's attitudes toward Party members' literary work range from assertions of indifference (because artists were considered "fickle and unstable") to distrust (because artists were viewed as "putative defectors and sentimental moralizers") (Schwartz 84; Aaron 299). Although Magil does not report distrust, he does report disrespect. Magil, who had a degree in English from the University of Pennsylvania, found literature to be of reduced value, as compared to other political efforts, in the eyes of Party leaders: "I had come to feel that the leaders of the Party had no respect for cultural activity or cultural expression, and it was a handicap to be known as a poet or a fiction writer or anything of that sort" (Buhle interview). He recalls a telling incident that occurred when he was writing for the *Daily Worker* in the late '20s. When Max Bedacht,[3] a Party leader, wanted something written for the paper, a staff member said he would give the assignment to Magil. Bedacht responded skeptically: "Magil? He's a *poet*, isn't he?" Attitudes such as this convinced Magil that to be a "professional revolutionary," as he intended, his work for the Party would have to be primarily political journalism (Buhle interview).

While reductive pronouncements grated on some of the foremost writers in *New Masses*, Gold's pronouncements became a central force in the development of American proletarian literature. In the September 1930 issue of *New Masses*, Gold dismissed "the bourgeois ultra-leftism of Trotsky in his *Literature and Revolution*, where he predicts there will not be time enough to develop a proletarian literature" and proclaimed, "this greatest and most universal of literary schools [proletarian] is now sweeping across the world." Gold declared himself "the first writer in America to herald the advent of a world proletarian literature as a concomitant to the rise of the world proletariat." A decade earlier his article "Towards Proletarian Art" had appeared in *The Liberator*. At that time he had been merely "feeling [his] way," but now he could rejoice that "the little path has since become a highroad" ("Notes" Sept., 4). Gold's confidence and enthusiasm were widely shared among *New Masses*' contributors.

The great certainty with which Gold announced the existence of proletarian literature resulted partly from the fact that his view of a potential proletarian literature remained unclouded by many of the subtleties marking Trotsky's more sophisticated view. For Gold proletarian literature could be reduced to a few "laws which seem to be demonstrable" ("Notes" Sept., 4). His first law, of no controversy to Marxists, was that "all culture is the reflection of a specific class society." From this he moved to the "law" that "bourgeois culture is in process of decay, just as bourgeois society is in a swift decline." From these two "laws" he went to a third: "The class that will inherit the world will be the proletariat." It was in the leap from these three "laws" to the fourth ("the law that this proletarian society will, like its predecessors, create its own culture") that Gold abruptly parted company with Trotsky ("Notes" Sept., 4–5).

Among Gold's few other laws is one with which Trotsky would have agreed in his discussion of working-class literary efforts. Gold argued that it was "dogmatic folly to seize upon any single literary form, and erect it into a pattern for all proletarian literature" ("Notes" Sept., 5). However, he did believe "a new form [was] evolving," a form "one might name the 'Proletarian Realism'" ("Notes" Sept., 5). As he articulated the "elements" of that form, he made it clear that his rejection of the impulse "to seize upon any single literary form" was far from Trotsky's toleration of multiple literary modes. In fact, some of the elements themselves, and the format in which Gold presented them, raise doubt as to Gold's distance from the "dogmatic folly" he claimed to deplore. Before discussing any one of the elements, I will reproduce them as they appeared in the pages of *New Masses* to indicate their full rhetorical force:

1.

Because the Workers are skilled machinists, sailors, farmers and weavers; the proletarian writer must describe their work with technical precision. The Workers will scorn any vague fumbling poetry, much as they would scorn a sloppy workman.

Hemingway and others have had the intuition to incorporate this proletarian element into their work, but have used it for the *frisson*, the way some actors try to imitate gangsters or men. These writers build a machine, it functions, but It produces nothing; it has not been planned to produce anything; it is only an adult toy.

2.

Proletarian realism deals with the *real conflicts* of men and women who work for a living. It has nothing to do with the sickly mental states of the idle Bohemians, their subtleties, their sentimentalities, their fine-spun affairs. The worst example, and the best of what we do not want to do is the spectacle of Proust, master-masturbator of the bourgeois literature. We know the suffering of hungry, persecuted and heroic millions is enough of a theme for anyone, without inventing these precious silly little agonies.

3.

Proletarian realism is never pointless. It does not believe in literature for its own sake, but in literature that is useful, has a social function. Every major writer has always done this in the past; but it is necessary to fight the battle constantly, for there are more intellectuals than ever who are trying to make literature a plaything. Every poem, every novel and drama, must have a social theme, or it is merely confectionery.

4.

As few words as possible. We are not interested in the verbal acrobats—this is only another form for bourgeois idleness. The Workers live too close to reality to care about these literary show-offs, these verbalist heroes.

5.

To have the courage of the proletarian experience. This was the chief point of my "mystic" essay in 1920; let us proletarians write with the courage of our own experience. I mean, if one is a tanner and writer, let one dare to write the drama of a tannery; or of a clothing shop, or of a ditch-digger's life, or of a hobo. Let the bourgeois writers tell us about their spiritual drunkards and super-refined Parisian emigres; or about their spiritual marriages and divorces, etc., that is their world; we must write about our own mud-puddle; it will prove infinitely more important. This is being done by the proletarian realism.

6.

Swift action, clear form, the direct line, cinema in words; this seems to be one of the principles of proletarian realism. It knows exactly what it believes and where it is going; this makes for its beautiful youthful clarity.

7.

Away with drabness, the bourgeois notion that the Worker's life is sordid, the slummer's disgust and feeling of futility. There *is* horror and drabness in the Worker's life; and we will portray it; but we know this is not the last word; we know that this manure heap is the hope of the future; we know that not pessimism, but revolutionary elan will sweep this mess out of the world forever.

8.

Away with all lies about human nature. We are scientists; we know what a man thinks and feels. Everyone is a mixture of motives; we do not have to lie about our hero in order to win our case. It is this honesty alone, frank as an unspoiled child's, that makes proletarian realism superior to the older literary schools.

9.

No straining or melodrama or other effects; life itself is the supreme melodrama. Feel this intensely, and everything becomes poetry—the new poetry of materials, of the so-called 'common man,' the Worker moulding his real world. ("Notes" Sept., 3–5)[4]

Gold rejected romanticism and symbolism, but modernism and formalism stand as the primary enemies in his outline of proletarian literature's elements. Implicit in Gold's elements is an orthodox Marxist portrait of modernism. In some of its manifestations—Eliot's poetry, for example—it had seen horror and drabness, it had portrayed "sickly mental states of idle Bohemians," it had acknowledged loss of purpose, and it had reacted with "pessimism," not "revolutionary elan." Against modernist literature's disillusionment Gold confidently placed a literature of realism that "knows exactly what it is and where it is going." Theories of literature growing out of the work of T. S. Eliot, T. E. Hulme, John Crowe Ransom, Allen Tate, Cleanth Brooks, among others, theories converging in what came to be known as New Criticism, stressed the close analysis of literature's formal properties and pitted the formal order of literature against what they considered the pervasive, immutable chaos of human existence.

Gold was among many Marxists who viewed this project as the study of "literature for its own sake." Against this project Gold set the theory and practice of "literature that is useful, has a social function." Embodying what the later New Critic W. K. Wimsatt (in the essay "The Concrete Universal" and elsewhere) approvingly identified as the criterion of complexity, much modernist literature could be seen by Gold and other Marxists as having been produced by "verbal acrobats," "literary show-offs," "verbalist heroes." While Gold was appropriately concerned with the social functions of literature, in his elements we find a complete rejection of modernism and formalism. Such wholesale rejection was far removed from Trotsky's position.

During the early '30s Gold was probably America's most famous Communist writer and critic, and at the 1935 American Writers' Congress he was hailed as "the best loved American revolutionary writer" (Rideout 168). His autobiographical novel, *Jews Without Money*, which has been translated into 16 languages, went through 11 printings in the first year of publication (1930) and six more printings by 1938. "Such was the book's resonance when first published," Bloom observes, "that Sinclair Lewis, in his [1930] Nobel Prize acceptance speech, paired Gold with Faulkner in prophesying a glorious future for American literature" (16). This novel is often referred to as a classic of the proletarian literature Gold believed possible.

A native of New York's Lower East Side, Itzok Isaac Granich (Gold's real name) was the son of impoverished Jewish immigrants.[5] In *Jews Without Money* Gold describes his pain and anger at being denied formal education beyond the ninth grade.[6] And years later, while in his sixties and writing for the *People's World*, Gold said simply, "Education haunts me" (cited in Folsom 224). As one of the editors from 1926 to 1932 of *New Masses* and as exemplar of a new proletarian tradition in American literature, Gold influenced leftist literary criticism and, by extension, affected the writing of Meridel Le Sueur and Tillie Olsen. In 1933 he transferred most of his considerable energy to his *Daily Worker* column, "Wake Up America," although his name continued to appear in *New Masses* in tributes from younger writers and succeeding editors.

Critics such as Gold who were members of or sympathizers with the CP were, in turn, influenced by the aims of the post-revolutionary Russian *Proletkult*, which sought a proletarian culture untainted by bourgeois elements. Following the 1917 revolution and until 1928, the year in which the first five-year plan was inaugurated, the Bolshevik Party had exercised little control over art, and various cultural movements enjoyed considerable autonomy. The prescriptive literary decrees, so thoroughly opposed by Trotsky in *Literature and Revolution*, began in 1928 and continued through the next three decades. Gold's elements thus echo a 1928 Bolshevik Party edict that "sent writers out to visit construction sites and produce novels glorifying machinery" (Eagleton, *Marxism* 37). This edict foreshadowed the doctrine of socialist realism adopted by the 1934 Congress of Soviet Writers, a direct organ of Stalin's control.

Michael Gold, Joshua Kunitz, and A. B. Magil numbered among the delegates to the previously mentioned 1930 Second International Conference of Revolutionary and Proletarian Writers in Kharkov in the Ukraine. A series of resolutions adopted at Kharkov became the dominant literary guidelines for American Communists for the next five years, including those adopted by *New Masses*, the John Reed Clubs, and the first American Writers' Congress. A basic message from Kharkov was to use proletarian literature as a weapon in class struggle. Thus Gold greeted the first novel of one young radical writer "not as literature at all but as a 'significant class portent,'" since the book, despite its limitations, "represented one more 'victory against capitalism'" (Pells 171–172).

In addition to Gold, Granville Hicks, as the literary editor of *New Masses*, served as an authoritative spokesman for proletarian literature. In 1933 Hicks published his *magnum opus*, *The Great Tradition*, which reassessed American literature since the Civil War—attacking one writer after another for not being adequately conscious of the class struggle or not joining the progressive side—and set simplistic standards for a revolutionary novel of the present. In 1942 Alfred Kazin declared *The Great Tradition* "a book of monumental naivete," and today it could be read as a parody of reductive Marxist criticism (324). Hicks's complaining, in another context, that there were not enough proletarians in Andre Malraux's *Man's Fate* gives one a sense of Hicks's standards for revolutionary art. *The Great Tradition* measures writers in terms of their understanding of socioeconomic forces and class struggle; moreover, their point of view must be sufficiently sympathetic to the working class and optimistic about possibilities for revolutionary change. The study barely addresses the subject of literary form.

Thus Hicks and Gold agreed on the terms by which literature should be judged. Writers' handling of socioeconomic issues, not their treatment of literary form, was to be the critic's fundamental concern. Although there was lively debate among Marxist critics about Hicks and Gold's position, these doyens of *New*

Masses literary policy exerted some pressure on contributors to *New Masses* to approach literature in a prescribed manner. These contributors generally thought formal considerations far less important than thematic ones, and many—but as we have seen, not all—regarded stylistic experimentation as bourgeois. Even David Peck's sympathetic account of the journal acknowledges that it often evaluated literature solely on the basis of its content or the class origin of its author. After 1933 "this practice became the judgment of literature on a categorical political scale: bourgeois or proletarian, revolutionary or counter-revolutionary, Communist or Fascist." One editorial characterized the sharpening class struggle that accompanied the deepening economic crisis after 1930 by this simple designation: "friends" or "enemies." In this climate, literary works were often evaluated "in terms of absolute political values" (Peck, "Development" 245, 246).

The John Reed Clubs played an important role in the American CP's emphasis on proletarian culture. Nationally organized in 1932, clubs sprang up in a number of small towns as well as in large cities and by January 1934, nearly 30 had formed. The clubs organized people at the grassroots by distributing leaflets and improvising skits, slogans, and group chants for protest rallies. They published various militant magazines featuring the work of unknown writers and provided an atmosphere in which would-be writers of working-class origin were warmly encouraged (Aaron 280–81). In an essay (composed of excerpts from *American Hunger*) included in Richard Crossman's *The God That Failed*, Richard Wright described his introduction to the Chicago John Reed Club, which he had visited skeptically, feeling that "Communists could not possibly have a sincere interest in Negroes." He was surprised at the greeting—"You're welcome here"— that he received from the first white man he encountered at the club. Wright reported that he met "men and women whom I should know for decades to come, who were to form the first sustained relationships in my life." They treated him uncondescendingly and were eager to publish what he termed his "crude" poems (116, 117, 120).

As part of its focus on working-class writing, the Party also promoted reportage, a generic sibling of proletarian realism (subsequent chapters will discuss some of Le Sueur's and Olsen's reportage). The classic anthology of proletarian writing, *Proletarian Literature in the U.S.* (edited by Granville Hicks, Michael Gold, Isidor Schneider, Joseph North, Paul Peters, and Alan Calmer; introduced by Joseph Freeman; and published in 1935 by the CP's publishing organ, International Publishers) informs us that the term "reportage" came to the United States from Europe, particularly from the Soviet Union, yet it became "a peculiarly American form. John Reed was a master of it; [Reed's] *Ten Days That Shook the World* is its classic example" (211). *Proletarian Literature in the U.S.* noted other practitioners of reportage, including John Dos Passos, Myra Page, Agnes Smedley, and John L. Spivak.

A form of journalism, reportage attempted to detail Depression conditions from the perspective of those most acutely suffering them—the hungry, unemployed, and homeless. Reportage intended to make the reader *"experience"* the event recorded. This "three-dimensional reporting" eschews the presumed objectivity of traditional journalism (*Proletarian* 211). According to Georg Lukacs, "at its best, it [reportage] makes the right connection between the general and the particular. . . . Genuine reportage is in no way content simply to depict the facts; its descriptions always present a connection, disclose causes and propose consequences" (49). William Stott uses "participant observer" to describe the role of the writer of reportage; the writer "used vicarious persuasion: the writer partook of the events he reported and bared his feelings and attitudes to influence the reader's own" (178–179).

Proletarian Literature in the U.S. reserves a special place in literary history for reportage:

> Every age produces its characteristic literature. . . . The twentieth century—history in seven league boots—has evolved a variety of forms, all characterized by the swiftness of the time. One of these—and it assumes greater importance as the tempo of this age increases—is reportage. (211)

More apparently linked to a specific historical period than many other literary forms, reportage was viewed as "a form which has sprung up because the revolution requires it" (212). Indeed, written under deadline pressure, while events and issues were still fresh, reportage was hardly the product of a protracted creative process. As we will see when I discuss Le Sueur's "I Was Marching" and Olsen's "The Strike," "a world making for the barricades" left little time for reflection, no time for arduousness (211).

Reportage was part of a rapidly changing socioeconomic and literary milieu in which the periodical form, with a relatively broad, popular journalistic base, dominated. Periods of crisis and transition have historically favored shorter literary forms, and some '30s writers, quite self-consciously, considered themselves pamphleteers. Muckraking journalism, one of reportage's predecessors, had been part of the Progressive Movement; but muckrakers had been a politically diverse group, and their journalism was not stamped by one political party or faction. Reportage, on the other hand, like proletarian realism, was adopted and fostered by the CPUSA (although liberal journals like *New Republic* and *The Nation* also published it in the early '30s).[7]

The Working Woman was one CP publication in which reportage was a mainstay, although *The Working Woman* (1929–35), along with its successor, *Woman Today* (1936–38), have been nearly obliterated from America's cultural memory. Examples of reportage featured in *The Working Woman* include Malvina Reynolds's "Recuerdo: A True Story of the Lettuce Strike in California" (August 1935); Vivian Dahl's "Them Women Sure Are Scrappers" (August 1934), about "colored and white" women farm workers' uniting to strike successfully for higher wages and for recognition of their union; Mary Heaton Vorse's "Hard Boiled" (May 1933), about the Scottsboro trial; and Lucy Parsons's "A Story of May Day" (May 1931), recounting Parsons's activity in the Chicago strike for an eight-hour day. In all cases, reportage linked individuals to oppressed groups or collective struggles.

As Charlotte Nekola has observed, "at the same time that reportage allowed for an expansion of ideas beyond the self, it also encouraged women to speak about themselves" (195). Nekola and Paula Rabinowitz's *Writing Red: An Anthology of American Women Writers, 1930–1940* (1987) includes a useful discussion of reportage and has reprinted leftist women's fiction and poetry as well as reportage.

The flourishing of proletarian writing between 1930 and 1935 and its subsequent decline corresponded to shifting cultural policies within the CP. Of the 70 proletarian novels published during the 1930s, 50 of them appeared before 1935 (Rideout 171). The years favorable to proletarian writing coincided with the Party's "proletarian period," also known as the Third Period (1928–35), when the CP concentrated its work among industrial workers, the unemployed, and African-Americans. The Party generally refused to work with the established American Federation of Labor trade unions, considering all liberals and non-CP socialists to be "social fascists," the chief enemies of the working class and socialist revolution. This "United Front from Below" policy advocated collaboration with the rank-and-file but not with the leadership of non-Communist organizations.

In 1935, responding to Hitler's rise to power, the Communist International reversed its strategy to the "Popular Front," calling for coalitions between workers' parties and liberal capitalist parties. The CPUSA changed its course accordingly, helping form the CIO and allying itself with the New Deal. Opposing fascism rather than agitating for socialism became its central strategy. The Party's literary policy changed with the general shift to the Popular Front. As the Party expanded its appeal to middle-class writers and intellectuals, it broadened its approach to literature, viewing favorably some work condemned as bourgeois during the Third Period.

The treatment of Archibald MacLeish's poetry suggests the extent of this shift in literary policy. In January 1934, Margaret Wright Mather (frequently a pseudonym for Granville Hicks) denounced MacLeish as "a Nazi, at least a kind of ur-Nazi." In December 1935, the poet, "now miraculously denazified," appeared as a contributor to the journal's Anti-Fascist Number, while in March 1936 Isidor Schneider praised his *Public Speech* as a "beautiful and moving collection of poems" (Rideout 242). A letter from Edith Anderson of *The Daily Worker* to poet H. H. Lewis also exemplifies the shift in literary policy from the Third Period to the Popular Front: "I like your poem 'Mass Movement March,'" she writes. But she feels "that the end of it is too aggressively red for right now when we have an immediate goal which absorbs most of our energy. It simply is not wise, not correct, not helpful to the war effort or to the opening of a second front, to talk of red marches" (cited in Cary Nelson 207).

From 1936 to 1937 the discussion of proletarian art gradually disappeared from the pages of *New Masses*. Conscious of the charge that the CP had abandoned proletarian art, Gold wrote in 1937 that revolutionary culture had not died; rather, there had been a "lull, perhaps, while the authors prepare themselves for new tasks." However, as James Gilbert points out, this "lull . . . was permanent" (160). Earl Browder's speech before the Second Writers' Congress,

held in New York in June 1937, indicated the Party's new attitude toward literature: "The greatest literature of our day," he declared, "will surely have at its
heart" a representation of the process of building "a broad democratic front and
the defeat of fascism" (Gilbert 160–161). The Popular Front's effect on proletarian writing is also suggested by Joseph Freeman's June 1936 reference to "those
radical writers who in the 'sectarian' days were engaged in advancing what used
to be called proletarian literature" (Rideout 243). Literature could no longer
emphasize the very class distinctions on which Gold's tenets of proletarian realism had been based. Art was still a weapon, but one to be used against fascism,
not against capitalism or the bourgeoisie.

In September 1934 the Party dissolved the John Reed Clubs to make way for
the League of American Writers—an affiliate of the International Union of Revolutionary Writers, the literary arm of the Comintern—which concentrated on
enrolling writers of "some standing" and excluded unpublished writers (Aaron
283). When a member of the Reed Clubs' executive committee protested that it
was undemocratic to liquidate an organization without consulting its membership, Alexander Trachtenberg, the CP's cultural commissar, replied that "first we
must carry out the decisions of the party, and then 'speak of democracy and what
not'" (cited in Aaron 282).

During the period in which the proletarian literature movement flourished
(1930–35), American Marxism included a force running counter to the programs
of Gold and many of the *New Masses* writers. Trotsky's *Literature and Revolution*
became a weapon for those who battled for freedom from Soviet orthodoxy, such
as V. F. Calverton and Max Eastman. The latter became known internationally—
and became a pariah in most American Left circles—for translating and
defending Trotsky's work. In fact, Eastman was singled out by Stalin himself as a
"notorious crook" and a "gangster of the pen" (Aaron 315).

Trotsky's influence was also evident in James T. Farrell's controversial *A Note
on Literary Criticism* (1936). Farrell, like many of his contemporaries, believed
that world revolution would create a new socialist society and that this transformation would affect all cultural spheres. Yet he opposed premature declarations
of the existence of "proletarian" or "socialist" culture.

> Socialism will slowly, gradually, permeate every sphere of human activity. . . . But
> this change is not going to be brought about by fiat; it will not come merely for
> our wishing, nor through stout assertion that it is already here. . . . The new cul-
> ture that will grow from a new society will not precede that society, for thought
> and culture do not precede social changes: at best they guide toward such
> changes. (186)

Farrell also resisted a didactic and mechanical Marxism, acknowledged the necessity of assimilating literary tradition, and defended the formal innovations of
modernists such as Joyce. Attacking Gold "as a revolutionary sentimentalist" and
Hicks "as a mechanical determinist," *A Note on Literary Criticism* drew praise
from the *Nation* and *Partisan Review* and condemnation from *New Masses* (cited

in Wald, *Farrell* 42). *New Masses* reviewer Isidor Schneider correctly asserted that *A Note on Literary Criticism* represented not the "work of a single malcontent" but "a current of thought on the cultural Left." Indeed, Schneider argued, it was "an indication of a new crisis in revolutionary literature" (cited in Wald, *Farrell* 42).

Farrell was politically aligned with those clustered around the *Partisan Review*, which enjoyed a wide European scope and carried articles by Georg Lukacs, Nikolai Bukharin, Andre Malraux, Andre Gide, John Strachey, and the like. *Partisan Review* had been launched in 1934 as the literary organ of the New York City John Reed Club, the oldest and largest club in the United States. The opening editorial statement announced the journal's intention to "participate in the struggle of the workers and sincere intellectuals against imperialist war, fascism, national and racial oppression, and for the abolition of the system which breeds these evils" (2). The statement also pledged to defend the Soviet Union. While the journal's viewpoint would reflect that of "the revolutionary working class," it would "resist every attempt to cripple our literature by narrow-minded, sectarian theories and practices" (2). The statement concluded by hailing other magazines of revolutionary literature "already in the field," singling out *New Masses*, "whose appearance as a weekly . . . is evidence of the growth of the new within the old" (2).

Although the names of such Party regulars as Joseph Freeman and Joshua Kunitz appeared on its masthead, *Partisan Review* was dominated by William Phillips and Philip Rahv, whose criticism of the Party's political and literary policies caused the journal to split from the CP in 1937. That split generated a bitter dispute. On October 19, 1937, *New Masses* published in its "Reader's Forum" section a letter signed by William Phillips and Philip Rahv. Their letter was a response to a September 14, 1937, *New Masses* editorial attack on the *Partisan Review*. In their response Phillips and Rahv articulate what they consider to be a major difference between *New Masses* and *Partisan Review*:

> What distinguished *Partisan Review* from the *New Masses* was our struggle to free revolutionary literature from domination by the immediate strategy of a political party. The *New Masses*, on the other hand, has always been part and parcel of the very tendency which the *Partisan Review* was fighting.

In reply to this letter, the editors of *New Masses* accuse Phillips and Rahv, the "Trotskyite editors," of having changed their political position and that of the *Partisan Review*, which they find "is now being used for purposes utterly opposed to those for which it was founded and maintained" (21).

The next day, October 20, 1937, the *Daily Worker* carried an article, "No Quarter to Trotskyists—Literary or Otherwise," by V. J. Jerome, whom Daniel Aaron characterized as "the party functionary in charge of the intellectuals" in the early '30s.[8] Jerome identified Rahv, Phillips, Farrell, and Lionel Abel with the "scribblers and unskilled intellectuals in the literary field, who have sneaked back to the bourgeoisie through the gateway of Trotskyism" (6). He argued that "it is time to recognize that Trotskyites, 'literary' or otherwise, are engaged in tearing down all that we are working to build up" (6).

In *The Partisan Reader*, published in 1946, Phillips and Rahv reflected on their "differences with the Party" during their term as editors of *Partisan Review* and reaffirmed some of the disagreements asserted in their 1937 letter to *New Masses*. They noted their "protest against the official idea of art as an instrument of political propaganda." Believing themselves to have been "responsive to Marxism as a method of analysis," they, nevertheless, could not "go along with our 'comrades' of the *New Masses* and other Communist publications in their practice of ignoring the difference between good and bad writing in order to judge it primarily on grounds of political expediency." They accused their "comrades" of being primarily interested in whether or not literature's "political content coincided with the current specifications of the party line" (680–681). Those in the *Partisan Review* orbit stressed the value of imaginative literature beyond its immediately apparent meanings and usages and were intrigued by the formal innovations of Joyce, Eliot, Yeats, Proust, Kafka, and other, primarily European, modernists. Partisan Reviewers were less inclined than CP literati to champion American proletarian literature. Thus the *Partisan Review* circle offered leftist writers a license not available from Gold and some of the *New Masses* group to learn from modernist formal experiments and to entertain subject matter that was not necessarily "party-line."

In 1937, with the help of Dwight Macdonald, Fred Dupee, Mary McCarthy, and the painter George L. K. Morris, Rahv and Phillips reorganized the *Partisan* on an independent, anti-Stalinist basis. "*Partisan Review*," wrote Dupee in the opening editorial, "aspires to represent a new and dissident generation in American letters" (quoted in Gilbert 159). Thereafter the journal served as a forum for writers estranged from the Party, like Lionel Trilling, Sidney Hook, Meyer Shapiro, and Clement Greenberg. Although American Trotskyists lauded the *Partisan*'s break from the Party and supported the journal's quasi-autonomy-of-art position up to a point, they criticized the extreme to which the *Partisan* proposed to carry it. The relation between literature and politics, the Trotskyists believed, "should neither be one of despotism and servile dependence, as the Stalinists demand, nor one of toplofty indifference and alienation as the Partisan reviewers think necessary" (quoted in Gilbert 198).

The *Partisan* gradually moved from militant Marxism to endorsing the established social order. Many of the historical forces that contributed to shifts in CP cultural policies also affected the *Partisan*'s gradual metamorphosis. By 1939 Rahv and Phillips argued that "the Left's most serious error had been its decade-long presumption that the artist would improve both his mind and his work by entering the political world" (Pells 340). For Rahv and Phillips, "detachment was a superior form of political, artistic, and moral commitment" (Pells 341). The Partisan Reviewers' sense of the intelligentsia as an ordained elite resembled Samuel Taylor Coleridge's conservative notion of a "clerisy," Matthew Arnold's schemes for cultural preservation, and T. S. Eliot and E. R. Curtius's shared "dream of a secret directorate for western cultural politics."[9]

A postwar alliance between many of this elite and the state emerged, as both Pells and Wald have shown. While these Parnassians cultivated their role as "non-partisan" cultural priests, governmental activity, such as constructing the Cold War, could go largely unchecked.

> Once the journal's editors and contributors began to question the value of revolutionary activities in the wake of Stalinist experience, and once they began to re-emphasize the traditional liberal belief that ideas and individuals should be totally free, it seemed natural for them to transfer their loyalties to America as the main defense against the totalitarian menace both of Germany and the Soviet Union. (Pells 345)

In *How New York Stole the Idea of Modern Art: Abstract Expressionism, Freedom, and the Cold War*, Serge Guilbaut chose as an epigraph a telling quotation from Clement Greenberg: "Some day it will have to be told how anti-Stalinism which started out more or less as Trotskyism turned into art for art's sake, and thereby cleared the way, heroically, for what was to come" (17). Thus these "apolitical" *Partisan Review* brahmins left in power the dominant social order they had once so strenuously opposed.

Significantly, the appellation for this group changed from "Trotskyist intellectuals" to "New York intellectuals." It includes such former Trotskyists as Saul Bellow, Sidney Hook, and Seymour Martin Lipset, who were associated, as Wald reports, with the reactionary "Committee for the Free World," a predominantly pro-Reagan organization led by *Commentary* editor Norman Podhoretz. Among other activities, it sponsored a *New York Times* ad (April 6, 1981) to "applaud American policy in El Salvador" (cited in Wald, "Intellectuals" 156). The Democratic Party has attracted many of the other surviving New York intellectuals. By the time of the resurgence of political activity during the '60s, "many of these intellectuals had hardened into apologists for American imperialism," but a few, such as Dwight Macdonald, Mary McCarthy, F. W. Dupee, and Philip Rahv, moved to the Left (Wald, "Intellectuals" 155–156; 179–180).

The leftist cultural contributions of the Partisan Reviewers are enduring, relevant components of a rich Marxist heritage, and those contributions deserve more examination than I can provide here. In *The New York Intellectuals* and in numerous essays, Wald has undertaken that examination, arguing that what is politically and theoretically useful in the Partisan Reviewers' legacy has been overlooked because contemporary radicals scornfully dismiss them for their movement to the Right. As Wald points out, their politics were not "tainted from the beginning," and their evolution to the Right was not the only possible trajectory ("Intellectuals" 167). A number of social and historical factors as well as anti-Stalinism caused these intellectuals' transformation.[10]

Neither those affiliated with the Party nor those on the anti-Stalinist Left had been prepared for the complexity of history's unfolding events. The Moscow Trials (1936–38) and the Nazi-Soviet Non-Aggression Pact (1939) brought on a debilitating disillusionment. By the close of the '30s, as Peck points out, many "felt betrayed, most certainly by Russia, but also by their own social, political, and economic ideas and ideals. They renounced both, and in the act of renunciation they jettisoned the literature which those ideas and ideals had created" ("Orgy" 379). By the end of the decade, proletarian literature became the subject of a number of obituaries. In "Proletarian Literature: a Political Autopsy," Rahv reduced proletarian literature to "the literature of a party disguised as the literature of a class," to an "episode in the history of totalitarian communism" (623, 628). This judgment persisted, defining—and, in effect, blacklisting—proletarian literature for decades.

Peck terms what followed the Moscow trials, the Non-Aggression Pact, and Rahv's autopsy an "orgy of apology," which undercut the premises of '30s criticism—that literature has material roots, that writers represent class interests, and that literature and criticism should respond to human needs. A referendum was called not only on Stalinist Russia but on history itself, and versions of formalist criticism (such as New Criticism and Chicago Criticism) which had emerged in the '30s and dominated criticism during the '40s, '50s, and early '60s, welcomed repentant revolutionaries into the fold. But, as we will see when we turn to Le Sueur's and Olsen's texts, writers attracted to the proletarian literary movement did not merely reproduce doctrinal directives, as Rahv charged.

As I have said, neither Le Sueur nor Olsen played a major role in the public literary debates of the '30s. The literary world, even on the Left, was chiefly a male preserve. Men generally staffed editorial boards of leftist journals of literature and criticism, although a few women writers, like Le Sueur, Josephine Herbst, and Grace Lumpkin, contributed regularly. As Rabinowitz notes, "a woman might be a reviewer—often of other women's books—because she had written a novel, but she was not expected to attempt to analyze the formal or ideological concerns of proletarian writing. . . . Serious criticism was left to men." (*Labor* 59). While Aaron, Gilbert, Pells, and Rideout have contributed valuably to the history of literary radicalism, they focused on "the head boys," to borrow Josephine Herbst's term (Madden, xxi), and on the period's major publications, such as the *Daily Worker*, *New Masses*, and *Partisan Review*. As Rabinowitz points out, for the writings of women and minorities, we must also examine more obscure, noncanonical Left journals.[11]

Le Sueur and Olsen were among the nine women (out of a total of 70) who signed the "Call for an American Writers' Congress" drafted by Granville Hicks and published in *New Masses* in January 1935.[12] They were also among the few women delegates to the Congress held later that year. A drawing of Olsen was one of the rare portraits of women writers to appear among the many renderings of male literary figures in the issue of *New Masses* (7 May 1935) that reported on the Congress. However, since James Farrell had informed her that she was one of "'the two flowers there,' compared with the other 'old bags'" (Rosenfelt, "Thirties"

395), we can only hope that she was noticed for some reason other than her youthful attractiveness. According to Olsen, remarks such as Farrell's were plentiful within the movement (Rosenfelt interview).

On the opening night of the Congress, organizers recruited Josephine Herbst at the last minute when they realized they needed a token woman on the program (Langer 185). Herbst once wrote to Katherine Anne Porter about the "gentle stay-in-your place" she received from her husband, John Herrmann, when she wished to join his political discussion with Michael Gold, Edmund Wilson, Malcolm Cowley, and others: "I told Mister Herrmann that as long as the gents had bourgeois reactions to women they would probably never rise very high in their revolutionary conversations but said remarks rolled off like water" (Langer 120).

While numerous instances of male-centeredness occurred on the literary Left, Gold's masculinist pronouncements about style and criticism were best known and most influential. The following excerpt from Gold's "America Needs a Critic" exemplifies what Alice Kessler-Harris and Paul Lauter have termed the Left's "hairy-chested polemics" (xii):

> Send us a critic. Send a giant who can shame our writers back to their task of civilizing America. Send a soldier who has studied history. Send a strong poet who loves the masses, and their future. Send someone who doesn't give a damn about money. Send one who is not a pompous liberal, but a man of the street. Send no mystics—they give us Americans the willies. Send no coward. Send no pedant. Send us a man fit to stand up to skyscrapers. . . . Send us a joker in overalls. Send no saint. Send an artist. Send a scientist. Send a Bolshevik. Send a *man*. ("Critic" 9; my emphasis)

In another example of Gold's rhetoric, Edmund Wilson's chest was, apparently, not only hairless but that of a "high-bosomed Beacon Hill matron" (cited in Klein 231). Out of this masculinist pride, Gold urged writers to pen "the new Communist man" and, in *New Masses* (April 1930), cast his previously mentioned crusade against Thornton Wilder in terms of a homophobic attack on Wilder's effeminate writing style: "That fairy-like little Anglo-American curate . . . . is a beautiful, rouged, combed, well-dressed corpse, lying among the sacred candles and lilies of the past, and sure to stink if exposed to sunlight" ("Toward" 12; "Notes" April, 4). In the *New Republic* (October 22, 1930), Gold continued his assault:

> But what is this religious spirit Mr. Wilder aims to restore? . . . It is a pastel, pastiche, dilettante religion. . . . a daydream of homosexual figures in graceful gowns moving archaically among the lilies. . . . Prick it, and it will bleed violet ink and *aperitif*. ("Wilder" 267)

Wilder's novel *The Cabala*, Gold observed, was narrated by "a typical American art 'pansy'" ("Wilder" 266).[13] Gold's version of proletarian realism demanded a "manly" style that would be lauded by "manly" critics.

Others belonged to Gold's fraternity. Walter Rideout noted the frequency in proletarian novels of the "charge that the bourgeois, in addition to indiscriminate sexualizing, have a penchant for the gaudier perversions. . . . One suspects that

for the proletarian novelist homosexuality came to stand . . . as a convenient, all-
inclusive symptom of capitalist decay" (218). Without apparently referring to
sexuality, Joseph North crowed in *New Masses* that he had finally met a college
man "about whom [he] had no doubt" because the student had punched a Harvard dean in the mouth. North lamented that he had "seen sons of workers . . . go
to college and stay to teach Latin and Greek and marry masculine women"
("College Men" 14). Gold and North were among a number on the androcentric
Left who likely would have appreciated the central image of the following piece
of leftist doggerel, expressing contempt for the emasculated liberal:

> While social tremblors rock the scene
> And sift us, man from man,
> He rides the bounding fence between
> —As only a eunuch can.[14]

Even 40 years later, when North edited a *New Masses* anthology in 1969, masculinity predominated. North's prologue praises *New Masses* for describing "the life
of the workingmen" and rendering "a daily nightmare that swallowed men up."
"Its [*New Masses'*] men," he says, "its writers and artists understood this kind of a
life existed" ("Prologue" 23–24).[15] North's anthology appeared a year after David
Madden's *Proletarian Writers of the Thirties*, a collection of essays. No woman
writer, as subject or author, figures in Madden's anthology (although Madden
had invited Josephine Herbst to contribute), and Harry T. Moore's preface begins
by suggesting we consider the volume as a companion piece to *Tough Guys in
Fiction*, which Madden also edited.

If "manly," "tough guys," and "proletarian" were synonymous, a "womanly" style
or point of view would be nearly as suspect as a "homosexual" one. In a review of
works by Edith Wharton, Willa Cather, and Ellen Glasgow (*The Modern
Quarterly*, 1932), Granville Hicks thus summed up the accomplishments of
American women writers:

> Talented some of them undoubtedly are—especially the three we have been con-
> sidering—but they lack the courage to strike out into the world of strife. Far more
> than the men with whom, in literary skill, they are comparable, they are the vic-
> tims of timidity, and, as a result, even their failures are minor failures. (100)

Apparently, success was possible only through "manly" courage.

Women themselves sometimes internalized the old-boy aesthetic. Leftist
writer Genevieve Taggard, for example, derided the journals of Katherine Mans-
field, a writer who had a "powerful influence" on Tillie Olsen, as "neat little
feminine cajolery . . . helpless, forlorn, honest, childlike, lost . . ." (Rosenfelt
interview; Dixler 45). Clara Weatherwax's *Marching! Marching!*, which won the
1934–35 *New Masses*-John Day Company contest for the best American novel on
a proletarian theme, refers to "College talkers swashbuckling up to large ideas"
who are "not men enough to take their pants down healthily to a working world"

(32). Le Sueur has complained that the Party "tried to beat the lyrical and emotional out of women" (Hedges 14).

Josephine Herbst was not so much beaten as "outwitted," as she put it (Langer 199), by those with "manly" courage. Herbst dates her withdrawal from the movement with her involvement in a skirmish between Farrell and Gold. Farrell's unfavorable reviews of "Communist favorites" such as Clara Weatherwax's *Marching! Marching!* and Clifford Odets's *Awake and Sing* (which Farrell privately called "Stumbling, Stumbling" and "Lay Down and Die") provoked Gold to denounce Farrell, an attack which, to Herbst, also seemed to be against "the very existence of criticism within the radical movement" (Langer 199). When Herbst and a number of other writers associated with *New Masses* wrote letters defending Farrell, she was summoned to a meeting with the journal's editors, who were disturbed by this display of division. As a result of the meeting, the group abandoned its protest, and when Herbst's letter appeared in *New Masses* (10 March 1936), it was a gentler version and was followed by a Gold rejoinder. Farrell, who "had 'loved' the 'punch' of the first letter, felt she [Herbst] had let it become 'emasculated,' and told her she had been 'out-maneuvered by the boys'" (Langer 199). Herbst concluded from this episode "that politics was essentially beyond her," although she continued to support and be sustained by the "mobilization of the people on their own behalf" (Langer 200).

When Gold challenged proletarian writers to "write with the courage of [their] own experience," addressing himself to machinists, sailors, farmers, weavers, tanners, ditch-diggers, and hobos, he thought he was speaking broadly, inclusively. Ironically, it is as if both Le Sueur and Olsen took Gold at his word and wrote "with the courage of [their] own experience." It is as if they knew that the "man" on an East Side soap-box whose revolutionary oratory awakened the boy at the end of *Jews Without Money* was, in Gold's actual experience, a woman (Elizabeth Gurley Flynn, then a Wobbly orator) (Folsom 223). Le Sueur's and Olsen's texts subvert the Party's productivism and sexism, legitimating the point of *re*production, work that Olsen terms "the maintenance of life" (*Silences* 217). They implicitly question the Marxist theory of the primacy of production, which defines production as *the* distinctively human activity and encodes activities carried out in the home, to which women have historically been disproportionately consigned, as less valuable than men's outside it. Le Sueur's and Olsen's writings suggest that the "new Communist woman" may be as worthy of our attention as the "new Communist man."

Yet Olsen and Le Sueur acknowledge a tremendous debt to the Party for fostering their writing; indeed, Le Sueur credits it for her very survival as a writer. And Olsen, who became "incited" to write because "so much of the human beings around me was not in literature," would concur with Gold's demanding, "Why should we artists born in tenements go beyond them for our expression? . . . Need we apologize or be ashamed if we express in art that manifestation of Life which is so exclusively ours, the life of the toilers?" (cited in Turan 56; "Towards Proletarian Art" 65). While acknowledging the Communist Left's androcentrism, we must keep in mind that it reflected that of the broader culture and that the CP offered more opportunities for women—especially working-class women—than did the dominant culture. As later chapters in this study will suggest, Le Sueur and Olsen maneuvered, consciously and unconsciously, on a boundary between their lived experience as radical women and a literary/political milieu that often voiced—but sometimes silenced—their concerns.

TWO

"Scratch a Communist . . . ":
Women and the American Communist Party
During the Depression

"Unfortunately it is still true to say of many of our comrades," he said, "'scratch a Communist and find a Philistine.' Of course, you must scratch the sensitive spot, their mentality as regards woman."
V. I. Lenin, quoted in Clara Zetkin, *Reminiscences of Lenin*

The androcentrism of Communist literary circles reflected that of the Party as a whole, but the CP's role in the struggle for sexual equality must be measured against the backdrop of the dominant culture. I begin this chapter, then, by (briefly) discussing the position of women in the United States during the '30s, indicating a few of the historiographical sources that provide a necessary complement to this study. I move quickly to this chapter's central task, examining the CP and "the woman question," and focus largely on Party publications during the period. However, the chapter's last section relies on four documentaries (*With Babies and Banners, Union Maids, The Life and Times of Rosie the Riveter*, and *Seeing Red*) that, with my own interview material, augment information derived from the Party press. The role of women in Party-related activities reminds us of Myra Jehlen's useful premise for analyzing women's history and writing: Women must be viewed not in "actual independence but [in] action despite dependence" (581).

Feminism was thwarted during the '30s by the national preoccupation with economic collapse and recovery. The previous decade's debate over the "new woman" was subsumed by anxiety over the unemployed man, and competition for a limited number of jobs reinforced cultural assumptions about the proper sexual division of labor. The public arena absorbed most attention, while issues seemingly unrelated to economic reclamation were ignored. Americans were reluctant to examine or tamper with traditional roles within the family at a time when it was viewed as perhaps the only remnant of stability. More than ever, many felt, the family needed to serve its purpose as the foundation of social order.

Married women workers faced a special form of discrimination. New York Assemblyman Arthur Schwartz represented the prevailing view when he announced in 1931 that the employment of married women was reprehensible and admonished "our federal, state and local governments [to] cooperate to remove these undeserving 'parasites'" (cited in Scharf 45). Section 213 of the 1932 Economy Act allowed the firing of one spouse if both husband and wife worked for the Civil Service, and nearly all of those fired before Section 213 was repealed in 1937 were women. Private industry likewise discriminated. In 1931, for example, New England Telephone and Telegraph fired all its married women employees. And most large companies, banks, and insurance firms refused to hire married women as clericals (Strom 361–362). "Seventy-seven percent of the nation's school systems refused to hire married women," Kessler-Harris reports, and half of them fired female teachers who married while on the job. The state of Texas established a "means" standard for females holding transportation jobs, firing those whose husbands earned more than 50 dollars a month (257).

Such discrimination continued throughout the decade. As late as 1939, 26 state legislatures were considering bills to ban married women from state employment, and in that year in *Current History and Forum* Norman Cousins articulated a popular solution to the unemployment problem: "There are approximately 10,000,000 people out of work in the United States today; there are also 10,000,000 or more women, married and single, who are jobholders. Simply fire the women, who shouldn't be working anyway," Cousins opined, "and hire the men. Presto! No unemployment. No relief rolls. No depression" (cited in Kessler-Harris 256).

The employment of married women, many people believed, had contributed to the unemployment crisis. As one leader of the National Woman's Party put it, in "this era of depression, the first impulse seems to be to 'wallop the ladies'" (Scharf 47). The assault on married women workers affected all employed women, married or not. As Sharon Hartman Strom observes, because most women eventually married, "the working woman was by default considered to be a young adult, or 'working girl'" (362). Only a temporary presence in the labor force, she should not have a voice in union policy equal to the man's. Employed married women were considered anomalies, working only due to a temporary financial necessity or personal selfishness. Work outside the home "was a stage, not a right" (362-363). African-American women workers, however, whether married or not, "had never been accused of working for 'pin money,'" as Nancy Woloch notes (450). Historically a greater part of the female labor force, they had long worked out of necessity, "a position new to many white middle-class women in the 1930s." While some Euro-American women entering the work force found white-collar and factory jobs, African-American women were barred from such work and were "relegated to the lowest-paid and most menial jobs, a situation that remained unchanged by [the] depression." Moreover, they "suffered a disproportionately high unemployment rate" throughout the decade; more than 50 percent lost their jobs, as compared to 30 percent of Euro-American women (Woloch 450).

Popular culture, as Alice Kessler-Harris observes, depicted husbands "endlessly hunt[ing] for jobs" and wives sitting passively by, "poignantly wringing their hands in despair." The opening scene of a 1935 film, King Vidor's *Our Daily Bread*, Kessler-Harris adds, offers just such a tableau: "Mary says to her husband, who has come in after yet another fruitless day of job-hunting, 'Oh, Jack, what shall we do?'" And mainstream women's magazines published articles with titles such as "You Can Have My Job: A Feminist Discovers Her Home" and "The Return of the Lady" (253).

The American CP held contradictory attitudes toward women during the Depression decade. To some extent the Party recognized the special concerns of women through a Women's Commission; a special magazine, *The Working Woman* (1929–35), which changed its title during the Popular Front to *Woman Today* (1936–37)[1]; a special column in the Party newspaper, the *Daily Worker*; all-women party units (which were not, however, organizationally autonomous); and the support of many strikes of women workers. Whereas a 1936 Gallup poll indicated that 82 percent of all Americans believed a wife should not work if her husband held a job, the CP insisted on the right of all women to work and, along with the League of Women Voters and the Business and Professional Women's Clubs, opposed state legislation forbidding the employment of married women. But fighting for gender equality was a relatively low priority for the Party. This can be explained partly by the absence of a viable autonomous women's movement to put pressure on the Party, which maintained that working-class women and men faced the same enemies: imperialist war, fascism, unemployment, poor working conditions, speed-ups, wage cuts, monopolies. The low priority can be further explained by the Party's focus, in the decade's early years, on workplace organizing (only about 20 percent of women worked outside the home in the '30s). The Party believed that basic industry, in which few women were employed, contained the element of the working class most central to the economy.

The CPUSA both misrepresented the status of women in the Soviet Union and exaggerated the advances women had made there, simplistically assuring its followers that, as one 1935 *Daily Worker* headline proclaimed, "Legend of the 'Weaker Sex' Effectively Smashed By the Position of Women in the Soviet Union: All Inequality Abolished by the October Revolution" (5).[2] "The Kitchen Under Socialism" (*The Working Woman*, October 1931) declared that because the October Revolution had "brought complete emancipation to women" and had given them "absolutely equal legal and social rights," it was "necessary to take them out of that 'proper' place, to enable them fully to benefit by their newly acquired freedom" (Yarros 4). "How We Live," by Soviet Women Workers (*The Working Woman*, April 30, 1934) included subheadings such as "Women Paid Same Wages as Men" and "Wages Constantly Rising" and featured a photograph of children, with the following caption: "BEST CARED FOR CHILDREN IN THE WORLD: Soviet

Children at Play in the Garden of the Nursery While Mothers Work" (8–9). Such idealizing served the attitude among many CP members that a socialist revolution would be requisite *and sufficient* for alleviating women's oppression. Complacency about male domination, then, appeared justified on two counts: The impending revolution would dissolve patriarchy in its wake, and little could be done to further sexual equality prior to the revolution, in any case.

What attention the Party gave to women during the Third Period centered on those who were paid laborers. It considered the grievances of female as well as male workers, although most Party publications (with *The Working Woman* the notable exception) used male figures almost exclusively as images of workers. During the Popular Front, following its general line, the Party broadened its approach to women's issues. But even though the emphasis on organizing in largely male industries shifted slightly after 1935, Party union activity still centered on the mining, steel, maritime, and auto industries.

Although Party leadership was overwhelmingly male, women composed a significant and growing portion of the rank-and-file. Only 1600 women belonged to the Party in 1931, but by 1933 that number doubled, with over 3000 women accounting for nearly 20 percent of the membership. According to a partial registration in 1935, women members numbered 6200, nearly one-quarter of the Party (Klehr 163). By the end of the decade, more than one out of three members was a woman (Woloch 450). Females constituted 16 percent of the students attending Party training schools in 1931; 21 percent in 1936; and 24 percent in 1938 (Dixler 225, 228–229). And, by 1940, women constituted between 30 and 40 percent of the membership (Shaffer 90). Unfortunately, these sources and others I consulted did not—and likely could not, given the information available—break down female membership according to race and ethnicity.

Questions about what the American Communist Party had done in the past and could do in the future to ease the dilemma of the working woman were the subjects of Rachel Holtman's "International Women's Day," published in *Communist*, the Party's theoretical journal, in March 1930. Holtman asserted, "So the woman is now under a double yoke: she is compelled to slave at home as well as in the factory for the man's wages are too meager to support the family" (204). A troubling fatalism lurks in Holtman's articulation of the double yoke and the potential for its being lifted. She says nothing of the possibility of men and women sharing housework and child care. Moreover, women will continue to wear their double yoke until the revolution, which Holtman, with many Communists, believed was imminent: "International Women's Day is a means of collecting strength, arming for the revolution, which may be nearer than anyone thinks. . . . The end of the capitalist system is sure to come." Holtman urges women to join in the struggle that will, among other things, free them of their double yoke (208–209).

Holtman's brief history of the Party's approach to women's problems provides perspective on her somewhat fatalistic view of the double yoke. Her history reports approvingly on the Party's attempts to discourage its members from joining forces with "the bourgeois suffrage movement" or "bourgeois feminism" (204). Holtman registers a common complaint of Communists against feminists of the period: "The main stress was laid by the suffragette on sex and not on class" (204). However, Holtman's attack on feminism sharpens as she describes the circumstances in which "American Socialist Women" developed "the idea of International Women's Day":

> In order to make their work in this field [socialist propaganda] more successful, the American Women called a conference in 1904 and decided to lay aside a special day for agitation among women. Equal rights was at that time a very popular idea. Therefore they put forward that, as their main point, and that was their slogan on Women's Day.
>
> At that time there were working among the suffragettes in America quite a few active women socialists. These soon resolved themselves into two groups and began to fight among themselves for the class line.
>
> One group of socialist women said that the working women in America should not collaborate with those women whose sole aim was equal rights. The other group was of the opinion that the feminists were good "comrades," for they did not make any distinction between rich and poor. That is why many of them joined the movement and with their active participation helped to strengthen the suffragettes.
>
> This goes to show how "class conscious" the American socialist women were. Instead of pointing out to the working women the evil consequences of getting together on one united front with the feminists, instead of pointing out that collaboration means doing away with the class line drawn between the bourgeois and working class, instead of all these, they tried to work together with their enemies, the bourgeois women. (205)

Aside from the dream that the revolution was just around the corner, Holtman's sectarian position held out little immediate hope for women wearing the double yoke.

The same issue of *Communist* carried a report, "Plenum of Women Workers' Committee of the RILU [Red International of Labor Unions]," that recognized more fully than Holtman the necessity that the CP attend to the needs of women wearing the double yoke. Comrade [Solomon] Losovsky argued that it had become fashionable in Party resolutions to pay lip service to the work and needs of women but that the Party continued to marginalize women in various ways. Losovsky considered the Party's mentioning of women and young workers in their resolutions "the usual bow" that "does not oblige those who have signed the resolution[s] to do anything." Organizing among women continued to be viewed as a "'sideline,' as an extra occupation." The "most simple" and "best" method for drawing women into the movement, Losovsky argued, is "that of bringing up before the women workers questions connected with their everyday needs and the everyday struggle" (224, 227).

A similar point was made by C. D. in the September–October 1931 issue of *Party Organizer*, a "how-to" organizing bulletin for activists: "It is about time the entire Party, men and women, got a new slant on how to draw the women workers into our campaigns and struggles. We should stop stating policy and then adding 'and the women, Negro, and youth'" (30). In February 1930 an unsigned article, "Women's Work in the Shops," appeared in *Party Organizer* arguing the necessity of factory organizers' attending carefully to "the type of women employed" in a given factory, "their social customs, their particular problems, hardships, and grievances in that factory, and their living conditions at home" (13). Thus some Communists at the beginning of the '30s urged the Party to recognize working women's everyday needs.

However, Dorothy Healey recalled the phenomenon of the Party's obligatory final paragraph: "'And there must be etc., etc., including women.' You know, all . . . oppressed minorities and women. [It was the concluding] paragraph of Party resolutions where all miscellaneous—the etceteras—were all gathered together" (interview). And the marginalizing of women was attested to by another former Party member, Harriet Magil, who recalled the Party's insensitivity during the late '30s and '40s to women's everyday needs and "conditions at home."[3] Magil was a social worker and a member of a union to which many other women belonged. She reports that women in the union "had a good deal of communication, a kind of communal interest as women, and saw ourselves as persecuted in many more ways than men." She notes that women in the union were "very much interested in reading, for example, [about] angles on the family and getting a whole new focus on life for Communists as women" (Buhle interview).

"Did you feel there was official recognition for your solidarity as women within the Party?" Buhle asked Magil. She responded emphatically:

> Absolutely not. Absolutely none. . . . The women in the leadership of the movement were not women's women; they were men's women . . . and they had no identification with the problems of the average woman. Their identification was totally in the male world, and we were very much persecuted by these women who expected the kind of discipline from us that was pretty shocking to people, particularly [those] trained in my field in emotional development of human beings and . . . [to] the people who had my frame of reference, that is that socialism was . . . a great means of achieving the goal of making better human beings, and that you didn't start making better human beings by . . . having terrible relations and oppressing people in the course of developing that movement, and so we were very much at odds with the leadership.

When Buhle asked for clarification, "And by oppressing people you mean . . . ?," Magil again replied emphatically:

> Arbitrarily telling people where they had to be when, irrespective of what their duties were in relation to childrearing [or] in relation to many other very vital and important life problems. And so that we had many, many grievances against the leadership. . . . We felt it was not a human leadership, and we felt it was theoretical and not in touch and much too related to revolutionary conditions in primitive societies and not related to American conditions at all. . . . And the epithet[s] [were] constantly slung at us—"middle class," "bourgeois"—and we had to fight against that all the time. (Buhle interview)

According to Magil, the Party did not recognize the "double yoke"—or "double standard" of domestic labor—under which women, and especially mothers, were exploited. Moreover, its failure to acknowledge the real conditions of women's lives caused the Party to place unreasonable demands on its women members. Magil was not arguing, of course, that the Party should not have expected women to be active, but that it should have responded more sensitively and flexibly to women already struggling under the "double yoke."

Two influential books written by women Party members during the '30s, Grace Hutchins's *Women Who Work* (1934) and Mary Inman's *In Woman's Defense* (1940), suggest the Party's conflicting attitudes toward women. Hutchins's book details the exclusion of women from many jobs, particularly skilled, higher-paying ones, and examines wage differentials between women and men, blacks and whites; white women earned less than white or black men, and black women earned the least of all. Hutchins discusses the "double burden" (Holtman's previously discussed "double yoke") of married working women who are responsible for domestic as well as paid labor, urging working women to organize for maternity insurance, cooperative kitchens, day-care centers, and school lunch programs. No more than Holtman does Hutchins advocate that men assume some of the burden of housework and child care. (In the women's column of the *Daily Worker* columnist Helen Luke dared to raise the question of women and men sharing housework, which "provoked sympathetic responses from women and sarcasm and hostility from men" [Ware 127].)

Hutchins properly locates the economic basis of women's subjection in the unpaid position of the housewife and in the lower pay and restricted employment status of women in the paid work force, which contribute to depression of all workers' wages. But she argues schematically that the American Federation of Labor unions support this system simply because they are pro-capitalist, failing to take into account that they represent the interests of male workers. Moreover, Hutchins begins the book by dismissing "women of the middle and upper classes," who, she claims, have already nearly achieved economic, political, and professional equality with men (7–8).

Mary Inman's *In Woman's Defense* was first published in 1939 in serial form in the *People's World*, the Party's West Coast newspaper, and reflects the broader character of the CP's work among women during the Popular Front. Unlike Grace Hutchins, Inman argues that all women are oppressed, not just wage-earning or working-class women, and considers housework productive labor, a linchpin of the capitalist system in which labor power is produced and reproduced. Drawing on Charlotte Perkins Gilman's conception of collectivized domestic labor, Inman demonstrates that housework is performed with outmoded techniques. The chores women do individually could be accomplished far more efficiently under a collective system, Inman suggests, freeing women for other pursuits. (Nowhere does Inman, any more than Hutchins, argue that men should share domestic labor, including the care of children.) Inman believed that one could be both a feminist and a Communist, and she attacked those sectarians in the people's camp whose opposition to all varieties of feminism "helped strangle all of woman's activity" (22–23). Inman acknowledged that cultural forms and attitudes unrelated to women's economic status could be oppressive, whereas most Communist theorists defined the exploitation of women in strictly economic terms. According to Earl Browder, for example, an adequate income was sufficient for marital harmony. "Abolish poverty," he insisted, "and the problem of divorce will largely disappear" (201).

The Party's response to *In Woman's Defense* is telling. While Inman's views represented the perspective of some Party members, including Tillie Olsen, who used *In Woman's Defense* when she taught a class on "the woman question" for the San Francisco Young Communist League, those views were not welcomed by the CP leadership. Representing the Party leadership, Avram Landy "disputed Inman's analysis of the housewife as an indirect employee of either the capitalist or of her husband," maintaining "that wage-labor was the defining economic relationship of capitalism"; argued the Third Period line that "trade unions are the main force for social change," even regarding housewives' concerns; and denied "any conceivable antagonism between working-class men and women" (Shaffer 86). In *Marxism and the Woman Question* Landy concluded: "it is because the husband is exploited that the housewife's position is wretched and miserable" (64). Landy's positions, in effect, discouraged struggles against sexism.

In 1939 and 1940 Mary Inman and Al Richmond, an editor of the *People's World*, renewed agitation for a national Women's Congress, which had previously failed, but their effort was squashed by the Party leadership (Weinstein 162). The negative response to Inman's attempt to conjoin feminist issues with Party concerns resulted in her leaving the Party, and her radical analyses of women's oppression were thereafter ignored (Ware 126).Conflict between men and women, it was assumed, had to be denied or minimized to strengthen Party unity, and women paid a higher price than men for this individual and collective repression.

One of the most forceful and prescient essays about women's rights that appeared during the '30s, Rebecca Pitts's "Women and Communism" (*New Masses*, January 19, 1935), anticipated Inman's positions as well as some concerns of contemporary feminists.[4] Pitts (a poet and a member of the Indianapolis John Reed Club) identified "a specific dilemma involved in being a woman . . . a conflict between *sex* (with its biological needs and social demands) and our *humanity*" (14). Pitts's concern about this dilemma was echoed over forty years later by Annie Gottlieb in *Mother Jones* (November 1976), in remarkably similar terms: "a woman must make an impossible choice—between her femaleness and her humanity" ("Feminists" 51). Pitts and Gottlieb addressed the same problem—a woman's desire to have children *and* to undertake meaningful work outside the home—and both saw the root of the problem as "*social* rather than biological" (Pitts 14).

"Women and Communism" was published in the twilight of the "proletarian" Third Period. However, Pitts's appeal, like Inman's, was far broader than that of Hutchins or Irene Leslie, who in *The Communist* (March 1936) termed bourgeois women "parasites upon parasites" and insisted that "the woman problem" included only "the toiling women and the wives of toilers" (245). Pitts, addressing "the oppressed industrial worker, to be sure; but also the professional woman, the ambitious college girl, the wife who has stifled her native talents in domestic slavery," urged readers to recognize "that sex and parenthood are important for women and men alike; but that while they *are* important they do not fill every need nor exercise every capacity" (18).

In an unorthodox move for a Communist, Pitts gives equal weight to psychological and economic factors in explaining women's oppression. She discusses the "psychology of [private] property," the "subtle" and "pervasive" forces that mold people, the complicity of women in their subordination, and the "mental anguish" and "crushing inner burden imposed not by nature, but by the social order" (14, 15, 17). Although the Party often considered psychological and emotional categories unmaterialist, unrelated to "real" politics, Pitts treats these categories as fundamentally political.

The role of women in the CP can be gauged partly by the extent to which they contributed to Party publications. Out of a list of some 50 contributors to *New Masses* in 1933, for example, only five were women. Its editorial board was composed wholly of men until one woman joined it in 1936, although some women—such as Meridel Le Sueur, Ruth McKenney, Mary Heaton Vorse, and Josephine Herbst—contributed regularly. In the Party's theoretical journal, *The Communist*, only two articles by women appeared in 1934, out of more than 50 contributors in 12 issues. The *Party Organizer* fared somewhat better; although in the early '30s articles by women averaged less than one per issue, by 1936 or '37 "it was not uncommon for almost half of the writers to be women." The greatest exceptions to the predominant pattern were *The Working Woman* and *Woman Today*, in which all but a few contributors were women (Shaffer 114, n70; 93).

The Working Woman, with a circulation of about 8000 at its peak, identified its primary audience as women working for employers and "housewives" working at home and attempted to address the multiple, pressing needs of these women.[5] From 1929–35 *The Working Woman* appeared in the form of a monthly newspaper and from 1933–35 in the form of a monthly magazine. In each form its circulation was both national and international. In addition to reports from its staff writers, *The Working Woman* published many stories, articles, interviews, and letters of women throughout the United States and other parts of the world. The multiplicity of voices of suffering and militant women constitutes a powerful record of the period. Moreover, the photographs in this publication provide a forceful visual record of working and living conditions and of activities such as strikes.[6] *The Working Woman*, whose masthead bore the slogan "Working Women! Demand Equal Pay For Equal Work; Higher Wages, Shorter Hours—For Negro and White Women," persistently addressed issues of civil rights, birth control, child care, health care, poverty, prostitution, and homelessness. Further, it recorded endeavors to organize across race, gender, and class lines.

Although *The Working Woman* emphasized the need for working-class men and women to "unite and fight," it occasionally addressed problems between men and women. For example, under the headline "WHAT WOULD YOU DO?," the December 1934 issue announced a contest, inviting readers to reply to the following letter received by its editor.

> *October 15, 1934*
> Dear Editor:
>
> I am interested in the working-class movement. I worked ten years in the two mills in our town. Now I would like to join a real working class organization and attend meetings.
>
> *But my husband won't let me.* I've been married five years and have two kids. Whenever I tell my husband (who has just gotten his third wage-cut) that I want to go to these meetings, we always quarrel. It's no use quarreling all the time and I don't know what to do. He has all kinds of interests outside work and goes to all kinds of meetings. But when it comes to me, that's different.
>
> I read your magazine for women and wonder whether you could tell me what I can do. I would surely appreciate it if you would.
>
> > Sincerely,
> > [name withheld] (5)

The letter was accompanied in the magazine by the following blurb, including the opening lines of replies *The Working Woman* had already received:

> Answers to the vital problem raised in this letter . . . have already come from women in ten cities in the North, East, South and West—from small mining towns, from farms, from large industrial cities. Here are replies from New York, Detroit, and Chicago.
>
> I would avoid discussing the matter of meetings for a while and bring literature home. . . .
>
> I would just express to him my opinion. I would tell him the time is over when a husband can boss his wife. . . .
>
> I would get in touch with the nearest Party unit which would assign a member best suited to approach my husband from the special angle of his interest. . . . (5)

Sixteen prizes were offered in the contest, including canned goods, an electric iron, a six-months' subscription to the *Daily Worker*, a year's subscription to the *Negro Liberator*, posters from the Soviet Union depicting Soviet life, and (your author's personal favorite) large glossy photos of Lenin, Stalin, and Marx. Rose Wortis, Margaret Cowl, Williana Burroughs, Clarence Hathaway, and Ella Reeve Bloor judged the contest.

The March 1935 issue announced the winners. First Prize, a "Hamper of White Rose Canned products," went to this reply from F. Reish, "a Bronx, New York housewife":

> I am going to tell you what I would do. The first thing, I would buy the Daily Worker every day and would give it to my husband to read. I would buy pamphlets and magazines to give him. I would not expect in the beginning that he would read everything, but I would pick out something to appeal especially to him. If he would not read it, I would not quarrel with him, but I would find out what organization is giving a good lecture and "just for fun" I would invite him to go. I would

tell him he doesn't have to join the organization, but "let us go anyway and hear what they have to say." . . . As to the children, mother and father should arrange not to go to meetings the same evening. They should share the time, as they share their bread. Perhaps two evenings a week father should go, and two evenings, mother.

Now, what would I do if my husband would ignore me; if he would not care to read anything that has to do with workers' life and would not want to go to mass meetings, and also would not let me go? I would stand for my rights. Finally, if he would refuse to let me go out, and the children are too small, I would bring the meetings to my house. I would give my children a proletarian education. . . . (13)

When she discusses the right to attend evening meetings while the children need caring for at home, Reish calls for equality (couples should "share the time, as they share their bread"). However, the First Prize winner's willingness to bring her meetings home, should the husband refuse to let her go out, suggests support for forms of accommodation.

Second Prize, a Westinghouse electric iron, was awarded to Anna Vera Bell, a miner's wife from central Pennsylvania, for the following, far less accommodating reply:

I am married eight years, have two children. . . . Now I am in the Communist Party four months. One day last week he [her husband] told me he would put a stop to all this meeting business. He thinks I'm out too much. But I told him there can't be a revolution without women. Our Party is the only Party interested in the working woman. No one could ever convince me to drop out. I told him rather than leave the Party, I would leave him. (13)

The article announcing the winners thus summarized the opinions expressed in other replies: "'The sanctity and peace of the home[,]' wrote one woman[,] 'is the most important thing of all. If you love your husband, you will please him, no matter what he requires.' The majority of women, however, declared that such a 'peace' would be distasteful to them" ("The Winners!" 13). The article drew the following conclusions from the contest:

The many letters show that a very important problem has been probed through this contest. The letters . . . reveal the ferment among women; their demand to be organized; to fight for their economic and political rights.

The letters show that this period is very ripe for the organization of women. They are waiting to be organized, and in many cases are organizing themselves. It lays a task upon the readers of the *Working Woman*. They must organize these women, bring them into the rank and file groups of the unions, into the unemployed organizations, into the fight against fascism and war, into the Communist Party. The women, these letters reveal, are demanding organization. As one farm woman writes—"Let's go to it!" ("The Winners!" 13)

The Working Woman, which clearly announced the importance of organizing women, despite resistance from some men, was a liberating force for women. This publication urged women to be politically active, and, in so doing, some women would necessarily resist male domination and insist on men's sharing, if only occasionally, "the double yoke." But it is important to acknowledge that inequality between men and women was almost never addressed *per se* by the editors (although it was occasionally addressed by letters from readers). Sexism was an annoying inconvenience, requiring women's attention only so they could be active in resisting *other* "genuine" forms of oppression.

Similar letter-writing contests were held by the *Sunday Worker Magazine*, part of the Sunday edition of the *Daily Worker*. The contests were announced in Ann Rivington's column, "Woman's Point of View," on January 12, 1936. She announced the first contest problem: "A Woman goes to work outside the home. Her husband feels that 'women's work' is beneath him and fails to help with household tasks, though he has as much time for them as she. What should she do?" (14). In her column of February 9, 1936, Rivington commented on responses received to that date: "Quite a number of letters suggested that the solution to the problem was for women to accept the inevitable and do all the work of the home in addition to the outside job, because men 'just aren't fitted for such things.'" Rivington expressed her impatience with such responses: "Nothing was ever accomplished in this world by accepting the 'inevitable'" (14). The prize-winning letter, published February 16, 1936, was also intolerant of the "inevitable." Mary of Cleveland observed that "women's work" "has been taken for granted for so long that we don't stop to think it out." In analyzing the problem she noted: "It is a bourgeois attitude that the man is superior, that the woman should look up to the man, and therefore woman's work is beneath him" (14). The prize-winning letter and two letters receiving honorable mention were published without editorial comment.

On July 5, 1936, the *Sunday Worker Magazine* contest series returned to a version of the question with which the series had begun. This time Rivington labeled the problem "Husband Trouble"—a man's refusal to share housework, even when his wife worked full time—and she proposed a "Dear-Mr.-Husband Contest": "Write a letter to Mr. Husband telling him in what ways he treats you as an inferior, why you think he does it, and in what ways he is harming himself by doing so" (14). This time, many of the letters in the contest expressed considerable hostility toward men. A letter from "Your Wife Betty," for example, published in *Sunday Worker Magazine* (2 August 1936), while ultimately blaming the "capitalist system" for her subordination, nevertheless speaks sharply:

> You do love to boss, don't you? At home, of course. On your job, you're being bossed. But at home there's no one to stop you, your wife being weaker, and as your manly ego would have it, inferior—after all, "only a woman". . . .
>
> I'll admit that all I do is take care of the children, sew, mend and do all the housework, including the wash. If my figures are right, a twelve or fourteen hour job, compared to your eight. Do I hear you say, "Just housework, a woman's job, not worth doing, not much of a job?"
>
> Yes, I believe I heard those words before. How you like to command the whole show! (15)

But the first of the two letters that appear under the heading "The Prize Letter" (23 August 1936), signed by "Your Comrade in Marriage," asserted that men and women alike have inherited their roles of male dominance and female subordination from their parents. "Your Comrade in Marriage" neither blamed nor accused her husband ("it really isn't your fault that you treat me as an inferior") but patiently explained the difficulty of her double burden. Implying that confronting her husband about housework is pointless, she concludes: "My energy should be directed towards helping to build a society where women's equal rights will be established" (13). Like Rachel Holtman's article in *The Communist*, discussed above, this letter expresses both optimism about the imminence of a socialist revolution and fatalism about the "double yoke"/"husband trouble." The author of the prize-winning letter, then, while "committed" to the principle of sexual equality, in effect accepted inequality in her own home.

Oddly, Rivington's note about "The Prize Letter" refers to it in the singular ("The author of the following letter will receive a copy of Granville Hicks's great biography of a great revolutionist, 'John Reed'"), even though two letters follow her note. The second letter published under "The Prize Letter," signed "Comradely yours, H. M.," is sarcastic and considerably more militant than the first:

> . . . But lo! There was I, wanting—ardently wanting—to do a bit for the Rothstein Strikers (remember those courageous girls and boys who fought for long months until they won): wanting to picket with them, to talk for them, to mother and encourage them. But no! Mr. Husband, no! Your precious little wife (poor, frail thing) her place was in the home, by the kitchen stove, on the lap of her Man, safe from the strife of the class-struggle . . . [ellipsis in the original] Adolph Hitler mustn't dictate! But you Mr. Husband? . . . [ellipsis in the original] And how you coddled me, smothered me with kisses, away from the Rothstein Strikers!
>
> Bosses, too, say nice things to the workers when they cut their wages. Mr. Mussolini (may the Pope bless him!) caresses babies before he gasses a defenseless people. We women, Mr. Husband, resent, yes resent, a sugar-coated stigma of inequality, of inferiority. . . .
>
> If "labor in a white skin can't be free while labor in a black skin is branded" the labor in pants will never break its fetters while labor in skirts sits shackled!" (13)

Beginning October 3, 1937, Elizabeth Gurley Flynn contributed a regular column to *Sunday Worker Magazine*'s "women's page." Flynn's column that day, titled "The Feminine Ferment," announced that "this column will be devoted to discussing labor organization, politics, economic and social problems from the woman's angle" (10). In the December 19, 1937, issue, Flynn thus directed her male reader: "Help her [his wife] at home, with the children. No good Communist thinks today, in this changing world, that 'women's place is in the home'" (10). Further, in the January 23, 1938, issue, Flynn referred to "the double burden": "No use to tell these new generations, 'Women's place is in the home!' Married women, who carry the double burden of domestic and factory work are joining auxiliaries and unions, going on strike and picketing, are participating in struggles to win for themselves the security they once expected from others" (10).[7]

A letter written by M. K. (*The Working Woman*, July 1933) deals poignantly with the relationship between "the double burden" or "husband trouble" and a woman's desire to become a part of an organized fight for rights:

> Dear Editor:
>
> I really don't know how to start my letter. But this is the only place where I can write all this out.
>
> I am Italian woman and all my life I am working, after a hard day's work I attend to the house and children. . . .
>
> Here starts my trouble. My place organized into an Industrial Union and now I am a union girl. My shopmates made me go to a meeting, to take part in union activities, to fight for conditions. I was elected as a delegate to conferences and every word became attached to my mind and entire being. I wish I could express the enthusiasm I feel now. If only I had more time to learn more—I am longing to develop. Now I never keep away from a meeting.
>
> But my husband is not in favor of all these new ideas and we have fights, he thinks that I do something wrong in back of him. I attend the house, the children better than before. I try my best to make him understand the present system which forces us to fight against wage cuts and our very bread. I want him to be closer to his own class, to read and go to meetings to see that no woman is wrong by going to meeting. I think that you will do much good for me and my family by helping me out. (13)

The unidentified editor of *The Working Woman* replied:

> The problem raised in M. K.'s letter is not an isolated one. The working class women who have awakened to fight for their own class interests, who are anxious to read, study and learn, meet with obstacles in their own homes.
>
> Many husbands and fathers, not only Italians, but American and other nation-alities, still cling to the old ideas that the woman's place is at home. They try to discourage the women from taking part in the fight to improve the conditions of her family. . . .

Unfortunately, a printing error omitted most of the rest of the editor's reply.[8] But after the truncated reply, the editor calls upon readers to "Give the Answer": "We would like to hear from our readers who had similar experiences to write and tell us what they have to say about it" (13). While not directly confronting sexism, *The Working Woman* can be credited for encouraging women to consider and voice possible "husband trouble."

With the publication of "An Open Letter to Husbands" (May 1936) *Woman Today* carried on *The Working Woman*'s tradition of airing "husband trouble" complaints. The writer begins her letter:

> A few words to the progressive husband. You married her to be your companion and partner in life and still you go out to educational lectures or to union meetings to inform yourself on shop conditions without giving your wife a chance to join a group of women—who are the wives of workers and workers them-selves—where she can meet and discuss the problems of today. (19)

"How come, Mr. Progressive Husband?" the writer asks. Like the editors of *The Working Woman*, those of *Woman Today* followed the letter with an invitation for both wives and husbands to respond.

Many Party members were aware of Lenin's position against what he termed "household drudgery": "woman continues to be a *domestic slave*, because *petty housework* crushes, strangles, stultifies and degrades her, chains her to the kitchen and to the nursery, and wastes her labor on barbarously unproductive, petty, nerve-racking, stultifying and crushing drudgery" (Lenin 56). Jessica Mitford, who came to the United States from England in 1939 and joined the Party in 1943, indirectly comments on the issue of "husband trouble," paraphrasing Lenin, whose words on "the woman question" she tacked above her kitchen sink: "A perennial complaint of some wives we knew was that their husbands kept them tied to unproductive, barbarous, arduous, petty housework and so prevented them from taking their place beside men in the world of work and careers."[9] When I asked Bill Bailey if in his memory this was "a perennial complaint," he replied: "I think it was. . . . I always felt that my role in the Party was more important than her [his wife's] role in the Party. In other words, my meeting was always more important than what she had to do." Party men, in general, Bailey thought, wanted women "to take care of" the "domestic things." In hindsight, Bailey adds, "it doesn't make you feel good, I'll tell you that much, and I've regretted quite a bit of it" (interview).

Accommodation to men, the tactic the Party press sometimes recommended to women, was endorsed in two pieces published in *Party Organizer*. In a May 1937 issue, a Los Angeles organizer described her frustrated efforts to recruit Latinas to the Party. The men "advance, they go to meetings, they join the Party, but the status of the wife is still the same at home. . . . The men don't let their wives go to meetings where there are other men. They are very jealous" (cited in Dixler 71). Instead of trying to change the men's attitudes, the organizer arranged to meet with the women during the day. The women could bring their children and did not have to ask their husbands to stay with them in the evening; a meeting attended only by women, moreover, did not rouse the husbands' jealousy. A Manhattan unit adopted the same strategy, according to an article in the July 1937 issue, meeting during the day in Central Park so members could keep an eye on their children: "we were up against husbands who refused to stay home with the baby, or husbands who were ignorant of the wives' new status, and would question and dictate" (cited in Dixler 72). Rather than confront male domination, then, women accommodated it. Although these women deserve credit for exercising one of their few options, the Party press treated such half-measures as genuine solutions.

Nevertheless, objections to half-measures and mere lip service occasionally appeared in the Party press. Ann Weedon complained in a letter to *New Masses* (July 16, 1935) about the position of women within the Party. Under the heading "Do We Recognize Women?" *The Working Woman* (September 1935) reprinted the letter:

I have had a number of discussions lately with Communists about the new deal Communism proposes to give women. So far as I can see it is equivalent, roughly, to the liberation the Negroes were given after the Civil War. . . . I am speaking of actual deeds and real results, not of the abstract policy which is beautiful enough. As an outsider looking in and seeing only through the window, I catch glimpses like this:

1. The current (July 2) New Masses is written 100 percent by men. . . .

2. The executive positions in the Party are held by men. . . . I see a predominance of women in the ranks and a man in every position of any consequence.

When I mention these facts to Communists they react in one of three ways. They point with pride to some lone women who holds a third-rate post, much as Mr. Roosevelt might point to Ruth Owen or Miss Perkins to prove that women get a square deal in America. Or they sneer, and say with fine sophistication, "What! still a suffragette?" to which one might well reply, "Yes, and still an abolitionist, also." The third reply is verbose, and, now that I have heard it so often, rather tiresome; it is a lengthy recitation of the whole attitude of Communism toward women, plus a retreat to Moscow for concrete examples. . . .

I believe the question should be put this way: Do you feel that women are lacking in ability, or do you admit that you have failed to recognize their ability? (13)

Apparently, Weedon's dissatisfaction represented that of a significant number of women. According to the editor's note, her letter "raises a question that is on the lips of hundreds of women."

Resistance to male domination was problematic partly because it countered the Party's concern that its members live like "ordinary workers" and observe the Victorian moral standards that prevailed among the rank-and-file. These Victorian moral standards included a conservative view of sexuality. Tillie Olsen recalls that Communists frequently quoted Lenin's challenge to Alexandra Kollantai on the issue of sexual freedom, favoring Lenin's position that "the chaos of an unruly love life seemed to be completely unproductive for socialist reconstruction" (Rowbotham, *Resistance* 153). Kollantai, the only female member of the Bolshevik central committee and the Soviet Union's first Commissar of Social Welfare, became notorious in the Soviet Union for advocating sexual freedom and the abolition of the bourgeois family. Most American Party members, if they knew about Kollantai at all, associated her merely with the "glass of water theory," the notion "that sex should be as easy and uncomplicated as drinking a glass of water" (Holt 13). In fact, Kollantai's ideas differed significantly from this "glass of water" caricature.

Kollantai believed that love would develop into a higher form under communism, echoing the views expressed by Marx and Engels in *The Origin of the Family*. She debunked "the hypocritical morality of bourgeois culture," which "resolutely restricted the freedom of Eros, obliging him to visit only the 'legally married couple,'" and contrasted bourgeois morality to "love-comradeship" or "winged eros":

Obviously sexual attraction lies at the base of "winged Eros" too, but the difference is that the person experiencing love acquires the inner qualities necessary to the builders of a new culture—sensitivity, responsiveness and the desire to help others. Bourgeois ideology demanded that a person should only display such qualities in their relationship with one partner. The aim of proletarian ideology is that men and women should develop these qualities not only in relation to the chosen one but in relation to all the members of the collective. . . . The ideal of love-comradeship, which is being forged by proletarian ideology to replace the all-embracing and exclusive marital love of bourgeois culture, involves the recognition of the rights and integrity of the other's personality, a steadfast mutual support and sensitive sympathy, and responsiveness to the other's needs. . . . With the realisation of communist society love will acquire a transformed and unprecedented aspect. By that time the "sympathetic ties" between all the members of the new society will have grown and strengthened. Love potential will have increased, and love-solidarity will become the lever that competition and self-love were in the bourgeois system. Collectivism of spirit can then defeat individualist self-sufficiency, and the "cold of inner loneliness," from which people in bourgeois culture have attempted to escape through love and marriage, will disappear. (cited in Holt 289–290)

Thus Kollantai speculated on the connection between change in personal relationships and other elements of social change, insisting that socialist theory and practice address this important question.

In the late '30s, Soviet suspicion of Kollantai's "subversive" views of sexuality, marriage, and the family turned to official condemnation. Her writings "were pronounced to be officially erroneous and then their very existence hidden from public view" (Holt 24). American Communism imported the official view. The way in which Kollantai's positions were popularly misunderstood and diminished in the CPUSA is suggested by a quote from Lenin on the "glass of water theory" that, according to Olsen, became a common rejoinder to any remark favoring Kollantai or "free love": "Of course, thirst must be satisfied. But will the normal man in normal circumstances lie down in the gutter and drink out of a puddle, or out of a glass with a rim greasy from many lips?"[10]

Lenin thus chastised Clara Zetkin for what he termed one of her "sins": "I was told that questions of sex and marriage are the main subjects dealt with in the reading and discussion evenings of women comrades. They are the chief subject of interest, of political instruction and education. I could scarcely believe my ears when I heard it" (cited in Zetkin 44). Lenin opposed anything that diverted energies from the revolution. In Victorian discourse he preached to Zetkin what historian G. J. Barker-Benfield (in another context) termed "spermatic economy": "Dissoluteness in sexual life is bourgeois, is a phenomenon of decay. . . . no weakening, no waste, no destruction of forces. Self-control, self-discipline is not slavery, not even in love." As if embarrassed by a momentary lapse into the preoccupation with sex for which he is scolding Zetkin, Lenin asks her to forgive him for straying from the starting point of their conversation, adding: "Why didn't you call me to order? My tongue has run away with me" (cited in Zetkin 50–51).

In a review of Zetkin's *Reminiscences of Lenin* (*New Masses*, 23 January 1934), Eugene Gordon repeated approvingly Lenin's warning that "dissoluteness in sexual life is bourgeois," a "phenomenon of decay" (26). Given their nineteenth-century cultural heritage, many American Party members also endorsed sexual moderation and self-control. Their own views did not parrot so much as genuinely correspond to Lenin's.[11] Although Upton Sinclair was not a Communist, he captured the view (at least the official one) of many Party members in "Revolution—Not Sex." To a query about the "correct revolutionary proletarian attitude towards sex," Sinclair replied: "Real revolutionary proletarians are recognized by the fact that they make sacrifices for the cause. . . . And their sex life will be tested by that attitude" (11).

But as much as Lenin's disorderly slip of the tongue, Sinclair's position suggests an important contradiction, which Sheila Rowbotham elaborates (although the passage refers to the Soviet Union, the problem extends to other revolutionary movements as well):

> Theoretically the revolution was committed to release, to the development of free, unrepressed human beings, but practically the immediate task of creating a communist society from the chaos of the Soviet Union in the twenties required a great effort of self-discipline—in fact the good old virtues of the bourgeoisie in early capitalism: hard work, abstinence and repression. (*Resistance* 153)

Rowbotham implicitly questions whether the very goals for which revolutionaries sacrifice can be achieved if social utility rather than human liberation becomes the central moral criterion. Further, Rowbotham argues that historically the Left has failed to attract numbers to its ranks partly because it has both feared and trivialized people's emotional needs.

> Why is there such a horror of cosiness, as if cosiness were almost more dangerous than capitalism itself? . . . The fear seems to be that cosiness means people get cut off from the 'real' politics. . . . If a version of socialism is insisted upon which banishes cosiness, given the attachment of most people, working-class men and women included, to having a fair degree of it around in their lives, this socialism will not attract or keep most people. (*Fragments* 67–68)

Spermatic frugality and Communist discipline notwithstanding, the CPUSA advocated birth control during the early '30s. In the May 1933 issue of *The Working Woman*, for example, Margaret H. Irish published an article titled "Childbirth—A Woman's Problem." While the article's title and content suggest that contraception is solely a "women's issue," it nevertheless urges "working and farm women" to demand "good free clinics with scientific contraceptive information" (17). Many articles about the need for contraception appeared in *The Working Woman* from 1934 to 1935; and both *The Working Woman* and the *Sunday Worker Magazine* discussed specific contraceptive methods. Party publications included articles by Margaret Sanger, and *The Working Woman* editorially supported the bill she sponsored to legalize the distribution of birth control information through the mails.

At the same time, however, the Party's orthodoxy refused to consider that the interests of men and women could fail to coincide. When letters from women readers of the Party press suggested that men's insistence on unprotected intercourse was oppressive, the official response emphasized that capitalism was the enemy, not men. Under the heading "Thinks Men Are to Blame," a letter to the editor appeared in *The Working Woman* (August 1935) from a "Western Farm Woman" expressing "boundless indignation against selfish, sensual husbands." She insisted that "men are not 'ignorant how to prevent getting that way.' Every man, young or old naturally knows how to prevent consequences. . . . But he will not deny himself" (11). *The Working Woman* replied:

> The cause for too many babies is poverty and ignorance—not the selfishness of men. . . . More and more working women—and men—are seeking birth control information, but they can't afford it and they have no way of getting it. At present there are laws which make it illegal to spread such information. But the rich, who can pay the price, can beat the law and get the information. (12)

According to the official voice of *The Working Woman*, "the cause for too many babies" was an issue exclusively of class rather than a complex problem involving sexual inequality as well.

Communist Party participation in the birth control movement diminished in the years following 1935, partly in response to Soviet policy on the issue. In the mid-'30s the Soviet Union began a vigorous campaign for larger families, justifying its "new family policy not on the grounds of necessity," but elevating it "into a communist morality" (Rowbotham, *Resistance* 160). The legislation of this new family policy reversed the revolutionary Family Laws passed in the 1920s, which had been intended to emancipate women, not strengthen the family. "Nobody talked anymore about the family withering," and "non-reproductive sexuality came to be seen as a deviation from socialist reconstruction" (160). Research into birth control methods was curtailed, homosexuality was made a criminal offense in 1934, and abortion, which Lenin had termed an elementary democratic right and which had been legalized in 1920, was outlawed in 1936. In *The Revolution Betrayed*, published in 1937, Trotsky noted:

> The triumphal rehabilitation of the family . . . is caused by the material and cultural bankruptcy of the state. Instead of openly saying, "We have proven still too poor and ignorant for the creation of socialist relations among men, our children and grandchildren will realize this aim," the leaders are forcing people to glue together again the shell of the broken family, and not only that but to consider it, under threat of extreme penalties, the sacred nucleus of triumphant socialism. It is hard to measure with the eye the scope of this retreat." (cited in Rowbotham, *Resistance* 160)

In 1936 the American Communist press reprinted some of the attacks on abortion from the Soviet press, while Lenin's widow, Nadezhda Krupskaya, argued in the July 19, 1936, edition of *Sunday Worker Magazine* that abortions were no longer necessary in the Soviet Union because so many positive changes had occurred in Soviet life since the Revolution. According to Krupskaya, the positive changes had produced a situation in which "the Soviet people are taking from the mother the burden of caring for children and motherhood will more and more give her joy, a deep and unshadowed joy" (2). In this new environment abortion was no longer necessary. The June 23, 1936, issue of *New Masses* signaled its approval of the Soviet Union's proposed law to encourage large families. The editors reprinted four Soviet satiric cartoons portraying the selfishness of those who did not want children. In one cartoon a young man sitting on a beach is flanked by two young women. He asks, "Why all this fuss about children? I prefer grownups, especially blondes. Brunettes, too" (16–17).

Some Party members protested the Soviet prohibition of abortion. The December 1936 issue of *Woman Today* carried the arguments of Margaret Sanger (who was not a Party member) against the new law. In "The Soviet Union's Abortion Law" Sanger asserted:

> The new law on Abortions and Aid to Mothers is at once a reversal of the earlier libertarian philosophy and a seeming contradiction within itself. Coupled with clear cut and adequate provisions for state aid to mothers and children, in the form of maternity allowances, confinement care, nurseries, kindergartens and so on, is a section forbidding abortions except for therapeutic reasons, that is, when the continuation of pregnancy endangers the life or threatens serious injury to the health of the pregnant woman. (8)

Sanger's analysis of the rationale for the "reactionary" new law included the observation that the Soviet regime had moved into its "second phase" in which it "no longer acutely needs women as laborers" but now finds that "their usefulness to the state is greater in the field of reproduction than in the field of industry" (8). Sanger declares, "As a feminist, I protest against any woman having children if and when she does not want them" (30). Sanger's position was echoed in angry correspondence from readers of CP publications.

But the anti-abortion law had its defenders. The January 1937 issue of *Woman Today* carried a long letter by Beatrice Blosser condemning Sanger's analysis. Blosser attacked Sanger's argument that the Soviet government now needed women as mothers more than as industrial workers. Sanger, who based her reasoning "on the logic of a capitalist world, not a socialist one," lacked "any understanding of the Soviet world" (26). In defense of the law, Blosser asserted: "The beauty of the abortion law, in the eyes of this feminist, is that under it the right is recognized of the woman to have both a career and motherhood—this conflict, so disturbing to the women of the capitalist world, no longer exists in the socialist world" (26). The *Sunday Worker* also defended the Soviet law. In the February 28, 1937, edition of the *Sunday Worker Magazine* Myra Page wrote a long article defending the change, observing, "to me, the new Soviet law further prohibiting abortions marks another step towards women's freedom and the stabilizing of the new Russia's family life" (5). In an interesting twist of logic, the rescinding of a fundamental right was touted as evidence of genuine freedom.

During the Popular Front the CPUSA began to work with a much broader range of groups to build the anti-fascist movement and mass industrial unions. As it did, it was careful not to antagonize potential allies on such issues as abortion and contraception. Like the Soviet Union, the CPUSA during this period stressed the merits of family life and increasingly idealized motherhood. Under Stalin it was as if a "new," but oddly familiar, place was being given to women.

> Just as the Victorians combined the spiritual elevation of 'womanhood' with an institutional framework which made her powerless, in the Soviet Union under Stalin the elevation of Soviet motherhood . . . provided a new form of paternalist containment. . . . While *Pravda* denounced 'free love' along with all 'disorderly sex life' as 'bourgeois', and claimed that the enemies of the people had introduced 'the foul and poisonous idea of liquidating the family and disrupting marriage,' Stalin visited his old mother in Tiflis, and the Soviet papers carried articles on his children's reaction to the jam their grandmother made. (Rowbotham, *Resistance* 161)

The American Party likewise made the mother's role central in its appeals to women.

Lenin had termed facilities such as public dining rooms and nurseries "*young shoots* of communism" and declared these shoots to be "the simple everyday means . . . which can *in fact emancipate women*" (56). However, despite the proclamations in the CPUSA press about child-care facilities guaranteeing female independence in the Soviet Union, Party publications did not make publicly funded child care a prominent demand. Occasional articles criticized capitalism for failing to provide for the children of working mothers, but the Party did not wage a major campaign on that issue, even though organizers frequently mentioned that Party women's units were handicapped by the lack of child care.

During its short life, *Woman Today* demonstrated some concern for child-care issues, but it was a concern marked by the ambivalence typical of the Party's general attitude about such issues. In the April 1936 issue, a letter signed "A Mother" called attention to a number of day nurseries in New York City supported by the WPA (the Works Progress Administration). Following the letter, the editors encouraged mothers to explore the WPA-sponsored programs and offered *Woman Today* as a clearinghouse for exchanging ideas about child care. In ensuing issues, three articles on child care appeared: "Have You a Nursery in Your Town?" (February 1937), "After the Nursery School" (April 1937), and "Do You Understand Your Children?" (May 1937). All three articles explained the WPA's efforts to support children and parents. However, none attempted to analyze the economic and cultural problems that, despite the WPA programs, rendered only negligible public assistance for child-care programs.

A revealing example of the Party's approach to child care during the '30s appeared in an article praising the ingenuity of the Cleveland Young Communist League, which "went so far as to offer volunteers among its girl comrades to take care of children of Fisher Body strikers so that the mothers could enter more freely into strike duty" (cited in Dixler 171). Significantly, only the female comrades were expected to volunteer. Moreover, although this article appeared in the Party's theoretical journal, *The Communist* (May 1937), the author said nothing about working women's general need for child care (Dixler 171). The CP failed to champion the child-care issue during the '30s for various reasons, including the influence of the dominant culture; the composition of Party leadership, which was nearly exclusively male; and the fact that its model, the Soviet Union, did not examine sex-role stereotypes relating to the care of children. During World War II, when women were desperately needed as factory workers, the Party more actively supported day care, as did mainstream America.[12]

The Party opposed the Equal Rights Amendment, which had been introduced by the National Woman's Party in 1923, because it would have removed the hard-won gains of protective labor legislation for women, including minimum wage laws, restrictions on the hours that women could work, and limits on night work. (For the same reason, such groups as the League of Women Voters, the National Women's Trade Union League, and the General Federation of Women's Clubs, also opposed the proposed Amendment.[13]) Publications such as *Woman Today* expressed the official Party view. The March 1936 issue carried an editorial, "Equal Rights Amendment," which began: "The *Woman Today* does not support the Equal Rights Amendment to the Constitution initiated by the Woman's Party in its present form" (11). The editors asserted that the proposal would create the risk of "a law by which all legislation in the interests of women who work (such as minimum wage laws and the prohibition of home work under sweatshop conditions) would be declared unconstitutional" (11). While they urged defeat of the ERA, the editors called on their readers to "become active in abolishing all legal discrimination against all women" (11).

The Party, however, supported efforts to adopt "The Women's Charter." The February 1937 issue of *Woman Today* carried an article by Mary van Kleeck, National Chairman of the Inter-Professional Association, about the Charter. Van Kleeck thus described the document:

> The basic principles are that women should have full political and civil rights; full opportunity for education; full opportunity for employment according to their individual abilities and without discrimination because of sex; and security of livelihood, including the safeguarding of motherhood. . . . [The Charter] is designed primarily to embody objectives for legislation. (3)

Van Kleeck traced the origins of the Charter movement to a 1935 resolution in the Assembly of the League of Nations "calling for facts as to the effect which the adoption of an 'equal rights' treaty might have upon labor legislation throughout the world" (3). Van Kleeck addressed the controversy over the ERA and said about the Charter's position on labor legislation: "The exploiting system . . . must be controlled by the setting of basic standards through legislation" (3).

"Statements from Leading Women on the Charter," compiled by Leane Zugsmith, appeared in the same issue of *Woman Today*. Among the women who contributed statements supporting the Charter were Ella Reeve Bloor, Genevieve Taggard, Rose Wortis, and Margaret Sanger. Zugsmith included a list of women (and their organizational affiliations) who also supported the Charter. The list indicates that the CP made some alliances at this time—with women affiliated with the United States Department of Labor, the National League of Women Voters, the Young Women's Christian Association, the American Federation of Teachers, the American Association of University Women, and the National Council of Catholic Women—that the Third Period would not have allowed (27).

Sunday Worker Magazine supported the Charter. In the January 10, 1937, edition, Myra Page, who one month later wrote in defense of the change in Soviet abortion law, published an article in support of the Charter. She observed: "In 1937 American women, together with women in all countries throughout the world, have decided to win other rights—even more far-reaching [than the right to vote]," and she notes, "they have embodied these rights in a declaration—a new Charter of Women's Rights" (12). While Page supported the Charter, she noted that it could be improved by attending more specifically to the needs of American "Negro" women.

The Party's conflicting views of women are evident in the contradictory images of women that appeared in the Party press. Numerous articles depicted women strikers and organizers. Others featured women who had distinguished themselves in the labor or revolutionary movement, such as Ella Reeve ("Mother") Bloor, Lucy Parsons, Clara Zetkin, Rosa Luxemburg, and Nadezhda Krupskaya. And the Party press objected to the exploitation of female sexuality by the motion picture industry. The April 1935 issue of *The Working Woman*, for example, carried the third installment of the story of "a Hollywood extra" who reported in "Broad Is the Path: Slave Market—Up to Date!" that "our constant battle is against the men who have an idea that every chorus and every extra girl is for sale." She asserted, "We must be on our guard every minute of the day and night against the professional procurer, who haunts the sets, getting his percentage for 'fixing it up' with visiting business men" (11).

But the Party did not magically escape influences from mass culture. In the late '30s, the *Daily Worker*, for example, like many mainstream newspapers, began to feature promotional movie photos. Some of these were of women, with captions like "Lovely to Look At." And the *Sunday Worker* occasionally included photos of bathing-beauty contest winners. The January 8, 1939, issue featured a photo of "Blonde Marjorie Moore." Perched on the back of an upholstered chair, her chest thrust forward, Blonde Marjorie models ("with effective attractiveness") a strapless bathing suit. The headline queries, "Wonder What Keeps It Up?," and the caption reads, "If this vogue continues, about the only place for straps will be in street cars and on harnesses."

In the May 21, 1939, edition, "a pretty bather," at the ready for either sunshine or showers, sports "a transparent mackintosh of cellophane over an attractive ribbed wool beach suit." Apparently, transparent fabrics were all the rage in '39: The July 1 edition depicted "Pretty Jean Foster" wearing a prize-winning bathing suit "of transparent oiled silk, to give [the] wearer complete benefit of the sun." In the June 4, 1939, issue, under the blurb "Not So Fast, Girls," two "attractive girls" are featured "toe dunking" in Atlantic City, and California's 17-year-old "Queen of the Beaches" adorns the June 9, 1939, edition. Under the heading "Beauty Before the 4th," the June 19, 1939, issue featured a photo of a "pulchritudinous" movie actress displaying a "patriotic costume" consisting of stars on her halter top and stripes on her short shorts.

All the photos depicting beauty or "best-dressed" contest winners that I surveyed in the *Sunday Worker* appear strikingly out of place, surrounded by articles concerning matters such as unionizing efforts, civil rights struggles, and opposition to fascism in Europe. For example, the June 25, 1939, issue ran a photo of the "pretty brunette" (posing in front of a beach umbrella), winner of a "Best Dressed" Contest that was part of the annual "Surf, Sun and Sand celebration" in Long Beach, California. This photo appears on the same page with a report of the CP's Harlem division's drive to improve health and housing and alleviate unemployment; an article about a Czechoslovakian military attache's suicide, which his wife attributed to the Nazi seizure of his country; a report of an effort to destroy the National Maritime Union in New Orleans; and an article about teachers planning a rally to save New York state aid to education.

Sometimes sexism was couched in remarks that passed for acceptable expressions of class or political antagonism. One columnist affected an inability to recall the name of "that little girl who reviews books" for the *Nation*, Mary McCarthy. Likely, such a slur would have been only partly motivated by McCarthy's Trotskyist sympathies. In *New Masses*, the idle, parasitic middle-class woman stood for capitalism's effete decadence, paralleling the homosexual's emblematic role in proletarian novels. "There seems to be much less resentment felt for owning class men than for owning class women," Mary Inman observed (33). A survey of short stories in the Party press bears out Inman's impression. In Edwin Seaver's "Afternoon of a Realtor," for example, "the title character lounged in his office, thought lecherously about his secretary, and planned to seduce the wife of a man he was evicting." But Seaver "explained carefully that the realtor's nature resulted from his class and occupation, not his sex" (Dixler 250).

The ideal of comradeship "transcended" the imbalance of power between women and men. Articles in the Party press contended that women's interests should extend beyond their men—as long as "beyond their men" meant support for their men's politics. In 1938 the *Sunday Worker Magazine* ran a series examining the marriages of American workers and their wives. Most of the stories were similar. A miner's wife mentioned her lack of participation in politics to the *Sunday Worker* interviewer: "'I'm sorry that taking care of Fred and the three children doesn't give me enough time to do more about fighting against the high cost of living,' she said, 'but my Fred does the fighting for both of us.'" A biography of Jennie Marx praised her "constant unfailing courage in the face of the greatest odds, silent shouldering of a terrific burden so that her husband's great work could continue with as few obstacles as possible" (Dixler 81). In the Party press, a married couple's "common cause," however honorable and progressive, was usually based, as in mainstream marriages, on the husband's work.

Because the Party had established its organizing priorities within male-dominated heavy industries, it could reasonably argue that an appeal to housewives rather than to women workers made sense. Yet one suspects that the Party lauded women's auxiliaries as it did partly because such organizations defined women's interests in terms of their husbands and families. Moreover, because auxiliaries supported men's unions, they reinforced the Party line that working-class men and women had identical interests. Participation in a women's auxiliary was not inconsistent with the bourgeois—and the CP—convention of a housewife's duty and devotion to "her man."

Yet the role of women's auxiliaries in labor struggles, and the extent to which individual women developed within these organizations, remind us, once more, of Myra Jehlen's useful premise for analyzing women's history and writing (cited above) and of a phrase from Thomas Mann that Tillie Olsen is fond of quoting— "audacity within confinement." Despite the Party's androcentric views, women often played important roles in demonstrations, the unemployed councils, labor-organizing efforts, and strikes.

Probably the United Auto Workers Auxiliary that emerged during the 1937 sit-down at General Motors contributed most to winning a strike. About 50 women formed the Women's Auxiliary after a street dance on New Year's Eve in front of the worker-held Fisher Plant Number 2. Eventually claiming about a thousand members, the Auxiliary fed several thousand strikers daily. The kitchen was managed by Dorothy Kraus, wife of Henry Kraus, a CP member and editor of *The Flint Auto Worker*, the union newspaper. The Auxiliary also organized around-the-clock picket lines; operated a first-aid station; ran a day-care center for children of women involved in the strike; distributed literature and publicized the sit-down; and visited wives who opposed the strike, hoping to convert them. The Auxiliary also organized entertainment in front of the plants, including singing, dancing, and "living formations" that spelled out slogans such as "Solidarity Forever" (Foner 324).

As Philip S. Foner reports, on January 11, "as workers were handing food in through the main gate of Fisher [Plant Number] 2, company guards suddenly appeared and overpowered them" (325). Then, in 16-degree weather, the company turned off the heat. While workers battled the guards, the Flint police advanced, hurling tear gas bombs. "News of this action brought more workers to the scene. Women pickets deposited their children at the union hall and raced to the plant" (325). In the midst of the battle, Genora Johnson, an Auxiliary member and a 23-year-old mother of two children, asked permission to speak over the union's sound-truck microphone. She believes that Victor Reuther, who was staffing the truck, acquiesced because the batteries were running down anyway.[14] Johnson first tried intimidating the police—"Cowards! Cowards! Shooting unarmed and defenseless men!"—and then appealed to the women in the crowd: "Women of Flint! This is your fight! Join the picket line and defend your jobs, your husbands' jobs, and your children's homes!" (quoted in Foner 325). Women responded by joining the picket line and defying tear gas and police with the men.

After proving themselves in this "Battle of Bulls Run," so called because by morning the "bulls" (police) had run, 50 women between the ages of 16 and 65 formed the Emergency Brigade as a "vanguard detachment" of the Auxiliary. Its purpose, leader Genora Johnson told reporters, was "to be on hand in any emergency and to stand by our husbands, brothers, sons. We will form a picket line around the men, and if the police want to fire, then they'll just have to fire into us" (quoted in Foner 325). Membership quickly grew to 350, and the organization became a model for similar brigades in other "auto" cities—Detroit, Saginaw, and Lansing. With its distinctive red armbands and berets, the Emergency Brigade lent drama as well as vital support to the strike.

The Brigade was actively involved when strikers seized several other General Motors plants late in January. "Creating a disturbance, they lured the police to Chevrolet Plant 9 at Flint, so that male strikers could seize Plant 4, the key to the motor assembly division. When Plant 9 was tear-gassed, the Emergency Brigade broke windows in the plant so that the strikers could breathe" (Foner 326). At a turning-point in the battle over Plant 4 and in the strike as a whole, a few Brigade members locked arms in front of Plant Number 4, standing off the police who had ordered them to disperse and stalling for time until reinforcements could arrive. "Over our dead bodies, you're going in," they announced defiantly (*With Babies and Banners*). Other Brigade members soon amassed at the plant, a flag bearer heading their dramatic procession. The women "formed a revolving picket line in front of the plant," marching to "the rhythm of such songs as 'We Shall Not Be Moved' while police looked on rather sheepishly" (Fine 270).

An analysis of the influence of auxiliary activity on women's lives must be partly grounded on the perception of the women involved. The wife of one Flint striker wrote:

> I found a common understanding and unselfishness I'd never known. These people are real people and I'm glad I'm one of them. . . . I'm living for the first time with a definite goal. I want a decent living for not only my family but for everyone. Just being a woman isn't enough any more. I want to be a human being. (cited in Vorse 80–81)

"A new type of woman was born in the strike," one of the members of the Emergency Brigade wrote after the sit-down. "Women who only yesterday . . . felt inferior to the task of organizing, speaking, leading, have, as if overnight, become the spearhead in the battle of unionism" (Fine 201). Eight veterans of the Flint Auxiliary and Emergency Brigade were reunited 40 years after the sit-down for a documentary, *With Babies and Banners* (1978), produced and directed by Lorraine Grey in association with the Women's Labor History Film Project.[15] The documentary combines archival footage with interviews of the women, who reveal that their participation in the strike indelibly marked them. In a representative remark, one woman declared: "If I had to do it again, I'd have *more* fight in me."

The reunited women were also aware of the limits of their victory. The UAW, recognizing the women's contribution in Flint, voted full support for all auxiliaries at its August 1937 convention. But in effect the union also said, in Genora (Johnson) Dollinger's words, "Thank you ladies very much. Now the laundry's piling up, the dishes are piling up, and the kids need attention." Some of these Brigade veterans were present in 1977 at the UAW's fortieth anniversary celebration of the strike. Wearing red armbands and caps as a tribute to the Brigade, women demonstrators chanted, "The UAW needs an ERA!" Appearing as militant as she had been during the "Battle of Bulls Run," Genora (Johnson) Dollinger again demanded the right to speak. Although *With Babies and Banners* included only a fragment of her speech, she urged the union to take up the pressing issue of preschool child care for working women.

That Communists were prominent in the Flint strike has been established. Except for Genora Johnson's membership in the Socialist Party, however, little is known about the political affiliations of the Auxiliary and Emergency Brigade members.[16] As Bert Cochran comments, "the Communists did not neglect this golden opportunity to 'politically develop' the workers" (for example, the *Daily Worker*, which covered strike events extensively, was distributed to the plants [121]), but it does not appear that the Party was involved in any systematic way with the Auxiliary and Brigade. It is difficult even to estimate the Party's efforts to politicize—or to contain—the Flint women. But at least the Party helped create circumstances in which isolated housewives had individual and collective opportunities that would not have been available to them otherwise.

Ties to the CP were more direct in the lives of three "union maids." A documentary by this title, made in 1976 by James Klein, Miles Moglescu, and Julia Reichert, alternates archival footage from the '30s with recent interviews of three women, Sylvia Woods, Stella Nowicki, and Kate Hyndman, who were union organizers and political activists during the Depression. Although the documentary focuses on the women's activities, not their organizational ties, all were Party members during the '30s. If we borrow Mari Jo Buhle's approach to the Socialist Party and apply it to the CP, we will look less at the Party's formal statements on "the woman question" and more at how women actually functioned within the movement. The CP was not a monolith; democratic centralism notwithstanding, the views and daily experiences of rank-and-file women often varied from those of male Party bureaucrats, as Tillie Olsen and Meridel Le Sueur insist. Yet the activity of rank-and-file women remains largely unrecorded. Documentaries made during the '70s and '80s, such as *Union Maids, The Life and Times of Rosie the Riveter*, and *Seeing Red*, have begun to fill this historical gap, taking up what historians in the late '60s called "a search for a usable past."

The three union maids started work as teenagers—Sylvia for the Great Western Laundry, where African-Americans earned less than their Euro-American counterparts; Stella in the stockyards, where women earned 15 cents less per hour than men; and Kate at Bauer and Black, a surgical supplies factory. Sylvia's father, who had been a union man, a Garveyite, and a member of the Universal Negro Improvement Association, had given her a mandate: If "there's a union, join it . . . if there isn't one, then organize one." When Sylvia's boss at the laundry hired an inexperienced white woman as a supervisor rather than promote a veteran black woman, Sylvia quickly organized one of the '30s first sit-downs. The women switched off the mangles (machines for pressing fabric) and refused to move. Police had to "throw us out bodily," Sylvia recalls. Eventually, she became an aggressive shop steward and CIO organizer, and, as a result of her union experience, moved away from a Garveyite view of whites.

Women took the lead in organizing at Stella's meat-packing plant. After a woman lost her fingertips because the machines lacked safety guards, "a bunch of us got together and we wrote out a leaflet . . . with certain demands." The women also asked the other workers not to operate the machines in question until the company provided safety devices. "The whole plant heard about it . . . [a] bunch of women actually organized and stuck together and went right up to the foreman and swore, in Polish or whatever . . . 'Fix the machines!' 'Safety guards!'"

Later Stella helped to organize the CIO Packing House Workers Union. She describes the drama of their first meeting, when the hall filled to capacity and yet people kept coming—"hundreds and hundreds, I don't know. Maybe 500 . . . . It was the most inspiring thing." But Stella comments that she could be as active as she was only because she did not have a family:

> These poor women would have to work all day and then they would have to come home and take care of the house. Now the union was a man's job. This is the way it was at the time. And the few of us that were active in the union, we were not married, we didn't have families . . . very few women who were . . . married and had children . . . were active in the union, very few. You only had so many hours in the day.

But it was also difficult for single women to be active in the union: "There was a real sexist attitude then in society in general [and among] the radicals themselves . . . the few women who aspired to be leaders, if you want to put it that way, didn't come by it easy. We had to take a lot of gaff."

Another example of women's taking the lead in organizing occurred at Bauer and Black. When Kate's superintendent announced a layoff of 50 percent of their workers, Kate wrote an article about it for the *Daily Worker*, calling for the Trade Union Unity League to organize Bauer and Black. She asked the newspaper to send her a half-dozen copies of the piece, which she posted in all the factory's departments.

> By the time I got back . . . to my own department it was bedlam. Somebody had shut off the machinery . . . . One woman was standing on a table and nobody was working. And one woman was up there reading the article, "Listen to this. Look! Look at this! It was printed in the newspaper and it's about us!"

When Kate was fired for taking such action, none of her fellow workers protested, but a few years later a friend from Bauer and Black telephoned her: "Kate, guess what. We've made it up to you, kiddo. We've finally made it up. We've joined the union and we're out on strike and I'm the picket captain! Now how do you like that?"

Kate also organized an Unemployed Council on Chicago's near West Side. Between 1932 and 1935 over 20,000 families were put out on the street, and the Unemployed Councils resisted these evictions. With characteristic elan, Kate describes one such episode. By the time she arrived, a number of police officers were on the scene, several truckloads of people fighting the eviction had already been arrested, and the patience of the officer in charge had been sorely tried. Waving his sawed-off shotgun from the top of the apartment steps, he threatened: "The first son-of-a-bitch that puts a foot on the steps is going to have their head shot right off!" Kate remembers asking herself, "Now Katie, is you is or is you ain't?"—and then she started up the steps. A white man and a black couple quickly joined her; together they passed the officer and began kicking the locked apartment door. Exasperated, the lieutenant yelled, "Damn it, I'm tired of this. Let's call it quits." Passing his hat among the other policemen, he ordered every officer to contribute and then thrust the rent at the landlord: "Here's your damn rent . . . . Now go ahead and open that door."[17] Kate, Sylvia, and Stella expressed no ambivalence about their radical pasts. Kate could have been speaking for all three when she declared: "We were fighting for justice and we gave our lives for it gladly"; moreover, "I felt there was purpose in my life."

The Life and Times of Rosie the Riveter (1981), directed by Connie Field, tells the story of thousands of women farmers, domestics, and shop clerks who were urged to join the factory labor force during the Second World War and then excluded from that work force when returning veterans needed jobs. The film includes segments from late '30s and '40s newsreels that were shown in movie theaters to sell women on the benefits of factory labor. The newsreel segments are spliced together with interviews conducted with five former Rosies, whose accounts of their lives as factory workers contrast with the newsreels' false promises of safe working conditions and child-care centers. Although these five women became skilled welders and took great pride in their work, they were forced out of their jobs when the veterans returned.

The film does not reveal that two of the Rosies interviewed, Lyn Childs and Lola Weixel, had been CP members. Few who have seen the film forget Lyn Childs, a small, fiery African-American woman who told how she once turned her welder's torch on a large Euro-American man who was kicking her male Filipino coworker. Childs's foreman, hearing the commotion, immediately summoned her on the intercom, and when she went to his office, he demanded to know "what kind of Communist activity" she was up to. She replied, "If it's 'Communist' to intervene when a fellow worker is being beaten, well, then, I'm a Communist, all right." Tillie Olsen believes that "those understanding, those sharpenings . . . [and Childs's] ability to act" resulted partly from her years in the Party, and that it similarly benefited others who as members or fellow-travelers grew to understand, articulate, and act upon their experience as working-class women (interview).

Because the documentarists who made *With Babies and Banners, Union Maids*, and *Rosie the Riveter* sought a popular audience, they may have considered discussion of their subjects' political affiliations a red herring. In *Seeing Red* (1984), James Klein and Julia Reichert, veterans of *Union Maids*, make that problem itself the subject of a documentary. The film gives Communism, "the great American taboo," a human face. Combining archival footage and interviews,

Seeing Red focuses largely on the rank-and-file members who joined the CP as young people during the Depression and remained in the Party for many years. For many of them, this was the first time they had spoken openly about their lives in the CP. The film includes important interviews of men—Howard ("Stretch") Johnson, Bill Bailey, Carl Hirsch, and Pete Seeger, among them—but how the women assessed their Party experience is more relevant here.

The documentary criticizes the Party's treatment of women. Rose Podmaka, a steel worker, recalls:

> I thought I was doing good work, I mean I was the leader of our youth organization. But they concentrated on my brother. They weren't recruiting any women . . . they would take him to Communist conventions and they would give him literature. But he wasn't that interested. So finally they decided they needed someone to take the minutes of the meetings and collect their dues, so they approached me.

Apparently aware of the irony, Podmaka smiles and adds, "And I was very thrilled that I had the honor of joining the Communist Party." The Party chose Podmaka to attend their national training school for six months. Her tutor at the school proposed marriage, insisting that they "would make a marvelous team." Assuming that her special training qualified her to be a "professional revolutionist," Podmaka agreed.

> So right at the end of school the Ohio State Convention of the CP was being held. So both of us went there and I asked what our assignments would be since we're both trained revolutionists . . . . They suggested that I go back to [work in] the mill and my husband become the section organizer and I support him.

Some of those interviewed commented on the Party's lack of democracy. Dorothy Healey, now a Vice Chair of the Democratic Socialists of America, was a Party member for 45 years and a leader for 25 of those years. She acknowledges that "the [Party's] bureaucracy . . . fell on all of our shoulders . . . . I was a little Stalin. I don't have to talk about other people." And Edna Whitehouse recalls: "If you *did* raise a question, they would simply say, 'Did you read the latest article in *Political Affairs* [a Party journal]?'" Whitehouse, Muriel Eldridge, Rose Podmaka, and Ruth Maguire were interviewed collectively, and there seemed to be a consensus for Maguire's view:

> I . . . sincerely believe today that there is a great connection between ends and means . . . . I think we could at one point say, "Well, as long as our objectives are all that great, we can do all these crappy little things on the way." . . . I don't believe that at all anymore. I think there's a direct relationship between how we might have built a party that was democratic and the kind of society that might have come out of *that*.

Yet the women benefited from their Party experience. Muriel Eldridge credits her many years in the movement for her abiding sense of political responsibility and involvement. In her old age, Rose Kryzak delivers rousing speeches on the plight of senior citizens. And Healey, to explain what she gained as a labor organizer during the '30s, refers to one representative experience:

> As I looked out at that audience there was a kind of joy. Here were people in the most desperate living conditions who had discovered what unity meant, what solidarity meant . . . . The speakers, the strikers, there was no "we" and "they." There was only "us" . . . . We [organizers] got more enrichment, we learned more, we acquired more ourselves than any other . . . experience had ever given us.

When I interviewed Ruth Maguire and Edna Whitehouse (together) in 1989, they stood by the assessment of their Party experience that they had expressed in *Seeing Red*. Again, they criticized the organization's lack of democracy as well as acknowledged the positive ways in which their membership had shaped their lives. With the following remarks, Whitehouse spoke for both women:

> I've often said, and I've heard other people say, that being in the Party during those formative years . . . was a college education that nobody really could duplicate in any university. . . . The sense of responsibility, the sense of feeling a part of a movement, the sense of feeling as though your participation did matter—all of those things, I think, were [a result of] . . . Party activities. . . . while there were a lot of feelings [about the Party] that were negative . . . still, my overall feeling has never been and probably never will be negative. I always feel on balance that I was the recipient of some pretty terrific stuff, which I wouldn't trade for anything. . . . The longer we live [and] the more independent [in our] thinking we get, the more critical we are of those years [in which] . . . we would submit to such ridiculous kinds of authority without question. But that has never upset the balance in my mind about whether or not it was a worthwhile experience to have lived through. It still remains part of my life.

Angela Ward, a union organizer and, beginning in the '30s, a Party member for 20 years, also criticizes the extent of her past subservience to Party authority. When asked if she would join the Party if she had it to do over again, she replied: "I think I would have preferred to be very *close* [laughing] to it, but not to have been so subservient to it" (Ward, Oral history 129). But Ward, like Whitehouse, describes her Party experience as generally "positive" and "educating," and, within the Party, Ward developed many "enduring and wonderful" friendships.

> There was a comradeship and a unity of purpose that was very helpful. And I think some of the reason that I was—*if* I was—successful in organizing workers was because of the support I did get from the Party in *thinking*, and in organizing my ideas and so on. I still believe in socialism. . . . I don't see how you can have a society that has any degree of fairness or justice unless we learn to distribute what the working people produce, to distribute it with some degree of fairness. I think the Soviet experience has been a very disillusioning one, but that needn't mean that socialism can't work. . . . *I* have faith, and I try to do what I can in my own small way now, without any organization. But you'll see me at all the meetings that I think are worth attending. (Ward, Oral history 120–121)

   Much like Angela Ward and the women depicted in the documentaries I've discussed, Tillie Olsen and Meridel Le Sueur maneuvered successfully within limits prescribed by both the patriarchal, capitalist culture and by a fundamentally undemocratic and male-dominated CP. Margaret Cowl, head of the Party's Women's Commission and a Party spokesperson on women during the '30s, concluded in 1974 that the leadership had paid only lip service to women's issues during that decade; that mass women's movements were not genuinely accepted as part of the U.S. working-class movement; and that "male supremacy" played a role in keeping Party women in their place (Ware 122). In the concluding chapter of her autobiography (1940), Ella Reeve ("Mother") Bloor, who served on the CPUSA central committee throughout the '30s, observed: "I do not minimize what our Party has done toward bringing about true equality, admitting no discrimination of race, color or creed in our ranks. But I have often felt . . . that there has been some hesitancy in giving women full equal responsibility with men" (308). When I asked Angela Ward if Party men differed from mainstream American men in their attitudes toward women, she replied: "Basically, I would say they weren't very different. They gave lip service" (interview); "they still had great bands of male chauvinism in their personality make-up" (Ward, Oral history 42). Elsa Dixler concludes that in the Party subculture of the '30s, woman's place was "on the picket line—and in [the] home" (127). But Peggy Dennis perhaps best reflects the views of Olsen and Le Sueur when she summarizes the contradictory experience of Party women: "Male Communists often responded to discussions of the 'woman question' with derision or condescension, but there were few other organizations in the country at the time in which women would even consider it their right to challenge such attitudes" (quoted in Isserman, *Which Side* 141).

   The CP's work among women in the '30s should be carefully evaluated as part of the struggle for women's liberation in the United States. Many women developed an awareness of their own potential, a sense of collectivity, and an understanding of America's social system through Party-related activities. That Party leadership was overwhelmingly male and that its bureaucracy functioned undemocratically "from the top down" is a matter of record. But the history of the rank-and-file, including its women, has yet to be thoroughly explored.

   One lesson, however, is already clear. The experience of CP women demonstrates, as does the experience of women in the Socialist Party before its sharp decline in 1919, that autonomous organizations of women are central to the development of a democratic socialist movement. During the '30s a viable feminist movement did not exist to pressure the CP on issues of concern to women, and the Party's structure has never allowed for autonomous women's organizations. As a result, the struggle for women's liberation—and for socialism, itself—was inherently constrained. When I asked former Party members if anyone had raised the possibility of establishing autonomous women's groups or women's caucuses within the Party structure, they responded much as Healey did: "Wouldn't have crossed our minds. . . . I can't remember one woman ever suggesting it. Ever. Not one." Healey now believes that such "independent, autonomous organization[s]" are "absolutely necessary" (interview).[18]

According to Johanna Brenner and Nancy Holmstrom, women's self-organization includes a women's movement fighting for reforms around issues particular to women, as well as women's caucuses within all mass organizations, including socialist organizations. A women's caucus allows the women in a given organization to meet at times separately from the men. Completely controlled by women who elect their own leaders, such a caucus often develops women's skills and self-confidence more effectively than does the mixed group and provides a power base from which women can struggle to keep their concerns from being marginalized within the parent organization (41, 45). The strategy of women's autonomous organization counters Marx himself, who in 1872 recommended the expulsion of the American section of the First International on the ground that they gave "precedence to the women's question over the question of labor." Unabashed, the American representative replied: "The labor question is also a women's question" (quoted by Buhle, xiv).

Tillie Olsen's and Meridel Le Sueur's biographies and literary texts speak to the contradictory experience of women within the Communist Left. As I have said, Deborah Rosenfelt has suggested the useful term "socialist feminist" for the literary tradition to which these writers belong. But such a term would have been derided by the Party, which denounced feminism during the '30s because it privileged issues of gender over those of class. And it is likely that even Olsen and Le Sueur would have rejected the label at that time. Their major commitment, like that of other Party women, was to class warfare and the "impending" revolution, which subsumed their hopes for sexual equality.

Yet their oeuvres can be read as a "double-voiced discourse," containing both a "dominant" and a "muted" story (Showalter 34). To borrow Sandra Gilbert and Susan Gubar's term, Le Sueur's and Olsen's canons constitute modern versions of a palimpsest, a document of classical antiquity inscribed on parchment and written upon several times, often with remnants of earlier, imperfectly erased writing still visible. As the following chapters discussing Le Sueur and Olsen will argue, an apparent literary and political orthodoxy recedes and an uneven heterodoxy emerges.

THREE

Meridel Le Sueur:
Biographical Sketch and
Reportage

I've spent all my life trying to conceal it.

Mary Antoinette Lucy's reproach to her granddaughter (Meridel Le Sueur) for writing the truth about women's lives, reported during an interview with the author, 1985

I haven't really revealed the brutality of . . . my own life.

Meridel Le Sueur, during an interview with the author, 1985

I survived [as a woman writer], maybe by camouflage.

Meridel Le Sueur, in an Afterword to Margery Latimer's *Guardian Angel and Other Stories*

Ourself behind ourself, concealed—
Should startle most—

Emily Dickinson

One of the most prominent women writers of the '30s, Le Sueur endured red-baiting, blacklisting, and 25 years of obscurity to become in the '70s a regional folk heroine and nearly an archetypal figure within some elements of the women's movement. For some of the Le Sueur faithful, her work seems to deserve uncritical celebration. Yet such celebration would have us ignore historically resonant problems in her work. For the vast majority of mainstream critics, on the other hand, Le Sueur's work merits little notice. This latter position is more damaging than the first because it denies Le Sueur's social and historical value as well as her significant formal experiments.

Le Sueur, herself, feels ambivalent about her Wonder Woman status. On one hand, she welcomes the readership and recognition that came after 25 years of obscurity and feels she has earned her self-imposed title, "Mrs. Lazarus." Yet she also hungers for genuine criticism of her work, and she refuses the role of "St. Meridel" that some people have imposed on her (Grossmann 3D). "I am not a writer, just a recorder," she insists. "The greatest poetry is in the people" (Grossmann 1D).

This chapter has three sections. The first sketches Le Sueur's biography, including information derived from my interviewing her and from her unpublished '30s journals. A second portion of this chapter places Le Sueur in the context of the '30s literary Left, extending the background provided by Chapter 1. A third section discusses two pieces of Le Sueur's reportage that number among the best known of that genre, "Women on the Breadlines" and "I Was Marching," and a little-known piece of her reportage, "Evening in a Lumber Town." In Chapter 4 I contrast this reportage to what I consider more heterodox Le Sueurian texts.

When I question in this chapter the position Le Sueur took on how radical writers create a literature of resistance ("The Fetish of Being Outside," 1935) or her presentation of ideology as merely superstructure ("I Was Marching," 1934), I am not, as I indicated in the Introduction, suggesting that she should have known better. These were the prevailing views among orthodox Marxists at the time. Gramsci's pathbreaking work on hegemony, for example, undertaken in a Fascist prison between 1927 and 1935, was not yet translated; Louis Althusser's generative essay "Ideology and Ideological State Apparatuses" did not appear until 1971. Since the '60s we have seen a proliferation of studies of ideology that were unavailable to '30s Marxists.

Meridel Le Sueur was born February 22, 1900, in Murray, Iowa, into a Euro-American, middle-class, and educated family. She has written extensively about her maternal grandmother, Mary Antoinette Lucy, a stern "third-generation Puritan" and "one of the first settlers, gun in hand, of the Oklahoma territory."[1] Lucy had divorced her husband for "drinking up the farms her father left her" ("The Ancient People" 22), which at least partly explains her active membership in the Women's Christian Temperance Union: she "laid" all problems "to drink" and became secretary of the Oklahoma WCTU under the leadership of Frances Willard. Le Sueur thus describes her indomitable grandmother:

> With her peculiar single courage . . . she packed her small bag every week, set out by buck board, into the miserable mining communities where she met in shacks and white steepled church[es] the harried, devout, half-maddened women who saw the miserable pay checks go weekly at the corner saloon, and who attempted to stave off poverty and the disappearance of their husbands by smashing the saloons. (*Crusaders* 39–40)

As a child Le Sueur "rode in hayracks in temperance parades, dressed in white and shouting slogans—'Tremble, King Alcohol: We shall grow up,' and 'lips that touch liquor shall never touch mine!'"[2]

Le Sueur's vivid memories of her grandmother, so full of the woman's courage and self-reliance, are nevertheless shadowed by a recognition of her emotional and sexual repression. Le Sueur has described Lucy's "graceless intensity," her "work-for-the-night-is-coming, dutiful labor." She was "earnest, rigid . . . spare as the puritan world" ("The Ancient People" 31, 33). Usually dressed in black, Lucy considered bright colors sinful. Her only emotional outlet was singing Protestant hymns, which she did with a telling fervor (Le Sueur particularly remembers "Jesus, Lover of My Soul, Let Me to Thy Bosom Fly"). In Le Sueur's words, through this hymn-singing, "my grandmother made love to Jesus."[3] Actually, the hymn-singing revealed many repressed feelings, she believes. "Only through these songs did I know the depths of her sorrow, her terrible loneliness, her wish to die, her deep silence. Sometimes I heard her cry in the night, but I could not humiliate her by going to comfort her. In the day there would be no sign" ("The Ancient People" 34).

Le Sueur has said of her mother and grandmother that "their experience of this world centered around the male as beast, his drunkenness and chicanery, his oppressive violence" (Hedges 44). *Crusaders* describes women as

> often left alone, the men gone to better fields. The pattern of the migrating, lost, silent, drunk father is a mid-west pattern, and accompanying that picture is the upright fanatical prohibitionist mother, bread earner, strong woman, isolated and alone. My grandmother raised her own children, my mother hers, and I mine. (39)

Meridel was ten when her mother, Marian Wharton, left her first husband, William Wharton, a Church of Christ minister. Marian could take the uncommon step of leaving her husband partly because her mother had boldly done the same. The Whartons were living in Texas, a state that denied a divorced woman custody of her children, so Marian and her children (Meridel was the oldest of three) fled at night to Lucy's home in Perry, Oklahoma. William Wharton's attempts to extradite his wife and children failed, and a divorce was granted him on grounds of Marian's desertion and interest in "dangerous literature" (*Crusaders* 45).

Lucy helped care for the three children and raised funds for libraries, believing that people consumed by reading would be less likely to be consumed by alcohol. As a single woman Marian Wharton earned a living by lecturing on women's issues, and sometimes the children would accompany their mother on the Chautauqua circuit. "'There was a big tent, and people would come and camp,'" Le Sueur recalled in one interview. "'You'd go for a week. It was a real cultural [event]. The women would come up to her [Marian] afterwards and ask her how not to have children'" (Gage 30). Marian was tried in Kansas City for giving birth control information to a woman who had 14 children but was acquitted when the mother refused to identify her in court (interview).

In *Crusaders* Le Sueur thus recalls the lecture circuit: "It was a daring and wonderful thing to take the road to talk about the rights of women, in the beginning to stand trembling with nervousness, to be the butt of jokes, to see the frightened, asking eyes of the women who packed the opera houses" (*Crusaders* 46). A Missouri paper carried the following item about Marian in August 1912:

> The Methodist Church reports a crowded house for Mrs. Wharton's physical culture lecture "The Glory of Superb Womanhood." In the evening she occupied the pulpit, speaking of Love and Bread. . . . "Women have been born and reared in ignorance, taught to feel shame toward the most sacred functions of life. Immorali-

ties in and out of wedlock, the terrible white slave traffic, ruined lives, blighted homes, all can be traced to inequality of the sexes, and ignorance." (*Crusaders* 46)

While a lecturer, Marian was also arrested for participating in the suffrage fight, and in 1918, with other suffragists, she chained herself to the White House fence.

Marian headed the English Department at the People's College in Fort Scott, Kansas, where she met and (in 1917) married Arthur Le Sueur. Arthur, an 1891 graduate of the University of Michigan's law school, had served four terms as socialist mayor of Minot, North Dakota, and had edited a radical newspaper, the *Iconoclast*. Arthur was president of the college and Eugene Debs, the chancellor. Marian and Arthur edited *People's News*, the college magazine, which bore the slogan "To remain ignorant is to remain a slave." The school strove to attract working-class students and to teach from a working-class perspective.

While teaching at the People's College, Marian wrote a grammar and usage book, *Plain English*, identified in its preliminary pages as "for the Education of the Workers by the Workers." Published by the People's College in 1916, this was no ordinary grammar book. To instruct its readers about complete sentences, it explained, as grammar books standardly do, that a sentence names a person or thing and then makes an assertion concerning that person or thing; but the book's examples of complete sentences were hardly standard textbook fare:

> 1. Two classes have always existed.
> 2. To which class do you belong?
> 3. Join your class in the struggle.

To teach the difference between active and passive constructions, *Plain English* used the following examples:

> 1. The system enslaves men.
> 2. Men are enslaved by the system.

To teach the substituting of pronouns for nouns, the book provided exercises such as the following: "The workers will succeed in gaining the workers' freedom if the workers learn solidarity." And to exemplify a sentence employing a dependent clause, *Plain English* exhorted: "If there is anything that cannot bear free thought, let it crack." Other exercises included phrases from "The International." Small wonder that Eugene Debs, as Le Sueur recalls with pride, had high praise for *Plain English*.[4]

Through her mother and her stepfather, both active socialists until their deaths in the early '50s, Meridel was exposed as a girl to Populists, Wobblies, anarchists, union organizers, and members of the Socialist Party, the Non-Partisan League, and the Farmer-Labor Party; through her parents she met luminaries such as Debs, Helen Keller, Emma Goldman, John Reed, Mabel Dodge, Margaret Sanger, Theodore Dreiser, Carl Sandburg, and Woody Guthrie.

The April 20, 1914, "Ludlow Massacre," the culmination of a coal miners strike against the Colorado Fuel and Iron Corporation owned by the Rockefeller family, profoundly affected Le Sueur at an impressionable age. Grievances of the 11,000, mostly foreign-born miners included low pay, dangerous working conditions, and the "feudal domination" of company towns (Zinn 347). In this period before the legalization of unions, the strike followed an all-too-familiar pattern. When the strike began in September 1913, the miners were evicted from their company-town shacks and, with help from the United Mine Workers Union, set up tents and carried on the strike. When the Baldwin-Felts gunmen hired by the Rockefellers failed to break the strike, the Colorado governor called out the National Guard, with the Rockefellers paying the Guard's wages (Zinn 347).

On the day of the massacre, the Guard machine gunned and later torched the miners' tents. Thirteen people were killed by the gunfire, and 13 (11 children and two wives of miners) died in the fire (Zinn 347–348). Le Sueur was 14 years old when "the grieving men came to Fort Scott to raise money," as she recalled for the *St. Paul Pioneer Press Dispatch* on the occasion of her ninetieth birthday. The newspaper article continues, citing an account Le Sueur had previously written of this dramatic moment in her life: "'They were starving,' she [Le Sueur] writes. . . . 'They had lost the strike. They marched down the street . . . silently. . . . The faculty of the People's College marched behind them. I held my mother's hand. We were weeping'" (cited in Grossmann 3D).

The "Ludlow Massacre" has continued to haunt Le Sueur. Indeed, her most recent publication, *The Dread Road* (1991), written largely while Le Sueur was in her eighties, tells the story of a woman's bus trip from Albuquerque along "the dread road" north into Colorado, past Trinidad (one of the mining towns involved in the strike) and Ludlow, where the woman's grandparents were killed in the massacre. As Le Sueur reported to the *Pioneer Press Dispatch*, the "Ludlow Massacre" was an event that "changed me forever" (cited in Grossmann 3D).

During the First World War Marian and Arthur were persecuted for their anti-interventionist views. People hurled stones through the windows of their Fort Scott home, threw yellow paint on their car, and burned antiwar literature on their front lawn. After vigilantes destroyed the People's College with "fire and ax," the Le Sueurs fled Fort Scott, moving along back roads under cover of darkness, to St. Paul, where the Non-Partisan League had an office.[5] The Le Sueurs' basement served as a clinic for removing tar and feathers from opponents to the war, and visitors to their home included Joe Hill, "tall and blond with amazing blue eyes"; Lincoln Steffens, who "secretly came to tell the people of what had happened in Russia"; Big Bill Haywood, "the one-eyed giant of the miners"; and Eugene Debs, "a man who expressed love boldly" (cited in Grossmann 3D).

Marian and Arthur continued to work in the Non-Partisan League as educational directors while Arthur, as a lawyer, defended free speech, the foreign-born who had come under suspicion, and people whose property had been damaged because of their opposition to the war. Arthur was frequently threatened and barely escaped many acts of violence, while Meridel and her brothers were ostracized at school. Meridel attended school irregularly, quit in the ninth grade, and never returned to formal education. Instead, her mother sent her to McFadden's Physical Culture School in Chicago, a progressive institution that concentrated on physical fitness, movement, and dance. In her late teens Le Sueur studied acting for one year at the American Academy of Dramatic Art in New York City. During this period she lived with Emma Goldman in the well-known Anarchist commune, where Le Sueur got caught up in the antiwar struggles and the trials that resulted in the deportation of Goldman, Alexander Berkman, and hundreds of other foreign-born radicals.

Le Sueur's dissatisfaction with the exploitation of women in the New York theater led her to investigate Hollywood's burgeoning film industry, and she remained in California from 1922 to 1928. Le Sueur landed bit parts and sporadic work as an extra and "stunt girl" (one memorable role was in *Perils of Pauline*, when she stood in for actress Pearl White in a fencing scene). But after refusing a studio's suggestion that she have cosmetic surgery done on her "Semitic" nose, Le Sueur left the film business for alternative theater groups in Sacramento and Berkeley, working with Harry Rice, a Marxist labor organizer she had known in St. Paul. For a while she played Betty Crocker on the radio but was fired, I had heard, because her voice sounded too sensuous for the kitchen. When I asked her if this was the case, she nodded and smiled, "My voice was" (Hedges 3; Grossmann 3D; interview).

Le Sueur joined the Communist Party in 1924.[6] By then she was writing regularly for the *Daily Worker,* and in 1927 her first short story, "Persephone," was published in the *Dial.* In that same year, while in jail for having protested against the Sacco and Vanzetti executions, Le Sueur decided to have a child. At the time she was married to Rice (born Yasha Rubonoff, in Russia, he had spent the war years in a Leavenworth prison as a conscientious objector). They had married "around 1926" (Grossman 3D). As reported in a St. Paul newspaper on the occasion of Le Sueur's ninetieth birthday,

> Le Sueur tells different versions of why she decided to get married. Recently, she said it was because she wanted her children to have birth certificates: "I didn't see any other reason to get married. I was never married in the sense of living together. I didn't fall in love with men who cared for permanent bourgeois marriage." (Grossman 3D)

To have a child, as Le Sueur said in "Annunciation," a story about her first pregnancy, was a choice for life in a world that was "dead and closed" (128). She recalls also having in mind a statement she attributes to Lenin: the "primal relationship between mother and child is the only communality left in capitalist society" (Hedges 4). Rachel was born in 1928, Deborah less than two years later.

When Le Sueur and Rice divorced in the early '30s, Le Sueur asked the court to allow her to take back her "maiden" name, an atypical request in that period. Rice, who has been mentioned only fleetingly in biographical material about Le Sueur, saw his daughters only irregularly until his death in 1948.[7] Mary Ann Grossmann, a reporter for the *St. Paul Pioneer Press Dispatch*, is not the first to note Le Sueur's proclivity for telling different versions of stories. In an unrecorded conversation, December 13, 1983, I asked Le Sueur if Harry Rice had fathered her children. She chuckled and replied mischievously, "I stole the seed." Yet in a journal entry Le Sueur revealed that she took her relationship with Rice [referred to as "Y," for Yasha] seriously: "I put my best truest most honest generous energy into it" (vol. 13, 1938–41, n. pag.).[8]

Le Sueur has remarked that her children were born before "Red-diaper" babies became fashionable.[9] She recalls that prior to the Popular Front, Party members were fond of quoting H. L. Mencken's line about the futility of providing "cannon fodder" for the next war. She also remembers that Anna Louise Strong, among others, criticized her for having children and thus making herself less effective as a political organizer. According to Le Sueur, Strong reacted in dismay when she met Rachel as a child: "Is this *yours?*" Strong demanded. "You're ruined!" (interview).

In 1991, Myra Page, a writer and Party member during the '30s, recalled "a prejudice against [Party] women's having children." She added, "I thought that [the prejudice] was wrong, and I still think it was wrong." Annette Rubinstein, another Le Sueur contemporary who was active in the Party, also observed in 1991: "it was generally felt . . . that it was not only foolish but even wrong to have a child in the '30s . . . it was not only foolish and wrong for the baby because you couldn't feed it . . . it also was wrong for a full-time activist because you wouldn't be able to do what you should be doing." Rubinstein then referred to two Le Sueur stories published in *Salute to Spring*, "Annunciation" and "Tonight Is Part of the Struggle." Rubinstein spoke approvingly of these stories' portraying two unemployed women in relation to motherhood (one is pregnant and one has recently had a baby): Le Sueur wrote, Rubinstein says, "without making a theoretical thing" of it, using "stream of consciousness" and the "first person through the woman."[10]

Peggy Dennis, an active Party member for 50 years and widow of Party leader Eugene Dennis, gave birth to a child in 1929, at Eugene's insistence. (He had regaled her "with visions of our travelling with babe on our backs from barricade to barricade, wherever the revolution called" [*Autobiography* 35]). Peggy Dennis's autobiography includes her mother's prophetic response to the news of Peggy's pregnancy: "Mama sat silent, looking out the trolley window. Then, without looking at me, she said in a flat voice, 'The pity of it is it will change your life, not his'" (*Autobiography* 37). Later Dennis would undergo several abortions when children would have interfered with her or her husband's political work, and she knew other women who reluctantly submitted to abortions on orders from the CP leadership.[11]

Zona Gale, a Wisconsin writer who encouraged Le Sueur to write and helped get her work published, viewed the birth of Le Sueur's children as interfering with her literary career (Hedges 6). In 1921 Gale was the first woman awarded the Pulitzer Prize (in drama, for *Miss Lula Bett*, which Le Sueur describes as "a kind of *Doll's House* of the middle west, with two endings, one in which Lula Bett stays, and the other in which she goes out alone, shutting the door behind her" [Le Sueur, Afterword 232]). Gale believed that "a woman must choose between the life of a creative artist and that of an ordinary married woman. One couldn't have both" (Loughridge 223). She "preached that sex was brutalizing, bestial, enslaving. And in her time it was," Le Sueur has written.[12]

Gale also influenced and promoted the writing of Margery Latimer, who in turn greatly influenced Le Sueur. Latimer, who appears in Le Sueur's '30s journals, published, among other texts, *Guardian Angel and Other Stories* (reprinted by the Feminist Press, 1984). Latimer, who married writer Jean Toomer, died in childbirth in 1932 at 33. "All my writing is like hers," Le Sueur asserts (Afterword 234). The following passage from Latimer's *This Is My Body*, a rewriting of the ritual of holy communion, strikingly resembles the form and content of some of Le Sueur's work ("Corn Village," for example, which I discuss in Chapter 4). The passage also expresses a desire that Le Sueur shared for a collective marriage far more encompassing than traditional coupling:

> Live in my body, O my town and my people! Do not perish! I partook of you and you partook of me, in this marriage, and it became two marriages—the marriage of myself to him, the marriage of myself to you and you to me, O town, O people. And inside you, Town, I had suffered, and from you, People, I had hidden and covered my face and walked alone. And now, through him and through you I have partaken of full life. Deep in us, living its strange life, we are ripe together and complete and round with this perfect taste of living fruit. And in this moment of marriage, of perfect tasting and absorbing and fulfilling, I received and ate the best of you, the marvelous fruiting of your lives, the complete willing surrender of you all, lifted for a moment into full bodied and sweet blooded giving with eyes and bodies radiant, never to die but always to live. (cited in Afterword 235)

Speaking of women such as Gale and Latimer and of her relationship to them, Le Sueur asserts that

> they wrote on the walls with their blood. . . . Carefully we must decipher these messages. Our lives depend on it. They cared enough about us to warn us. Margery was willing to go through fire for illumination. As we bonded together, escaping refugees along an unknown road, so they wrote for you not born yet. The three of us [Gale, Latimer, and Le Sueur] might not have survived without each other. . . . I survived, maybe by camouflage. (Afterword 233)

In her '30s journals, which appear to have no "camouflage," Le Sueur did not express the feeling that her children had ruined her life, as Anna Strong had thought they would, or had interfered with her literary career, as Zona Gale believed they would. Le Sueur expressed tenderness, affection, and compassion for her children, found comfort in them, and took pleasure in their activities. Rachel Tilsen has cared for Meridel in her old age (Meridel now lives with Rachel and her husband, Kenneth Tilsen, a progressive St. Paul attorney, in Hudson, Wisconsin); but the '30s journals provide some evidence that, as a child, Rachel (the older of the two children) had already assumed the role of caretaker for her mother. "R[achel] is such a love," Le Sueur writes in one typical journal entry, "knowing . . . when I am sad" (vol. 7, 1933, 27). In another entry Le Sueur writes, "I can't even look sad because R[achel] is watching me like a hawk to see if there is any danger" (vol. 7, 1933, 26).

As if making notes for a story, Le Sueur writes in the third person about her relationship to Rachel:

> A mother who feels that her child is like herself—torn, frightened, and passionately moved. [A mother] who sees . . . [that her daughter] will have all the struggles. . . . A mother who realizes compassionately the struggle of her daughter, like her own, to know.

In a subsequent note, Le Sueur adds, a "story of a woman remembering her own childhood with her daughter" (vol. 13, 1938–41, n. pag.). And Le Sueur thus describes a response to Deborah: "I had the strangest tearing tenderness and passion for her, it was painful and pure passion, with that tragedy that things of pure passion give you, that ache of fullness and yet want" (vol. 10, 1935–37, n. pag.).

Referring to both Rachel and Deborah, Le Sueur writes, "they bear me so simply, so tenderly." In the evening of the same day, Le Sueur notes: "I am going to wake the children to see the orange moon at ten. I promised I would" (vol. 7, 1933, 27, 28). Again referring to both children, she writes, "their bodies, their speech is like a myth to me, like a legend, something great, simple, and utterly communicable to me, instantly imaged on my blood, on my flesh" (vol. 10, 1935–37, n. pag.). At one point, listening for her children to come home, Le Sueur notes: "So here I am waiting as if they were going to be born again, waiting to see them, to touch them; and I feel my body all aglow with the most extraordinary love and anticipation for them." And in the same entry Le Sueur writes, "I keep knowing why I had children. I keep knowing what a good instinct it was" (vol. 7, 1933, 170).

Le Sueur's commitment to a "communal" sensibility derived partly from her living so passionately *in relation to* her children: "I cannot help but feel the superiority of this kind of collective feeling to anything I feel myself alone" (vol. 13, 1938–41, n. pag.). Le Sueur longed to extend the love she felt for her children to all of humanity: "To pick up R[achel] and feel her body and feel her flesh and the slim sides warm . . . my child—one should feel this about all the bodies of the world—one should feel this" (vol. 5, 1929–32, 159). Le Sueur writes that she had her children "with the best emotions, the most generous, sweet, and tremendous emotions." And she wonders why those feelings are "never, never spoken to anyone" (vol. 13, 1938–41, 17).

During the Depression, Le Sueur, her children and parents, and other family members sustained themselves by living together in Minneapolis and pooling resources. Of that period Le Sueur has written:

> We had no key to our door or latch to the ice box. My mother and I came down in the morning and looked on the couch to see what fresh emissary from the east or west would be asleep in the living room. Sometimes we didn't know them. Word had gone out to some Oklahoma ballad singer . . . WPA worker, or striker without a bed. (*Crusaders* 57)

Marian and Arthur Le Sueur worked in the educational component of the Farmer-Labor Party, which was especially strong with Floyd Olson as governor of Minnesota, and helped edit that party's newspaper, the *Leader*. In 1934 Olson appointed Marian to the State Board of Education and to the State Planning Board. In 1936 Governor Elmer Bensen appointed Arthur, by then an attorney for the CIO, a municipal judge.

In the '30s Meridel Le Sueur's hopes, like those of many others, centered in the CP and the assumed potential of the working class. Leftist organizations, most affiliated with the Party, provided a framework for Le Sueur's literary and political expression and development: the John Reed Clubs; the *New Masses*, whose staff she joined; the Workers' Alliance, an organization of artists and workers that helped unemployed men and women obtain jobs in the arts and to whose newspaper she contributed; the New Deal Federal Writers Project; the 1935 and 1937 American Writers' Congresses; and *Midwest* Magazine, a regional publication she and Dale Kramer founded in 1936.

Through reportage and fiction, Le Sueur became the biographer of ordinary, "anonymous" men and women, especially the economically destitute. She produced over two dozen pieces of reportage; 30 short stories; a novel; some poems and miscellaneous articles; daily journal entries; and pieces written for *Vogue*, *Harper's Bazaar*, and *True Confessions* in order to earn a subsistence income.

Le Sueur received substantial recognition during the '30s. Her work was praised by such prominent writers as Sinclair Lewis, Nelson Algren, and Carl Sandburg and published by prestigious journals—*Dial*, *Scribner's*, and *Yale Review*, among them. Sixteen of her short stories were either reprinted or cited in Edward O'Brien's annual collections of best short stories, and one of her pieces of reportage, "I Was Marching," was reprinted three times. Le Sueur was the lone woman among the 28 scheduled speakers at the 1935 American Writers' Congress (although, as noted in Chapter 1, Josephine Herbst was recruited at the last minute for the opening session because the organizers suddenly noticed the absence of women on the program). Le Sueur was also the lone female member of the 1935 Congress's 16-member Presiding Committee, which included Malcolm Cowley, Joseph Freeman, Michael Gold, Granville Hicks, Isidor Schneider, Edwin Seaver, and Alexander Trachtenberg, among others (Hart 165). At the conclusion of the 1937 American Writers' Congress, along with such distinguished writers as Van Wyck Brooks, Malcolm Cowley, Erskine Caldwell, Upton Sinclair, Langston Hughes, Ernest Hemingway, and Archibald MacLeish, Le Sueur was elected one of several vice-presidents of the League of American Writers (Schwartz 62).

The publication in 1940 of *Salute to Spring*, a collection of Le Sueur's '30s reportage and stories, marked the high point in her career. Alfred Kazin, who was quick to point out what he termed the "limitations and bigotry" of proletarian literature, said in his review of *Salute to Spring* that "Le Sueur is in some respects the most intense and self-consciously workmanlike artist proletarian literature has produced" (Smith 15). Until the mid-forties Le Sueur continued to find ready publication for her work. When the United States entered the war, she wrote both journalism and fiction defending the war effort. In 1943 Le Sueur won a Rockefeller Historical Research Fellowship, which enabled her to write *North Star Country*, an impressionistic "history" of the North Central States. It was part of the American Folkways Series edited by Erskine Caldwell and was chosen as the Book Find Club selection for March 1945. But *North Star Country* received mixed reviews. As folklore, it received acclaim as "spirited" and "poetic"; as history, it was viewed as "highly misleading" and "woefully inadequate" (cited in Smith 17). (Le Sueur intended it as "mythical history" [Smith 16]). *North Star Country's* message—"the people, yes"—was harmonious with a long tradition of Midwestern populism and with the CP's position during the Popular Front.

Yet for the 25 years following the Second World War, Le Sueur all but disappeared. With the arrival of the Cold War period in 1947, she moved into what she has described as her "dark time," when she was blacklisted from most publishing outlets, although she continued to publish in the CP journals *Mainstream* and *Masses and Mainstream*, successors to *New Masses*. Linda Ray Pratt has usefully surveyed Le Sueur's publishing record prior to the "dark time":

> While a complete bibliography of Le Sueur is not available, Mary K. Smith's 1973 master's thesis compiles 135 items, excluding what Smith terms "much ephemeral journalistic writing" (41). Of the 86 stories, articles, poems and reviews listed between 1924 and 1946, only a little more than 20 per cent of them are in journals such as *New Masses* or the *Daily Worker*. . . . While Party publication was an important part of Le Sueur's early publishing history, and the response she got from it perhaps even more important to her sense of development as a writer, her access to an audience was not dependent on the CP during this period. . . . Nothing could more vividly reflect the effectiveness of blacklisting than this bibliography, so varied in scope until 1947, so limited thereafter. ("Woman writer" 255)

As a result of relentless FBI harassment, Le Sueur and her family found it difficult to find or keep jobs. "I was surrounded, lassoed," Le Sueur wrote in her journal. Her house was bugged, her phone was tapped, and "two FBI agents sat outside day and night" (cited in Schleuning, *America* 108). While Rachel and Ken Tilsen were under constant FBI surveillance, their car was stolen from in front of their house. "Now what would *you* think?" Rachel laughed, when she reported this incident to me in 1992. "The car's getting stolen was even worse than our discovering sugar in the gas tank. It's funny now," she added, "but it certainly wasn't amusing then."[13]

Carl Bernstein's *Loyalties: A Son's Memoir* is one quite sober account of the vicious and absurd nature of McCarthy Period harassment. *Loyalties* records some of the questions loyalty-board members asked of governmental employees after Truman issued the Loyalty Order, March 21, 1947:

> "Do you read a good many books?" "What magazines do you read?" "What newspapers do you buy or subscribe to?" "Do you think that Russian Communism is likely to succeed?" "How do you explain the fact that you have an album of Paul

Robeson records in your home?" "Do you ever entertain Negroes in your home?". . . . "Have you ever discussed the subject of the dance in Russia?" "Did you ever write a letter to the Red Cross about the segregation of blood?" (205)

A memorable description of the House Committee on Un-American Activities [HUAC] appears in Jessica Mitford's A *Fine Old Conflict.* "An instrument of terror," HUAC at its inception in 1938 was received "with a certain light-hearted contempt," and "in its early days . . . pulled some delightful boners," including naming "Shirley Temple, then aged nine, as an unwitting dupe of the Communists" and "the indisputably accurate designation of Christopher Marlowe as Un-American." But, as Mitford reminds us, "the jokes stopped after the war":

> In *Inquisition in Eden*, Alvah Bessie, himself a victim of the Committee, attributes some dozen suicides and numerous premature deaths from heart attack to persecution by the witch-hunting committees in the postwar years, not to speak of "permanent ostracism, divorce and voluntary exile—a list that numbers many hundreds if not thousands." (195)[14]

During this "dark time" Alfred Knopf informed Le Sueur that she had been blacklisted but that he would continue to publish her children's books; between 1947 and 1954 she produced several of them, based on such figures as Davy Crockett, Johnny Appleseed, Abraham Lincoln, and Lincoln's mother, Nancy Hanks. The books were banned by some libraries and were the subject of red-baiting reviews (the *Milwaukee Sentinel*, for example, referred to her book on Abraham Lincoln as having "pink-tinged" pages).[15] Although the sale of these children's books provided some income, Le Sueur earned much of her living from 1935 to 1950 by teaching creative writing classes—sometimes at the YMCA, sometimes in rented offices, and sometimes at home.[16] But the FBI's harassment of Le Sueur caused her to lose students, and this source of income dried up.

Sick and partially blind, Arthur practiced law until his death in 1950. In 1952, despite McCarthy Period repression, Marian ran (unsuccessfully) for Senator on the Progressive Party ticket to protest the Korean War: "She was seventy-five years old, had still to make her living; she went to the Progressive Party office every morning, wrote speeches, toured the countryside, spoke in the houses and the little halls again, recorded radio programs, mimeographed leaflets" (*Crusaders* 74).

Marian died in January 1954, in the same week that Le Sueur's daughters, Deborah and Rachel, and Rachel's husband, Kenneth Tilsen, were "named" by a witness for the Senate Select Internal Committee. FBI agents followed the Le Sueur family members to and from Marian's hospital. "The agents didn't follow us to my grandmother's bedside," Rachel Tilsen recalls, "but we *felt* as if they were there." And for a week, while the family mourned Marian's death, Deborah, Rachel, and Ken's names were in the headlines of the Minneapolis-St. Paul newspapers.[17] To add to Le Sueur's sense of loss, her companion of 25 years, painter Robert Brown (whom I will discuss subsequently), died in June of the same year. Le Sueur wrote *Crusaders* shortly after her mother's death to commemorate Marian and Arthur Le Sueur's activism and to "reaffirm her own faith in the Midwest populist tradition" (Hedges 16). *Crusaders* was an act of reclamation during the "dark time"; the book's jacket aptly termed it an "antidote to fear."

Le Sueur remained in the CP and took a leading role in salvaging the Minnesota state party, even when 85 percent of the national membership left in response to the Khrushchev revelations and the Soviet Union's invasion of Hungary, both in 1956.[18] The Party, which had about 20 thousand members in January of that year, lost at least half of them by the summer of 1957 and shrank to 3000 members by the following summer. Le Sueur accepted what came to be known as the Party's "five minutes to midnight" line, which predicted imminent economic depression, the triumph of fascism in the United States, and war between the United States and the Soviet Union.

As Hedges points out, "Tillie Olsen has referred to any woman who manages to write as a 'survivor,'" and the term aptly applies to Le Sueur at this time (18). As the '50s drew to a close, she was nearing 60 and was still without a steady income. After Marian's death in 1954, Le Sueur had taken over the operation of her mother's boarding house. But again, business was adversely affected by FBI surveillance, which frightened away prospective boarders, and by the close of the decade Le Sueur felt forced to sell the house. By living frugally she sustained herself for some time on the proceeds from the sale. Traveling extensively by bus and by her Volkswagen van (which she used as a kind of "mobile home"), Le Sueur talked to many "ordinary" people, recording their stories, and "thus continuing the work as a social historian that she had begun in the thirties."[19] She also earned a modest income from chauffeuring a disabled woman who commuted between Iowa and Santa Fe, and, as a volunteer, attended women in the Minneapolis State Asylum.

Because of the freer political climate of the '60s and '70s, however, and especially as a result of the women's movement, Le Sueur's work has enjoyed a revival of interest. Much of it has been reprinted, including three collections of short stories—*Salute to Spring* (International Publishers, 1940, 1977), *Song for My Time* (West End Press, 1977), and *Harvest* (West End, 1977). A revision of the novel *The Girl*, drafted in 1939, was published by West End in 1978 (although sections of the manuscript had been published as short stories). In 1982 the Feminist Press issued a Le Sueur anthology edited by Elaine Hedges, *Ripening: Selected Work, 1927–1980*. The Minnesota Historical Society reprinted *Crusaders* in 1984; in the same year West End published *I Hear Men Talking* (a novel revised from a manuscript begun in the late '20s and probably completed by 1940) in a volume by the same title also containing two reprinted novellas, "The Bird" and "The Horse." From 1985 to 1992 Holy Cow! Press reprinted the children's stories first published by Knopf from 1947 to 1954. In 1990 West End Press published *Harvest Song*, reprinting '30s short stories and reportage that had not been included in other editions of Le Sueur's work. Nearly all of Le Sueur's short works can be found in a combination of three volumes—*Ripening*, *Salute to Spring*, and *Harvest Song*.

In 1956 Le Sueur edited *The People Together*, a collection of poetry, stories, and songs about Minnesota farmers and workers, for the state's centennial celebration.[20] Since the '50s Le Sueur has published new material in a volume of poetry, *Rites of Ancient Ripening* (Vanilla Press, 1975); "The Ancient People and Newly Come," a chapter in *Growing Up in Minnesota: Ten Writers Remember Their Childhoods* (University of Minnesota Press, 1976); and, most recently, a novella, *Winter Prairie Woman* (first edition, the Minnesota Center for Book Arts, 1990) and *The Dread Road* (West End Press, 1991). Much of Le Sueur's writing has been in her unpublished journals, which span the period from 1917 to the present and number over 140 volumes.[21]

Like her grandmother and mother before her, Le Sueur became active in the '70s and '80s on the "lecture circuit," speaking on political issues, especially those related to women; talking about her life; and reading from her writing. While apparently Le Sueur remains a member of the CP, it has been ostrich-like regarding "the woman question" in recent years, and she seems to identify more closely with the women's movement than with the Party. For example, while in her eighties, Le Sueur traveled to the international women's conference in Nairobi, "where she reveled in the sense of global sisterhood" (Grossmann 3D).

In 1987 Le Sueur established the Meridel Le Sueur Library, now housed at Augsburg College in Minneapolis, near the Meridel Le Sueur Center for Peace and Justice. The library includes many books and magazines from Le Sueur's private collection, concentrating on American literature, Native American history, African-American history, and women's issues. Many of the books are by or about women and record the history of progressive movements of twentieth-century America. In February 1990 the Meridel Le Sueur Library and the Center for Peace and Justice joined with numerous other progressive organizations, family members, and friends to celebrate Le Sueur's ninetieth birthday. A concert featuring Pete Seeger, Ronnie Gilbert, and a 40-member Children's Cantata was held in the Orpheum Theatre in Minneapolis, followed the next day by "Meridel and 90 Years of Struggle," a community festival held at the College of St. Catherine's O'Shaughnessy Auditorium and sponsored by many progressive organizations.[22]

When I interviewed Le Sueur in 1985 and 1989, she was noticeably sensitive about some topics and in discussing them was, consciously or unconsciously, less than direct. Her reluctance to talk openly might be partly explained by old habits of Party membership (even before the McCarthy Period's persecution of Reds, many members did not reveal their affiliation); by the sexist treatment she received for many years from male editors; and by the red-baiting and harassment to which she has been subjected. Her reticence probably results, as well, from a lifelong shyness. Although diffidence is not a quality that interviewers and admirers generally attribute to Le Sueur, her journals and her daughter Rachel confirmed my sense of her as a shy person. Le Sueur feels at once a common, understandable uneasiness about full disclosure and a responsibility to record the severity of women's lives, including her own.

This issue of openness is further complicated by Le Sueur's unconventional relation to time. From the mid-fifties until the mid-seventies she occasionally lived among Native Americans, including the Oglala Sioux at the Pine Ridge Reservation in South Dakota and the Hopi in northern Arizona, and was attracted by their conception of time as more fluid than that of the dominant culture. Le Sueur has little tolerance for what she terms "linear" time and resisted my attempts to date some of the events in her life and beliefs she has held.[23] She can also be mischievous with time, collapsing what she believed in the '30s with what she came to believe decades later. "This indifference to the mechanics of living," acknowledged the *St. Paul Pioneer Press Dispatch*, "can drive her friends [and sympathetic critics, I might add] to loving distraction" (Grossmann 3D). John Crawford, Le Sueur's publisher at West End Press, tells an amusing—and representative—anecdote about driving Le Sueur to a Minneapolis party one night in subzero temperature: "I was new to the Twin Cities, and I asked her for directions. She said, 'That's very linear; we'll get there the way the Indians did.' Basically, we drove around the cities in concentric circles. I remember crossing Cedar Avenue four times. Eventually, we found it" (cited in Grossmann 3D).

As I mentioned earlier, Le Sueur has achieved Wonder Woman status. On the basis of her long, admirable life as a radical, writer, and feminist, Le Sueur has become an emblematic figure, variously termed "Mother Bard," "Mystic," "Goddess," "High Priestess," "prophet," "Renaissance woman," "Earth-Mother," "socialist tribal mother," "the essence of mystery," "St. Meridel."[24] But, she admits, "I haven't really revealed the brutality of . . . my own life. And I think the women's movement has helped me to cover it up." She provided *Ms.* magazine as an example: "They want to present you as what they call a role model who made it, who succeeded. That's a locker room boy philosophy to me." They "don't really tell the horrible—like it's just coming out, like the battered women—the horrible violence of women's lives" (interview). When I have asked this sometimes reserved woman about the brutality of her own life, she has directed me to her journals, even though she understandably has some misgivings about allowing people access to them. In some publications about Le Sueur, passages, including some with intimate information about her mother, have been excerpted out of context and hence misrepresented. But "I can't close [the journals] up," Le Sueur concludes, "because I really wrote for women not yet born" (interview).

Housed under restriction at the Minnesota Historical Society, these unpublished journals, as well as letters, await revelation in a full-length biography of Le Sueur, which to my knowledge has yet to be undertaken. And Le Sueur has not yet released to an archive 20 boxes of letters, including her correspondence with Margery Latimer and a 50-year correspondence with her closest friend, Irene Paull, a writer and long-time Party member. Piecemeal—conducting interviews, reading her journals from the '30s, and sampling other papers at the Minnesota Historical Society—I have gathered enough information to believe that a comprehensive biography of the Le Sueur family would contribute richly to the history of U.S. radicals and feminists.

Published biographical material about Le Sueur has not addressed, for example, the impact that both the presence and absence of Le Sueur's biological father may have had on her life and writing. Le Sueur describes him as "a charming rascal, a lovely, wonderful dancer, a beautiful seducer. . . . a womanizer . . . an orator, beautiful speaker, preacher" as well as very violent, a heavy drinker, and physically abusive (interview). Le Sueur obliquely refers to psychological scars from physical abuse. For example, when trying to account for her uncharacteristic behavior when she was televised in 1980 with two male poets (despite a lifelong feminism, a "little girl" emerged, "terrified" and "wounded," who began "to throw the questions" to them), she conjectured that her "body remembered all that terrible oppression of men. . . . The body just never, never forgets" (interview). Threatening male protagonists such as Butch in *The Girl* and Bac in *I Hear Men Talking* may have been partly modeled on Robert (Bob) Brown, her lover for 25 years, or on her biological father; dead fathers figure in *The Girl* and "Our Fathers." The importance of Le Sueur's absent father is suggested cryptically in the following journal entry: "I had no father and could not be impregnated then with my own womanhood. I could not be a woman—I could not let myself flower with no male stalk over me . . . [her ellipsis] broken off one part of me. . . . to go unchartered—without a trail—I feel gutted at the core somewhere" (vol. 5, 1929–32, 118).

Le Sueur has also said little about Bob Brown, an artist until his death in 1954, and about his impact on her life and writing. Le Sueur dedicated *The Girl* to Brown "and that dark city of St. Paul," but she was unwilling to talk about him at length in our interviews.

> I'm willing to give the experience of it [her relationship with Brown], [but] I don't want to talk *about* him. I chose a creative man who wasn't going to support [me] or have [my] children. I [chose him] because he had a great creative mind, a great male mind, which fed me. But I had no security from him. . . . not in the sense of bourgeois living. I mean, who needs that? That's not a pattern necessary for creative people. . . . our relationship had nothing to do with possessions or property or owning. It had to do with our [being] creative. He was the only person that really honored a female creative mind, and I honored his male mind. I never cooked his breakfast or had a house. . . . He honored my creativeness . . . which was unusual for a man. (interview)

Sharon Doubiago's tribute to Le Sueur's eightieth birthday, written in the form of a journal entry, included a revelation about Brown. Doubiago describes herself sitting in Le Sueur's chair, reading a photocopied essay:

> . . . as I read I find notes in Meridel's handwriting on the back of the xeroxed pages: "Madness to react to male confinement. I was mad . . . around the terrible light of Bob, like a moth. Female reality extremely different than accepted reality. What kept me home? I am shocked back into my servitude and fright. . . ." And

then I read it, surely the saddest, the most haunting line in all her writing. I'm uneasy for having come across something perhaps terribly private and yet, how much more I know of her . . . in this one line: "Mac [Le Sueur's brother] and Bob hated my writing." (McAnally n. pag.)[25]

"He [Brown] didn't think I was a very good writer," Le Sueur acknowledged without bitterness in 1989. But "he supported [the] feminine creative feeling that he got from me" (interview). However, at age 83 Le Sueur remarked that she "never knew a man who wanted a relationship with a woman equally creative" (Pratt, "Afterword" 227).

In Le Sueur's '30s journals Brown appears as a powerful, complicated force in the writer's life.[26] Many entries, like the following two, suggest that Le Sueur valued Brown as an inspiriting and loving presence:

> I cannot describe this physical sense of the world that B[ob] gives me . . . [her ellipsis] this sense of things existing solid, real, wonderful, the sounds, the sights. . . . When he lets me feel him fully . . . when he opens to me . . . then there is nothing better. (vol. 9, 1934–35, 143)

> I can't help but feel that B[ob]'s love for me has dissolved my neurosis of fear and grief and failure. Something in it has given me—actually GIVEN me a physical glowing ease—a sentient way to feel life in my being, in my body. (vol. 8, 1934–35, 2)

Another entry declares, "I know in my white bones that he is the only thing standing up in this world" (vol. 5, 1929–32, 85). And on many occasions Le Sueur felt a rare kinship with Brown:

> He has the power of opening up the wounds and darknesses of the past and making me disgorge them. . . . A marvelous thing to open up those wounds and cauterize them. I can't do it myself, they heal over dangerously. But he—there are places in him beyond any human being. . . . Sometimes when he talks I listen in amazement to hear him, sheer amazement. I cannot believe it. I cannot believe that anyone is saying these things but myself. He becomes then a brother, a male counterpart of myself as if nurtured in the same womb. . . . it surpasses his being a man to me. It surpasses that kind of love, goes beyond it. (vol. 5, 1929–32, 81)

Yet the journals also reveal that Brown was "the weapon of destruction" as well as "the weapon of love"; his "sculptured nature," Le Sueur wrote, "is at once a boon to me and a barb" (vol. 5, 1929–32, 96; vol. 8, 1934–35, 76). Brown drank heavily and was sometimes hateful and physically violent when he was drunk. Le Sueur's ambivalence is evident, with both "Browns" often present on one journal page. The following two comments are representative. First Le Sueur comments on Brown as a unique positive force in her life:

> What made me think, what made me feel this astounding thing . . . that a great resurrection lay in him? But it has been true, there is no denying that it has been true. I have felt it. I have something imposed upon me that I can't forget.

She then describes Brown in negative terms:

> This world of suspicion, this fine edge of hate he has. His eyes glitter, his mouth cuts down as if a jagged knife had cut it in his face with hate. . . . what a force, what a chisel cutting away the world. If love could ever be half the force. If he could ever speak from his love with half that force—throw the force of love as he throws the javelin of his keen black hate. (vol. 5, 1929–32, 153)

Many journal entries describe Bob's dramatic mood swings, usually associated with drinking. "He says when he is sober that he will not drink or strike again. He says when he is drunk [that] everything is foul" (vol. 7, 1933, 251).

Brown's erratic behavior deeply affected Le Sueur's emotional equilibrium, and what she experienced for many years can be summed up with the following entry: "This swing . . . [her ellipsis] coming together tenderness . . . [her ellipsis] miraculous love passion and then something snaps in him and he goes wild and dark and mean" (vol. 7, 1933, 244). In her afterword to Margery Latimer's *Guardian Angel*, Le Sueur acknowledges Latimer's—and, implicitly, her own— "split desires." "We still feel the fright without the old dominance," Le Sueur explains, adding that "the prisoner can long for the prison" (233).

The family biography is also complex and incomplete. *Crusaders* says that the Le Sueurs "never had a nervous breakdown. [They were] very un-neurotic because there were no choices" (75), yet Le Sueur has revealed that Marian attempted suicide twice in one year while married to Arthur and that she herself tried to take her own life during the '20s, after contemplating suicide a number of times (interview). About that period she says simply, "I was insane, I think" (*Crusaders* 75; interview; Pratt, Afterword 227). There is no reason to doubt Le Sueur's sincerity in the dedication of *Crusaders*—"To my mother and father: valiant leaders in the people's struggle for peace, freedom, and justice"—but even *Crusaders* raises some questions about the private lives of these public figures. Le Sueur thus depicts Marian's position soon after her marriage to Arthur:

> Marian found herself back in the cage of marriage she had tried to escape. She was no longer Comrade Wharton, head of the English Department, with her own house and life. She was now doubly servant; she went to the office at nine after getting her children off [where she worked as Arthur's secretary], she came back at four, cleaned the house, and got supper; in the evening she ran up and down between the apartment they occupied upstairs and the children's lessons in the front room. (52)

When I questioned Le Sueur about this passage, she confirmed that Arthur was, at least in one respect, no exception to most men of his generation: He did not consider domestic labor and child care his responsibility.

Only fragments are known about Le Sueur's personal relationship to her mother and stepfather. Le Sueur has said, for example, that she and Arthur "didn't get along" and that he was jealous of her close relationship to her mother; Elaine Hedges has described the relationship between Marian and Meridel as "intense and often ambivalent"; Le Sueur described her mother as being "awfully domineering" and has said that she wrote her first short story ("Persephone") at a time when her mother was "antagonistic and controlling."[27] As a young woman Le Sueur once impulsively traveled from Los Angeles to St. Paul to tell her mother about her first love affair. When she arrived home, however, Marian talked incessantly about one of her own affairs without inquiring about her daughter's state of mind, and Meridel left without telling her mother the reason for her visit (interview). Le Sueur also remembers her parents' "telling her they wouldn't love her unless she behaved a certain way. 'My love related to pleasing, to serving them. I always felt they were wiping me out'" (Pratt, Afterword 227). Ambivalence about one's parents is common, but *Crusaders*, our main source of information about Le Sueur's relationship to her parents, reveals little of that complexity.[28]

One exchange I had with Le Sueur about her relationship with her mother was amusing. "My mother was a fierce mother," Le Sueur told me in 1989. "She was like an elephant," she continued, "as if he [the elephant] were going through the jungle [and] saw a wren's nest, abandoned, with eggs in it. And he said, 'Well, don't worry, I'll hatch you.' So he sat down on the eggs. That was my mother's passion for her children. She'd hatch 'em even if she killed 'em." Then she asked me what my response would be to someone's sitting on me and trying to hatch me. "Ambivalence," was my cautious reply, to which Le Sueur laughed and said, "No it's not—it's terror!" (interview). "In *Crusaders* you talked about your mother," I persisted, "but you talked about her in ways that were appropriate for a tribute to her. You haven't told the story of her being an elephant, hatching eggs. Have you made a decision about that—that you're not going to tell that story?" Le Sueur responded as she often did: "I tell it all in my notebooks."

The following journal entry from the late '30s expresses admiration for—and some misgivings about—Marian's capacity to "feel strongly":

> M[other] attracts everyone, attracts them because underneath is her strong feeling, and they do not know how to have strong feeling—they don't have strong feeling and there is no worse hell on earth than not to feel, not to feel strongly—to feel only in pieces—only partly—people who feel strongly no matter what they do are alive—people who feel luke warmly are never alive—they are the true murderers. M[other] murders you and then snatches you from death. Her passion is never niggling or clever, that is the great beauty and vitality of her—her passion is strong, beyond her, outside her own memory, even—it snatches her like a storm. It's a chemical compound of her own groping suffering just as the beautiful storms all summer were a chemical compound of great winds, light, currents of air rising from water, meeting heat—and a storm, natural, terrific—and then calm—her storms are not compounded of cleverness or deceit, and she remembers nothing—nothing. Now she thinks that everything was always peace between herself and A[rthur], that they were always at peace like now—she does not remember the terrific storms—the awful struggle between them. (vol. 13, 1938–41, n. pag.)

And Le Sueur's journals acknowledge another important element in the legacy her mother left her: "What I owe to M[other] is that I did not belong to any milieu of society. I seemed to be wrenched OUT of it" (vol. 7, 1933, 235).[29] In 1989 Le Sueur said, "I don't think I'll ever . . . write a study of my mother, [although] I'd like to really—I see the horror of her struggle, what a bold and terrible thing it was, and [at that time] there wasn't a women's movement" (interview).

When Le Sueur speaks candidly about her life, as she does in her journals, she supplies details that add dimensions to the persona promoted by elements of the women's movement and the radical press. As her journals reveal, Le Sueur struggled courageously against a deep sense of melancholia—and even despair—much of her life, and she wrote partly to alleviate this terrible sadness. "I feel miserable in my body and somewhere far inside the bone of me," Le Sueur writes (vol. 9, 1934–35, 300). In another representative entry, she notes: "I know there is a deep incessant pain in me. . . . Something gets very weak and tired inside me like when I was a child" (vol. 13, 1938–41, 105). But with a few exceptions she has been treated as "politically correct," as an ideal without contradictions.[30]

Such treatment, however, shortchanges not only Le Sueur but also students of women's history and of the American Left. In contrast, the candid biographies of Emma Goldman by Candace Falk and Alice Wexler that include the personal correspondence between Goldman and her lover Ben Reitman have revealed Goldman to be more, not less, intriguing as a historical figure and a socialist feminist. And Elinor Langer's biography of Josephine Herbst, who was widely regarded in the '30s as one of the most important women writers of the decade, is all the better for its sympathetic directness. Aptly subtitled *The Story She Could Never Tell*, the biography confronts the problematic aspects of Herbst's life and the personal dimension of CP political and literary activity during the '30s. Perhaps the most powerful portion of Langer's biography results from her juxtaposing, on the same page, excerpts from Herbst's tough-minded notes on the Cuban revolutionary movement (written from Havana for several U.S. publications) and her desperate letters to John Herrmann as their marriage disintegrated. Herbst seemed "to divide herself in two," Langer observes (165).

In Le Sueur's novel *The Girl* (1939), one woman confides in another: "We can't tell what happens to us in secret even" (135). Over 50 years ago, then, Le Sueur tentatively anticipated what would become a working assumption of the women's movement in the '60s and '70s—that is, that women must confront the unacknowledged truth about their experience. In the poem "Kathë Kollwitz" (1968), Muriel Rukeyser suggests the personal and political significance of such disclosure: "What would happen if one woman told the truth about her life? / The world would split open" (1786).

Although Le Sueur seldom engaged in the literary debates carried out in such journals as *New Masses* and *Partisan Review*, she has, despite some significant disagreements with Michael Gold that I will discuss, several things in common with the exemplar of proletarian literature. Both Le Sueur and Gold attributed their success as writers to the Party. Similarly, whereas the mainstream publishing world felt alien to Le Sueur, "nourishing" is her word for the leftist organizations (most affiliated with the Party) that supported her literary and political development. The John Reed Clubs perhaps most fostered her writing.

Moreover, Gold and Le Sueur shared a hostility toward middle-class intellectuals, resulting at least partly from their own lack of formal training. As discussed in Chapter 1, in his autobiographical novel, *Jews Without Money*, Gold describes his pain and anger at being denied formal education beyond the ninth grade. He also makes his feelings about intellectuals quite clear in a 1927 *New Masses* tribute to John Reed. Gold defends Reed posthumously against accusations that he was an adventurist and a playboy revolutionary by arguing that Reed's physical activity (athletic endeavors as well as boyish hijinks) coupled with his political activism distinguish him from "pale, rootless intellectuals . . . careful men with perpetual slight colds who write for the *New Republic* and the *Nation*." In contrast, Reed "was a cowboy out of the west, six feet high, steady eyes, boyish face; a brave, gay, open-handed young giant." Gold reminds us that "in the IWW the fellow-workers would tar and feather (almost) any intellectual who appeared among them; the word 'intellectual' became a synonym for the word 'bastard,'" and, Gold acknowledged, some of this feeling persisted "in the American Communist movement" ("Reed" 7). In 1937, in his *Daily Worker* column, Gold attacked John Dos Passos and, implicitly, all intellectuals critical of the CP. He concluded: "Intellectuals are the most unstable and untrustworthy group in modern society, one often is forced to believe" ("Change the World" 7).

Similarly, Le Sueur, whose formal education also stopped at the ninth grade, candidly admits suspicion of intellectuals. A strong regional identification, moreover, in some cases compounds her bias: Eastern, and particularly New York, intellectuals are the least trustworthy of all. Le Sueur felt trebly vulnerable to the Party leadership—as a woman, as a person with rural roots, and as a person lacking formal education. The most cowardly and insipid character in her fiction is the protagonist of "A Hungry Intellectual" (originally published in *American Mercury*, 1935, and reprinted in *Salute to Spring*, 1940). And *The Girl* suggests, as do other Le Sueur texts, that actual experience is the *only* teacher ("Nobody can tell you anything, girl. You have to live it" [43]).

A romanticizing of workers often accompanied such anti-intellectualism. Their experience seemed somehow purer, more human, closer to "reality" than that of intellectuals, and their "intuitive" knowledge was considered superior to formal education. Accordingly, Sherwood Anderson with self-deprecation wrote from the World Congress Against Imperialist War in Amsterdam, Holland, attended largely by workers: "Always the workers speak better, more directly, than the intellectuals," he declared in *New Masses* in 1932. "It is amazing how well the workers and the peasants speak. There is a kind of force, a strength that shakes the nerves. . . . There is something alive here, glowingly alive" ("Amsterdam" 11). In "Let the Voice of the People Be Heard" Le Sueur expressed a similar view when she noted that "the poetry of the people is full of muscle, straight from the forge, hot off the griddle" (*Pavement Trail* 3).

Such views of the proletariat's strengths and intellectuals' weaknesses resulted in self-deprecation on the part of many radical intellectuals. Most pronounced in the early '30s, this tendency was already present in 1927, when Genevieve Taggard thus responded to a *New Masses* poll, "Are Artists People?"

> Practical men run revolutions, and there's nothing more irritating than a person with a long, vague look in his eye to have around, when you're trying to bang an army into shape, or put over a N.E.P. If I were in charge of a revolution, I'd get rid of every single artist immediately; and trust to luck that the fecundity of the earth would produce another crop when I had got some of the hard work done. Being an artist, I have the sense that a small child has when its mother is in the middle of house-work. I don't intend to get in the way, and I hope that there'll be an un-molested spot for me when things have quieted down. (6)

Anderson even called for a form of group suicide (*New Masses*, August 1932): "My own feeling now is that if it be necessary, in order to bring about the end of a money civilization and set up something new, healthy and strong, we of the so-called artist class have to be submerged, let us be submerged. Down with us" ("A Writer's Notes" 10).

Because of the skepticism with which they viewed middle-class intellectuals, Gold and Le Sueur shared the opinion that it was desirable, and even creatively necessary, for middle-class writers to "proletarianize" themselves. Gold based his *New Masses* tribute to Reed on his belief that Reed had successfully crossed class lines. Reed had "identified himself so completely with the working-class . . . [that] there was no gap between [him] and the workers any longer" ("Reed" 7).

Le Sueur's desire to abandon her class stemmed partly from a contempt, much like that of Anderson, for individualistic values. In "The Fetish of Being Outside" (*New Masses*, 1935), a reply to Horace Gregory's defense of some middle-class writers' reluctance to join the CP, Le Sueur confessed: "I do not care for the bourgeois individual that I am. I have never cared for it" (22). Notes for "The Fetish" appear in Le Sueur's journal (the ellipses are hers unless otherwise noted):

> The passional vitality of belief, extreme belief. Write this for the New Masses in answer to Gregory . . . write it right away today . . . the peculiar physical childish-ness of the type that wants to be safe . . . to be a man you have to have some not caring in you, some daring, some point where you step off. . . . [ellipsis mine] I want to give over the individual not because I want to side step that responsibility but because that responsibility is too small, too minute, and pertains to myself alone. I can no longer live without communal sensibility, I can no longer write, and the Communist party is the only nucleus of that . . . [ellipsis mine] communal feeling. (vol. 8, 1934–35, 63)

Le Sueur's language in "The Fetish" suggests rebirth, a baptismal cleansing of original sin, a Kierkegaardian leap of faith: "you cannot leave it [your class] by pieces or parts; it is a birth and you have to be born whole out of it. It is a complete new body. None of the old ideology is any good in it." The "creative artist" must be willing to "go all the way, with full belief, into that darkness. . . . In a new and mature integrity" the writer does "not react equivocally." Using Biblical allusions, she asks rhetorically: "Why want to be an outsider when . . . you admit sight of the promised land as Gregory does; why choose to walk around the walls of Jericho . . .?" (22–23).

The view expressed in "The Fetish" was popular among Party members, especially during the early '30s. Joseph Freeman's autobiography, *An American Testament*, for example, attempted to show that an intellectual committed to proletarian revolution could break irrevocably with the middle class. That such a metamorphosis can occur is questionable, however. Political artists and intellectuals, rather than passing as a matter of will from one class to another are "suspended between classes, lost in contradictions of belief and obligation—'an impossible place,' as Walter Benjamin called it" (Foster 54).

In "The Fetish of Being Outside" Le Sueur links her attacks on bourgeois individualism to "the problem of objectivity" (22). A pernicious version of the fetish of being outside is, according to Le Sueur, the desire of many artists to live "outside the demarcations of economic and political positions" (22). Such desire often produces attempts at "objective writing" which, Le Sueur says, "can never provide will or purpose and is related to the liberal formal ideal of neutrality and disinterestedness" (22). But, as we will see, the "problem of objectivity" haunted some of Le Sueur's writing, especially her reportage.

In "The Fetish of Being Outside" Le Sueur speaks often of "communal discussion," "communal interaction," and "communal participation." More than any other term, "communal" has remained for over 50 years Le Sueur's trademark, and for many of those years she identified the Party with "the communal" just as strongly as she did in 1935 when she proclaimed: "I do not feel any subtle equivocation between the individual and the new disciplined groups of the Communist Party . . . I can no longer live without communal sensibility" (22). Communal sensibility could thrive on the level of the "cell," the smallest organizational unit of the Party's structure, in a way that it often did not at the top. As a Midwesterner, Le Sueur was removed from the often bitter quarrels of the East Coast Party members, who were more affected by the shifts in the Party line taking place at Party Headquarters in New York City. She deliberately remained a "maverick," as she called herself, and identified with Midwesterners and Midwestern writers such as Jack Conroy, Nelson Algren, and Richard Wright.

Perhaps an unlikely source for insight into Le Sueur's relation to the Party is Wright's contribution to *The God That Failed* (1949), in which six writers recount their conversion to Communism and their subsequent disillusionment. In the introduction, editor Richard Crossman observes that all the writers made a conscious sacrifice of personal and professional status in accepting Communist discipline, except for Richard Wright, who came from the Chicago slums. His sacrifice came, Crossman suggests, when Wright *left* the Party, and Crossman quotes in his introduction that unforgettable passage near the conclusion of Wright's contribution to the book: "For I knew in my heart that I should never be able to write that way again, should never be able to feel with that simple sharpness about life, should never again express such passionate hope, should never again make so total a commitment of faith" (9).[31] The daughter of "Crusaders," Le Sueur absorbed as a youngster the IWW ideal of the worker-writer and may have needed the Party for sustenance even more than Wright.

As is evident in the following journal entry, for Le Sueur communism meant an emotional, familial connection to others:

> I know how it is to hunger and long for your father and your mother, to feel that split in the universe. I think I would go crazy without the communist party, which is like a father to me, something strong and paternal, and binds me to a large and tender family. (vol. 10, 1935–37, n. pag.)

And in another journal entry, Le Sueur writes: "It isn't any wonder people feel religious about the party. It is love, wife, children to us" (vol. 13, 1938–41, 23). Le Sueur still harbors a total commitment of faith to "a large and tender family," to "the people," and to "people's culture." But Le Sueur is not receptive to the suggestion that "the people" and "people's culture" are no longer readily definable terms, if ever they were.[32]

On the other hand, Le Sueur's journals express some concern about the Party's response to personal feelings. In one entry she admits "always feel[ing] strange" at party meetings, which make her feel "drained," "betrayed," "impersonal," and "torn apart." "Who cares about anyone's personal feeling," she adds, "but it is dangerous to abstract it. That is what alarms and hurts me in the movement. You cannot abstract personal feeling. It is dangerous. You will have nothing" (vol. 13, 1938–41, 103). Writing several years earlier about another meeting, Le Sueur asserts,

> There is no life in the sensual sense in revolution, perhaps that's what was in the room. There was Ruth Shaw, sleepy with having a baby. I imagine she must have felt very much as I did. . . . Here she was having a baby. She was not organizing anything to them. I suppose she is kind of out of it. I felt they had kind of dropped her until she was through with this [the pregnancy]. . . . In fact, you were not living now unless organizing was living. It may be to some people but not to me. (vol. 9, 1934–35, 312)

Writing near the close of the Depression decade, Le Sueur asserted, "I am only just beginning. . . . It takes a long time if you want to go underground, feel along these dangerous underground passages of our life where thousands of people disappear" (vol. 13, 1938–41, n. pag.). Many of those "anonymous" people were women like the pregnant Ruth Shaw, removed from organizing efforts and other standard Party activities.

Le Sueur often felt a kinship with such women, while noting in her journal that "Gold and Freeman have lost their contact with the backwards America. They are attached—and possibly want to be—to the advanced revolutionary worker" (vol. 10, 1935–37, 342). In an earlier entry Le Sueur associates Dos Passos with "the man speech," observing that "we need, too, the woman speech. I would like to say the woman speech" (vol. 7, 1933, 112). She felt alienated from those at the American Writers' Congresses who delivered "great theoretic ideological speeches," attempting to make "a bureaucratic, intellectual, inhuman . . . kind of thing of Marxism" ("Interview" 10). "There is no use building the Communist party on dogmatism and leaving out the tenderness, the essential touch," Le Sueur believed (vol. 9, 1934–35, 314).

When reading some of Le Sueur's work, however, one feels the pressure of the Party's early '30s literary guidelines. The Party considered the style of some of Le Sueur's writings "undisciplined" (Hedges 14). Even "Women on the Breadlines," a relatively orthodox piece of reportage originally published in *New Masses* in January 1932, is followed by a reprimand from one of the journal's contributing editors at that time (identified in a West End Press reprint of "Women on the Breadlines" as Whittaker Chambers, of all people):

> This presentation of the plight of the unemployed women, able as it is, and informative, is defeatist in attitude, lacking in revolutionary spirit and direction which characterize the usual contribution to *New Masses*. We feel it is our duty to add, that there is a place for the unemployed woman, as well as man, in the ranks of the unemployed councils and in all branches of the organized revolutionary movement. Fight for your class, read *The Working Woman*, join the Communist Party. (7)[33]

When asked about Chambers's public rebuke, Le Sueur claimed not to have changed her writing to accommodate *New Masses*, which she termed "often very doctrinaire" and "male supremacist": "I fought them. I kept my lyrical style. Sometimes I was almost blacklisted by the Left, [which] often commented on my lyrical style. They wanted . . . socialist realism" (interview).

Elaine Hedges has also recorded Le Sueur's response to Chambers's editorial finger-wagging:

> Although Le Sueur, who accepted such criticisms as necessary in the development of any movement, later wrote reportage showing women actively involved in Unemployed Councils and the Workers['] Alliance—pieces that more obviously conformed to what the Party wanted—she continued to write about the suffering of women. For she saw suffering, not as negative and passive, but as a source of solidarity. (11)

And Irene Paull, who was active in the CP during the '30s, wrote the following to Neala Schleuning in 1976:

> Our imaginations were stifled in the interests of immediate propaganda. . . . Meridel did the agit-prop work that was needed all through the Thirties and Forties and into the Fifties, but at the same time she maintained her literary integrity with what she wrote in her notebooks [journals]. (Schleuning, *America* 119)

One journal entry comically parrots a local Party organizer's trying to involve Le Sueur in activities other than writing:

> "We've got to collect money, we've got to make contacts here, we've got to hurry, we've got to be on the move, we've got to get busy. Organize the writers' union, the office workers' union. We can't be subjective about this, about collecting money. . . . Listen, I don't want to interfere with your writing."

"Like hell, you don't," I say, "of course you do. You don't give a god damn about writing, really. . . . Alright, I'll write at night, I'll write in the middle of the night, sometime after the CP is in bed." (vol. 9, 1934–35, 313)

The contrast between the texts discussed in the remainder of this chapter and those addressed in Chapter 4 suggests that Le Sueur's deep Party loyalty was indeed seasoned by an accompanying resistance to its aesthetic and its contradictory attitudes toward women. As a feminist within a male-dominated movement, she herself experienced, and expressed in her writing, the conflicting impulses for which "The Fetish of Being Outside" does not allow. Several of those conflicting impulses are associated with Le Sueur's uses of literary forms. As her interest in "communal discussion" suggests, she saw the need for forms that would promote what Bakhtin has termed "heteroglossia," forms that would allow writing to serve as a vehicle for the emergence of multiple suppressed voices. As I will show, in a few of her works she conducted significant experiments with forms embodying heteroglossia; yet in others she remained allied to monologic literary forms.

Le Sueur produced over two dozen pieces of reportage, a form of journalism popular among many leftists during the '30s (see pp. 27–29). The remaining portion of this chapter discusses "Women on the Breadlines" (1932), "I Was Marching" (1934), and, less extensively, "Evening in a Lumber Town" (1926).

"Women on the Breadlines" is a moving account of the women Le Sueur met during the '30s in a Minneapolis unemployment bureau. Her relationship to these women was not that of Party emissary, but of one who, to a certain extent, shared their fate. Despite her middle-class origins, Le Sueur's own life during the Depression was economically marginal. For a time she lived with her two children in a single room and, after working all day, would thrust her head under the cold water faucet to stay awake and write. She met women in relief agencies and unemployment bureaus because she too needed welfare and employment, and, in some cases, she lived collectively with the women whose experiences she recorded.

Le Sueur's journals at this time document her precarious economic status. In one entry she wonders "if we can get through Monday, Tuesday, and Wednesday, if we can get enough food and fuel for then." In another entry she writes,

I am broke; we haven't a cent. . . . we have no stove, no wood, no way to make a fire, to cook food. . . . It's an awful sensation to have nothing to eat . . . fear and defeat sit in you. Tonight I feel actual fear of the evening coming down, of the night, of the grocery man. . . . nobody knows the awful fear of the dispossessed, the way the world looks different. (vol. 9, 1934–35, 222, 140, 141)

As Le Sueur notes in the preface to a recent edition of "Women on the Breadlines," her accounts "are not stories, but epitaphs marking the lives of women who . . . leave no statistics, no record, obituary or remembrance" (n. pag.). "Women on the Breadlines" contributes to American literature and social history a valuable record of people whose lives have rarely been chronicled.

Some of the women portrayed in "Women on the Breadlines" have been deserted by their unemployed husbands and have children to support. The following description of Ellen, who has been out of work for eight months, is representative:

> A young girl who went around with Ellen tells about seeing her last evening back of a cafe downtown, outside the kitchen door, kicking, showing her legs so that the cook came out and gave her some food and some men gathered in the alley and threw small coin on the ground for a look at her legs. And the girl says enviously that Ellen had a swell breakfast and treated her to one too, that cost two dollars. . . .
>
> "I guess she'll go on the street now," a thin woman says faintly, and no one takes the trouble to comment further. Like every commodity now the body is difficult to sell and girls say you're lucky if you get fifty cents.
>
> It's very difficult and humiliating to sell one's body. (139, 140)

Ellen's desperate exchange of a glimpse of her legs for "a swell breakfast" is unforgettable, but the last two sentences of the passage could not have better fit proletarian realism's mold if they had been penned by Michael Gold himself. Redundantly, didactically, Le Sueur presents the requisite "social theme" of Gold's formula (see p. 24). And the didacticism continues:

> Perhaps it would make it clear if one were to imagine having to go out on the street to sell, say, one's overcoat. Suppose you have to sell your coat so you can have breakfast and a place to sleep, say, for fifty cents. You decide to sell your only coat. . . . The street, that has before been just a street, now becomes a mart, something entirely different. You must approach someone now and admit you are destitute and are now selling your clothes, your most intimate possessions. . . . It is even harder to try to sell one's self, more humiliating. It is even humiliating to try to sell one's labor. When there is no buyer. (140)

In harmony with Gold's dicta, the language of Le Sueur's reportage is also unadorned, suggesting that reportage requires little or no artifice or craft, "no straining or melodrama or other effects; life itself is the supreme melodrama. Feel this intensely, and everything becomes poetry—the new poetry of materials, of the so-called 'common man'" (see p. 25).

In her reportage Le Sueur relied upon a clipped, staccato prose, with an abundance of short declarative sentences and monosyllabic words. The sentences that begin "Women on the Breadlines" serve as an example: "I am sitting in the city free employment bureau. It's the women's section. We have been sitting here now for four hours. We sit here every day, waiting for a job. There are no jobs. Most of us have had no breakfast. Some have had scant rations for over a year" (137). At different times and to different degrees, Le Sueur was affected by Gold's tenets, including the slighting of form. Unadorned prose was considered an act of good faith, a break from bourgeois writers who "believe in literature for its own sake" (see pp. 23–25).

But in Le Sueur's hands, as in those of many other writers, reportage's seeming lack of artifice—its "straightforward," "transparent" representation—is deceptive, raising problems of "objectivity" Le Sueur made prominent in "The Fetish of Being Outside." Although her reportage's messages oppose the dominant culture and politics, her work often relies on a monological rhetorical model from the dominant culture. In reportage, despite the desires of those who saw the form as a potential departure from traditional notions of "objectivity," the author often writes objectively, directly addressing the readers, anticipating their responses and deflecting their objections; meanings are seen as delivered, unchanged, from source to recipient. Like workers under capitalism, readers are merely to consume, suppressing any consciousness of their role as active producers.

Antithesis, a monological rhetorical structure that Le Sueur and other writers often employ, "may well have been the earliest invention of rhetorical practice," Aldo Scaglione observes (31). It is capable of a wide array of applications. Antithesis may appear at the local level of the sentence and/or it may stand at the core of the organization of an entire discourse. It may be employed to describe physical and/or psychological conditions. In some of its classical applications, antithesis is used to establish the polarities between which a given discourse operates, the parameters of a discourse's world.[34]

In "Women on the Breadlines" Le Sueur uses antithesis in some traditional ways. The last sentence of the first paragraph sets the antithetical parameters of the world in which women on the breadlines exist: "Is there any place else in the world where a human being is supposed to go hungry amidst plenty without an outcry, without protest, where only the boldest steal or kill for bread, and the timid crawl the streets, hunger like the beak of a terrible bird at the vitals?" (137). Our narrator sees the range from hunger to plenty and sees among the hungry the scope of reactions from bold to timid. The narrator of "On the Breadlines," like Blake's narrator in the following passage from "Holy Thursday (II)," sees the full antithetical sweep:

> Is this a holy thing to see
> In a rich and fruitful land,
> Babes reduced to misery,
> Fed with cold and usurous hand? (324)

For both Le Sueur and Blake part of the power of social commentary lies in the writer's ability to display the parameters of a world in which poverty coexists with its antithesis.

The following passage from "Women on the Breadlines" further illustrates the full antithetical range of the narrator's view.

> She lives alone in little rooms. She bought seven dollars' worth of second-hand furniture eight years ago. She rents a room for perhaps three dollars a month in an attic, sometimes in a cold house. Once the house where she stayed was condemned and everyone else moved out and she lived there all winter alone on the top floor. She spent only twenty-five dollars all winter.
>
> She wants to get married but she sees what happens to her married friends, being left with children to support, worn out before their time. So she stays single. She is virtuous. She is slightly deaf from hanging out clothes in winter. She has done people's washing and cooking for fifteen years and in that time she saved

> thirty dollars. Now she hasn't worked steady for a year and she has spent the thirty
> dollars. She had dreamed of having a little house or a houseboat perhaps with a
> spot of ground for a few chickens. This dream she will never realize. (138–139)

The antithetical parameters of this discursive universe are starkly set. The harsh reality of the world in which the woman lives contrasts sharply to the world of which she dreams, a world "she will never realize." Further, the antithesis of her reality versus dream is a microcosm for the macrocosmic antithesis of the world of the exploited versus the world of the exploiters. What provides us the full sense that this discursive universe is closed off and delivered whole to the seemingly passive reader is the narrator's position in relation to the antithetical parameters. The narrator "stands above" the antithetical extremes, "objectively" observing them. She has both ends of the spectrum in her view and can deliver that view to us whole.

In addition to antithesis, the quoted passage relies on other classical devices that relegate the reader to the role of passive consumer. The repetition of the she-plus-verb syntactical pattern lays out with reductive clarity the woman's condition and droningly dramatizes that condition. "Women on the Breadlines," like much reportage, is marked by antithetical structures, an uncontested authorial voice, a conventional narrative order, and a completion and closure of meaning.

This monolingual/monological cultural form is related to the tendency among '30s Marxists to envision American political and cultural life as clearly divided between the exploiters and the exploited, a view that in hindsight appears reductive. In her statements about her work—as opposed to some of her practice as a writer—Le Sueur has not refined that view, however. In an interview published in 1978 and again, when I interviewed her in 1985, she steadfastly held her 1935 position that a "people's culture" exists wholly apart from and opposed to the dominant culture, denying that such a subculture exists only *in relation to* "high" and popular culture: "all culture comes from the oppressed. . . . the oppressed are the only repository of culture in monopoly capitalism" ("Interview" 12). She has been more specific: "All lyricism, poetry, symbols, archetypes [come] from the working class" (Schleuning, *America* 129). Ambiguity in literature is a mark of a high, now moribund culture and synonymous with "sludge . . . an elitist way for a magician, some Merlin, to trick the readers" ("Interview" 9).

Mary Jacobus and Rachel Blau DuPlessis, in their work on other women writers, help illuminate this fundamental problem in Le Sueur. As Jacobus argues, women writers, "at once within this culture and outside it," must simultaneously challenge cultural terms and work within them ("Difference" 20). Acknowledging Jacobus's work, DuPlessis notes that women writers experience a "split between alien critic and inheritor." They are "neither wholly 'subcultural' nor, certainly, wholly main-cultural, but negotiate difference and sameness, marginality and inclusion in a constant dialogue" (43). (DuPlessis reminds us that W. E. B. DuBois first postulated this double consciousness for African-Americans, who constantly negotiate with the dominant culture.)

Such a split occurs with radical writers as well, especially with radical women writers, who are doubly marginalized. Moreover, radical women writers must cope with yet another version of divided consciousness as they oscillate "between complicity and critique" within male-dominated leftist organizations. These women agree with the group's opposition to the political mainstream but must be vigilant about their inferior status within the Left organization itself. But when Le Sueur talks about writing, she allows for no "movement between complicity and critique" (DuPlessis 33), allows for none of the "contrary instincts" that Alice Walker ascribes to African-American women writers (235). Le Sueur continues to assert positions she held in "The Fetish of Being Outside." Rather than acknowledge that women and leftist writers negotiate with divided loyalties and consciousness, simultaneously within and outside the patriarchal class culture, Le Sueur has repressed, displaced, and denied whatever tendencies keep her "within," declaring herself by fiat an ex-officio member of the politicized element of the working class.

Gramsci's notion of "hegemony" may help us here. Hegemony has been traditionally defined as political rule or domination. Gramsci, however, made a distinction between "direct [political] domination" and "hegemony":

> What we can do . . . is to fix two major superstructural "levels": the one that can be called "civil society," that is the ensemble of organisms commonly called "private," and that of "political society" or "the State." These two levels correspond on the one hand to the function of "hegemony" which the dominant group exercises throughout society and on the other hand to that of "direct domination" or command exercised through the State and "juridical" government. The functions in question are precisely organizational and connective. (12)

While "direct domination" appears overtly in political forms and actions, especially when the state feels threatened, "hegemony" is a ubiquitous, intricate interlacing of cultural and political influences that shape people's daily lives. Gramsci recognized dominance and subordination as a complex social process intruding into even the most private aspects of our lives. They are dynamic processes, constantly altered and regenerated. Hegemony is also a site for dissent, for "counter hegemony" and "alternative hegemony" (Williams, *Marxism* 113). Thus hegemony can be, in Bakhtin's terms, a site for "heteroglossia" with multiple voices resisting the dominant, monologic discourse of power.

Le Sueur explored forms of heteroglossia as disruptions of hegemony, as I will demonstrate in the next chapter. However, when she talks about the artist in relation to the dominant culture, the notion of hegemonic processes—perpetually conflicting, negotiating, and appropriating—are as foreign to her today as when, in "The Fetish of Being Outside," she insisted that the artist "cannot take a double course and be part of it [bourgeois culture] and still apart from it." Only "full belief" can save her and other writers from a "middle class malady—common to all . . . nourished on rotten bourgeois soil" (22, 23). Implied here is the misconception that "rotten bourgeois soil" *can be left*, when the question to address, as Gramsci and others have clarified, is how to maneuver while mired in it. The overthrow of capitalism does not seem imminent, as it did to Le Sueur and many others in the '30s, and current strategies for cultural resistance should reflect the current historical period, one Raymond Williams has termed "the long revolution."

Another piece of reportage, "I Was Marching," originally published in *New Masses*, illustrates the all-pervasiveness of hegemonic forces, a point I will turn to again in a moment. "I Was Marching" was written in 1934, a year of unusual working-class militancy, as nearly 1.5 million workers engaged in industrial actions. Le Sueur participated in the Teamsters Strike in Minneapolis, which closed down the trucking industry and tied up the entire city, using motorized "flying squadrons" of pickets. Most businesses were affected by the strike, and pickets patrolled roads into the city, refusing entry to non-union trucks. Other Minneapolis workers, including taxi drivers and 35,000 construction workers, lent their support to the strike. The militant Farm Holiday Association contributed substantial amounts of food, and "hundreds of non-Teamster workers showed up at strike headquarters daily saying 'Use us, this is our strike'" (Brecher 162).

The Citizens' Alliance, a powerful employers' association that for a generation had kept unionism out of Minneapolis almost entirely, mobilized in response to the strike. They developed their own strike headquarters with barracks, hospital, and commissary, and to break the strike they organized a citizens' army. "With an unusual clarity, two organized social classes stood face to face, poised for battle" (Brecher 163).

On July 20, quickly dubbed "Black Friday," police opened fire on pickets in the central market, wounding 67 (including 13 bystanders) and killing two (Brecher 165). But even as the wounded returned to headquarters for treatment, supporters gathered. A protest meeting of all Minneapolis workers was called for that night and culminated in a march of 10,000 on City Hall. Farmer-Labor Governor Floyd Olson (who had been Arthur and Marian Le Sueur's candidate and "had personally contributed $500 to the strike fund," announcing "I am not a liberal . . . I am a radical") declared martial law and had the strike leaders arrested (Brecher 166). But the arrest of the leaders infused the movement with greater fury. Since the strike had been organized in a democratic fashion—a rank-and-file committee of 100 Teamsters formed the official strike authority—leaders quickly emerged from the ranks to replace the Trotskyist organizers who went to jail. Unable to intimidate the strikers, Olson released the leaders and ordered a raid on the Citizens' Alliance, hoping "to save face with his labor constituents" (Brecher 166). The employers surrendered, opening the way for a Teamster organizing drive throughout the Midwest.

This was Le Sueur's first experience in a strike, and the following passage from "I Was Marching," which suggests themes of "The Fetish of Being Outside," also describes her self-consciousness and the fear of losing her identity:

> The truth is I was afraid. Not of the physical danger at all, but an awful fright of mixing, of losing myself, of being unknown and lost. I felt inferior. I felt no one would know me there, that all I had been trained to excel in would go unnoticed. . . . I felt I excelled in competing with others and I knew instantly that these people were *not* competing at all, that they were acting in a strange, powerful trance of movement *together*. (158–159)

Despite her political experience and her assertions in "The Fetish of Being Outside," Le Sueur feels awkward crossing class lines; the faces that express "the same longings, the same fears" as hers belong to artists, writers, and other professionals sympathetically but hesitantly standing across the street from strike headquarters (158).

In her journal Le Sueur described her fears—and her resolves—about writing about the strike:

> The strike is to be at midnight. I won't be held off from it. I won't be left out. I won't look at it lyrically. I'm afraid I won't be able to be IN it. I'm afraid I will withdraw and not really see anything. . . . It's like a terrific test. I'm afraid I won't know how to bore in deep enough to what is happening. I would like to write . . . [a] terrifically hard, real, factual and yet emotional account with every implication in it external and internal at the same time. It's a kind of hoax to write about it looking AT it. I must be part of it. That's the devil about being a writer in America. Reporting is objective observing, and writing is subjective and each is only half—without being a part so you become a special creature of a sort, neither fish nor fowl nor good red herring. So special and LOOKING ON. I am determined to get IN, to have an experience with it, in it and not just look at it. I am determined. (vol. 8, 1934–35, 68)

However, despite her determination, Le Sueur did not fully solve the problem of "be[ing] IN" versus "looking AT" the strike.

When Le Sueur finally dares to enter the headquarters, she has "an awful impulse to go into the office . . . and offer to do some special work" (159). Instead, she finds herself wearing a butcher's apron and washing tin cups in the kitchen, where she realizes she has "never before worked anonymously" (160). Just how anonymously she worked can be gleaned from other accounts of the strike: "A crew of 120 prepared food day and night; at the peak of the strike, 10,000 people ate at the headquarters in a single day" (Brecher 162). Le Sueur writes about Black Friday's terror and of the mass funeral for one of the slain pickets, attended by an estimated 50,000 to 100,000, including "one thousand more militia [who] were massed downtown" for the event (Brecher 166; "Marching" 158). The march that takes place at the story's conclusion is in response to Black Friday, and by this time Le Sueur, electrified by the communion of thousands protesting together, feels she has overcome her self-conscious individualism.

Yet the very form of her reportage, while attempting to portray the narrator as being at the heart of the event, simultaneously holds that narrator above and apart from the event that has appeared to render her collective and anonymous. As in "Women on the Breadlines," the narrator of "I Was Marching" begins her report with an Olympian view of the antithetical parameters within the universe her discourse describes:

> . . . in American life, you hear things happening in a far and muffled way. One thing is said and another happens. Our merchant society has been built upon a huge hypocrisy, a cut-throat competition which sets one man against another and at the same time an ideology mouthing such words as "Humanity," "Truth," the "Golden Rule," and such. (158)

Opposites abound in a world in which "man" is set against "man" as the result of an ideology that says one thing and means its opposite.

Even as the intensity of the action increases, the narrator of "I Was Marching" maintains her ability to stand above and see objectively the full range of antitheses within the scene. The narrator reports:

> From all over the city workers are coming. They gather outside in two great half-circles, cut in two to let the ambulances in. A traffic cop is still directing traffic at the corner and the crowd cannot stand to see him. "We'll give you just two seconds to beat it," they tell him. He goes away quickly. A striker takes over the street.
>
> Men, women, and children are massing outside, a living circle close packed for protection. From the tall office building business men are looking down on the black swarm thickening, coagulating into what action they cannot tell.
>
> We have living blood on our skirts. (162)

As in "Women on the Breadlines," antithesis is central to the portrayal of "I Was Marching"'s universe. Here the antithesis is one of the "low point" and the "high point." Down is the "living circle" of the men, women, and children. Up are the businessmen peering down. This antithesis is bolstered by a further antithesis of action versus inaction. The workers "are coming," "they gather," they are "massing." This action is set in opposition to the inactivity of the businessmen who are "looking down." Further antitheses, such as outside versus inside, support the depiction of a macrocosmic antithesis like that found in "Women on the Breadlines": the exploited versus the exploiters. The narrator of "I Was Marching" is in a now-familiar position. She stands above the antithetical poles of the discourse's universe and gives us, as seemingly passive readers, the completed objective picture of that universe.

The narrator's position in relation to the parameters of the universe she depicts, and the accompanying proliferation of the "I," place the text within the very mode of production it attempts to oppose, at odds with the very collectivity it espouses. James Kavanagh's following observation, made in reference to another text, also illuminates "I Was Marching": "it is the 'I'. . . with its necessary, strained connection to the 'every,' that bears the weight of ideology—[that is,] the weight of a lived relation to the world that forms and deforms the text—and us." Perhaps as much as any form, reportage produces an "ideological mirror-relation"—an "empirical world 'out there' [which] functions to reflect the individual subject's subjectivity back onto him or her" (37–38). "I Was Marching" at once lauds a subsuming of the individual by the collective and affirms individual subjectivity and perception. The marching "I," fixed at the text's center, undercuts the dialectical process, which has no individual at its fulcrum and constructs people as they construct the system.

The problem of the narrator/subject as source and center and the fear of loss of self mark an earlier piece of reportage by Le Sueur, "Evening in a Lumber Town" (*New Masses*, July 1926). In that work the narrator stands in the town, observing its streets, its houses, its people:

Now the whistle screams. Now the workmen come from the mill, down the streets close together, huddled together. Their black loose clothes are all alike. Like a dark moving mass they come shuffling along heavily, heads lowered, arms hanging, their dark half-drunken faces thrust out. They look drunk, drunk with a deadening concentration. There is the unnatural flush and sullenness of drunkenness. Their concentration is the concentration of themselves against everything, against hungers and terrors . . . and hourly fears. It is a hard combative identity in them . . . [ellipses Le Sueur's]. (22)

In a manner typical of reportage, the narrator moves from the pictures of these particular people to the general conclusions that "poverty is grotesque" (articulated twice) and that "poverty humbles a man low so that nature has her way with him" (22, 23). As in "I Was Marching," the form of reportage in "Evening in a Lumber Town" traps the narrator at the center of the event: "Three men exactly like the others come from the far end of the street, walking together, their heads bent as if all were listening to the same sound. They come up to me and pass me, veering a little from their path" (23). Like the narrator in "I Was Marching," this narrator is located simultaneously at the heart of the scene and above the scene, and this narrator too provides us, as seemingly passive readers, the completed objective picture of the scene.

As in the other Le Sueur reportage I have discussed, antithetical structures play a role in shaping an "I" that locates "Evening in a Lumber Town" within the very mode of production it attempts to subvert. Immediately following the previously cited passage we find:

I see their faces quite close—the dead look, the humble half-comic look. I think a queer thing as they pass me. I am shocked at first by such a thought. Then it seems quite natural. I think that they remind me of Charlie Chaplin. He may be a wag but he says a great deal about these men, about the exigencies of poverty, the humiliation, the tragic, comic pathos. The shoes, the trousers, the shy defenceless attitude—all Chaplin's, in the best sense, terrible comedy. (23)

This "I," simultaneously inside and outside the scene, is oddly antithetical to the very people with whom the writer is attempting to identify, as is suggested by the simple fact that she is an obstacle in the workers' path, requiring their "veering a little." The individual "I"—in opposition to the "mass" about whom she says, "No excess consciousness, only the blindness of necessity"—has a lively consciousness, as she demonstrates by comparing the workers to Charlie Chaplin and the scene in the town to a Goya painting (22). Further, within the Chaplin comparison we find classical antithetical points of reference in the "tragic" and the "comic." The antithetical structures inadvertently contribute to rendering the workers' lives as the sort of commodified artifact an audience goes to see when it desires the entertainment of a Charlie Chaplin film.

This narrator/subject as source, as center, is a product of ideology. Yet Le Sueur's limited understanding of ideology, revealed not only in the following (and previously cited) opening of "I Was Marching" but also at numerous points

in her work, is characteristic of '30s working-class writers, even those who acknowledge its importance:

> Our merchant society has been built upon a huge hypocrisy, a cut-throat competi-
> tion which sets one man against another and at the same time an ideology
> mouthing such words as "Humanity," "Truth," the "Golden Rule," and such. Now
> in a crisis the word falls away and the skeleton of that action shows in terrific
> movement. (158)

Ideology is not merely a superstructure produced by an economic base. Rather,
the contradictions within a network of structures—such as politics, culture, ideology, and economics—weigh upon the contradictions of the others. Gramsci's
concept of hegemony suggests that one class rules not only by economic and
physical force but also with moral, political, and cultural values: workers actually
experience themselves in terms prescribed by the bourgeoisie. In developing his
ideas of hegemony, Gramsci explicitly noted his debt to Lenin, who stressed the
importance of a change in consciousness, or what Gramsci refers to as "episte-
mological" change, in producing a revolution (365).

One disciple of Gramsci, Louis Althusser, defines ideology as a set of socially
determined representations of "the imaginary relationship of individuals to their
real conditions of existence" (162). In the conception of the "free worker," for example, we see the way in which the system (production of surplus value and its
appropriation by capital) necessarily distorts itself to the individual worker. Ideology here becomes no less than "the way in which the individual actively lives
his or her role within the social totality" (Coward and Ellis 67).

According to Althusser, ideology is not merely a system of beliefs or false consciousness; there is no "'cloud of ideas' floating above" society's "real" structures
(Coward and Ellis 72). This position separates Althusser from the humanist version of Marxism prevalent in working-class writing produced during the '30s, in
which an otherwise free subject is alienated by social structures, and the advent of
communism will reinstate the free subject's essence. In the passage from "I Was
Marching" quoted above, ideology, "in a crisis," suddenly "falls away"—as if it
were a facade distinct from other societal structures. The text dangerously underestimates the all-pervasiveness of ideology.

Le Sueur's reportage contributes to American literature and social history a
record of "anonymous," "voiceless" people, opposing the dominant culture's capacity to homogenize and repress difference. Readers of reportage encounter an
economic system that has transformed humans into commodities and a state
stripped of its guise of neutrality, providing for some the first shock of recognition.
However, reportage's often-monological rhetorical model conforms to rather than
disrupts the narrative and social order. Le Sueur's "I Was Marching" affirms collective resistance while its traditional first-person narrative and antithetical
structures undialectically plant the individual subject at the center of experience.
And the deliberately unembellished prose of "Women on the Breadlines," especially the predominance of simple, subject-verb-object sentences, intends to

minimize form, as if it were a nuisance obstructing the *"real* stuff," the politically oppositional content. But form is not simply an artifice or, as Robert Maniquis once unceremoniously remarked, "form is not a bucket."[35] Literary forms are historically limited by the content they embody, and they break down and transform as that content changes. Forms, as well as content, bear history and ideology. Many '30s Marxists rightly opposed those versions of literary formalism that focus on technique at the expense of historical significance. But some of these Marxists read literary texts chiefly for their political content, dangerously minimizing form's ideological baggage.

Moreover, many '30s Marxists also defined ideology as Le Sueur does in "I Was Marching," as a false consciousness that, once recognized, can be readily discarded, shed like old skin. Such a view seriously underestimates ideology's power and complexity. Althusser's definition of ideology supplied above, however, grants it too much force, without allowing sufficient space for ideological struggle. Gramsci's related concept of hegemony is not only more dialectical but also more useful for strategists building a culture of resistance. While potent and complex, pervading the most private areas of our lives and consciousness, hegemony is also a site for dissent.

FOUR

Le Sueur's *The Girl*, "Our Fathers," "Annunciation," and "Corn Village"

Who cares about anyone's personal feeling, but it is dangerous to abstract it. That is what alarms and hurts me in the movement. You cannot abstract personal feeling. It is dangerous. You will have nothing.

From Meridel Le Sueur's journals, 1938–41

I never looked upon the Left as being something that you just submitted to. I fought them. I kept my lyrical style. Sometimes I was almost blacklisted by the Left, [which] often commented on my lyrical style. They wanted . . . socialist realism. . . . I considered it a struggle. [But] I would have died, literarily and personally, without the Communist [movement] . . . and the people in it.

Meridel Le Sueur, during an interview with the author, 1985

"I've never heard anything about how a woman feels who is going to have a child," observes the pregnant narrator of Meridel Le Sueur's "Annunciation" (130), a story Le Sueur wrote in the form of notes scrawled intermittently on scraps of paper for her first, unborn child. When a *Scribner's* editor rejected the story, suggesting to Le Sueur that she write more like Hemingway, she quipped: "But fishin', fightin', and fuckin' were not my major experiences" (interview). Like Le Sueur's retort, the reportage discussed in Chapter 3 counters writing of the dominant culture. Other Le Sueur texts, however, subvert not only writing of the dominant culture but elements of the '30s leftist subculture as well. This chapter addresses some of Le Sueur's most subversive writing—the novel *The Girl* and three short stories, "Our Fathers," "Annunciation," and "Corn Village."

The Girl is a heterodox reply to Mike Gold's brawny "new Communist man"; to a male-dominated literary/political Left; and to the good-housekeeping, comradely Communist wife. But *The Girl* also subscribes to a strain of biological determinism, suggesting that men are inherently competitive and violent while women are naturally nurturing and regenerative because of their procreative capacity.[1] To the extent that *The Girl* promotes woman as myth, it supports the very system it seeks to oppose. But the novel also offers a counter-myth that challenges some of the Victorian and patriarchal values prevalent during the '30s among leftists as well as mainstream Americans.

The subjects of "Our Fathers," "Annunciation," and "Corn Village" — pregnancy, familial relations, and emotional and sexual repression — would have been considered ersatz by many of the Party's orthodox critics during the early '30s. And the texts' evocative, poetic language contrasts sharply with the unembroidered prose characteristic of reportage and proletarian realism. Moreover, these stories implicitly subvert the position Le Sueur later assumes in "The Fetish of Being Outside" (1935) on how leftists should approach building a culture of resistance.

As discussed in Chapter 3, "The Fetish" posits that to join a revolutionary movement, middle-class writers must wholly leave the class of their origin, exorcising any residual bourgeois tendencies. "The Fetish" allows for no blurring, ambivalence, or negotiating at the boundaries between class-based cultures. In "Our Fathers," "Annunciation," and "Corn Village," however, Le Sueur adopts the very double consciousness — that of "alien critic and inheritor," to repeat DuPlessis's terms — that "The Fetish" condemns. Further, in these stories and in *The Girl*, Le Sueur explores literary forms that promote heteroglossia.

Le Sueur revised *The Girl* in 1977–78, especially the beginning and end, although much of the original manuscript remained unchanged. It has been a bestseller for West End, the small press that published it in 1978, nearly 40 years after it was written.[2] The following few paragraphs summarize the novel.

During the Depression, the young, naive narrator of *The Girl* moves to Minneapolis/St. Paul from an impoverished farm, seeking work, and takes a waitressing job in a speakeasy. Never identified by name, she is referred to by the other characters as "girl." The Girl's anonymity serves to undermine the narrator/subject as source, as center, and to underscore the universality of her experiences, which are common to the women of her class and time — and, in certain respects, to other women as well. The speakeasy is operated by Belle and her husband, Hoink. Clara, a waitress in the speakeasy, also works as a prostitute. The tavern is frequented by Amelia, a member of the Workers' Alliance who is partly responsible for the Girl's eventual awakening to working-class consciousness. Butch, another tavern regular and a scab at the local foundry, becomes the Girl's lover (when she eventually gets pregnant, she refuses home abortion remedies). Ganz, who pays the police to protect the bootleg operation, is the novel's chief villain: He treats women with even more habitual brutality than do the other men and involves Hoink and Butch in the bank robbery on which the plot turns. All three die as a result of the robbery, which is foiled by an arriving customer.

When new operators assume management of the tavern, Belle, Clara, Amelia, and the Girl go on relief and move to an abandoned warehouse to survive the Depression, creating a collective strength. The Girl, however, has difficulty getting welfare, despite her pregnancy. While a relief officer is momentarily away from her desk, the Girl scans her own file, which concludes: "She should be tested for sterilization after her baby is born. In our opinion sterilization would be advisable" (129). Urged to sign a form authorizing this procedure, the Girl revolts—screaming, running, swearing, and reeling into office desks. Two police officers subdue her and drag her to the state relief maternity "home," where she meets Alice, who, like Amelia, belongs to the Workers' Alliance. Alice is deaf, but she and the Girl communicate by notes:

> I wrote, *What does it do, the Workers Alliance?*
>
> *They demand food, jobs,* she wrote quickly.
>
> I looked at the word demand. It was a strong word. I didn't know what to write. I looked at it for a long time. She looked at me, and when I looked at her she smiled and nodded, like she was going through woods and I was following her. She leaned over and the light shone through her thin hand. She put her hand under her cheek, closed her eyes which I saw meant sleep, and then she wrote in a bold hand and turned the tiny light on it.
>
> *Wake tomorrow!* (133)

By now the Girl is ripe for political conversion.

When Amelia intervenes in the Girl's behalf, she is released from the maternity institution, only to find Clara dying from electric shock treatments forcibly administered at a mental institution. While Amelia organizes a demonstration to demand from Welfare the milk and iron pills that might save Clara, the Girl's conversion becomes complete: "I knew then I was one of them" (136). At the novel's conclusion, three dramatic events occur almost simultaneously: the demonstration, Clara's death, and the birth of the Girl's daughter.

A brief entry in Le Sueur's journal reveals that the writer was actually involved in opposing sterilization in the Twin Cities:

> That fight . . . about sterilization did more for me than anything. I acted then against them, against shoddy thought, against idealistic half measures. I saw and felt the class lines. It entered into my blood and along with it a kind of temper I never had before, a temper that acts and is not defeated, that is not individualistic. . . . (vol. 9, 1934–35, 27–28)

Another journal entry describes Le Sueur's response to participating in Workers' Alliance demonstrations:

> It's like going to a rendezvous, it's like love, it's like some fearful and strong test of your personal calibre. You are meeting something, you are going towards something, something that is in the future. . . . It's very frightening. You change, every part and parcel of you undergoes a chemical change, a challenge in the blood. (vol. 13, n. pag.)

Especially considering when it was first drafted, *The Girl* is exceptional. Its emphasis on the physiological and sexual events that shape women's lives—sexual initiation, battery, pregnancy, sterilization—is remarkable at a time when these topics seldom appeared in literature, including leftist literature. Indeed, some Party members who read the novel in manuscript form considered it politically suspect. CP leader Elizabeth Gurley Flynn, for example, questioned Le Sueur's writing about prostitutes rather than "virtuous Communist women," declaring *The Girl* a "lumpen" rather than a bona-fide proletarian novel.[3]

Drafted during the Popular Front, when the CPUSA, following the Soviet Union, stressed the virtues of family life, *The Girl* represented a departure from the Party line. As noted in Chapter 2, the CP held up the Soviet Union as the model on "the woman question," even though the legislation that constituted family policy in the Soviet Union during the '30s completely reversed the laws passed in the '20s intended to emancipate women, not strengthen the family. For example, the Soviet Union outlawed abortions in 1936, and although the Girl refuses to attempt one, the novel is not unsympathetic to Belle's having undergone as many as 13. The novel's one conventional living arrangement—that of the Girl's family, which she visits when her father dies—is hardly a model one. Frustrated by his inability to support his large family, the Girl's father had physically and verbally abused his wife and children. Relaxed communication among family members becomes possible now that the volatile patriarch has died. The younger children subvert all rules of propriety by laughing and bantering about their father's incompetence while his corpse is lying in the next room. Even their mother, who protests, cannot resist their playfulness. That such familial camaraderie is possible only after Father's fortuitous death, however, has a contradictory effect: The problem of the patriarchal family appears at once instantly resolved and yet eternally unresolvable.

The Girl is also subversive to the extent that Victorian values—hard work, delayed gratification, sexual repression, self-improvement, sobriety—are absent from or explicitly opposed by the novel. These were the values of Le Sueur's tight-lipped grandmother—and, to an extent, of her mother and stepfather—as well as those required to maintain order and productivity under capitalism. These values, significantly, were also embraced by many members of the CPUSA as necessary for making a revolution. The Party would have regarded *The Girl*'s recreational sex as Bohemian, reminiscent of the self-indulgent 1910s and '20s.

The formal experiments that Le Sueur attempts, with mixed success, also make the novel exceptional. As I will note later, Le Sueur does not completely abandon in *The Girl* the structure of antithesis on which her reportage so heavily relies, but she clearly recognizes that such classical structures, with their potential for closing off worlds and presenting meaning whole to passive readers, will not do the work she wants done in *The Girl*. Far from the position of the narrators in the reportage, the Girl stands among a heteroglossic crossfire of voices. The Girl narrates the story, but, as the Girl's namelessness suggests, Le Sueur struggles to make her not dominant over, but the vehicle for, the multiple voices she encounters.

The following representative passage, which includes the voices of some of the Girl's family members, appears in the novel when the Girl has returned home for her father's funeral.

> My sons are good, mama said. Henry is nervous but not a bad boy. Papa always wanted his boys to do the right thing. When you were all little, she said, we had less trouble. But Stasia, O Stasia was bad to her papa. She would come home and see him sitting at the table and she couldn't look at him.
>
> Stasia stood up. He wanted to be king, to boss, she said. Because he was a failure he wanted others to be so that they wouldn't be better than him. When he read the paper out loud we couldn't say a word, he said, we should not talk but listen. . . . [ellipsis Le Sueur's]
>
> Helen said, But if papa tried to whip you, you would go dancing around waving your arms and this made him mad. You should let him whip you.
>
> Stasia began to cry. He beat me before people. Now he'll never beat me again. I'm glad he's dead.
>
> Nobody said anything.
>
> Mama said, I think the home needs love.
>
> Nobody said anything. (36)

The narrative tags, "he said," provide occasional reminders that the Girl is reporting, but the absence of quotation marks and the often extended speech of any given voice leave the impression of voices speaking for themselves.

This experiment with narration signals an important move by Le Sueur to resolve the ideological and literary problems of the "I" as source and center in her reportage. One move she makes, as I will show more fully, is to constitute the narrator as a heteroglossic repository of the voices around her. While Le Sueur was unaware of Bakhtin, this is a highly Bakhtinian move. Fundamental to Bakhtin's interest in heteroglossia is his recognizing ways in which an understanding of heteroglossia undermines traditional bourgeois notions of individualism.

Wayne Booth has articulated this Bakhtinian interest well:

> He [Bakhtin] conducts a steady polemic against atomized, narrowly formalist or individualistic views of selves. His targets here—all "monological" views—are shared with other Marxists. . . .
>
> For him, as for more orthodox Marxists, what I call my "self" is essentially social. Each of us is constituted not as an individual, private, atomic self but as a collective of the many selves we have taken in from birth. We encounter these selves as what he calls "languages," the "voices" spoken by others. . . . We are constituted in polyphony. (51)

Many passages from well-known works by Bakhtin could exemplify what Booth is discussing, but I will cite two from a lesser-known work, "From Notes Made in 1970–71":

> Everything that pertains to me enters my consciousness, beginning with my name, from the external world through the mouths of others (my mother, and so forth), with their intonation, in their emotional and value-assigning tonality. I realize

myself initially through others: from them I receive words, forms, and tonalities for the formation of my initial idea of myself. (*Speech Genres* 138)

"From Notes Made in 1970–71" further discusses the permeability of the "I": "The *I* hides in the other and in others, it wants to be only an other for others, to enter completely into the world of others as an other, and to cast from itself the burden of being the only *I* (*I-for-myself*) in the world" (147). I cite these passages because they, more than similar, better-known Bakhtinian formulations, speak to Le Sueur's (and, as I will later show, Olsen's) desires to explore the possibilities of a narrator who is a heteroglossic "I."

To return to *The Girl,* the impression of a heteroglossic narrator is intensified in some passages where Le Sueur withholds narrative tags for long periods of time.

> Don't think about it. Stop thinking about it.
>
> All right, you stop too.
>
> What time is it?
>
> Almost four.
>
> This time tomorrow we'll be through with it.
>
> It will be all right. Everything will be all right.
>
> Yes.
>
> It won't though. It will be stinking. Lousy.
>
> Don't say that.
>
> Might as well look yourself in the eye.
>
> It will be all right. We'll make it.
>
> We'll be dead.
>
> No, no.
>
> We'll be dead and forgotten.
>
> O, we will live forever, I cried. (90–91)

For a sustained time, the voices stand on their own, equally vying for our attention without the intrusion of a narrator. Clearly, Le Sueur is searching for forms that will permit heteroglossia, forms that will allow a multiplicity of voices to speak for themselves in the recognition that all selves are interdependent. In *The Girl* the voices emerge in many modes—they speak, sing, appear in letters and notes.

In an afterword Le Sueur claims that the novel, intended as a memorial to the women of the Depression,

> was really written by them. As part of our desperate struggle to be alive and human we pooled our memories, experiences and in the midst of disaster told each other our stories or wrote them down. We had a writers' group of women in the Workers Alliance and we met every night to raise our miserable circumstances to the level of sagas, poetry. . . .

> There was no tape recorder then so I took their stories down. Some could not write very well, and some wrote them out painfully in longhand while trying to keep warm in bus stations or waiting for food orders at relief offices. (n. pag.)

Although a reading of *The Girl* suggests that Le Sueur's role as a writer must have been more active than her remarks imply, the novel nonetheless records one of the dialects that has generally been excluded from American literature. In this sense, *The Girl* parallels the work of Olsen's *Yonnondio*, another novel recovered from the '30s; Harriette Arnow's *The Dollmaker* (1954); the work of Alice Walker and Zora Neale Hurston; Denise Giardina's *Storming Heaven* (1987); and the fiction of Carolyn Chute, who speaks the dialect of poor whites in rural Maine.

The multiple voices repeatedly rely on two common structures, the imperative and the question, through which Le Sueur portrays difficulties the voices have in their attempts to connect with one another. Further, these structures contribute to the novel's heteroglossic exploring of forms of power and powerlessness. Imperatives and questions have long interested scholars of speech acts who have examined in both of these structures the implied presence of a power imbalance between the speaker and the person addressed. Mary Louise Pratt notes that "both questions and imperatives . . . presuppose, among other things, that the speaker has a very specific motive. His point is to generate a specific action on the part of the hearer. . . . Questions are requests or commands to *tell* something, imperatives request or demand us to *do* something" (132–133). In Pratt's analysis it is the speaker who attempts to exercise a form of control over the hearer. Yet, in the structure of questions potential exists for a very different version of power imbalance. Often a questioner attempts to exercise the form of control described by Pratt because he or she believes the hearer to have knowledge or information the questioner lacks. Dialogue in *The Girl* explores some of the parameters of these power imbalances.[4]

The structure of imperatives is highly compatible with Gold's "manly," direct style, and in *The Girl* Le Sueur often employs commands in a manner suggestive of Gold's "manly" style. Butch more than once describes his passion for winning: "I'm a natural winner. It's got to be. I feel it in my bones. Look, I want to win. I'm strong. I feel good. It ain't natural I shouldn't be winning. I like to beat everybody. I like to beat everybody in the world" (17–18). Not surprisingly, Butch often speaks in commands: "Shut up," "Mind your own business for God's sake," "Don't tell me what to do," "Don't put on airs." Given his view of the world, we expect to hear such commands from Butch. We are prepared to see him attempting to take charge of the world he often sees as his.

Yet, another group of commands are somewhat less expected from Butch. The oddity of these commands is not that they are out of keeping with Butch's view of the world; rather, the oddity lies in the fact that they appear in situations in which something other than a command would be appropriate. We know that Butch is capable of moments of genuine tenderness toward the Girl. Yet, even in some of those tender moments, Butch cannot escape the command structure: "Gee, love me a little kid," and "Listen, honey . . . you be good to me," he insists

(28, 17). The command structure, all-pervasive in Butch's view of the world, can appear in any situation. As the last example suggests, the command has become one of Butch's most basic conversational devices. In addition to Butch's utterances that begin with "Listen," we hear, "Look . . . look honey, we'll do it, get away from everything. Look honey, that's our out" (15). The command structure frames Butch's "manly" style and "manly" view of the world.

As is suggested by the heteroglossic "voice" of the novel's narrator, *The Girl* employs structures that stand as alternatives or resistance to the overt attempts at control inherent in the command structure. One such alternative structure is the question, a structure prominent in Chapters 10 and 11, when the Girl returns home after her father's death. Because the domineering patriarch can no longer delimit the family's discourse with versions of the command structure employed so often by Butch, the Girl feels free to coax her mother, through questions, into talking frankly about her life for the first time. The conversation between daughter and mother becomes part of an initiation into womanhood for the Girl, who is all the more attentive to her mother's revelations because of her own pregnancy.

> Maybe she would tell me something. Maybe out of all the words something would come through and I would see what to do. Whatever you say, mama had something, she had her life, her children, she knows what it is even if she can't say it right out. She knows something. She knows what it's about. She has felt something. (40–41)

Throughout these chapters, the Girl persistently questions her mother: "What did you do, mama?," "That was me?," "Was he, mama?," "What is a man when he is good to you?" These questions serve what I described earlier as the potential double function of the question structure in relation to a balance of power. The Girl controls the situation by asking questions in her attempt to learn from her mother what the Girl does not know. The Girl has power over the situation, but she exercises that power out of the perception that her mother has the power of knowledge the Girl lacks.

On the level of the story's narration, the questions function in yet another way, a way in keeping with the novel's heteroglossic impulses. At this point in the novel, as at similar points in many other works by Le Sueur, the narrator is intent upon someone else's exercising her memory for the sake of telling her previously untold story from which others might learn. The simple, intermittent questions function as prods and signposts for the mother. The questions aid the mother's telling of her story, serving as vehicles for her voice's being heard and recorded. The voice of the Girl recedes to the background as the voice of the mother telling her story fills two chapters of the novel.

The power of memory and of heteroglossic voices speaking their memories is structurally underscored by Le Sueur in Chapter 39 where she conflates the command and question structures in a scene dealing with memory. Just before Clara dies, the narrator desperately tries to communicate with her.

> Clara! Clara! I cried—remember me, remember how you took me on your wanderings, how you showed me everything.
>
> She didn't even smile. Those pupils leapt out though, as if to tell me something terrible. They told me. I saw it all, what they had done to her.
>
> Clara! remember the German Village and those Saturday nights with the Booya and Bill, I cried, Bill and Butch, those pretty fellows, those wonderful foxes you used to call them, those slick cats you said. . . . Remember?

Are these "remembers" commands? Are they questions? Clearly they are both and more. They are commands, they are questions, they are urgings, they are pleas. "I held her, I shook her, I caressed her, I shouted at her" (142).

This heteroglossia of speech acts suggests all the voices of the novel's oppressed "community" coming together for a moment urgently trying to find a way to get one of their own to record her story before she dies. We hear in the "remembers" echoes of the frequent command structures of Butch, for whom such structures had become a way of individualistically and competitively arranging his world.

But in this moment of heteroglossia we hear, too, the Girl's and the women's desire to find, in the story of one of their own, alternatives to Butch's reductive ways of talking about and seeing the world.

> Memory is all we got, I cried, we got to remember. We got to remember everything. It is the glory, Amelia said, the glory. We got to remember to be able to fight. Got to write down names. Make a list. Nobody can be forgotten. They know if we don't remember we can't point them out. They got their guilt wiped out. The last thing they take is memory. Remember, Amelia says, the breasts of your mothers. O mama help us now. Clara remember your mama like you told me, going from city to city, to lousy jobs and getting children and taking them on her back, and locking them in rooms while she waited on tables, did laundry, Clara you got to remember your mama, I'll help you. (142)

The Girl refers here to elements common to working-class women's experience—jobs with low pay and poor working conditions and the difficulty of caring for children without societal resources and support. And here, in a moment of resistance, the heteroglossia of the community's voices attempts to help Clara to help the struggling women in return.

Particularly in the ways in which Le Sueur permits the multiple voices of women to speak, we find her challenging some of the assumptions of Gold's kind of proletarian realism and attitudes about women reinforced by those assumptions. The "manly" style Gold argued for in proletarian realism, the very kind of style Le Sueur often approximated in her reportage, becomes a target in *The Girl*. In Chapter 13, the Girl and Butch fall into a dispute. With something close to a labeling of the novel's heteroglossic impulses, Butch, wanting the Girl's exclusive attention, complains, "you got words for everybody. You can weep for the Chinese, the Ethiopians, and I can go to hell." When the girl retorts "Sure you go to hell," the dispute begins to embody the subject of "manly" style in relation to "manly" action. Butch replies,

Now that's more like it. Let's know positively kid, let's have it, what are you going to do? Say it. Give out. I can take it. Go ahead hit me. I've been struck before and I'll be struck again.

I don't want to strike you, Butch.

O.K. by me, let it go, let's have it, let her fly I can take it. I been on the bench before this. Can't you shoot straight girl?

I'm not shooting or hitting or striking.

All right, can't a woman give it from the shoulder. Always pussyfooting around.

As the argument continues, the Girl interjects, to the apparent surprise of Butch, "After all, my papa was a good man." Butch responds, "There you go. That's what I mean about women. Talking of one thing, they bring up another" (49–50).

Alone this passage would stand, against the background of the full context of *The Girl*, as forceful commentary on proletarian realism's constraining assumptions about women and "manly" style. Significantly, however, the passage does not stand alone. In Chapter 29, after Butch has been shot and just before he dies, he breaks into a delirium of associative discourse, the very kind of disconnected discourse he had objected to the Girl's using. Further, he begins that associative discourse by blurting out something about his father.

> *No, he wasn't my father, Butch said. Do I owe my father any grief? Answer me that, he said. You don't owe your father anything. Here we are kicked around all our lives, what do you owe your father, spawning you in it. . . .*
>
> *I'd be coming down driving the truck, all bent out of shape with my kidneys killing me, and there'd be Joe warming up running like a dog. You can't hurt him now. Why should I be quiet? Can't I even speak? He's been knocked over so often his brains are addled.* (101)

Butch's "Can't I even speak?" serves as a delirious confession to the limitations of his uses of language and his competitive view of the world. Butch is redeemed to heteroglossia, but he is so only in death.

Although the novel experiments successfully with the collective voice, in other ways it is flawed. The bank robbery is an artificial structure on which to hang the real story—that of the Girl's pregnancy, the brutality of men and the Depression, and the generative power of women. (In Le Sueur's defense, pregnancy was not a saleable theme for a novel, as she had learned when she wrote a book-length manuscript about the experience of having her first child, an extended version of "Annunciation." When she sent the manuscript to *Scribner's* and *Atlantic Monthly* for possible serialization, editors who had previously published her work commented favorably on the style but questioned the content. Giving birth, she was told, is not a "suitable" subject.)

The presence of the Workers' Alliance organizers—just what Whittaker Chambers had ordered in his editorial finger-wagging—also contributes to the novel's awkwardness. Amelia and Alice constitute a projection of a superego—that is, their activity represents what ought to be taking place as opposed to what is actually going on. With the mechanical addition of these two characters and the narrator's obligatory conversion, it is as if the Party has stepped in to ghostwrite, an intrusion the text does not easily accommodate. For example, when, toward the end of the novel, the Girl asks Alice to define the Workers' Alliance—thereby providing Le Sueur a forum for propaganda—one marvels at the Girl's ignorance; after all, Amelia, never without her black linoleum bag of leaflets, had appeared at the novel's beginning and had befriended the Girl throughout.

The novel is most disfigured, however, by its stereotyping of men. Although some men are as sexist, negligent, violent, and incompetent as those the novel depicts, the novel caricatures its male characters—all of them. Except for Butch's heteroglossic soliloquy before he dies, the novel provides little narrative or dialogue—other than describing the Depression's cruelty, which also affected women—that might partly redeem the male characters, who provide nothing positive for the women other than sporadic sexual gratification. Moreover, Butch and the other men respond to economic victimization by embracing the very capitalist values that enslave them:

> There's plenty good things to want. . . .
>   There's winning all the time and the good feel it gives you and doing things, you know with the English on it, know what I mean? And driving a fast car. And having a girl who likes it and knows how to do it.
>   I could feel the bright blood in me.
>   It takes guts, he said, that's what it is, to go through the night. You got to be tough and strong alone.

The female characters' solidarity contrasts so sharply with this competitive individualism that we are reminded of Le Sueur's reliance on antithetical structures in her reportage. The dialogue between the Girl and Butch continues:

> I don't like it alone, I said. I don't want to be alone. I want to be with others.
>   He looked at me. Gee, women are funny eggs, he said, my mother's a screwy dame too! (17)

In contrast to Butch's competitive individualism, the Girl "embodies the longings and abilities, hungers and strengths, of her sex and class," as Jan Clausen notes (3). She also possesses the capacity to recognize this commonality.

The elimination of all male characters by a *deus ex machina*, however, renders the women's unity—like that of the Girl's family after her father's death—merely fortuitous and implies that cooperation among women and freedom from sexual domination are possible only in a world where men no longer exist. Le Sueur's intended "progressive" resolution, then, is ultimately defeatist, perversely to borrow Whittaker Chambers's term. Moreover, by employing such a mechanical plot device, *The Girl* evades the very questions raised by its female characters' subordination to men. First, the novel fails to confront its own evidence—as if paralyzed by the categorically antithetical nature of that evidence—that, in the face of economic oppression, all working-class women cooperate while all working-class men compete. Second, the novel in no way addresses the (limited) range of working-class women's options in the Depression decade; to what extent could they have freed themselves—and helped liberate one another—from oppressive relationships?

The last part of the novel is an espousal of what we now term separatism without announcing itself as such, thereby avoiding discussion of such a radical restructuring of society. (Conveniently, the Girl's baby, the novel's chief symbol of hope and regeneration, had been conceived before the men were whisked away.) Moreover, this final section is undercut by earlier evidence that men are anything but dispensable: The Girl is constantly preoccupied by thoughts of Butch; the women's conversations often revolve around men; and the women submit to the men's indifference and abuse out of a fatalistic sense that this is the way things have always been and must be. And, whereas the women in Charlotte Perkins Gilman's utopian socialist novel *Herland* have no sense of sexual passion (parthenogenic births produce only female children), Belle and the Girl are partly defined by their active, and often pleasurable, sexual experiences: The Girl says about sex with Butch that "his body had been good to me. It seemed like there was everything else bad, and our bodies good and sweet to us" (106). And Belle confides to the Girl "how good [Hoink] was and how it was even after the terrible years, how good it was for them. And you could always feel it in the [speakeasy] when they had it good together, as if some great rowdy light shone on us, and some love of the flesh had poured in to liven us all" (52).

This approbation of heterosexual passion is incongruous in what becomes a separatist novel. Structurally, the novel would have worked better had Le Sueur consistently depicted for its female characters what Adrienne Rich terms a "double life"—a life with men in which sex is both pleasurable and destructive and a separate life among women who provide mutual material and emotional support. This "double life" of heterosexual women is common in contemporary women's writing—for example, Toni Morrison's *Sula*, Alice Walker's *The Color Purple*, and Marilyn French's *The Women's Room*.

A reading of the 1939 manuscript reveals that the novel became slightly more, rather than less, schematic as a result of its 1977–78 revisions. In the 1939 manuscript, Amelia, the voice of authority, at one point explains behavior as an effect of the Depression rather than gender-determined: "It isn't the man. A man is a mighty fine thing, there is nothing better than a man. It's the way we have to live that makes us sink to the bottom and rot" (204). Elsewhere in the 1939 draft Amelia seems to be echoing, in muted form, the Party's "unite and fight" position of the Popular Front, which held that all special-interest groups should subordinate their particular concerns to a united opposing of fascism: "There is no use saying it is this and that, it is men, it is women, it is one thing and another. We all got to be alive, and not lay down, and *fight* for it. We got to be men and women again and want everything and dream everything and fight for it" (222). The most flagrant instance of anti-male bias is altogether absent from the 1939 draft. It occurs on the last page, when the Girl's baby is born: "It's a woman, Belle was shouting, a sister a daughter. No dingle dangle, no rod of satan, no sword no third arm, a girl a woman a mother" (148). In fact, in the 1939 version the baby is male.

The binary oppositions of *The Girl*—man/woman, subject/object, predator/ prey, life-threatening/life-giving, competitive/cooperative, and negligent/nurturing—are perpetuated by a strain of biological determinism apparent in cultural feminism. This current within the women's movement considers feminism's primary goal as liberating women from the imposition of "male values" and creating an alternative culture based on "female values." A closely related current within the women's movement, a turn to *féminité*, has been supported variously by Kristeva, Cixous, Irigiray, and other French and American feminists and posits that Western thought is organized around categories that repress women's experience. A discussion of an exclusively female experience or "female nature" initiates, for them, a deconstruction of patriarchal culture, including its language, philosophy, psychoanalysis, and social practices.

Some feminist theory, however, suggests that *féminité* is idealist, essentialist, determinist. Gayle Rubin, Nancy Chodorow, and Dorothy Dinnerstein, for example, argue that sexuality, rather than being an inherent quality in women or men, is socially developed. A given society's sex-gender system, they believe, is systematically reproduced and yet subject to historical change. The categories "woman" and "man" are economic and political, not natural and immutable. Monique Wittig, who subscribes to such a position and writes from a perspective of "materialist lesbianism," insists that women define their oppression in materialist terms. She observes that such a definition

> certainly seems to be an impossibility since materialism and subjectivity have always been mutually exclusive. Nevertheless, and rather than despairing of ever understanding, we must recognize the *need* to reach subjectivity in the abandonment by many of us to the myth "woman" (the myth of woman being only a snare that holds us up). This real necessity for everyone to exist as an individual, as well as a member of a class, is perhaps the first condition for the accomplishment of a revolution, without which there can be no real fight or transformation. But the opposite is also true; without class and class consciousness there are no real subjects, only alienated individuals. (xiii, 19)

In the course of linking her work to other language theorists, Wittig notes, "among linguists, the Russian Bakhtin . . . is the only one who seems to me to have a strictly materialist approach to language" (78). Like these materialist feminists, I find suspect the language and logic through which *féminité* defines men as solipsistic, predatory, and committed to a sterile rationalism and characterizes women, by nature of their contrasting sexuality, as nurturing, empathetic, and intuitive. We must question rather than celebrate this male-female opposition and subvert binary logic, not employ it. Rather than essential strata, masculine and feminine "natures" are social, historical constructs. Jonathan Culler recognizes that for feminists there is "an urgent question: to minimize or to exalt sexual differentiation?" Following some deconstructionist leads, he suggests "the importance of working on two fronts at once, even though the result is a contradictory rather than unified movement" (172, 173). Similarly, Ann Rosalind Jones sees *féminité* and *écriture féminine* as useful *partial* strategies.[5]

To the extent that *The Girl* promotes biologism, binary logic, and woman as myth, the novel supports the very system it seeks to destroy. In its concluding pages, *The Girl* declares by fiat the existence of a magical, female "island on the land" with no reference as to how to achieve such a colony within the empire, and in fact itself supplies the evidence—a powerful heterosexual drive and a desire to procreate among some of its female characters—that such a colony does not offer a viable alternative.

On the other hand, the novel provides a counter-myth that questions some of the most basic assumptions of our present socioeconomic order. It promotes co-operation rather than competition, equality rather than domination/subordination, and alternatives to the nuclear family. The novel also exposes the limits of a welfare state at a time when the CP officially approved the New Deal's liberal reforms.[6] And, to an extent, *The Girl* subverts the ascetic Protestantism embodied by Le Sueur's grandmother and the Victorian values embraced not only by Le Sueur's parents but also by many CP members.[7] Most important, the novel depicts a version of women's self-organization. Of course, neither living collectively to survive the Depression nor separatism qualify as the autonomous political organization favorably discussed at Chapter 2's conclusion. But Le Sueur reveals some sense of the need for women to organize independently of men, a need the Communist Party did not recognize. That the novel can pose only a separatist alternative to the established order—an alternative, moreover, made possible only by a *deus ex machina*—suggests the limits of progressive change possible for working-class women during the Depression and hints at the contradictory quality of women's experiences within the CP.

"Our Fathers," "Annunciation," and "Corn Village" number among Le Sueur's most subversive texts. These stories counter elements in Le Sueur's own writing— the Party aesthetic, operating most apparently in her reportage; the biological determinism and sharp male/female opposition of *The Girl*; and the binary logic of "The Fetish of Being Outside." In these three stories Le Sueur frankly examines her own divided loyalty which "The Fetish" proscribes. The didacticism evident in some of her writing is noticeably absent from these three texts. Moreover, they acknowledge the complexity of "the people," who were often romanticized in Party—and in Le Sueur's own—discourse.

Le Sueur has described "Our Fathers" as "one of the few [of my] stories that's not covered up. . . . It [is] really a naked cry" (interview). Through the fictional characters, she confronts her grandmother's, her mother's, and her own emotional deformation. She insists on knowing and feeling what her mother and grandmother have repressed, forgotten, denied. (Le Sueur's grandmother reproached her for writing the truth about women's lives. "I've spent all my life trying to conceal it," she complained, viewing her granddaughter as a saboteur [interview].) "Our Fathers" is more critical of the "upright fanatical prohibitionist mother," to borrow Le Sueur's phrase from *Crusaders*, than it is of men (39).

"Our Fathers" takes place before the funeral for Penelope's father, Tim, who had been active in "the unemployment council" and shot in a demonstration. It was Tim, not the mother or grandmother, who, despite his irresponsibility toward his family, fostered Penelope's "communal sensibility." Penelope's mother, Mona, addresses Tim at his death, "I knew you wouldn't come to no good, always talkin'," but Penelope took seriously what she had overheard him say:

> "We've got a right to be living, see?"
> "Sure, you said it."
> "It was us made this country, it was us, the bones of my people lie along Hill's railroad and there was a man dead for every tie laid and that's a fact. . . ."
> "That's a fact all right . . . that sure is true."
> "My fathers dug in the earth, threw up bridges, that's what they done, tilled the god-damned soil, that's what, froze on the prairies. We've been buckers and loggers and made nothing while those that held the land became wheat, lumber, coal kings and us lean to the guts."
> "Yes sir, that's right, Tim. . . ."
> "Stand together. Be together. I got brothers to my fathers who joined up with John Brown, stormed Harper's Ferry. Lie now face up in Kansas dirt but they done something, showed us something. . . ." (114; all ellipses Le Sueur's)

In contrast, we are intended to see Mona as having acquisitive, individualist aspirations. She mourns Tim's death "not for him but for some obscure loss more terrible, because they had not been 'successful,'" because "she never had any of the things she might have had, an automobile, a silk dress for Sunday" (115). "Our Fathers" counters *The Girl*'s schema (men are typically competitive, women instinctively communal) without, however, merely inverting it: Both a male (Tim) and a female (Penelope) can be politically progressive.

Penelope is especially troubled by her grandmother's bitterness. Looking at a photograph of Samuel, a man she left after 20 years of marriage, the old woman sneers, "'Samuel that no account. If I'd known what I do now about men it would a been different. Men . . . men . . . .' She was only glad to remember in order to deride him" (120). Penelope wants desperately to know the stories of the forebears in the old photographs, to feel some connection to them, but the grandmother

> seemed like a woman triumphant, flushed with victory because she had them all buried, and they giving her no meaning to trouble her. She was proud of this, and wore it like a banner of death and silence more terrible than the dead father at the undertaker's, so that a fear came into Penelope of her own future, lest it fall into such an abyss and touch nothing. The fear was in her for those she did not know and for those she knew, walking like sleepers that one word of rebellion could awaken. (120)

The old woman begins to quaver, "Jeeesus lover of my soul / Let me to thy bosom fly." Her love of Jesus was "her only urgency." She could pledge to "go where you want me to go, dear Lord," but "never [go] an inch along with Samuel," Penelope observes. She was "like a spouse of the Lord being betrayed by earth's little men" (122).

Tim's death has intensified Penelope's adolescent search for her identity. Studying the old photographs, she tries to comprehend her past and imagine her future by placing herself in a genealogy of immigrants, settlers, bitter women, professionals, rakes, and rebels. As a result "Our Fathers" has a searching, dreamy quality strikingly different from reportage. Moreover, the didacticism characteristic of proletarian writing in general, and "Women on the Breadlines" and "I Was Marching" in particular, is muted in "Our Fathers," except for the dialogue in which Tim identifies the class struggle and the proper side to support. Rather than providing slogans, solutions, and clear demarcations, "Our Fathers" permits questions, doubts, and fears to emerge and suggests that some aspects of life may remain mysterious to Penelope, despite her craving to know.

The enemy is not simply the "wheat, lumber, and coal kings" about whom Tim sermonizes: Penelope senses that she will not escape the "bitter drouth" so affecting Mona, her grandmother, and the stern and angry women in the photographs. She sees that these women "were made that way by the hatred of their men, but she could not ask why feeling that brew would be in herself and then she would know and never be cured of it" (117). "Cured" associates this hatred of men with disease, suggesting that such bitterness is something to be feared, not worn triumphantly "like a banner of death and silence" (120). While "Our Fathers" is not without sympathy for what women have endured (the grandmother's "broken pelvis hung half to her knees from childbearing, from working in textile mills, from berry-picking and tobacco-hoeing" [115]), it sharply attacks the hostility toward men and emotional repression that constituted Penelope's—and Le Sueur's—legacy.

The contrast between "Our Fathers," written in Le Sueur's late twenties, and the biological determinism of *The Girl*, completed in draft form when she was 39, is striking. Le Sueur's problematic relationship to Bob Brown may partly explain the contrast. In any case, one can wish that Le Sueur had further explored in her published writing, as she does in "Our Fathers," the marks left on her— and, by extension, on other women of her generation—by the towering presence of an absent father and by a grandmother who could not cry unless "her bad eye" ran water, "as if weeping alone, unknown to her" (115). Le Sueur explains that she became a writer to speak for the "oppressed or silent or mute or forgotten," specifically identifying her grandmother: "My grandmother was mute. [She] had no word for her terrible life" (interview). One wonders about the additional contribution Le Sueur might have made to radical women's writing had she devoted more words in her published writing to the contradictions that affected her own life.

Although the position on class struggle in "Our Fathers" and its sympathy for the working class would have pleased Gold, Hicks, and other *New Masses* doyens, it is much less in harmony with their literary formulations than Le Sueur's reportage. "Our Fathers" contains poetic language—employing metaphor, alliteration, and long sentences involving several dependent clauses—rather than the shorn, staccato prose and short declarative sentences of "Women on the Breadlines." The following passage, which describes what Penelope sees while studying a photograph of a forebear, is representative:

> Penelope saw a woman whose old body was like a pod where the seed has flown, frail in age, delicate again and insubstantial as a girl—as if instead of being matured and made abundant by bearing five sons and four daughters she had been ravaged by a ghost, worn away by a dream at once fatal and tender, inwardly ravished by a melancholy that became like love, sublimated in longings that could never be fulfilled in this world. (116–117)

Language has a more ambitious task in "Our Fathers"—to capture a precocious adolescent's state of mind—than it does in "Women on the Breadlines," which at points merely lists concrete details of economic deprivation. The first paragraph of a previously cited passage provides an example: "She lives alone in little rooms. She bought seven dollars' worth of second-hand furniture eight years ago. She rents a room for perhaps three dollars' a month in an attic, sometimes in a cold house. . . . She spent only twenty-five dollars all winter" (138). This piece of reportage catalogs surface journalistic details, and while we get a valuable account of deprivation, we do not come to know these women as we come to know Penelope and her grandmother. Le Sueur's reportage is perhaps also delimited by her class origin. She does not penetrate the consciousness of the characters in "Women on the Breadlines," for example, but does so acutely in "Our Fathers," whose characters were based on people she knew only too well.

The formal elements in "Our Fathers" show that despite Le Sueur's description of it as a "naked cry," the story is not that, but an experiment with forms that give the impression of a naked cry. Penelope's cry is that of a girl who has heard a heteroglossia of voices, but cannot make out what they say.

> Penelope heard voices talking in the day and sleepwalking voices murmuring in the night, but not one of them said where they were, or what they would be doing in that long and tangled journey and a darkness would come over her asking of that space they traveled. Who are we? Where have we come from? (114)

The formal problems Le Sueur faces are complex ones. Unlike *The Girl*, this is not discourse in which the heteroglossia can be unleashed. Instead, it is the discourse of muffled voices, somewhere between audibility and silence.

Le Sueur's experiments with forms in "Our Fathers" include the development of a narrator who stands somewhere between the narrator of *The Girl* and the typical narrator of her reportage. The narrator of "Our Fathers" is rarely, as the Girl often is, the vehicle for a variety of competing voices, nor is she ever in the position of full omniscience, seeing the parameters of the world, a position in which Le Sueur often places the narrators of her reportage. The narrator of "Our

Fathers" knows some of the conditions "they" are in, but it is only a partial knowledge. This narrator rarely rises above the perspective of the child, Penelope, straining to hear what the voices are saying. When the narrator asks of the figures in the photographs, "Who are you? What did you have to say? What did you know?," these are very much Penelope's questions.

Near the end of "Our Fathers" we find just how incomplete the narrator's knowledge is. With Penelope, she has strained to discern the voices of the past, but she has absorbed only pieces of Penelope's questions and fragments of information grudgingly yielded by Mona and the grandmother. The narrator has become a logjam of their fragments of discourse. As the logjam suddenly breaks, the narrator pours out:

> YOUR HUSBAND IS DOWN BEHIND THE HEDGE. LET HIM LIE. HE IS
> DRUNK BEHIND THE BROOM BUSHES AND THE SUN IS GOING
> DOWN. WON'T YOU GO? DON'T LET THE POTATOES BURN, MARK.
> DON'T LET THE BEANS BOIL DRY, LUCE. . . . WHERE? WHERE?
> THERE? RIGHT BEHIND THAT FLOWERING BROOM TO THE RIGHT
> OF THE PEAR TREE. HE'S WAITING. TRIM YOUR WICKS. FILL YOUR
> LAMPS WITH OIL. THE BRIDEGROOM COMETH. . . . THAT COULDN'T
> BE HIM BEHIND THE HEDGE NOW COULD IT? THAT BUM? THAT
> WASTREL? THAT LIVING MAN? THAT NO ACCOUNT SAMUEL. THAT
> COULDN'T BE HIM. . . . (122)

Here we get no perspective on the past but merely the reflection of a bitter fragmenting of the present. At the end of the story, as the narrator reports Mona's and the grandmother's beating of Penelope, we hear Penelope scream the only piece of knowledge she has or the narrator has about the men whose voices Penelope has strained to hear: "'My father . . .,' she screamed crouching down, 'Our fathers . . .,' she screamed, 'Our fathers. . . .'" (123).

"Annunciation," like "Our Fathers," frankly examines Le Sueur's own experience, and its unnamed narrator, like Penelope, is open to life, searching. "Annunciation" departs even more than "Our Fathers" from typical proletarian writing. The title alludes to the angel Gabriel's announcement to Mary that she will give birth to the Son of God (Luke 1:26–38), and Le Sueur originally wrote the story, as I have mentioned, in the form of notes scrawled intermittently on scraps of paper for her unborn child. Set in the Depression, this narrative prose poem represents a pregnant woman's dream-like state of mind, imposing a theme of fertility and regeneration upon a secondary theme of contrasting deprivation. The unnamed narrator lives with Karl, the unborn child's father, a minor, oddly irrelevant character. He fits the pattern Le Sueur describes in *Crusaders* of the "migrating, lost, silent, drunk father" (39). But Karl is not a Butch or a Ganz; he is neither a dominant, threatening presence nor a preoccupation for the unnamed narrator. Her preoccupation is her unborn child.[8]

"Annunciation" is about meaning and lack of it, about connection and lack of it. From the point of view of Gold's version of proletarian realism, its themes are every bit as bourgeois as those of "The Waste Land," and Le Sueur, no less than Eliot, experiments with forms that allow her to explore fragmentation. However, unlike Eliot who often sets fragments in stark juxtaposition, Le Sueur places her juxtaposed fragments within a cyclical, lyrical flow. Near the beginning of the story the narrator says, "It is strange, I notice all these things, the sun, the rain falling, the blowing of the wind. It is as if they had a meaning for me as the pear tree has come to have" (124). We begin with the knowledge that at least one fragment of the narrator's world, the pear tree, has come to have meaning for her and may help draw other fragments into a pattern of meaning. At the end of the story we have come full circle, with the narrator speaking of meaning supplied by the pear tree: "It seems a strange thing that a tree might come to mean more to one than one's husband. . . . I listen to the whispering of the pear tree, speaking to me, speaking to me" (132). In the circular journey through the story, we discover *how* fragments have been drawn into patterns of meaning.

At the beginning of the story the connections among fragments remain submerged in "a rich powerful haze," a "mist" (124). Far more clearly than any connections among them, we see the juxtaposed fragments themselves: the scraps of paper, a magnolia tree, broken settees, a sick woman. At first all that seems to connect them is a musing narrator's movement among them. But as the story progresses and the narrator draws our attention increasingly to the child she is carrying, we begin to see connections among the juxtaposed fragments. The narrator writes:

> "Tonight, the world into which you are coming"—then I was speaking to the invisible child—"is very strange and beautiful. That is, the natural world is beautiful. I don't know what you will think of man, but the dark glisten of vegetation and the blowing of the fertile land wind and the delicate strong step of the sea wind, these things are familiar to me and will be familiar to you. I hope you will be like these things. I hope you will glisten with the glisten of ancient life, the same beauty that is in a leaf or a wild rabbit, wild sweet beauty of limb and eye. I am going on a boat between dark shores, and the river and the sky are so quiet that I can hear the scurryings of tiny animals on the shores and their little breathings seem to be all around. I think of them, wild, carrying their young now, crouched in the dark underbrush with the fruit-scented land wind in their delicate nostrils, and they are looking out at the moon and the fast clouds. Silent, alive, they sit in the dark shadow of the greedy world. There is something wild about us too, something tender and wild about my having you as a child, about your crouching so secretly here. . . . We, too, are at the mercy of many hunters. On this boat I act like the other human beings, for I do not show that I have you, but really I know we are as helpless, as wild, as at bay as some tender wild animals who might be on the ship.
>
> "I put my hand where you lie so silently. I hope you will come glistening with life power, with it shining upon you as upon the feathers of birds. I hope you will be a warrior and fierce for change, so all can live." (127–128)

The pregnant woman's address to the unborn child articulates connections among the two of them, the pear tree, and other elements and creatures in the natural world.

But what about connections between the two of them and other human beings? The narrator offers no simple answer to this question. In the passage above, she restricts her application of "beautiful" to the natural world, and with apparent reservations says, "I don't know what you will think of man." And yet she hopes that her child "will be a warrior and fierce for change"— change that encompasses all life ("so all can live"). On the one hand, the narrator believes most people incapable of seeing the only pattern of connections she has presented us thus far, the connection of life between herself and the child she is carrying and the natural world: "You can tell by looking at most people that the world remains a stone to them and a closed door" (129). On the other hand, her vision of natural connections is at times extended to include human beings: "The people coming and going seem to hang on the tree of life" (129).

It is immediately after this extension of vision that some new meaning, some new sense of how people are connected to natural patterns emerges: "I am standing here looking at the blind windows of the house next door and suddenly the walls fall away, the doors open, and within I see a young girl making a bed from which she had just risen having dreamed of a young man who became her lover . . . she stands before her looking-glass in love with herself" (129). The narrator sees more than she has seen before, and the seeing generates this response:

> Why should I be excited? Why should I feel this excitement, seeing a woman waving to her young husband, or a woman who has been nursing a child, or a young man sleeping? Yet I am excited. The many houses have become like an orchard blooming soundlessly. The many people have become like fruits to me, the young girl in the room alone before her mirror, the young man sleeping, the mother, all are shaking with their inward blossoming, shaken by the windy blooming, moving along a future curve. (129–130)

To the question of why she is excited by the extended vision, the narrator provides an answer, but it is an answer that does not have complete meaning.

The narrator's partial answer is one in which romanticism reverberates. The natural world offers human beings the potential for connections. This partial answer is couched in romantic similes and in romantic devices of animation: "Stand still like a fat budding tree," she says to herself, and she observes "the bony skeleton of the mountains, like the skeleton of the world jutting through its flowery flesh" (130, 128). However, the answer has little meaning if the people being offered the connections cannot see them. The narrator has found a way to see the young girl more fully, but what she has seen is someone not looking back at her or trying to speak to her, but a young girl in the narcissistic world of her own looking-glass. Having had the extended vision, the narrator realizes that people are not likely to be able to take advantage of the potential for connection, that they are likely to remain in the closed worlds of their own looking-glasses, and that her extended vision itself is fleeting: "But there will come a time when the doors will close again, the shouting will be gone, the sprouting and the movement and the wondrous opening out of everything will be gone. I will be only myself" (130).

Le Sueur's journals indicate that human isolation and disconnectedness were subjects about which the writer had thought extensively and was prepared to develop in several works. "I thought I would write an article for the *New Republic* entitled 'The Village,'" she records, and her notes for the article observe, "A good civilization gives the greatest possible scope to the common passions and makes them intelligible between the greatest number of people. But these people [of the village] seem isolated" (vol. 7, 1933, 68).[9] And in another journal entry she writes,

> In all these little houses there are people—you would hardly know it. They have no or little contact. . . . In each of these little houses there is a man—or a woman, almost isolated. You can tell by the way they look that they feel lost and isolated. . . . They walk along the road with every line of their body showing where they have been wrenched off the body politic. Their bodies do not flow easily—do not move easily—they move as if they [are] wound inward and not outward. (vol. 7, 1933, 121)

The realization the narrator of "Annunciation" comes to is not one of romanticism, but one akin to the modernism of *The Waste Land*. In fact, it is a realization that produces a response approximating, "These fragments I have shored against my ruin." After the narrator contemplates the time "when the doors will close again," she says, "I try to write it down on little slips of paper, trying to preserve this time for myself." To this she adds, "it is hard to write it down so that it will mean anything. . . about how a woman feels who is going to have a child, or about how a pear tree feels bearing its fruit" (130). But the narrator's child creates a significant difference between the narrator and *The Waste Land*'s isolated people. Her child provides the reference point for a vision, however fleeting, of connectedness and meaning. Her child provides the hope but not the certainty of a future in which the narrator finds connection with at least one other human being.

Set against the background of *The Waste Land* on the one hand and Gold's version of proletarian literature on the other, "Annunciation" is an interesting experiment in form. Le Sueur opts neither for Eliot's stark juxtapositions nor for Gold's reductive realism. Instead she employs a flowing, circular lyric style that stands in contrast to the disconnectedness with which the story is concerned. Le Sueur leaves us with the question of whether the lyricism belies the disconnectedness or the disconnectedness belies the lyricism.

Because pregnancy, labor, the moment one's child is born, and nurturing a newborn are among life's most profound experiences, it is striking that they appear so rarely in literature.[10] One explanation for this silence is supplied by Hortense Calisher, who, in referring specifically to labor and delivery, also describes the experiences surrounding them: "Childbed is not a place or an event; it is merely what women do" (quoted by Olsen, *Silences* 230). "Annunciation" suggests the powerful, inexplicable bond between mother and unborn child, a bond at once common and singular in women's experience and yet almost entirely excluded from canonical literature. And "Annunciation"'s lush, sensual, evocative language is hardly the stuff of Gold's masculinist proletarian literature:

> I look at myself in the mirror. . . . My hips are full and tight in back as if bracing
> themselves. I look like a pale and shining pomegranate, hard and tight, and my
> skin shines like crystal with the veins showing beneath blue and distended. . . . I
> am a pomegranate hanging from an invisible tree with the juice and movement of
> seed within my hard skin. I dress slowly. I hate the smell of clothes. I want to leave
> them off and just hang in the sun ripening . . . ripening. (130)

Toward the end, the text almost sags under its own weight, the lush, natural
images becoming nearly excessive, overripe.

And yet we see an emerging "feminine" form—developed more self-consciously by Le Sueur half a century later in *Rites of Ancient Ripening* (1975), a
volume of poetry, and in *Memorial,* an experimental novel-in-progress—that may
account for what appears to be excess and repetition. Images move in circles—
the magnolia tree, pear tree, and landlady appearing, disappearing, and
reappearing, for example—as opposed to the linear progression Le Sueur associates with masculine form. The pear tree heavy with fruit becomes an analog for
the pregnant woman:

> The leaves twirl and twirl all over the tree, the delicately curving tinkling leaves. . . .
> Far below straight down the vertical stem like a stream, black and strong into the
> ground, runs the trunk; and invisible, spiraling downward and outward in powerful
> radiation, lie the roots. (131)

As Elaine Hedges notes, "Annunciation"'s multilayered style "communicates not
so much through conventional narrative form and causal sequences as through
the creation of a matrix of event, symbol, and meaning." Le Sueur intends this
style as the "antithesis of what she sees as the male style of linear movement
toward a 'target,' or a conclusion to be 'appropriated'" (251). However controversial the quest for a "feminine" expressive form may be, a relationship clearly
exists between "Annunciation" and Le Sueur's more recent work. Le Sueur's affiliation with the Party would not have encouraged such experimentation with
"feminine" form.

"Annunciation" has become a Le Sueur classic, a piece frequently reprinted. It
has been called "a small American masterpiece," as Hedges notes (75). It was
included in Edward O'Brien's *Best Short Stories of 1936* and more recently in *The
Norton Anthology of Literature by Women* (1985) and *The Heath Anthology of
American Literature* (1990). "I've never heard anything about how a woman feels
who is going to have a child," observes the story's narrator (130). At the time
Le Sueur wrote "Annunciation," pregnancy was considered unacceptable as a
literary subject, probably as much by *New Masses* as by the magazines that gave
that reason for rejecting her manuscript (*Scribner's* and *Atlantic Monthly*). Other
women writing "merely what women do" were similarly censored—for example,
male editors excised from Edith Summers Kelley's novel *Weeds* the portion
depicting childbirth ("Billy's Birth") when Harcourt Brace originally published the
novel in 1923; the Feminist Press restored the childbirth portion when it reprinted
the novel in 1982. As Annette Kolodny argues, such "female" literary subjects

did not lack merit but lacked a critical readership that could understand and appreciate them. Editors such as Le Sueur's—who were overwhelmingly male—did not question their ability to read; instead, they criticized women's ability to write.[11] A favorite Le Sueurian anecdote, with which I began this chapter, recalls her retort to the editor at *Scribner's* who, as he rejected "Annunciation," suggested she write more like Hemingway: But "fishin', fightin', and fuckin'," she quipped, "are not my major experiences" (interview). "Annunciation" similarly defies protocol.

"Corn Village" also examines Le Sueur's own experience in an evocative, prose-poem narrative. Le Sueur lived her "impressionable years" in Fort Scott, Kansas, but "corn village" is obviously intended to represent many Midwestern small towns that experience harsh winters. In the "underworld dusk of the phantom prairie world," the landscape is colorless and lifeless—all whites, grays, "emptiness and ghostliness" (13, 10). It is "as if some malignant power were in the air . . . the winter madness coming on, the winter death" (11). And yet the prairie winter embodies an eerie, powerful beauty: "the black, cold prairies, the shocks of corn desolate in the fields, the earth upturned in the cold sunlight, the smell of loam . . . and the wild embodied wind of the prairies like a presence among the fields" (11).

Like *The Girl*, "Our Fathers," and "Annunciation," "Corn Village"—in which sexual and emotional repression are the human equivalent of the barren, frozen landscape—challenges some of the tenets of American Victorianism and ascetic Protestantism that affected Le Sueur's family, the CP, and the capitalist order. "Corn Village" also subverts the us/them, aggressor/nurturer oppositions of biological determinism. Men and women alike are subject to the cruel weather and are victims of a repressive culture. "The Yankee woman nagging her men" is hardly depicted as inherently nurturing, and the description of Le Sueur's grandmother resembles that of the grandmother in "Our Fathers":

> . . . my grandmother never kissed us. She was embarrassed by any excess of feeling and had a way of turning down her lips bitterly. She had that acrid, bitter thing too about her body, a kind of sourness as if she had abandoned it. . . . She never took a bath except under her shift. . . .
>
> Pleasure of any kind was wicked, and she never lay down in the daytime even when she was dreadfully tired. It would have been a kind of licentiousness to her to have done so. (20–21)

In this rural community only the "foreigners" are "loose" and comfortable with their bodies, their sexuality. The Yankee bodies are awkward, "always ungiven, held taut for some unknown fray with the devil or the world or the flesh" (15). Like Penelope's (and Le Sueur's) grandmother, those at the church revival have no love song other than "Jesus, Lover of My Soul," and, as in "Our Fathers," the sexual and sensual repression horrifies Le Sueur. The "mystery of the slim tenuous Yankee body" has haunted her since adolescence (13).

Other "excessive" forms of expression are also taboo. Only the "foreign girl prostitutes" are allowed to wear bright, expressive colors, and communication among the townspeople, "untinged by humor," is "muffled and silent." The Yankee has "his will set on not caring, not thinking, not attending to life at all" (23, 17, 15). The Protestant ethic, coupled with the severity of conditions, has caused these struggling, joyless farmers to "put themselves aside," and in their relation to the land and to one another there hovers a "strange emptiness and fear that no one admits" (17, 13). Many, like Le Sueur, are closed, wary, emotionally deformed:

> Like many Americans, I will never recover from my sparse childhood in Kansas. The blackness, weight and terror of childhood in mid-America strike deep into the stem of life. Like desert flowers we learned to crouch near the earth, fearful that we would die before the rains, cunning, waiting the season of good growth. Those who survived without psychic mutilation have a life cunning, to keep the stem tight and spare, withholding the deep blossom, letting it sour rather than bloom and be blighted. (9)

First published by *Scribner's Magazine*, "Corn Village" appears in *Salute to Spring*, a collection of Le Sueur's work from the '30s issued by the CP's publishing organ, International Publishers (1949, 1977, 1979). But "Corn Village" has little in common with proletarian realism or reportage, although it does indirectly comment on them. In writing in 1930 about Midwest farmers, Le Sueur was not writing about workers considered by the Party during the Third Period to be the key to revolution; as noted above, the Party gave priority in this period to organizing efforts among workers in basic industry because of its assumed importance to the economy. Moreover, in "Corn Village" Le Sueur has consciously or unconsciously almost wholly discarded the Party discourse. "Official optimism" and its corollary, what I term "official certainty" ("we know that not pessimism, but revolutionary elan will sweep this mess out of the world forever") are noticeably absent from the text (Gold, "Notes" Sept., 5). Mystery, uncertainty, and fear prevail. "Corn Village" depicts the "terrifying beauty" of severe weather conditions, with "the sun leaving the earth and a terrible insecurity at the bottom of every man's soul." Even in mild weather few venture far onto the prairie, the source of "mysterious forces" (11, 15).

Eventually, however, the trees thaw and bud, the bleak sky turns "corn-blue," spring scatters tiny wildflowers, and "a mist of greening come[s] on the thickets" (24). The birds return from the south; delicate grasses, prairie dogs, and rabbits appear. Life, color, and warmth return to a region that the writer at once chooses not to leave and cannot escape. The story does not conclude, however, with the advent of spring, on some upbeat note discordant with the tenor of the piece as a whole. Rather, the concluding paragraphs resemble an Old Testament Psalm, the text strategically adopting the authority of Biblical language and addressing Kansas with the cadence, repetition, and humility of King David's meditations on God's mighty deeds. Kansas is God the Father—punishing, unfathomable, a presence not dependent on geography for its power. "I have come from you mysteriously wounded," Le Sueur laments. "I have waked from my adolescence to find a wound inflicted on the deep heart" (24). In "Corn Village," then, Le Sueur both critiques Christian myth and appropriates one of its forms for her own purposes.

In a letter to Neala Schleuning in 1976, Le Sueur acknowledged her conscious borrowing of Hebraic forms. At times, she says, she wrote "like a prophet, a conduit for the suffering of [her] people." And she compares her literary form to that of "Hebraic prophets who were educators, singers, warners and opened the bundles of grief" (cited in Schleuning, "Regionalism" 26).

Le Sueur prescribed in "The Fetish of Being Outside" (1935) how radicals create a literature of resistance; she held the same position as recently as August 1989, when I last interviewed her. Yet if we accept Wendell Berry's definition of regionalism as "local life aware of itself,"[12] "Corn Village" qualifies as an extraordinary piece of regionalist writing precisely *because* Le Sueur adopts the double consciousness and the "movement between complicity and critique" that "The Fetish of Being Outside" condemns as neither possible nor desirable for the radical writer. Le Sueur resides at once within the corn village culture and outside it, negotiating "difference and sameness, marginality and inclusion" with divided loyalty and consciousness (DuPlessis 43).

"Corn Village" is strikingly different, stylistically and thematically, from Le Sueur's consciously "proletarian" writing. Subverting the Party aesthetic, "Corn Village" prefigures Le Sueur's more recent quest for a new and feminine form. Like "Annunciation" it is less a short story than a prose-poem, a matrix of incident, image, and symbol. Narration is circular, not linear, with images of natural and emotional/sexual frigidity and barrenness appearing, disappearing, and reappearing. Yet Le Sueur's experiments with form in "Corn Village" show her attempting to reach her audience in a manner distinct from that of "Annunciation."

The story opens with this previously cited sentence: "Like many Americans, I will never recover from my sparse childhood in Kansas" (9). As in *The Girl* and "Annunciation," we encounter a first-person narrator, but there is a significant difference between this first-person narrator and those of the other two texts. The narrators of *The Girl* and "Annunciation" begin in a manner common in stories of first-person narration, tacitly marking a difference between us as listening audience and them as speaking storytellers simply by launching into their first-person narration. The first-person narrator of "Corn Village," however, begins by marking a sameness. The narrators of *The Girl* and "Annunciation" begin in a manner suggesting that they are primarily conscious of their own stories; the narrator of "Corn Village" begins in a manner suggesting that she is chiefly aware of how her story is the same as, or is "like," the story of "many Americans."

With this opening, Le Sueur has in effect asked many of us as audience: "Will you find this to be your story too?" Le Sueur has extended an unexpected invitation to join her and her narrator in negotiating sameness and difference. She has structured the story in such a way that to accept the invitation is to relinquish the role of a passive listening audience and to agree to work on filling out the story.

The story develops two events at length—a murder and a church revival—and the strange ways in which they enliven the town. These two events, apparently so different, are not so for the narrator. As she moves from the tale of the murder to the tale of the revival, the narrator offers this simple and abrupt transition: "Another violence—the revival" (20). For the narrator, the sameness in the difference of these tales is violence. Clearly, we as readers are challenged to inquire into and fill out this sameness in the two occurrences.

To draw us into exploring the sameness, Le Sueur structures the report of the seemingly separate incidents in parallel verb-tense shifts. Much of the report of each incident is in the past tense. But in each case the narrator slips into the present tense to complete the report, bringing her past story into the present. Moreover, Le Sueur uses the term "purging" to describe the murder's effect on the villagers, a word we would more likely associate with the revival's effect on participants. But a difference exists within the parallel structure. The past tense report of the revival includes a few subjunctive "woulds," giving us the sense that this is a report, not just of one revival, but of the sameness of all revivals the narrator has attended in her town. Thus, one difference in the sameness of the two incidents' violence is the implied repetition of the revival's violence.

Le Sueur demands that readers explore other matters in "Corn Village," and, as she has done with the subject of violence, she provides structural signposts for the exploring. "What does an American think about the land . . . ?" and what is "the meaning of people in the Midwest towns?" are questions that loom large in the story (12, 16). Le Sueur prods us to examine these matters by providing an interestingly structured demythification of an American dream about the Midwest and its people and a major critique of that dream.

The deconstruction of myths on which American culture had relied was no less a priority for Le Sueur than it was for leftist writers in general. In "Formal 'Education' in Writing" (1935) Le Sueur discusses these myths in terms of cultural "images" that are products of "old ideologies," asserting that the "university preserves with exquisite care the corpse of an old image whose spirit has long been dead." Noting that "when a first-rate writer manages to come out of the schools it is by miracle only," she argues that it is the job of the writer "to dynamically resist the habitual images and fetishes of his time and cut through the dying corpse with ruthless precision and create a *new* image, a new body of life" (208–209). The new image is to be associated with the "communal." Describing the rebirth of Midwestern literature in "Proletarian Literature and the Middle West" (1935), Le Sueur observes that "now the Middle Western mind is finding a place, sensing a new and vigorous interrelation between himself and others" (206). Thus far, her discussions of the need to deconstruct the cultural myths glorifying individualism and the replacement of those myths with images of collectivism ring in concert with Gold's brand of proletarian realism.

However, as Le Sueur turns to the question of what will replace the old myths, we begin to see discrepancies between her vision and Gold's. In *North Star Country* Le Sueur describes what must be observed if the people's myths are to be articulated: "The broken trail of the people must be followed by signs of myriad folk experiences in story, myth, legend, reflecting the struggle to survive." This trail is not direct; it wanders; it disappears and reappears. She notes, "The trail must be followed in the spore, in the blood stains and the marks of struggle: the desolation of tar-paper shanties, windows gaping still like the eyes of mad women who could not stand the solitude" (33–34). There is warning here that Gold's interest in "as few words as possible . . . clear form, the direct line" may not be suited to the forms of indirection Le Sueur finds necessary to generate the people's myths.

Further warning of essential disagreements with Gold appear when she describes the "communal bond" the new myths attempt to foster. In "Proletarian Literature and the Middle West" she characterizes that communal bond in terms of a "subjectivity" linking the people of "a rising class" (206–207). In "The Ancient People" Le Sueur characterizes that vital subjectivity in terms of the feminine, opposing it to the "linear movement" she associates with the masculine. Of the women sustaining her as she grew up, Le Sueur says, "they lived a subjective and parallel life, in long loneliness of the children, in a manless night among enemies" (23). Gold's direct, "manly" style is not appropriate for the "feminine" subjectivity that Le Sueur wants her work to express.

It is in her exploring of this deeply prized, if vaguely articulated, communal subjectivity that Le Sueur employs the poetic language condemned by the Party's orthodox critics, the uses of language Le Sueur describes when she says, "I fought them [the Party critics]. I kept my lyrical style" (interview). The "new image" with which Le Sueur replaced the old was often a new communal myth sometimes pervaded by a brooding subjectivity and spirituality far removed from the "elan" Gold believed would sweep away the mess of capitalism.

For Le Sueur, demythifying and remythifying is a process of exposing meaninglessness and re-establishing meaning. While she never fully articulates her concept of "meaning," allowing it, along with her concept of "subjectivity," to remain vague, it is possible to derive from her various texts one central characteristic of her notion of "meaning." As for Bakhtin, for Le Sueur the problem of meaning is linked to the struggle between bourgeois individualism and communal ways of life. Meaning for Le Sueur does not lie in individual entities; it resides in relationships among entities. The process of demythification and remythification is an exploring of what prevents and what enables the interconnectedness on which the production of meaning depends.

In "Corn Village" Le Sueur's first task in demythification is to chip away at the traditional image of Lincoln as the man closely identified with the Illinois plains.

> Remember the sadness and innate depression of Lincoln as symbolic. He was naturally a lover, but he never loved the land, though he walked miles over it, slept and lived on it, and buried the bodies of those he loved in it; and yet he was never struck with the poetry and passion that makes a man secure upon his land, there was always instead this convulsion of anxiety, this fear. (12)

The narrator compares the body of the farmer, Simonson, to the body of Lincoln. "Lincoln too had this—the loose frame, the slight droop, the acrid, bitter power and tenuosity, the sense of hanging on in bad seasons, of despondency from lack of nourishment, that well-known Yankee form and the mystery of it" (14). But clearly her concern is not simply with the "form" of the body, but also the character, the "meaning" joined with that form and how that character connects with other characters. As she continues what began as a comment on Lincoln's body, the narrator shifts her commentary, "and the sudden tenacious sentimental sympathies, that would start wars for quixotic idealisms, provoke assassins' bullets and leave a wife embittered and maddened a little, left out always, never wholly warmed at that breast, the flesh never really warm and hanging from the tree of life, always a little acrid and ghostly, and the tenderness not enough to warm" (14). In this passage Le Sueur returns Lincoln from the level of myth to the plane of human mystery, to a husband in relation to his wife.

The demythifying of Lincoln invites us to view Lincoln and other American myths and "heroes" in terms of some kind of "realism," but what sort of "realism"? Could it be the proletarian realism of Gold? Could it be more sophisticated versions of realism being explored by other American leftist writers in the '20s and '30s? Here the story, in a section that parallels the demythifying of Lincoln, takes a forceful turn. "I am baffled to know the meaning of people in the Midwest towns. Lewis has not been right. He has portrayed their grimaces, a seeming reality, but still only their faces in a mirror. Anderson of course has apprehended them with love, but that too has left out a great deal" (16). This critique of leftist writers who engage in forms of realism to do, in part, the very kind of work Le Sueur has done in demythifying Lincoln, stands as an assertion that neither the myth nor the current Left literary attempts to find forms of realism that will counter the myth have got it right. Further, the demythifying of Lincoln and of the demythifiers of Lincoln and other American dreams assigns us as readers the very active role of thinking anew about the land and the people.

In this section of the story another pattern emerges. Those who have been demythified and critiqued are men—Lincoln, Lewis, Anderson. By withholding identification of the narrator's gender and by including a reference to "the Yankee woman nagging her men," Le Sueur is careful not to suggest that Corn Village's emptiness and fear is solely a man's world or simply caused by men (13). However, she does suggest that the realm of American dream and myth is male dominated, and, more important, that a male-dominated critique of that realm will not get the job done.

The question of why a male-dominated critique is insufficient returns us to matters of "form" with which the narrator was so concerned in demythifying Lincoln: "the slim tenuous Yankee body, hard and gawky like a boy's, never getting any man suavity in it, but hard and bitter and stubborn, always lanky and illnourished, surviving bitterly" (13). This "form" is akin to the literary form called for by Gold in his claims for proletarian realism. But what Gold identifies as a manly style, Le Sueur here suggests is more a boyish style, lacking "man suavity." Insofar as Gold's proletarian realism and other more sophisticated versions of re-

alism have confined themselves to the hard and slender manly style, they have—
in their attempts to "know the meaning of the people" and what they think about
the land—"not been right"; they have "left out a great deal."

Le Sueur's journals contain cryptic references to leftist male writers' limitations. In one entry she notes, "Sandburg—why didn't he say enough? Anderson,
where are you? They peter out, sort of, as if they were not men enough, as if they
did not grow up men enough." As she explores the kind of writing she wants, she
rejects "the smart young boy writers," saying, "let us be warm and vital" and "now
I am warm, let me be myself always a woman" (vol. 7, 1933, 154). In another
entry Le Sueur muses on the "sense" required for America to discover its own
culture: "Perhaps at first it must be a woman sense. The men with their little
narrow bodies go hard and bitter like Faulkner and Jeffers. . . . Perhaps only a
woman can give America birth" (vol. 7, 1933, 110). The same year she notes:
"Dos Passos—the man speech. We need too the woman speech. I would like to
say the woman speech" (vol. 7, 1933, 112).

In addition to the previously mentioned "What does an American think about
the land?" "Corn Village" poses the following questions:

> . . . what dreams come from the sight of it [the land], what painful dreaming? Are
> they only money dreams, power dreams? Is that why the land lies desolate like a
> loved woman who has been forgotten? Has she been misused through dreams of
> power and conquest? (12)

Surely capitalist ideology cannot properly engage these questions, but do the
available versions of leftist realism adequately do so? Male writers and their manly
style may not be able to prevent the situation of the "forgotten woman" simile
around which the last two questions are structured.

What then are the forms Le Sueur offers in "Corn Village" as alternatives to
the constraints of realism's manly style? As we have seen, one answer Le Sueur
provides is "myth." At the end of the story, in the tribute to Kansas (referred to as
being "like a strong raped virgin"), the narrator says, "And the mind scurrying like
a rabbit trying to get into your meaning, making things up about you, trying to
get you alive with significance and myth" (24). Prominent among the characteristics of this myth concerned with meaning and significance are the connections
and relationships with which she is concerned in "Annunciation." Elements of
the Kansas landscape provide natural connections: "I know all your little trees. I
have watched them thaw and bud and the pools of winter frozen over, the silos
and the corn-blue sky, the wagon-tracked road with the prints of hoofs" (24). The
landscape's elements connect, in turn, first to one person—the narrator—and
then to other people: "I have come from you mysteriously wounded, I have
waked from my adolescence to find a wound inflicted on the deep heart. And
have seen it in others too, in disabled men and sour women made ugly by ambition, mortified in the flesh and wounded in love" (24–25). As in "Annunciation," the natural world offers human beings potential for connections, but
here those connections result in a common "wound."

As in "Annunciation," we must raise the question of whether the people see the range of potential connections among themselves. The answer in "Corn Village" is not simple. Corn Village, seemingly without life at the moment of the murder, is brought to life by the event. As the people react to the situation, "The town is woven in this lovely dream. . . . Love awakens in the town. Every one is drawn into the great warp of myth" (19). After the revival, the night is "sweeter than a nut, at last with the stars now with meaning, the town now close and beloved, broken open with love, and all the rich juices flowing out as from some ripe sweet fruit" (23). Unfortunately, when the murder and revival have passed, "the lethargy looms again, everything closes up, the streets are as they were before." The townspeople resume their lives as isolated workers ("become again only traders, movers, buyers, sellers, farmers") rather than sustaining a sense of community (20). The people return to their individual lives of "ambition," connected to each other only by the common "wound."

What seems the near perversity of generating myth out of two acts of violence is similar to "breeding/Lilacs out of the dead land." However, a major difference exists between Eliot's modernist myth-production and Le Sueur's myth-production. While *The Waste Land* stands as relentless testimony to the fragmenting of meaning, the myth in "Corn Village," though quickly forgotten, draws people temporarily out of their individuality into a communal group.

Le Sueur sets her own approach to demythifying conventional American myths in contrast to the available approaches of realism. Insofar as realism relies on the principle of reducing myth to hard reality, it leaves things out, it misses much of the meaning. An alternative to demythifying the American dream, Le Sueur's approach in "Corn Village" is to demythify it and then remythify it. Le Sueur has not replaced myth with reality. She has replaced the abstract and hollow American myth, like that surrounding Lincoln's life, with "ordinary" Midwesterners' myths and dreams.

Le Sueur is intent on portraying the mysterious and sometimes surprising connections between the difficult lives of "ordinary" people and the dreams they manage to dream. Again, both of "Corn Village"'s dream-like, myth-like states have been generated by forms of "violence." Is Le Sueur commenting on the source of the myths and the dreams? Certainly. But she is also observing the stubborn fact that the dreams and myths continue to be generated, even out of the most unlikely circumstances. We cannot rest comfortably with the dreams that emerge out of the forms of violence in the story. But these are not the only possibilities. The greater possibility lies in what we have observed the narrator doing, her continuing to search for myths and dreams that yield meaning. And our minds are invited to join in the narrator's activity: "And the mind scurrying like a rabbit trying to get into your [Kansas's] meaning, making things up about you, trying to get you alive with significance and myth" (24).

As in "Annunciation," in "Corn Village" Le Sueur relies on some "bourgeois" lyrical forms to explore myths and dreams. As in "Annunciation," Le Sueur sometimes uses animation devices to weave human beings and the natural world into a web of lyricism. The narrator of "Corn Village" says, "I was born on these prairies while the land was lying low in this mid-winter solstice, lying low like this and dreaming" (12). Here the land, no less than the narrator, seems bent on the quest for dreams. As in "Annunciation," romantic similes appear: "the town, now close and beloved, broken open with love, and all the rich juices flowing out as from some ripe sweet fruit" (23).

Le Sueur's experiments with and borrowings from "bourgeois" forms in *The Girl*, "Our Fathers," "Annunciation," and "Corn Village" clearly indicate that Le Sueur was at once repudiating reductively simplistic plans for proletarian realism and complicating her own simplistic views in "The Fetish of Being Outside." "Corn Village"'s conclusion is exemplary. It must be viewed as one significant moment in Le Sueur's search for "feminine" forms that will stand as alternatives to reductive forms of proletarian realism and to a "manly" style. In concert with Trotsky's view of revolutionary art, the conclusion shows us that the search for "feminine" forms should not disregard the enormous legacy of bourgeois art's tradition. It should be a search for old forms out of which new meaning can be produced.

The concluding address to Kansas has such forms. It is at once a psalm-like structure, singing praise and love, and an address to the muse (Kansas) on whom the mythic-minded poet depends not only for inspiration, but for life itself.

> I have seen your beauty and your terror and your evil.
>
> I have come from you mysteriously wounded. I have waked from my adolescence to find a wound inflicted on the deep heart. And have seen it in others too, in disabled men and sour women made ugly by ambition, mortified in the flesh and wounded in love.
>
> Not going to Paris or Morocco or Venice, instead staying with you, trying to be in love with you, bent upon understanding you, bringing you to life. For your life is my life and your death is mine also. (24–25)

Le Sueur has demythified the raped land and its people, accomplishing what proletarian realism would have writers do. However, she has decisively parted company with proletarian realism in her experiments with traditional forms and in her search for "feminine" forms that will give new life and meaning to the land and its people through their remythification.

"Corn Village" is not constrained by the limited understanding of ideology that characterizes much of proletarian realism and reportage. For example, in "I Was Marching," ideology is merely a superstructure produced by an economic base, a false consciousness obscuring society's "real" structures. In contrast, ideology pervades this text, prefiguring ideology's more recent definition (cited in Chapter 3) as "the way in which the individual actively lives his or her role within the social totality" (Coward and Ellis 67). "Corn Village" supports Gramsci's notion of dominance and subordination as a "whole lived social process" saturating even the most private areas of our lives and consciousness. "Corn Village" acknowledges the complexity of "the people," who were sometimes romanticized in Party—and in Le Sueur's own—discourse.

"Corn Village" seems as authentic as it does, I suspect, largely because it examines Le Sueur's own experience. She chronicled the lives of other oppressed people sometimes at the expense of exploring her own oppression as a middle-class woman. "I don't know how to write about women. I feel I have to learn to write a final book about myself as a woman," Le Sueur told me, even though she has been writing about women for over 80 years, ever since she first recorded bits of conversation while hiding under the quilting frame as a 10-year old (interview). As noted elsewhere, Le Sueur has "even lied about" her life, softening its "brutality" (interview). Yet we sense that in "Corn Village" Le Sueur's untold story begins to emerge.

Le Sueur's motives for adopting the working class as her literary milieu were overdetermined: Surely a strong sense of justice and collective responsibility sparked her concern; she also disliked the strains of ennui, nihilism, and self-absorption in twentieth-century American literature; and she was influenced by the Party's focus during the Third Period on the proletariat as the key to overturning capitalism and by its contradictory attitudes toward women. Many CP leaders as well as many of the rank-and-file did not consider middle-class women oppressed; when they spoke of the "woman problem," they meant "the toiling women and the wives of the toilers" (Shaffer 88). Perhaps we should also consider Le Sueur's adopting the working class as partly an act of displacement. As discussed in Chapter 3, Le Sueur's journals reveal her courageous, life-long struggle against a deep sense of melancholia and even despair, and her own internal coping mechanisms may have made it difficult for her to write for publication about her own fear, anger, doubt, defeat.

It is instructive here to draw a parallel between Le Sueur and Rebecca Harding Davis, the author of an early American working-class novel, *Life in the Iron Mills* (1861), which I discuss in more detail in Chapter 7. Davis's sympathy for the mill workers depicted in her novel was the result of her own circumscribed life as a woman, albeit of the middle class. Davis used the working class safely to protest her own oppression, partly displacing a latent feminist voice. History may have precluded Davis's even conceiving of human relation as undefined by gender and class hierarchies, whereas Le Sueur was born generations later into a radical milieu that encouraged her to question such hierarchies. However, responding to pressure from various sources, Le Sueur, like Davis, has not fully confronted the cruelty of her own life. Adopting the personae and subject matter of the working class (and Native Americans, in the case of *Rites of Ancient Ripening*) to an extent relieved Le Sueur of that burden—at some cost, perhaps, to her readers. As a whole, Le Sueur's work contributes to American literature and social history a valuable record of people whose lives have rarely been chronicled. Yet in pieces such as "Our Fathers," "Annunciation," and "Corn Village," a different Meridel Le Sueur emerges, moving toward the oracular voice she sought but did not achieve in her reportage.

We can understand why demarcations seemed clear in the midst of the sharpening class struggle that accompanied the economic crisis in the '30s. However, we must move beyond '30s Marxist assumptions about working-class literature that place a resistance culture in binary opposition to bourgeois culture. Leftist criticism must try to account for the conscious and unconscious movement of working-class writing "between complicity and critique" and view working-class writing relationally, gauging which of its forms oppose, which strategically adopt, and which unconsciously borrow the forms of "high" and mass culture.[13] Working-class literature is, at best, a subspecies of bourgeois literature, just as any culture of resistance remains, for the historical moment, a subspecies of bourgeois culture.

As we have seen, some of Le Sueur's own texts subvert the reductive opposition she established in "The Fetish of Being Outside" and support a more contemporary view of how we might usefully approach elements of a resistance culture. In "Our Fathers," "Annunciation," and "Corn Village" we see that discourse lives, to borrow Bakhtin's language, "on the boundary between its own context and another, alien, context" (*Dialogic* 284). As Bakhtin indicates, it is at such boundaries that individuals and cultures can gain identity only by becoming entangled in "others."

FIVE

Tillie Olsen:
Biographical Sketch and
Thirties' Publications

We knew about Dachau very early, we knew about the concentration camps, the Left press was full of it. . . . It made my kind of book [*Yonnondio*] more and more difficult to write. . . . You remember how people felt after Allende? You remember how people felt after things were not ending in Vietnam, and you were so *personally* identified with it? . . . It was so much of one's being. . . . You lived with it in every room of your house . . . in every conversation whether it came up or not. It was a living, actual presence and force. We had that kind of consciousness [during the '30s], so many of us. . . . [it] made other concerns seem trivial by comparison.

Tillie Olsen, during an interview with Deborah Rosenfelt, 1980

Time on the bus, even when I had to stand, was enough; the stolen moments at work, enough; the deep night hours for as long as I could stay awake, after the kids were in bed, after the household tasks were done, sometimes during. It is no accident that the first work I considered publishable began: "I stand here ironing, and what you asked me moves tormented back and forth with the iron."

Tillie Olsen, from *Silences*

This chapter has three sections. The first sketches Tillie Olsen's biography. The second places Olsen in the context of the '30s Communist Party, extending the background provided by Chapters 1 and 2. The third discusses her publications from the '30s, which all appeared in 1934, when she was only 21. (Because it later became part of *Yonnondio*, "The Iron Throat," published as a short story in 1934, is discussed in Chapter 5.) Olsen's 1934 publications—"I Want You Women Up North to Know," "There Is a Lesson," "Thousand-Dollar Vagrant," and "The Strike"—to an extent resemble Le Sueur's reportage. Whereas the content is culturally and politically agitational, the discursive model has been borrowed from dominant modes of representation, although Olsen does modify those modes more than Le Sueur. These texts foreground the *message* rather than the *production* of meaning, although these two categories are less distinct than orthodox '30s Marxists believed. Frankly tendentious, Olsen's early '30s texts are marked by closure—that is, a restricting of meaning potentially available from the text. Like "Women on the Breadlines" and "I Was Marching," Olsen's writing during this period was intended to spark political resistance once the reader "experienced" the reported conditions or event. At the same time, however, its didacticism, like that of Le Sueur's more tendentious writing, actually limits involvement by undercutting the reader's role as an active producer of meaning.

Tillie Olsen's parents, Samuel and Ida Lerner, who were never formally married, were Jewish immigrants. They participated in the abortive 1905 Russian revolution, and, after Samuel escaped from a Czarist prison, fled to the United States. They settled first on a Nebraska farm; when it failed about five years later, they moved to Omaha. Despite laboring long hours as a farmer, packinghouse worker, painter, and paperhanger, Samuel Lerner became State Secretary of the Nebraska Socialist Party and ran in the mid-twenties as the socialist candidate for state representative from his district (Rosenfelt, "Thirties" 375). Ida Lerner, who was illiterate until her twenties, was one of the people who inspired the highly acclaimed "Tell Me a Riddle." The strong bonds she had with her mother, Olsen has said, "are part of what made me a revolutionary writer" (Rosenfelt interview). Olsen's conviction that capitalism blights human development, which she has often expressed in relation to the enormous potential evinced by young children, originated in the painful witnessing of her mother's deformation.

> If you [could see] my mother's handwriting, [in] one of the few letters she ever wrote me . . . she could not spell, she could scarcely express herself, she did not have written language. Yet she was one of the most eloquent and one of the most brilliant . . . human beings I've ever known, and I've encountered a variety of human beings in recent years, some of whom have a lot of standing in the world. (interview)

When Olsen was 11 or 12, Ida Lerner wrote the following letter to her English instructor:

> *2512 Caldwell Street*
> *Omaha, Nebraska*
> *December 10, 1924*

Dear Teacher:

> I am glad to study with ardor but the children wont let me, they go to bed late so it makes me tired, and I cant do my lessons. It is after ten o'clock my head dont work it likes to have rest. But I am in a sad mood I am sitting in the warm house and feel painfull that winter claps in to my heart. I see the old destroyed houses of the people from the old country. I hear the wind blow through them with the

disgusting cry why the poor creatures ignore him, dont protest against him, that souless wind dont no, that they are helples have no material to repair the houses and no clothes to cover up their bodies, and so the sharp wind echo cry falls on the window, and the windows original sing with silver-ball tears seeing all the poor shivering creatures dressed in rags with frozen fingers and feverish hungry eyes.

It is told of the olden days, the people of that time were building a tower, when they were on the point of success for some reason they stopped to understand each other and on account of misunderstanding, their hopes and very lives were buried under the tower they had built. So as a human being who carries responsibility for action I think as a duty to the community we shall try to understand each other. This English class helps us to understand each other, not to feel helpless between our neighbors, serves to get more respect from the people around us. We are human beings trying to understand, we learn about the world, people and our surroundings. This class teaches us to understand each other and brings better order in the every day life of the community.

IDA LERNER[1]

Moreover, Ida Lerner "was very conscious of the situation of women." Olsen remembers in particular a photograph of a statue—featuring a woman on all fours with an infant "chained" to her breast—that her mother had clipped from a leftist journal (interview).[2]

In her adult life, Olsen saw her mother only three times. They were separated by a continent, "by lack of means," and by Olsen's jobs and responsibility to her own children. Ida Lerner, who "had no worldly goods to leave," nevertheless left her daughter "an inexhaustible legacy," Olsen writes, a "heritage of summoning resources to make—out of song, food, warmth, expressions of human love—courage, hope, resistance, belief; this vision of universality, before the lessenings, harms, divisions of the world are visited upon it" (*Mother* 263–264).

Olsen's birth was not recorded, although she has determined that she was born either near Mead or in Omaha, Nebraska, in either 1912 or 1913 (however, her father once declared: "You was born in Wahoo, Nebraska" [interview]). Olsen has compared the harsh conditions on their Nebraska farm to those depicted in the film *Heartland*, which was based on letters written by a turn-of-the-century woman homesteader, concluding, "It's difficult to conceive how hard those women worked" (interview).[3] In her family, as she reported to Erika Duncan, "economic struggle was constant. There was never a time when she was not doing something 'to help the family out economically.'" As a 10-year-old, for example, Olsen had to work shelling peanuts after school (209).

But the political commitment and activism of her socialist parents provided a rich dimension to her upbringing. "It was a rich childhood from the standpoint of ideas," she insists (quoted in Duncan 209). Like Le Sueur, Olsen was profoundly influenced at an early age by the message and the rhetorical skills of socialist orators, some of whom stayed in her home while attending meetings in Omaha (Duncan 209). Like Le Sueur, Olsen particularly remembers admiring Eugene Debs. Both writers recall their excitement as children when Debs gave them affection and when they were chosen to present him with red roses at one of his speaking engagements.

The second oldest of six children, Olsen was burdened with the care of younger siblings, and "she remembers from an early age that sense of never having enough time" and solitude that "has haunted her most of her life, that sense of most women and her own mother feeling starved for time" (Duncan 210). It was only because she was often sick that she had any opportunity to read, although her parents could not afford to buy books (Olsen first saw a home library when, as a teenager, she worked for a Radcliffe graduate) (Rosenfelt interview). But she read "old revolutionary pamphlets" and journals she found lying "around the house," including *The Liberator*, a socialist journal of art and politics edited by Max Eastman; *The Comrade*, which published international revolutionary literature; and *Modern Quarterly*, a nonsectarian Marxist journal that "denied the distinction between intellectual and worker and between pure art and propaganda" (Rosenfelt, "Thirties" 376–377; Duncan 209; Aaron 323). *The Cry for Justice: An Anthology of Social Protest* (1915), edited by Upton Sinclair and introduced by Jack London, also influenced Olsen as a child. And she had access to the Haldeman-Julius little Blue Books, which were published in Girard, Kansas, in the teens and '20s on the premise that "all the culture of the past . . . is the worker's heritage" (interview). Designed to fit into a worker's shirt pocket, the five-cent Blue Books introduced Olsen to modern poetry and to established writers such as Thomas Hardy, who became a lifelong favorite. Novels by South African feminist Olive Schreiner, *Story of an African Farm* and *Dreams*, also influenced Olsen. Determined to read all the fiction in the Omaha Public Library, she would pick up a book, read a few pages, and, if she did not like it, move on to the next (interview; Duncan 210–211).

Olsen was one of few in her working-class neighborhood to "cross the tracks" to attend an academic high school, where an exceptional teacher introduced her to Shakespeare, De Quincey, Coleridge, and Edna St. Vincent Millay and made sure she was present when Carl Sandburg came to Omaha to read his work. Olsen avidly read *Poetry*, a journal edited by Harriet Monroe that was available in the school library. Although the high school stimulated Olsen intellectually, it "crucified her socially, setting up 'hidden injuries of class'" (Duncan 210). The necessity to work forced her to drop out of school after the eleventh grade, although she is careful to remind interviewers that few women in her generation enjoyed even that much educational opportunity.

Olsen stuttered as a child, something she considers "part of [her] luck" because the peculiar quality of her own speech made her curious about the "intoxicating richness" of other speech patterns: "Just the music, the varieties . . . of speaking . . . all had a magical tone" (quoted in Turan 56). Listening attentively to immigrants who had to be creative with limited vocabularies, she developed a keen ear for various dialects of "non-standard" English, a skill she later used in her writing. Yet Olsen found that "not only the speech but so much of the human beings around me was not in literature. Whitman's indictment of the aristocratic bias of literature was still true: Most of the people who wrote books came from the privileged classes." She became "incited to literature," she says, adding that the "factor which gave me confidence was that *I* had something to contribute, *I* had something which wasn't in there yet" (quoted in Turan 56).

Olsen became politically active in her mid-teens as a writer of skits and musicals for the Young Socialist League. In 1931, at 18, she joined the Young Communist League (YCL), the CP youth organization, and the next 18 months were a period of intense political activity. She attended the Party school for several weeks in Kansas City, where she helped support unemployed comrades by working in a tie factory. During this period Olsen was jailed for a month for distributing leaflets to packinghouse workers and, while in prison, was beaten up by one inmate for attempting to help another. She was already sick with pleurisy, probably contracted as a result of the tie factory's poor ventilation. Her station was next to both the factory's only open window and one of its few steam radiators; "I got overheated and 'overcold' all the time," Olsen explains (Rosenfelt interview). In jail she became extremely ill, and the Party sent her back to Omaha to recuperate.

Olsen moved to Faribault, Minnesota, early in 1932, a period of retreat from political work and wage-earning to allow for her recovery. She thinks of her illness, which had developed into incipient tuberculosis, as a blessing. As a result of it she was bedridden, and since she could not be politically active and was "in every way taken care of," something women of her class rarely experience, she was free to write (Rosenfelt interview). While in Faribault she began to write *Yonnondio* and completed its first three chapters fairly quickly. She became pregnant, however, in the same month that she started writing and bore a daughter, Karla, at nineteen. Olsen does not enjoy discussing her personal life between 1932 and 1935; even the weary tone of her voice suggests that it was a stressful period, financially and emotionally. "We were terribly, terribly poor," she has said. "When you [couldn't] pay your rent you just moved." The pregnancy had been unplanned. She had a "rough time of it," living only sporadically with Karla's father, who "left several times."[4]

The reception of "The Iron Throat," a short story published (and titled) by *Partisan Review* (April–May 1934), is especially relevant to Olsen's biography. When Robert Cantwell described his survey of 200 stories in 50 literary magazines (*The New Republic*, 25 July 1934), he singled out "The Iron Throat" as the best among them, "a work of early genius."[5] In a letter published in *The New Republic* on August 22, 1934, Cantwell drew even more attention to Tillie Lerner, who for some months had been submerged in the politics surrounding the Maritime Strike. Cantwell recounts that after his July 25 article appeared, the editors of two publishing houses wired him asking for help in locating Tillie Lerner. They had read "The Iron Throat" when it first appeared in *Partisan Review* and had tried to locate the author, but their letters and telegrams had been returned. "There was, however, a good reason why the publishers who wanted to see Tillie Lerner's unfinished novel had trouble reaching her," Cantwell explains in his letter.

> She was in jail. . . . [And] meanwhile, two more publishers and a literary agent were trying to locate her in order to see about publishing her novel. . . . I mention this because I now feel that in my article I minimized the difficulties that impede the progress of the young writers. To the difficulties of finding hospitable publishers must now be added the problem of dodging the police. (49)

"The Iron Throat"'s literary promise and the publicity resulting from her arrest caused Olsen to be "discovered," in her word, and she signed a contract with Macmillan. But Bennett Cerf and Donald Klopfer, founders of Modern Library and Random House, were so impressed with "The Iron Throat" that they negotiated with Macmillan to get her released from that contract. She then signed with Random House, which offered her a monthly stipend in return for completing a chapter every month. In 1935 she sent two-year-old Karla to live with her parents and moved to Los Angeles to write. However, she felt uncomfortable in Hollywood Left circles, where as a bona-fide member of the working class, she was "considered a curiosity," although she was befriended by screenwriter Marian Ainslee and enjoyed literary discussions with Tess Slesinger (Duncan 212; Rosenfelt interview). Unhappy at being separated from "her own kind of people," she occasionally traveled to several California towns for three- or four-day periods to help organize farm workers (Martin 10). The separation from Karla affected her most of all. In 1936, although she "felt like a terrible failure" for not having finished the novel, she forfeited her contract, moved back to San Francisco, and brought Karla home. Nearly 40 years later, examining *Yonnondio*'s "rough drafts and trying to figure out where she was when she wrote them," Olsen "realized that most of her best writing was done" after her reunion with her daughter (Duncan 212–213).

In 1936 Tillie Lerner began to live with her YCL comrade, Jack Olsen (with whom she had been arrested in 1934); they married in 1944, just before Jack entered the military (Orr 38, n36). Tillie had three more daughters—Julie, Kathie, and Laurie.[6] Between 1936 and 1959 she worked at a variety of jobs—waitress, shaker in a laundry, transcriber in a dairy equipment company, capper of mayonnaise jars, secretary, and "Kelly Girl"—and, against tremendous odds, tried to keep her writing alive.

She copied passages from books she could not afford to buy and tacked them on the wall by the kitchen sink for inspiration. She seized every moment she could:

> Time on the bus, even when I had to stand, was enough; the stolen moments at work, enough; the deep night hours for as long as I could stay awake, after the kids were in bed, after the household tasks were done, sometimes during. It is no accident that the first work I considered publishable began: "I stand here ironing, and what you asked me moves tormented back and forth with the iron." (*Silences* 19)

When the demands of Olsen's life—which included wage-earning, mothering, political activism, housework, and writing—resulted in her "having to give primacy to one part of her being at the expense of another," the children came first

(Rosenfelt, "Thirties" 380). *Silences* memorably records Olsen's experience and that of many mothers:

> More than in any other human relationship, overwhelmingly more, motherhood means being instantly interruptable, responsive, responsible. Children need one *now* (and remember, in our society, the family must often try to be the center for love and health the outside world is not). The very fact that these are real needs, that one feels them as one's own (love, not duty); *that there is no one else responsible for these needs*, gives them primacy. It is distraction, not meditation, that becomes habitual; interruption, not continuity; spasmodic, not constant toil. . . . Work interrupted, deferred, relinquished, makes blockage—at best, lesser accomplishment. Unused capacities atrophy, cease to be. (*Silences* 18–19)

When Olsen learned she was pregnant with her second child she made an appointment with an abortionist and then, at the last minute, walked out of his office. After Julie's birth, Olsen reports, she gave up her thwarted attempts to complete *Yonnondio*; although she had "fragments for another 70 pages of the novel," she had to go to work "typing income tax forms" (interview). Only her last pregnancy was "voluntary" (Rosenfelt interview).

Yet Olsen insists that the demands of mothering four children did not fracture her selfhood. Being female and an artist are complementary, not contradictory, she believes. Certainly a woman's experience is not antithetical to art, despite the view expressed by Le Sueur's editor at *Scribner's* who rejected "Annunciation" for its "ersatz" subject matter, and Olsen's texts provide ample evidence that parenting richly fed her writing. However, since writing requires time and solitude, the practical question arises: Why did Olsen have as many as four children when she had the ambition and talent "to be a great writer" (Rosenfelt interview)? The answer lies partly in Olsen's firm belief that motherhood is not only the "*core* of women's oppression" but an extraordinary source of "transport" for women as well (*Silences* 202). Children and art "are different aspects of your being," she told me. "There is . . . no separation." A life combining meaningful work and motherhood "could and should be" possible for women (interview).

Silences acknowledges that "the maintenance of life" (34)—an activity not limited to mothers but including all who in myriad ways attend to caring for others—is often an impediment to literary productivity. Significantly, however, *Silences* also expresses Olsen's hope that a "complex new richness will come into literature" as "more and more women writers . . . assum[e] as their right fullness of work *and* family life" (32). Reeva Olsen,[7] who was married for many years to a brother of Jack Olsen and who has been close to Jack and Tillie for over 50 years, indirectly spoke to this issue of "the maintenance of life" as both an impediment and a benefit to writing. She acknowledged that Tillie's "involvement with people and with her children and with family . . . has, in many ways, kept her from writing." On the other hand, Reeva added, Olsen's experiences "with people are what have made her the kind of writer she is. I don't think that she could have written the way she does sitting up in some ivory tower," removed from her characteristically "deep, deep involvement" with others (interview).

During the '30s and '40s Olsen was aware of "a real difference between [writers] who were 'rank-and-file,' so to speak, involved in struggles right around us," and those who considered themselves cultural activists, were in some instances funded by the Federal Writers' Project, and had the mobility to visit other countries to report on events (interview).[8] This second category, although dominated by men, included such women as Josephine Herbst, Anna Louise Strong, and Agnes Smedley. Largely because of her children Olsen could not make her writing her activism, as these childless women did, and writing could not be counted on to provide the steady income Olsen's family required. Moreover, the jobs Olsen took to support her children led naturally to a different form of political activism, union organizing, which in turn affected her daily life in positive, practical, and immediate ways—with higher wages, better working conditions, and more control of the workplace. As a parent, Olsen also became increasingly involved in educational issues and in the activities related to the particular schools her children attended.

Class was also a barrier to Olsen's becoming a full-time writer during the '30s. As noted above, during her stay in Los Angeles from 1934–36, Olsen had felt awkward around the sophisticated Hollywood Left (or "the cocktail set," as she put it[9]) and unhappy separated from "her own kind of people." She felt similarly out of place in what she terms the "Carmel crowd" of writers, to whom she was introduced when Lincoln Steffens and Ella Winter invited her to their home after her release from jail in 1934. Although Olsen was attracting a lot of attention at this time (as noted above), she did not feel at home in urbane literary circles. She has asked herself why she "didn't move heaven and earth to become part of that [writers'] world," since it was her ambition at that time "to be a great writer," and remembers feeling "an intimidation and wonder," based not only on gender but also on her class and "first-generation" background (Rosenfelt interview).

Class identification in a positive sense also contributed to Olsen's choosing a rank-and-file existence over a "literary" life. Olsen's comments in 1980 about her working-class comrades suggest both the depth of her loyalty to them and how different from them she sometimes felt because she aspired to be a writer:

> They were my dearest friends, but how could they know what so much of my writing self was about? They thought of writing in the terms in which they knew it. They had become readers, like so many working class kids in the movement, but there was so much that fed me as far as my medium was concerned that was closed to them. They read the way women read today coming into the women's movement who don't have literary background—reading for what it says about their lives, or what it doesn't say. And they loved certain writings because of truths, understandings, affirmations, that they found in them. . . . It was not a time that my writing self could be first. . . . We believed that we were going to change the world, and it looked as if it was possible. It was just after Hindenburg turned over power to Hitler—and the enormity of the struggle demanded to stop what might result from that was just beginning to be evident. . . . And I did so love my comrades. They were all blossoming so. These were the same kind of people I'd gone to school with, who had quit, as was common in my generation, around the eighth

grade. . . . whose development had seemed stopped, though I had known such in-herent capacity in them. Now I was seeing that evidence, verification of what was latent in the working class. It's hard to leave something like that. (quoted in Rosen-felt, "Thirties" 383)

Clearly Olsen did not share the problem of the enlightened middle-class writer who, like Meridel Le Sueur, contemplated in the '30s how best to identify with the working class. Hers was a different dilemma: Whereas our social system defines Olsen's intellectual and professional aspirations as middle class, her personal and emotional identification remained, profoundly, with the class of her birth. Olsen appreciated the power of class origin, which, as I have argued earlier, Le Sueur un-intentionally trivialized in "The Fetish of Being Outside." Both "intellectual" pursuits and the struggles of working people to improve their lives were crucially important to Olsen, and how to live in both worlds remained her insoluble riddle.

While Olsen's writing career was obstructed by her gender and class origin, and by the demands of wage and domestic labor, the historic conditions of the '30s also pulled her from writing into activism. The Depression, the rise of fas-cism in Europe, the threat of world war, and the apparent success of socialism in the Soviet Union instilled a sense of urgency and possibility for radical change that competed along with everything else for Olsen's energies. "Every freedom movement has . . . its roll of writers participating at the price of their writing," she comments in *Silences* (143). This was for Olsen a period of collective effort in myriad forms—Party meetings, union organizing, picket lines, demonstrations, leafleting—not the solitude necessary for sustained writing. About the threat of fascism in Europe, she says,

Sometimes [in conflict] with what needed to be done at home was an inter-national sense and an anti-war sense, the threat of war in the world. . . . We knew about Dachau very early, we knew about the concentration camps, the Left press was full of it. . . . It made my kind of book [*Yonnondio*] more and more difficult to write. . . . You remember how people felt after Allende? You remember how people felt after things were not ending in Vietnam, and you were so *personally* identified with it? . . . It was so much of one's being. . . . You lived with it in every room of your house . . . in every conversation whether it came up or not. It was a living, actual presence and force. We had that kind of consciousness [during the '30s], so many of us. . . . [It] made other concerns seem trivial by comparison. (Ro-senfelt interview)

Yet, as Rosenfelt points out, passages such as the following one from a '30s journal express Olsen's frustration at the amount of time required for things that took her away from writing, including political work and the necessity to write pieces on demand for various political activities: "Struggled all day on the Labor Defender article. Tore it up in disgust. It is the end for me of things like that to write—I can't do it—it kills me" (quoted in Rosenfelt, "Thirties" 384). "There came a time," Olsen tells us in *Silences*, when the "fifteen hours of daily realities became too much distraction for the writing" (20). But Olsen never entirely gave up the struggle to save her writing self.

Her determination to return to writing only deepened after the bombing of Hiroshima. Olsen vividly remembers one article, in what had been a series of horrific ones in the *San Francisco Chronicle*, that described "the ninth night," the first night without moonlight after the holocaust. Even without moonlight, the newspaper reported, the sky above Hiroshima had been eerily illuminated by bodies still burning from radiation. At that moment Olsen pledged "to write on the side of life," although it would be eight years before she could act on that re-solve (interview).

Olsen remained politically active in the '40s and '50s, serving as head of the CIO's Allied War Relief program and as president of organizations as diverse as the California CIO's Women's Auxiliary and the Parent-Teachers Association. In 1946 she authored a women's column in *People's World*, "writing articles like 'Wartime Gains of Women in Industry' and 'Politically Active Mothers—One View,' which argued like [Mary] Inman that motherhood should be considered political work" (Rosenfelt, "Thirties" 406, n44). In the late '40s and early '50s, Olsen was active in the international peace movement that petitioned against governmental testing of nuclear weapons. During the same period, she also worked within the PTA to oppose civilian defense maneuvers, which sent school children scurrying under desks in the absurd "duck and cover" exercises so ef-fectively satirized in the film *Atomic Cafe*. Both "I Stand Here Ironing" and "Tell Me a Riddle" include disturbing references to a child's innocent acceptance of this Cold War hysteria.

During the late '40s and '50s, like Le Sueur and her family, the Olsens were victims of the harassment typical of the McCarthy Period. In June 1950, the night before Olsen was going to attend a human relations workshop with a stipend she had been given as president of the Kate Kennedy Elementary School PTA, she happened to turn on the radio during the broadcast of a San Francisco Bay Area gossip program. "I was standing here ironing . . . literally," she smiles, when she heard the following: "Tillie Olsen, alias Tillie Lerner, alias Teresa Lansdale [a name she had used when arrested during the '30s] . . . is a paid agent of Moscow [trying] to take over the San Francisco Public School System by tunneling in the PTA." Tillie and Jack believe that teamsters who were trying to take over the Warehousemen's Union paid the gossip-program host to "get at Jack," the Union's Educational Director, "through" Tillie (interview).

As a result of the broadcast, some of Olsen's closest friends shunned her. Even a "beloved" next-door neighbor to whom the Olsens had been especially close for years, declared: "'I know about double agents . . . that . . . in these days . . . they're just everywhere'" (interview). Four people named Tillie to the House Un-American Activities Committee (Jack was subpoenaed by the Committee, but neither he nor Tillie testified).[10] One of the four was Al Addy, a Warehousemen's Union member whom Jack, as the Educational Director, had schooled in writing and editing. Another of the four, Lou Rosser, was a special friend of the Olsens, who had recruited him to the YCL. Tillie compassionately explained that Rosser's drug problem made him especially vulnerable to the FBI, which financed his addiction in return for his information and would have prosecuted him if he had refused to supply it. "We're haunted by what happened with Lou, the destruction of that human being," Olsen said sadly.[11] During this period the FBI systematically contacted Jack and Tillie's employers, and they each lost a series of jobs. One manager cautioned Tillie when he fired her that "one had to be like the grass and be as inconspicuous as possible and bow with the wind" (interview).

When her youngest child entered school in 1953, Olsen was at last free of some of the responsibilities of child care, and she enrolled at 41 in a creative writing course at San Francisco State. Lois Kramer, a neighbor with whom Olsen could confidently exchange child care, was also instrumental in her beginning to write again. "That tumult I had in my head about what was going on with my kids subsided" because they felt as much at home in the Kramer household as they did in their own (interview). An unfinished manuscript of "I Stand Here Ironing" (at that point titled "Help Her to Believe") won Olsen a Stanford University Creative Writing Fellowship in 1955–56, even though the lack of a college degree had made her technically ineligible for admission, let alone funding.

A favorite Olsen anecdote reveals how that important fellowship nearly eluded her. At an initial screening intended to eliminate most of the applicants, one of the reviewers for the competition, after reading a few pages of "I Stand Here Ironing," tossed it in the wastebasket in disgust, muttering, "'Can you imagine? That woman went on for *pages* just about *ironing*. Standing there ironing!'" Procedurally, at that point the story would have been eliminated from the competition. However, Dick Krause, the one person on the screening committee with a working-class background, happened to overhear the remark and asked to see the piece; he was so moved by it that he delivered it personally to Wallace Stegner, the director of the program. After reading the manuscript, Stegner declared: "'Well, we have to have her'" (interview). Although housework and a full family life still required attention, for eight months Olsen did not have to hold a wage-earning job: "I had continuity, three full days [per week], sometimes more—and it was in those months I made the mysterious turn and became a writing writer" (*Silences* 20).

Another silence closed in, however, when she had to return to a nine-hour work day. Two years later, in 1959, a Ford Foundation grant "came almost too late":

> Time granted does not necessarily coincide with time that can be most fully used, as the congested time of fullness would have been. . . .
>
> Drowning is not so pitiful as the attempt to rise, says Emily Dickinson. I do not agree, but I know whereof she speaks. . . . (*Silences* 21)

Even so, the grant allowed Olsen to finish and publish "Tell Me a Riddle," which won the prestigious O. Henry Award for Best Short Story of the Year (1961). "Tell Me a Riddle" became the title story of a volume of Olsen's short stories that also includes "I Stand Here Ironing," "Hey Sailor, What Ship?," and "O Yes"; *Time* included *Tell Me a Riddle* on its "best-ten-books" list in 1962. *Tell Me a Riddle* "went out of print in 1963 or 1964 until 1971" but, as its devotees reported to Olsen, it "was kept alive by being passed hand to hand and photocopied by teachers" (interview).

Since 1962 Olsen has worked at intervals within the academy, earning an impressive number of appointments and awards.[12] Her work has been anthologized more than 85 times and published in 12 languages. But Olsen has remained politically active. In the spring of 1985, for example, along with writers Alice Walker, Maya Angelou, Lawrence Ferlinghetti, and Susan Griffin, she was cited at Berkeley's Sproul Hall for protesting the University of California's investments in South Africa. And when I arrived at Olsen's apartment to interview her in July 1989, I found her living room cluttered with the placards she and others had recently carried while demonstrating against repression in Beijing.

Olsen has also worked to restore eclipsed, out-of-print women's writing. She influenced several Feminist Press reprintings, including Rebecca Harding Davis's *Life in the Iron Mills* (1972), for which she wrote an extensive afterword; Agnes Smedley's *Daughter of Earth* (1973); Charlotte Perkins Gilman's *The Yellow Wallpaper* (1973); and Moa Martinson's *Women and Apple Trees* (1985). Olsen also reclaimed *Yonnondio* (1974)—the novel she had begun, as noted above, in 1932 and abandoned in 1937—by the arduous process described in Chapter 6.

And yet *Yonnondio's* reclamation and "Requa I," a story included in *The Best American Short Stories, 1971*, edited by Martha Foley, compose the sum total of Olsen's published fiction since *Tell Me a Riddle* appeared in 1961. *Silences* (1978), a nonfictional testimonial to the factors—including gender, class, and race—that obstruct literary productivity, derived partly from Olsen's struggle with her own silence. Informal literary criticism and literary history, *Silences* draws on writers' letters and diaries "to expand the too sparse evidence [about] the relationship between circumstances and creation" (262). Olsen contributed the foreword to *Black Women Writers at Work*, edited by Claudia Tate (1983) and edited *Mother to Daughter Daughter to Mother* (1984), published by the Feminist Press as the first in a series of books commemorating the fifteenth anniversary of the founding of the Press in 1970. The book is an unusual collection of 120 writers' work, including diary entries, letters, poetry, fiction, autobiography, memoirs, songs, and even gravestone epitaphs. With Julie Olsen Edwards, Olsen published an introductory essay in *Mothers and Daughters: That Special Quality: An Exploration in Photographs* (1989), and she contributed "The '30s: A Vision of Fear and Hope," a retrospective on the decade, to a special anniversary issue of *Newsweek*, January 3, 1994.

My biographical sketch of Tillie Olsen would be inadequate without some information about Jack Olsen beyond what I have provided thus far. Jack, who died at 77 in 1989, was born in Kiev, Russia, and emigrated to the United States as a small child. By all accounts an unflagging friend to leftists and Left causes, Jack came to San Francisco in 1933 after organizing homeless youth in Los Angeles. From 1933 to 1942, while working on the San Francisco waterfront as a warehouseman, he helped organize the warehousemen's branch of the International

Meridel Le Sueur's maternal grandmother, Mary Antoinette Lucy, c. 1900. One of the first settlers of the Oklahoma territory and secretary of the Oklahoma Women's Christian Temperance Union, she divorced her husband for "drinking up the farms her father left her."

(Below, left) Meridel Le Sueur's mother, Marian (Wharton) Le Sueur, c. 1935. Lecturer on behalf of women's rights—including suffrage and access to birth control information—and member of the Socialist Party, Non-Partisan League, and Farmer-Labor Party. In 1952, despite McCarthy Period harassment, Marian ran (unsuccessfully) for Senator from Minnesota on the Progressive Party ticket to protest the Korean War.

(Below, right) Meridel Le Sueur's stepfather, Arthur Le Sueur, c. 1915. Served four terms as socialist mayor of Minot, North Dakota; with Marian, whom he married in 1917, he worked as an educational director for the Non-Partisan League and the Farmer-Labor Party; served as an attorney for the CIO and as a municipal judge.

Meridel Le Sueur, c. 1908.

Meridel Le Sueur, aspiring actress, c. 192●
Le Sueur landed bit-parts and sporadic wo●
as an extra and "stunt girl."

Women preparing food at the strike commissary during the Minneapolis Teamsters Strike, 1934. Le Sueur's "I Was Marching," a piece of reportage discussed in Chapter 3, describes work in the commissary and strike events. *(Minnesota Historical Society)*

Strikers, including a few women (front, center), defy police during the Minneapolis Teamsters Strike, 1934. *(Minnesota Historical Society)*

July 24, 1934 funeral for Henry Ness, first striker killed by police gunfire (on July 20, known as "Bloody Friday" or, as Le Sueur refers to it, "Black Friday") in the Minneapolis Teamsters Strike. Striker John Belor also died and 67 people, including 13 bystanders, were wounded on the same day. The funeral procession, described at the conclusion to Le Sueur's "I Was Marching," was over a mile long; the Minneapolis *Labor Review* reported attendance of 100,000. *(Minnesota Historical Society)*

(Above) Meridel Le Sueur with daughter Rachel Le Sueur, c. 1935.

(Left) Meridel Le Sueur with daughters Rachel (standing) and Deborah Le Sueur, c. 1940.

(Right) Bob Brown, artist and Le Sueur's companion for 25 years, c. 1938.

(Below) Meridel Le Sueur, c. 1960.

Meridel Le Sueur, St. Paul, 1980. *(Jerome Liebling)*

(Right) From left: Tillie Olsen's paternal aunt Chaika, paternal great aunt Soglow, and mother Ida Lerner, early 1920s.

(Below) Tillie Lerner (alias Theta Larimore), 1932. Tillie Lerner preferred "T. L." names for her aliases. "Thousand-Dollar Vagrant" (an essay discussed in Chapter 5) chronicled her arrest for her role in the 1934 San Francisco Maritime Strike; at that time, Lerner adopted the alias Teresa Lansdale.

THE OMAHA BEE-NEWS, FRIDAY, FEBRUARY 5, 1932

ΙAMED HEAD OF NEV
'resent Demands -:- For Relief WORL

THETA LARIMORE

yed are shown present-
tergard in front of the
Jefferson Square was
ber fin-

Theta Larimore, 2023 Burt street, was one of the speakers demanding an extensive program of relief for the unemployed. "What becomes of the women who lose their jobs?" she shouted. "Save their respectability."

Planned for 70,000 SOVIET
ief Area

(Facing page) The man in the foreground carries a flag—"ILA [International Longshoremen's Association] Women's Auxiliary"—as part of the silent funeral march, 9 July 1934, honoring Howard Sperry and Nick Bordoise. Tens of thousands of silent marchers along Market Street formed, as the *Chronicle* reported, a "stupendous and reverent procession that astounded the city." *(Courtesy Labor Archives and Research Center, San Francisco State University)*

(Above) Bloody Thursday, 5 July 1934, during the San Francisco Maritime Strike. The *Chronicle* proclaimed "War In San Francisco!" as "blood ran red in the streets." "The Strike" (a piece of Lerner/Olsen's reportage discussed in Chapter 5) describes Bloody Thursday and other events of the strike. Striking longshoreman Howard Sperry (right) was killed by police gunfire; Gene Olson (left) survived. Strike supporter Nick Bordoise, a Communist, was also killed by police. *(Bancroft Library)*

(*Right*) Tillie Olsen when she was photographed as president of McKinley Elementary School PTA, San Francisco, 1941.

(*Below*) Tillie Olsen collecting razor blades as part of the Congress of Industrial Organizations' war relief effort in San Francisco, 1943 (identity of sailor unknown).

(*Above, left*) Jack Olsen at his desk at the International Longshoremen's and Warehousemen's Union Local 6, where he served as Director of Publicity and Education, San Francisco, c. 1946. (*ILWU Library, San Francisco*)

(*Above, right*) From left: Tillie Olsen, father Samuel Lerner, and daughter Julie Olsen, walking on Market Street in San Francisco, 1956.

Tillie Olsen's daughters. From left: Karla, Julie, Kathie, and Laurie, San Francisco, c. 1954.

(*Above, left*) Tillie Olsen at the MacDowell Colony in Peterborough, New Hampshire, 1968.

(*Above, right*) Tillie Olsen, 1973. (*Rob Edwards*)

(*Left*) Tillie Olsen, Stockholm, 1979. (*Dagets Nygheter*)

Jack Olsen with grandchildren (Kathie Olsen's daughters), Eleanor Lerner Hoye ("Noli," left), and Juanita Laurel Hoye ("Laurie"), c. 1979.

Extended family singing at Tillie Olsen Day (proclaimed by the San Francisco mayor and board of supervisors), 18 May 1981. From left: Tillie Olsen, Laurie Olsen, Mike Margulies, Rob Edwards, Julie Olsen Edwards, Rebekah Edwards, Eleanor Lerner Hoye (held by Kathie Olsen), Juanita Laurel Hoye, Jack Olsen.

(Left) Tillie Olsen with a young friend (wearing a Fort Point Gang sweatshirt, a gift from Tillie) at the MacDowell Colony in Peterborough, New Hampshire, October 1992.

(Below) From left: Julie Olsen Edwards, Laurie Olsen, and Tillie Olsen on Olsen's 80th birthday, at Fort Point on the San Francisco Bay, 1993.

Fort Point Gang, gathered near Golden Gate Bridge, May 1994. The Fort Point Gang originated in 1978 with seven men—Joe Passen, Bill Bailey, Al Richmond, Lou Goldblatt, Frank Jones, Jack Olsen, and Jim Kendall—all lifelong labor activists, union leaders, and former members of the American Communist Party. The group, so named because it walks weekly along the shore of the San Francisco Bay to Fort Point, has grown to about 25 and now includes women (some credit Tillie Olsen with first crashing the gender gate). Chapter 5, note 13 provides more information about the Gang.© Phiz Mezey, 1994.

Publicity poster for a 1986 benefit performance for the Foot of the Mountain, a feminist theater in Minneapolis. Meridel Le Sueur introduced Tillie Olsen's reading from *Tell Me a Riddle*. *(Leslie Bowman)*

Longshoremen's and Warehousemen's Union, encouraging women's participation in the union and action on women's issues. He taught classes for warehousemen in literacy, labor history, and politics, becoming the first educational director of ILWU Local 6, and edited the Local's bulletin. After serving in World War II, Jack returned to San Francisco, and in 1952 was subpoenaed to testify before the House Committee on UnAmerican Activities, as noted above. When he refused, he was denied work on the waterfront and in his 40's became an apprentice printer. As a commercial printer he was active in the Bay Area Typographical Union Local 21, served as a delegate to the San Francisco Labor Council, and became active in developing the Martin Luther King Apprenticeship Training Program to increase the number of minority apprentices in the printing trades. In 1973 Jack was instrumental in establishing the labor studies program at the City College of San Francisco. Appointed its founding director, he was also a teacher in the program ("Jack Olsen" B6; "Bread" n. pag.).

Jack and Tillie lived in St. Francis Square, a cooperatively owned apartment complex built with ILWU pension funds (dubbed "Red Square" by the San Francisco police, Tillie told me). Jack was its president for two years and editor of its newsletter, *Circling the Square*. Jack was also a founding member of the Fort Point Gang, a walking/support group that has expanded to about twenty "regulars" from the original seven who shared a history in the San Francisco labor movement.[13] After his death, San Francisco honored Jack when the Mayor and the Board of Supervisors proclaimed Jack Olsen Remembrance Day, and on January 15, 1990, the Martin Luther King Civic Committee gave him their Distinguished Service Award "in grateful recognition of his outstanding and lasting contribution to organized labor and all of humankind" ("Bread" n. pag.). At the time of Jack's death, a letter addressed "TO ALL COOPERATORS" of the St. Francis Square apartments from its board of directors describes Jack as I heard him described repeatedly when interviewing people who knew the Olsens: "Like a loving parent, he cherished the worth of each individual and was tolerant of their failings. Long years of struggle and inevitable disappointment seemed to enrich, rather than embitter him, and [he] did not fall prey to that cynicism which too easily comes with age."[14]

Both Jack and Tillie have considered their achievements and many years of struggle not as individual efforts but as part of a social movement. In *Silences*, interviews, lectures, and correspondence, Tillie has deliberately deconstructed her own success story. She stubbornly refuses the heroine's guise that some admirers would have her wear. "The rule is simple," she declares: When those denied enabling circumstances because of sex, class, or color nevertheless survive as writers, "it is not by virtue of special capacity, courage, determination, will (common qualities) but because of chancy luck, combining with those qualities" (*Silences* 223). She wants the circumstances of her own "chancy luck" to be a matter of record.

Olsen says frankly of her writing self: "I am a partially destroyed human who pays the cost of all those years of not writing, of deferring, postponing, of doing others' work" (Martin 11). But Margaret Atwood more accurately assesses Olsen's career:

> Few writers have gained such wide respect based on such a small body of pub-
> lished work. . . . Among women writers in the United States, "respect" is too pale
> a word; "reverence" is more like it. This is presumably because women writers,
> even more than their male counterparts, recognize what a heroic feat it is to have
> held down a job, raised four children and still somehow managed to become and
> to remain a writer. The exactions of this multiple identity cost Tillie Olsen 20
> years of her writing life. The applause that greets her is not only for the quality of
> her artistic performance but, as at a grueling obstacle race, for the near miracle of
> her survival. (1)

Olsen's affiliation with the Communist Party affected her writing, politics, and personal life in contradictory ways. As Rosenfelt has pointed out, the nature of Olsen's commitment to the Party in the early '30s is suggested by a letter she received from a fellow YCL organizer while recovering from pleurisy in Omaha, ostensibly on leave for months from League duties:

> Read. Read things that will really be of some help to you. The Daily Worker every
> day . . . the Young Worker. All the new pamphlets . . . and really constructive
> books. . . . You'll have time to now, and you've got to write skits and plays for the
> League. This you can do for the League, and it will be a great help . . . . have only
> one thing in mind—recovery, and work in the League, and if you pull thru, and
> are working in the League again in a few months, I will say that as a Communist
> you have had your test. (quoted in Rosenfelt, "Thirties" 382)

The comrade concludes by inquiring about Olsen's play-in-progress, urges her to send it quickly, and then adds a postscript: "How about a song for the song-writing contest?" Reflecting on this letter in a journal kept at the time, Olsen resolves to "abolish word victories. . . . let me feel nothing till I have had action—without action feeling and thought are disease" (quoted in Rosenfelt, "Thirties" 382–383). Another journal entry reveals that she sometimes considered her emotions "neurotic"—elements of an Old Adam that Party activity will purge—and hints that she may have occasionally questioned the political "correctness" of her desire to write:

> I shall only care about my sick body—to be a good Bolshevik I need health first.
> Let my mind stagnate further, let my heart swell with neurotic emotions that lie
> clawing inside like a splinter—afterwards, the movement will clean that out. . . . I
> don't know what it is in me, but I must write too. It is like creating white hot irons
> in me & then pulling them out. . . . so slowly, oh so slowly. (quoted in Rosenfelt,
> "Thirties" 384)

Olsen's resolutions in these journal entries reflected the movement's tendency to value action over deliberation and introspection, even though Marx himself had criticized the separation of thought and activity. As Richard Pells points out, even established writers, who generally had little choice but to continue the work for which they had been trained, manifested during the '30s a "persistent habit of regarding art and thought as vaguely inferior to social and economic issues" (169).

The prevailing Party attitude favoring collective, active, and immediate resistance over the often solitary, "passive," protracted endeavor of fiction-writing and other intellectual work was an understandable, even appropriate response to an economic crisis that left more than one third of the U.S. labor force unemployed and millions of Americans hungry. But a mechanical application of the Marxist principle that practice must accompany theory, a by-product of a peculiarly American anti-intellectualism, has plagued the American Left historically. Although Olsen's lived experience for 29 years led her to workplace organizing rather than writing, she did not harbor long (unlike Le Sueur and Gold) the anti-intellectualism she expressed in the journal entries above. Olsen came to define activism broadly, considering endeavors as diverse as full-time writing and mothering to be viable political work.

Olsen insists that she was independent of Party literary circles in other ways as well. Although she was occasionally obliged during her years as an activist to write short pieces "on demand" for political events, her early '30s publications were not consciously written to accommodate the Party literary credo: "I was not a person, excepting maybe that first Kansas City-Omaha year [1931–32, when she first joined the YCL], who was trying 'chapter and verse'" to follow the Party-line "prescribers," and "I was not a part of any of those literary wars" (Rosenfelt interview). Olsen was well aware that proletarian realism was "the standard that was set . . . by the leading columnists and polemicists" of *New Masses*, which she read "faithfully—sometimes lovingly, sometimes angrily." But she insists the Party literary line "did not touch" her (Rosenfelt interview; interview).

Nevertheless, Olsen's writing during the early '30s resembles proletarian realism, which the CP promoted from 1930 to 1935. Her writing shows "the *real conflicts* of men and women who work for a living," serves "a social function," and emphasizes that "not pessimism, but revolutionary elan will sweep this mess out of the world forever" (see p. 24). Perhaps the tenets of proletarian realism did not so much shape Olsen's writing as coincide with her own inclinations, reinforcing her belief—which had been confirmed earlier by her discovery of Rebecca Harding Davis's novella, *Life in the Iron Mills*—that art can be based on the lives of "despised people" (*Silences* 117). Gold's tenets of proletarian realism are easy to indict, she said, but she saw as "healthy" the Party's "special attention to those who wrote about what hadn't been written about before" (interview).

Like Le Sueur, Olsen recognizes the debt she owes the Communist Left for nurturing her writing. The Party provided publishing outlets for beginning writers and established the John Reed Clubs specifically to encourage unknown young writers and artists. The Party was perhaps most important for leftist writers from the working class—such as Michael Gold, James Farrell, Richard Wright, Langston Hughes, and Erskine Caldwell, as well as Olsen—who brought to their work "the pride of that first victory against middle-class society" which had given them the opportunity to become writers at all (Kazin 294). Although *New Masses* tended to romanticize writers from the working class ("novelists writing after long days in shops and offices, poets polishing their verses as they stand in breadlines" [cited in Kazin 294]), this journal and other organs of the CP should be credited with encouraging them. Olsen was one of seven women, out of a total of 69 contributors, represented in the classic anthology of proletarian writing, *Proletarian Literature in the U.S.* (1935), which was produced by International Publishers, the CP publishing organ.[15] And all but one of Olsen's '30s pieces appeared in Party publications.

During the '30s Olsen "certainly thought of [herself] as a feminist, including the word," and she taught a class at the San Francisco YCL headquarters on "the woman question," for which she used Mary Inman's prescient and controversial *In Woman's Defense* (for a brief summary of Inman's book, see pp.45–46). Olsen argues that Party schools and meetings gave "special attention to the situation of women," and she adds that "we [Party and YCL members] all read" W. E. B. DuBois's assertion in *The Damnation of Women* that "the great question of the Twentieth Century . . . was race, and after that it was the woman question" (interview).

However, as noted in some detail in Chapter 2, the CP had contradictory attitudes toward women's oppression during the Depression decade, and no viable feminist movement existed to exert pressure on the Party. For example, few Party members, including women, viewed domestic labor and child care as responsibilities to be shared equally by women and men. When a man worked in a full-time, unpaid leadership position, he often expected his wife not only to shoulder housework and child care but also to support the family by taking a wage-earning job. Le Sueur, who was critical of this practice, termed these wives "the Party housekeepers" (Hedges 14). Under these circumstances, Olsen points out, the men became far more developed politically than the women (Rosenfelt interview).

Tillie herself qualified as a "Party housekeeper" during Jack's tenure as a full-time Party functionary.

> I never acted on [my] feelings . . . of absolute anger about my situation compared to Jack's situation and the other men. . . . We did a lot of quoting of Lenin about this barbarous, petty, degrading housework, and how it had to be eliminated. But like our women's movement now we have been furthest behind in [regard to] . . . what women do at home. (Rosenfelt interview)

In Vivian Gornick's *The Romance of American Communism*, another "Party housekeeper" thus describes her marriage:

> Three nights out of the five when we weren't having a meeting or throwing a party he'd show up at eleven at night with a mob of people, and guess who had to feed them and keep trotting out the drinks? "Who the hell does all the goddamn work?" I'd yell. "While you sit on your ass making the revolution, *I'm* out there in the kitchen like a slavey. What we need is a revolution in this *house*." But, of course, he simply ignored me, and of course I simply went on doing it. (133)

Like mainstream Americans, many leftists considered domestic labor part of "women's sphere."

Contraception and unwanted pregnancies were also considered by most Party members (as by most birth control advocates of the '30s) to be a "women's issue." Olsen, who has remarked upon "the terrible penalties for sexual freedom before Margaret Sanger," recalls that unwanted pregnancies were a major concern for many of the Party women she knew.[16] She herself underwent several abortions and, as noted, only one of the four pregnancies she brought to term was "voluntary" (Rosenfelt interview). Federal legal bans on birth control were not removed until 1938, and, even so, many state laws against it remained on the books (Gordon 321). According to Olsen, Party women tried to "inform uninformed women about birth control," but it "was a struggle that fell into abeyance except in a personal sense" (Rosenfelt interview). Most of the Party women Olsen knew, like those of America's mainstream, were "ignorant about their own bodies" and "few women knew about the diaphragm" (interview).

Olsen trusts the accuracy of Peggy Dennis's autobiography, which suggests the extent to which at least the Party leadership failed to consider the personal as political.[17] In referring to women like herself whose husbands had been imprisoned under the Smith Act, Dennis wrote: "As to the personal problems each of us had, none of us was equipped by our Party experience to respond to each other on a simple human level. Like the other wives, officially and outwardly I was too calm, too impersonal, too political. Within myself, I cried silently" (*Autobiography* 215).[18] Eugene Dennis died while General Secretary of the Party, and condolence cables poured into Party Headquarters from all over the United States and from dozens of foreign countries. But of all his comrades of some 20 and 30 years, only Elizabeth Gurley Flynn expressed grief to Peggy or comforted the widow in hers.

> Was there no one to mourn the man without first weighing the political consequences, or to reach out in friendship to their comrade's wife and son? Instead, the funeral was being planned as efficiently and matter-of-factly as a political rally. . . . What was wrong with me? I seek more than that official eulogy praise. . . . I want, instead, the simple embrace, the words, "I miss him, too"; "I have lost a friend"; "Let me weep with you." (*Autobiography* 251–253)

Peggy refused to attend Eugene's funeral. While "eulogy speakers downtown paid a fine tribute to Gene's Marxist leadership," she sat alone in an empty apartment, "deliberately conjuring up more personal images" of the sympathy shown her by the postman, her "beery, loquacious" apartment-building manager, the neighborhood street-gang leader, a neighboring Puerto Rican mother of "four babies," and the clerk in the corner tobacco shop (*Autobiography* 254–255).

What former Party member Vivian Gornick found "most striking" about the Communists she had known and the former Party members she interviewed in the '70s was that their "gift for political emotion [was] highly developed, [their] gift for individual empathy neglected, atrophied."[19] One former member Gornick interviewed joined the Young Pioneers during the '30s at the age of 10. (The "CP version of the Boy Scouts," the Young Pioneers' slogan was "Smash the Boy Scouts" [Gornick 55; Kelley 96].) At 15 he joined the Party and left it 15 years later, in the early '50s. What he described to Gornick seems to have been a fairly common experience among the former Party members she interviewed:

> As close as we all were, living together as we did for years, we never discussed anything remotely connected to our emotional lives. We would have been mortified to reveal our sexual or emotional confusions to each other, we all pretended we didn't have any. All personal doubts or pains got submerged beneath Party language. If you stopped talking that language you felt guilty, confused, trivial. (58)

Gornick thus describes another former Party member, who joined in 1934 and served as one of the state chairmen of the Party for 23 years:

> [He] is neither the first nor the last Communist I will meet who, ask him a political question and he comes to instant, vibrant life, ask him a question having to do with his own feelings or emotional experience and he draws a painful, quizzical blank. . . . [He] came of age in a time when his kind of wraparound political response was the mark of a serious person; as Communists, particularly, they sneered at any other kind of response to human experience, calling all else "bohemian." (92)

Olsen disagrees with Gornick's general assessment of Party people as politically developed but emotionally deformed. The "gift" for "empathy," to borrow Gornick's words, varied widely among Olsen's rank-and-file associates and was highly developed in some of them, Olsen insists. But even a cursory review of Party publications from the '30s reveals a hostility to Freudianism and psychoanalysis and an approval of "simple" common sense and self-sufficiency; introspection was associated with the Bohemian '20s.

And Olsen acknowledges that it was the sort of insensitivity to which Gornick refers—manifest, in Olsen's view, in such things as unnecessary and brutally handled expulsions and demands that members sustain a consistently high level of activity regardless of their personal circumstances—which caused her to leave the Party. (Olsen's criticism of the Party's insensitivity to members' "personal circumstances" echoes Harriet Magil's criticism, cited in Chapter 2.) Olsen first left the Party "sometime in the '30s." She returned to it for a while after the Second World War and then, because of "all the attacks against" it, remained a member "for a year or so" longer, despite misgivings: "To abandon this organization at this time was a betrayal of much that I believed in," she explains (interview). Olsen, who remains "convinced that the CP was far more accurate in its analysis of what had to be done nationally and internationally than any other single force," did not leave the Party because of "ideological differences." Rather, she was disturbed by its callous treatment of people and by its justifying "terrible wrongs" out of political "exigencies." "I was most troubled by" the lack of "feeling . . . [and] consideration for people, and I didn't want to be around that," Olsen has commented. The Women's Commission censured Olsen for bringing her young daughter Laurie to meetings. On a lighter note, she recalls that the Commission also censured her for ironing during meetings ("I stood there ironing," she laughs).[20] But Olsen is serious when she observes about the Party: "There wasn't a human enough structure" (interview).

Olsen's leaving the Party the second time can be dated around 1948 because she remembers being deeply troubled at the time that she left by the Party's expulsion of gays and lesbians, which happened that year;[21] she also recalls that daughter Laurie, who was born in 1947, was "a very tiny child" at the time. During this period, the Control Commission "was expelling people left and right." At one point, overhearing a meeting in her home in which Jack was participating, Olsen realized that a comrade whom she and "most of the people there cared for and honored and respected" was "being discussed as someone who perhaps should not be in the Party anymore." "Absolutely furious," she interrupted the meeting to defend the person in question (interview). Despite the zealousness of her journal entries and early '30s publications, Olsen insists: "I could never have been eligible for inclusion in *The God That Failed* because for me it [the Party] never was a God . . . I was an atheist's daughter from the beginning" (quoted in Duncan 209).

In responding to a draft of an article Deborah Rosenfelt had written about Olsen's life and work (later published as "From the Thirties: Tillie Olsen and the Radical Tradition"), Olsen urged her not to delete from the final version a quote from Peggy Dennis's 1976 letter of resignation from the Party, which states that Dennis deplored the Party leadership's "explicit, deliberate, and reprehensible sexism" (Rosenfelt interview). Party members—especially male Communists—often ignored, trivialized, or repressed the domestic, personal, and emotional dimensions of their lives, and, as Olsen observes, "those things having to do with . . . the maintenance of life and the bearing and rearing of the young" received the least attention of all (Rosenfelt interview).

That Party women could at least challenge sexist attitudes, however, put the Party, in Olsen's view, "absolutely ahead of anywhere else" (Rosenfelt interview). Women "benefitted enormously" from CP membership, Olsen insists, adding that "the Party developed many working-class kids. . . . I could go on and on with example after example" (interview). Olsen rightly calls for more examination of the Party's contradictions regarding women, contending that for women the Party was "a mixed place . . . in a far deeper and [more] complex sense than anybody has begun to approach" (Rosenfelt interview). Moreover, Olsen quite correctly points out that some of the Old Left's failures regarding sexism (an equitable sharing of responsibility for children, for example) have not yet become successes for the current women's movement. "It drives me mad," Olsen says angrily,

> when women historians take our understandings now and apply them to the past, to indict . . . when actually many of them in their own lives are going through the same things. . . . I've never since I was a child lived in a country of such exhausted women. . . . I'm talking about [our] screaming right now. . . . We have not made that exhaustion visible. It's not in any forms of the media. (interview)

Olsen is referring here to "the anguish of women [in the United States] who say, 'I am going to have both [meaningful work and children] in my life.'" Because we still lack government-funded maternity and parental leave, child care, and health care, women today do not fare much better than did women of her generation, Olsen believes, observing that this unnecessary destruction—"the cost to your work, the cost to yourself, the cost to your children, and the cost to society"—remains "largely undocumented" (interview).[22] When I asked her how she would mobilize people around these issues, she replied, smiling, with a movement slogan—"Agitate, educate, organize"—insisting that "we can understand the past if we start with our own lives and struggles because that past is too terribly present" (interview; Rosenfelt interview).

As Olsen began her writing career, workers started pouring into the available unions. New Deal legislation included the National Industrial Recovery Act (1933), and Section 7A guaranteed workers the right to organize and bargain collectively. "Many workers," James Green observes, felt "the tide of history had finally turned" (even though the NRA was skirted far more often than it was enforced by the establishment of "company" unions and was declared unconstitutional in 1935 [143]). Three major strikes of 1934 demonstrated the great potential for working-class militancy. In February, 900 National Guardsmen failed to break a massive picket of 10,000 workers from the community surrounding the Toledo Auto-Lite plant. Significantly, the striking electricians alone could not have defied the Guard. Their strength came in sheer numbers, and those numbers came from other workers willing to join the picket in solidarity. The Maritime Strike on the West Coast, which involved Olsen directly, began in May. And in July, Minneapolis Trotskyists led the teamster strike that inspired Le Sueur's "I Was Marching," closing down the trucking industry and tying up the entire city (see Chapter 3).

Such was the dramatic setting in which young Tillie Lerner, "fierce for change," was writing.[23] As much as a youthful zealousness and what I term the CP's "official certainty," this expanding unionization and increasing working-class militancy affected her writing. As noted above, Olsen has said of the '30s: "We believed that we were going to change the world." As one might expect, then, Olsen's 1934 publications are more polemical, more akin to orthodox proletarian writing than her more recent writing. Their settings and subjects, for example, are standard for proletarian writing—conditions in a (garment) factory; the murdering of socialists by a fascist regime; an exploited mining community; an arrest of Communist labor organizers; and a strike.

When Olsen was 21 and an active YCL member, her first publication, a poem titled "I Want You Women Up North To Know," appeared in *The Partisan* (March 1934), a magazine of the West Coast John Reed Club. This poem grew out of a letter to *New Masses* (9 January 1934) from a Texas woman, Felipe Ibarro, indicting the owners of the Juvenile Manufacturing Corporation who exploited workers—in this case, Chicanas—in the San Antonio garment industry.

Ibarro reports that Catalina Rodriguez, "in the last stages of consumption, works from six in the morning till midnight," never earning more than three dollars a week. Ibarro adds that she no longer wonders "why in our city with a population of 250,000 the Board of Health has registered 800 professional 'daughters of joy' and in addition, about 2000 *Mujeres Alegres* (happy women), who are not registered and sell themselves for as little as five cents." Ibarro reports that the Chamber of Commerce has dubbed San Antonio "Where Sunshine Spends The Winter" as part of its campaign to compete with Florida and California for tourists. "I don't know whether the tourists came," she adds, but "Capital came and let out the children's dresses for home work" (22).

Olsen's basing her poem on Ibarro's letter locates "I Want You Women Up North to Know" loosely within the genre of workers' correspondence poems (although Ibarro was not herself one of the workers, she knows the "bloody facts" because she had "spoken to the women" workers [22]). The *Daily Worker* identified Harry Alan Potamkin as the first to use workers' correspondence as a theme for poetry.[24] Gold, another practitioner of this genre, crafted poems from letters sent to the *Daily Worker*. The correspondence from Ibarro included many specifics—names, ages, wages. Olsen repeats many of these details in her poem, which begins:

> I want you women up north to know
> how those dainty children's dresses you buy
>   at macy's, wanamakers, gimbels, marshall fields,
> are dyed in blood, are stitched in wasting flesh,
> down in San Antonio, "where sunshine spends the winter."
>
> I want you women up north to see
> the obsequious smile, the salesladies trill
>   "exquisite work, madame, exquisite pleats"
> vanish into a bloated face, ordering more dresses,
>   gouging the wages down,
> dissolve into maria, ambrosa, catalina,
>   stitching these dresses from dawn to night,
>   in blood, in wasting flesh.
>
> Catalina Rodriguez, 24,
>   body shriveled to a child's at twelve,
> catalina rodriguez, last stages of consumption,
>   works for three dollars a week from dawn to midnight. . . .

And it ends:

> And for Catalina Rodriguez comes the night sweat and the blood
>   embroidering the darkness.
>   for Catalina Torres the pinched faces of four huddled
>   children,
>   the naked bodies of four bony children,
>   the chant of their chorale of hunger.

And for 2800 ladies of joy the grotesque act gone over—
    the wink—the grimace—the "feeling like it baby?"
And for Maria Vasquez, spinster, emptiness, emptiness,
    flaming with the dresses for children she can never fondle . . . .
        fondle. . . .

Women up north, I want you to know,
I tell you this can't last forever.

I swear it won't. (cited in Burkom and Williams 67–69)

Like much reportage, this poem foregrounds fundamental antitheses: the abstract
women up north who have the money to shop at "gimbels, marshall fields" versus
the particular "maria, ambrosa, catalina," "down in San Antonio," "stitching these
dresses from dawn to night, / in blood, in wasting flesh." In the concluding two
lines (taken verbatim from the concluding sentences of Ibarro's letter), the poem
embodies the "official certainty" characteristic of '30s proletarian literature, while
another line describes the Soviet Union as "heaven . . . brought to earth in 1917."
Like many Party members, Olsen believed in an American socialist future with
the buoyancy Lincoln Steffens expressed upon his return from the Soviet Union:
"I have seen the future and it works."

In the following passage from the poem Olsen opposes herself to what she
terms "the bourgeois poet" by moving abruptly from a parody of traditional lyrical
poetry, which in her view would ignore or distance the reader from the plight of
these exploited workers, to prosaically announcing their low wages and their only
available alternative for employment, prostitution:

> White rain stitching the night, the bourgeois poet would say,
> white gulls of hands, darting, veering,
> white lightning, threading the clouds,
> this is the exquisite dance of her hands over the cloth,
> and her cough, gay, quick, staccato,
>   like skeleton's bones clattering,
> is appropriate accompaniment for the esthetic dance
>   of her fingers,
> and the tremolo, tremolo when the hands tremble with pain.
> Three dollars a week,
> two fifty-five,
> seventy cents a week,
> no wonder 2800 ladies of joy
> are spending the winter with the sun after he goes down—
> for five cents. . . .

In this poem Olsen parodies a long bourgeois tradition of "romanticizing" the
worker while displaying the mental agility of the poet. Olsen could easily have
had Wordsworth's "The Solitary Reaper" in mind:

> Whate'er the theme, the maiden sang
> As if her song could have no ending;

I saw her singing at her work,
And o'er the sickle bending;—
I listened, motionless and still;
And, as I mounted up the hill,
The music in my heart I bore,
Long after it was heard no more. (351–352)

Olsen could also have been thinking of the no-less-condescending Yeats poem, "The Lover Tells of the Rose in His Heart":

All things uncomely and broken, all things worn out and old,
The cry of a child by the roadway, the creak of a lumbering cart,
The heavy steps of the ploughman, splashing the wintry mould,
Are wronging your image that blossoms a rose in the deeps of my
    heart.

The wrong of unshapely things is a wrong too great to be told;
I hunger to build them anew and sit on a green knoll apart,
With the earth and the sky and the water, remade, like a casket of
    gold
For my dreams of your image that blossoms a rose in the deeps of
    my heart. (620)

These are only two of many such examples from the bourgeois tradition at which Olsen's poem takes aim. An amalgam rather than a blend of poetry and reportage, "I Want You Women Up North to Know" is nevertheless at points sensitive to the richness and rhythm of language. The free verse form and the repetition of words and phrases may represent a debt to Whitman, while a bold central metaphor transforms the women into the clothing they embroider—that is, into commodities.

But the discomfort this poem causes its readers is ambiguous. While the text succeeds in its intention to force us to confront the agony and injustice of these garment workers' lives, it is also unsettling because it preempts our emotional and moral responses. It bludgeons us, its exhortatory language announcing a distrust that the reader will respond appropriately to the garment workers' suffering. The language announces itself, too, as "movement" discourse, which in practice turns back on itself, speaking to itself rather than to a general audience—that is, the already converted speak to the already converted in the special discourse of converts. Because those who might have been persuaded are, in effect, excluded by this discourse, the poem's intention is undercut.

Even so, in this first publication we already see emerging in Olsen's writing a tendency, which will later become dominant, that competes with her desire for monological authorial and pedagogical control. In this "workers' correspondence" poem, she gives others a voice, straining toward a collective form. The poem is a vehicle for the stories of exploited Chicanas, as *Tell Me a Riddle* will be permeable to multiple oppressed voices. And in nascent form, "I Want You Women Up North" prefigures *Silences*' maverick intertextuality. Olsen "yields the floor" to

Felipe Ibarro as she will to dozens of other writers in the later text, and she allows Ibarro's words to conclude the poem, as she will give the "last word" in *Silences* to Rebecca Harding Davis.

Olsen's "There Is a Lesson" is another incendiary poem. First appearing in the *Daily Worker* (5 March 1934) and reprinted in *The Partisan* (April 1934), the poem concerns the murdering of Austrian socialists by the fascist Dollfuss government:

> Keep the children off the streets,
>   Dollfuss,
> there is an alphabet written in blood
>   for them to learn,
> there is a lesson thundered by collapsed
>   books of bodies.
>
> They might be riddled by the bullets
>   of knowledge,
> The deadly gas of revolution might
>   enter their lungs,
> in the streets, the hazardous streets.
>
> In a week, in a month, let them out
>   of their corners,
> it will be safe then . . . (safe Dollfuss?
>   safe Bauer and Seitz?
> there is a volume written with three
>   thousand bodies that can never
>   be hidden,
> there is a sentence spelled by the
>   grim faces of bereaved women,
> there is a message, inescapable, that
>   vibrates the air with voices of
>   heroes who shouted it to the last:
> "Down with Fascism!
> Down with Social Democracy!
> Long live our Soviets")
>
> Keep them off the streets, Dollfuss,
> It will quiver your fat heart with terror
> The alphabet written in blood out there
>   that children are learning.
> (cited in Burkom and Williams 70)

"There is a Lesson"'s condemning of fascism and social democracy in one breath marks the poem as a product of the Third Period, during which (as noted in Chapter 1) the CP considered liberals and non-CP socialists to be the main enemies of the working class and socialist revolution ("social fascists"). In the muckraking and reportage tradition, Olsen wants her readers "to see and feel the facts" — to "*experience*" — oppression's iron heel (Hicks et al. 211).

A principal structure in the poem appears first in the lines "there is an alphabet written in blood / for them to learn." The structure appears again in "lesson thundered by collapsed books / of bodies"; "bullets of knowledge"; "volume that can be written with three / thousand bodies"; "sentence spelled by the grim faces of bereaved women"; and again in the repeated but varied "The alphabet written in blood out there / that children are learning." The repetition of the structure has a blatant effect, as Olsen clearly intends. Yet the effect is achieved through a rather complicated structure that has a considerable history in the bourgeois literary tradition. Alphabet, sentence, lesson, volume, and so on are aligned against blood, bodies, faces of bereaved women, and so on. These are competing classes of the material causes of understanding. However, the first class, when set in opposition to the second, seems far less material, far more abstract than the second, which is evidently material. In a version of competing metonymies, the second category (blood, etc.) triumphs as the true set of material causes for "The Lesson" learned.

This competition of material causes of understanding is at the heart of Gold's version of proletarian realism, and "The Lesson" is the kind of writing for which Gold had called. However, the competing structures central to "The Lesson" were also employed in a wide variety of ways in the bourgeois tradition Gold rejected. A version of this device is central, for example, to Wordsworth's "The Tables Turned," although it lacks Olsen's forceful social commentary:

> One impulse from a vernal wood
> May teach you more of man,
> Of moral evil and of good,
> Than all the sages can. (38)

Wilfred Owen's "Arms and the Boy," in sharp contrast to "Tables Turned," employs competing metonymic structures in powerful antiwar commentary.

> Let the boy try along this bayonet-blade
> How cold steel is, and keen with hunger of blood;
> Blue with all malice, like a madman's flash;
> And thinly drawn with famishing for flesh.
>
> Lend him to stroke these blind, blunt bullet-heads
> Which long to nuzzle in the hearts of lads,
> Or give him cartridges of fine zinc teeth,
> Sharp with the sharpness of grief and death.
>
> For his teeth seem for laughing round an apple.
> There lurk no claws behind his fingers supple;
> And God will grow no talons at his heels,
> Nor antlers through the thickness of his curls. (718)

A "bayonet-blade," "blunt bullet-heads," and "cartridges of fine zinc teeth" try to claim a boy whose "teeth seem for laughing round an apple" and who naturally would not grow weapons "behind his fingers supple" or "through the thickness of his curls." We see in "There Is a Lesson," then, an effort to do what Trotsky recognized as necessary in *Literature and Revolution*: to write in calculated relation to bourgeois poetry, appropriating its forms for an oppositional literature.

Olsen's "Thousand-Dollar Vagrant" chronicles her arrest, with Jack Olsen and two other male members of the YCL, for their role in the 1934 Maritime Strike (Tillie helped produce the *Waterfront Worker*, the union newspaper, among other duties). Lincoln Steffens had urged Tillie to write "Thousand-Dollar Vagrant," she tells her readers: "'People don't know,' he informed me, 'how they arrest you, what they say, what happens in court. Tell them. Write it just as you told me about it.' So here it is" (67). The essay appeared in *The New Republic* (29 August 1934) one week after Robert Cantwell's published letter about Olsen's arrest had made her something of a cause célèbre (see pp.145–146). The piece describes the arrival of five police officers, the ransacking of the apartment where the Communists were gathered, the interrogation and beating.

> They asked Jack: "You a Communist?"
>
> "Yes," he answered, "that's legal, isn't it?"
>
> "Yeah? You're gonna find out how legal that is, you red bastard. This country's not good enough for you, huh? You don't like our Constitution, huh?" . . . They tell me to go into the other room . . . I know why they want me out of the kitchen. I hear the questions. "Where were you born? In Russia?" Silence, a thud of something soft on a body. "What are you doing here?" Silence. A thud. "Who's the girl?" Silence. A thud. . . . "What nationality are you? Come on—lie, we know you're all Jews or greasers or niggers." (68)

One of the officers remarks to Tillie, "You know what would've happened if we wouldn't 've come. You'd probably been raped. Don't you know these guys aren't any better than niggers?" (68). This officer's racist remark reflected the prevailing belief that black men

> were drawn to Communism because it meant having access to the dominant society's greatest treasure—white women. Wrote one observer, "In the eyes of Coloured men, complete equality with the Whites, as proclaimed by Moscow, *means free possession of White women*." Some of the Party's detractors even suggested that the Communists planned to wage a sexual revolution alongside the class struggle. During the 1934 strike wave the Birmingham White Legion issued leaflets asking white citizens, "How would you like to awaken one morning to find your wife or daughter attacked by a Negro or a Communist!" (Kelley 79)

As Kelley argues, Communism was linked to the dominant culture's twin phobias about sexuality and miscegenation. This "peculiar myth" functioned "as a powerful buffer against Communism" (79).

Tillie and her comrades were taken to jail where the men were beaten a second time. At the jail she gave a false name and address to protect her family:

If you give any names of members of your family they see that they lose their jobs; if you give your address they raid the place and wreck the furniture in the process of "searching." And even if you do show your "visible means of support"—you're still a vagrant. (68)

When the police discovered that she had given a phony address, they booked her on a vagrancy charge and set bail at $1000.

"Thousand-Dollar Vagrant" does not have as many of the marks of proletarian realism as the poems, but it is not without elements of the sort of proletarian realism typical of reportage. One antithetical structure is basic to the entire piece: the opposition between humans and nonhumans. Of the "bulls" who make the arrest the narrator says, "Only the two harness bulls looked a little human. The other faces were distorted and bestial." The head bull had "small pig eyes." One of the bulls was a "gorilla," and another was a "weasel-faced bull" (67–68). What complicates the antithesis between human and nonhuman in this piece is that some of the figures we would expect to be on the nonhuman side are allowed into the human category. The matrons at the jail were "nice," and "the fingerprint guy was human too" (68). This slight complication serves the piece well. Our narrator is not absolutely predisposed to unyielding antithetical categories. In her willingness to make somewhat thoughtful judgments about people despite their presence in the oppressive power structure, she displays more humanness than do the animal bulls who say of the people they are arresting, "we know you're all Jews or greasers or niggers."

"Thousand-Dollar Vagrant" has at least one telling silence. Although Olsen has said that Party literary criteria did not affect her ("I had my own standards," she has noted [Rosenfelt interview]), "Thousand-Dollar Vagrant" fails to mention that Olsen was living alone with her first child, who was not yet a year old, at the time of her arrest. Olsen remembers vividly that "part of the horror about being arrested" was not knowing who would care for Karla (Rosenfelt interview). Yet not a hint of that concern appears in the essay. Olsen has said that she was "critical of all" the '30s proletarian literature because it "left out a lot of 'mother content'" (Rosenfelt interview). Nevertheless, she excluded the "mother content" from "Thousand-Dollar Vagrant."

Olsen's "The Strike" appeared as the lead article in the September/October 1934 issue of *Partisan Review*, at that time a bi-monthly of revolutionary literature published by the New York John Reed Club. A piece of reportage, "The Strike" describes from the workers' perspective some of the events leading to the 1934 Maritime Strike, which on May 9 spread from San Francisco up and down the coast, cutting off nearly 2000 miles of coastland.[25] The chief grievance was the "shape up," a system of hiring that required longshoremen seeking a day's work to line up at 6 A.M. along the Embarcadero, where foremen would pick out those they wanted for the day. This hiring system demeaned and angered the workers, who could not count on steady work; were obliged to play up to or even bribe the foremen; and had to work to exhaustion or risk not being hired again. When the International Longshoremen's Association failed to challenge this practice, the more militant workers, some of them from the CP, formed a rank-and-file movement under the leadership of Harry Bridges to replace shape-up with a union hiring hall.

A battle between police and 5000 strikers and sympathizers took place on July 5, or "Bloody Thursday." When the police could not control the crowd with tear gas, they opened fire, leaving two strikers and a bystander dead and 115 people hospitalized (Brecher 153). The killing of unarmed strikers heightened the resentment of the city's workers, and on July 16 virtually all other San Francisco unions joined the longshoremen in the first general strike in the United States since the Seattle General Strike in 1919.[26] As a result of the strike "the longshoremen won the right to have union dispatchers in hiring halls, though employers officially retained the final choice of workers"(Green 145). Even so, as Mike Quin wrote in *The Big Strike*, hiring was "to all intents and purposes controlled by the union through the dispatcher" (cited in Green 145).

The monological rhetorical model in which meanings are delivered from source to recipient, a model relied on so heavily by Le Sueur's reportage, appears in "The Strike": "HELL CAN'T STOP US. That was the meaning of the lines of women and children marching up Market with their banners" (3–4). Structures of antithesis so common in Le Sueur's reportage are also present in "The Strike." Like Le Sueur's "I Was Marching," "The Strike" includes antitheses of action and inaction: the marching strikers versus those who stand and watch; the marching strikers versus the strikebreakers sitting on trucks "like corpses sitting and not moving, holding guns stiffly"; the marching strikers versus the sitting narrator, "up in headquarters," writing about the events (7). There is the antithesis inherent in the "police 'protecting lives'" by "smashing clubs and gas bombs into masses of men like themselves" (5). Even the narrator's emotions are at times portrayed in antithetical form: her happiness to be working in the movement versus her hatred of and anger at the police, the newspapers' "screaming lies," and the shipowners (5).

However, because Olsen complicates reportage's model of "straightforward," "transparent" representation, "The Strike" differs from much reportage. Although the piece includes instances of monological rhetoric, there are also moments that undermine the monological rhetorical model, and questions about meaning draw the reader into some active participation. In the opening, ambiguously directed command, the narrator suggests that she cannot do what she is about to do: "DO NOT ASK ME TO WRITE of the strike and the terror" (3). Is this directed at us as readers? At her editor? At her comrades? In a passage that comments ironically on leisurely bourgeois writing, the narrator notes, "if there were time and quiet, perhaps I could do it. All that has happened might resolve into order and sequence, fall into neat patterns of words" (3). Thus, from the beginning, a tension exists between what she is doing and her reported recognition of the near impossibility of what she is doing.[27] And, from the opening sentence, Olsen implies that readers must help her to construct meaning about "the strike and the terror." It is as if she is saying, "Do not ask me to do this alone."

Given the seeming impossibility of her task, this narrator employs a form of indirection quite foreign to reportage's concern with "straightforward," "transparent" representation. The story is framed with the narrator's assertions: "I am on a battlefield" and "I write this on a battlefield" (3, 9). Yet the narrator interjects between these two assertions, "I was not down . . . [ellipsis Olsen's] by the battlefield. . . . I sat up in headquarters . . . I sit there, making a metallic little pattern of sound in the air, because that is all I can do, because that is what I am supposed to do" (7). Why the contradiction? There is validity to Rosenfelt's observation that the double setting reveals a conflict between Olsen's role as a writer and "her guilt at not being on the real battlefield herself—between the word and the deed" ("Thirties" 385). While Rosenfelt's analysis does not go far enough, William Stott's suggestion—that when the narrator is in the headquarters, she is removed from the strike's immediacy—fully misses the point.[28] There are two battlefields, each equally real and completely connected to each other. One is the battlefield of the strikers. The other is the battlefield of the mind trying to find meaning in the swirl of action, the mind struggling with myriad fragments, "the pictures I pieced together from words of comrades, of strikers, from the pictures filling the news papers" (7).

Olsen chooses to have her narrator report from the battlefield of the mind that is, in turn, reporting from a location close to the battlefield of the strikers' action. This precarious position allows her to work in a form in which there are moments of direct assertion of meaning (typical of reportage's monologic rhetorical model) and moments of inconclusive grasps for meaning. At one moment the narrator can assert:

> That was the meaning of the lines of women and children marching up Market with their banners—"This is our fight, and we're with the men to the finish." That was the meaning of the seamen and the oilers and the wipers and the mastermates and the pilots and the scalers torrenting into the river, widening into the sea. (3–4)

But at another moment she must acknowledge, "But I hunch over the typewriter and behind the smoke, the days whirl, confused as dreams" (3). This narrator is as certain as the narrators in Le Sueur's reportage that capitalism is the source of the strikers' oppression. However, this mixture of forms captures capitalism's psychic as well as brutal physical consequences.

As we move back and forth with the narrator between assertion of meaning and search for meaning, we recognize that Olsen is experimenting with forms that Gold would associate with decadent bourgeois literature. This narrator is not one of the "masturbators of bourgeois literature" reporting her "sickly mental states of the idle Bohemians," but she is willing to report sickly mental states generated by the brutal opposition to the strike: "Weeks afterward my fists clench at the remembrance and the hate congests so I feel I will burst" (5). For this narrator the *real conflicts* of men and women who work for a living" cannot in Gold-like fashion be confined to the strikers' battlefield. They exist no less in the battlefield of the mind trying to make sense of the battlefield of the strikers.

This is a modernist narrator, not as fragmented as the narrator of *The Waste Land*, but far from the typical monolithic narrator of reportage. The fragmented mental state of "The Strike"'s narrator recalls narrators of the early modernist experimenter Wilfred Owen—narrators who, like the narrator of "Dulce et Decorum Est," move between moments of chaos ("Dim, through the misty panes and thick green light, / As under a green sea, I saw him drowning") and moments of recognition of meaning ("The old Lie: *Dulce et decorum est / Pro patria mori*") (719). Owen's war-torn narrator, by virtue of his concluding assertion of meaning, expresses more certainty than "The Strike"'s narrator, who must end by saying, "Forgive me that the words are feverish and blurred. . . . But there is so much happening now. . . ." (9; second ellipsis Olsen's). This ending, like the piece's beginning, calls on readers to get involved—to complete the sentence, to complete this story and others like it. "There is so much happening" that one writer/activist cannot do it alone.

At points, Olsen's narrative form—more so than the form of much reportage—requires us as readers actively to construct meaning. At times the narrator can give us the meaning of the pieces; but at other times she can give us only the fragments themselves:

> Law . . . and order . . . will . . . prevail [ellipses Olsen's]. Do you hear? It's war, WAR—and up and down the street "A man clutched at his leg and fell to the sidewalk" "The loud shot like that of the tear gas bombs zoomed again, but no blue smoke this time, and when the men cleared, two bodies lay on the sidewalk, their blood trickling about them."—overhead an airplane lowered, dipped, and nausea gas swooned down in a cloud of torture, and where they ran from street to street, resisting stubbornly, massing again, falling back only to carry the wounded, the thought tore frenziedly through the mind, war, war, it's WAR—and the lists in the papers, the dead, the wounded by bullets, the wounded by other means— W–A–R. (6)

What must we do with these fragments? Like the narrator, we must take these fragments—these "pictures . . . from words of comrades, of strikers, from the pictures filling the newspapers"—and "piece [them] together." She has done some of the piecing for us. We must do the rest.

One of the few literary critics since the '30s to address reportage, William Stott objects to its emotionalism, using the opening lines of "The Strike" as an example. Stott argues that if reportage had been spoken "direct" via radio rather than written, the emotions might not seem excessive. He illustrates his point with Herbert Morrison's description of the May 1937 Hindenburg disaster, considered one of broadcasting's greatest eyewitness reports. Although Morrison's claims were extreme, says Stott ("Oh my, this is the worst catastrophe in the world!"), they were thoroughly convincing: "He went to pieces right before the listener, sobbing, sputtering ('the people! All the humanity!'), fighting to control himself; and the listener could not fail to recognize the honesty of his feelings" (182). In an indirect medium such as print reportage, however, such "extreme emotion is less plausible," Stott maintains.

> A writer, by the fact of writing, has moved from the immediacy of his experience; his rhetoric should acknowledge as much. To be trustworthy a print reporter needs

to have more control of himself and the topic; be able, however obliquely, to see the experience as the reader must—from the outside. The absence of such control suggests to a reader that the writer either has been demented by his experience or is indulging his emotions to try to move the audience. (182–183)

Because much of proletarian writing could be characterized by its votaries as well as by its detractors as emotional or melodramatic, I would like to address Stott's criticism. Writer Carl Hirsch's experience while covering a sharecroppers' strike in the area around Sikeston, Missouri, illuminates this question of "emotionalism." Hirsch, who was interviewed for the documentary *Seeing Red* (discussed in Chapter 2), reported during the '30s for the *Midwest Daily Record*, a Communist-sponsored Chicago newspaper. The evicted black and white sharecroppers, Hirsch recalls, moved all their belongings to the side of the highway, hoping to call attention to their plight. Huddled in flimsy, improvised shelters, these tenant farmers and their families faced starvation.

When the interviewer in *Seeing Red*, who had read Hirsch's newspaper accounts of the strike, comments that "it was a dramatic story," Hirsch replies as if anticipating a familiar criticism: "Well, it certainly was very dramatic for me . . . I wrote it without trying to be melodramatic but the conditions . . . were such that I couldn't write it any other way." Hirsch reads aloud a letter he had written to his wife about the strike, which, like his journalism, resembles '30s reportage. At the time he read the letter to the documentarists videotaping him, he had not seen it for many years:

> All day long I hear the talk of planters and their stooges, deputies, state troopers, bureaucratic small-time officials, and when they say "nigger" and "nigger-lover" and "lynch" and "agitator" and "communist," they mean violence. And all of it is directed against a few hundred mild and wonderful people. Simple, quiet, intelligent, honest, loving people who are starving in a swamp. It's all too damned ominous like something horrible were about to happen. I've been feeling this way all day. This morning I went out to a dismal bog where the sharecroppers are. It rained continuously and I sat in one of those excuses for a tent and talked and talked and helped them move the pans around to where the water was dripping in worst. Something sings inside of me when I'm with these people and it runs, "Arise ye wretched of the earth." (PAUSE) I heard stories today that would make your blood freeze and through it all ran the same (CRYING) savage depravity about a planter who whipped a sharecropper's hog to death because it was on his land. About a sharecropper who was tied to a post and beaten to death. About a little Negro boy who was starving and stole some beans and was beaten and forced to work in the field for a week to pay for the damage. By intervals this thing has ripped the heart out of me and inspired me as few things ever have. The colossal guts of these people bucking a set-up as cruel and hide-bound, as ruthless and powerful as the planter autocracy. It's a story that I'll tell you for weeks if I ever get back.

If few progressive people viewing *Seeing Red* would consider Hirsch's letter overblown, Stott might plausibly attribute their response to Hirsch's understated but powerful reading.

Yet the issue is more complex than Stott would have it. Literature written during an economic collapse is difficult to evaluate from the vantage point of relative prosperity. Hirsch's words bear repeating: "the conditions . . . were such that I couldn't write it any other way." Moreover, far from being absolute, textual meaning is affected by many factors, including the political perspective, class, gender, and race of the reader. Ishmael Reed implicitly comments on the need for such a reading model when he expresses the frustration of the undervalued African-American writer: "Art is what white people do. All other people are 'propagandists'" (quoted by Kostelanetz 243).

Like most reportage, Olsen's "The Strike" was written under deadline pressure, with a passion and sense of purpose appropriate for what seemed to be "a world making for the barricades" (Hicks et al. 211). Impending revolution is a given: At the funeral for the two unarmed strikers killed by the police, Tillie Lerner "saw the people, saw the look on their faces. And it is the look that will be there the days of the revolution" ("The Strike" 9). The following passage, which captures the electricity of collective resistance, resembles the conclusion to Le Sueur's "I Was Marching":

> There was a night that was the climax of those first days—when the workers of San Francisco packed into the Auditorium to fling a warning to the shipowners. There are things one holds like [a] glow in the breast, like a fire; they make the unseen warmth that keeps one through the cold of defeat, the hunger of despair. That night was one—symbol and portent of what will be. We League [YCL] kids came to the meeting in a group, and walking up the stairs we felt ourselves a flame, a force. At the door bulls were standing, with menacing faces, but behind them fear was blanching—the people massing in, they had never dreamed it possible— people coming in and filling the aisles, packing the back. Spurts of song flaming up from downstairs, answered by us, echoed across the gallery, solidarity weaving us all into one being. (4)

And yet "The Strike"'s concluding words suggest a conflict between two kinds of writing: "the quick, fervent, impressionistic report from the arena of struggle" and the careful "rendering that, ironically, would require for its full development a withdrawal from the struggle" (Rosenfelt, "Thirties" 385). These hurried, concluding words—"The rest . . . must be written some other time, must be written later. . . . there is so much happening now"—were also prophetic in the history of Olsen's writing career. "The Strike" would be her last publication for over 20 years.

That hopes for a socialist America were high among CP members in 1934 is evident in the notes about contributors when "The Iron Throat" appeared in *Partisan Review*.

> Tillie Lerner is at work on a novel of mining life. She is a 21 year old Nebraska girl at present living in Stockton, Calif. Last year she took a leave of absence from the Young Communist League to produce a future citizen of Soviet America. (2)

With a Soviet America just around the corner—and, indeed, with a world to win—propaganda, battle cries, and calls to revolution could be the stuff of literature, but there was not time for the painstaking editing that later became a hall-mark of Olsen's work. Her images are not as compressed, as controlled in her early writing as they would later be. She also deals less with the complexity of consciousness and more with the economic causes of oppression than she does in her "second period." In 1933–34 Olsen wrote propaganda, not to fulfill specific Party assignments, but in a passionate, buoyant response to a working class that was on the move. Her early '30s writing had many of the qualities of muckraking and reportage—a forthrightly anti-establishment point of view; a sense of immediacy; a narrator "intruding" into the text; exposure of corporate and governmental corruption and inhuman working and living conditions; and the attempt to involve the reader in the reported issue or event. This early writing is also marked by a didacticism, an "us/them" opposition, and a political certainty absent from Olsen's later texts.

SIX

Olsen's *Yonnondio:*
From the Thirties

Bang!

    Bess who has been fingering a fruit-jar lid—absently, heedlessly drops it—aimlessly groping across the table, reclaims it again. Lightning in her brain. She releases, grabs, releases, grabs. I can do. Bang! I did that. I can do. I! A look of neanderthal concentration is on her face. That noise! In triumphant, astounded joy she clashes the lid down. Bang, slam, whack. Release, grab, slam, bang, bang. Centuries of human drive work in her; human ecstasy of achievement; satisfaction deep and fundamental as sex: *I can do, I use my powers*; *I! I!* Wilder, madder, happier the bangs. The fetid fevered air rings with Anna's, Mazie's, Ben's laughter; Bess's toothless, triumphant crow. Heat misery, rash misery transcended.

Yonnondio: From the Thirties

    "Mazie. Live, don't exist. Learn from your mother, who has had everything to grind out life and yet has kept life. Alive, felt what's real, known what's real. People can live their whole life not knowing. . . . But there is more—to rebel against what will not let life be."

Elias Caldwell to Mazie Holbrook, *Yonnondio: From the Thirties*

Yonnondio: From the Thirties, which provides a bridge between Olsen's writing published in 1934 and her more recent writing, constituted her most important literary effort during the '30s. Her promising short story, "The Iron Throat," became 60 percent of the first chapter, and she completed the first four chapters, or almost half, of the novel before abandoning it in 1937. As in Olsen's "second period" work, the central theme of *Yonnondio* is the tension between the human drive to learn, assert, and create and the social forces that obstruct that drive. But varying tendencies coexist uneasily within *Yonnondio*—some elements adhere to the tenets of proletarian realism while other elements subvert them. These conflicting tendencies hint not only at Olsen's increasing ambivalence about what I have loosely termed "the Party aesthetic" but also at fundamental problems within the '30s CP and orthodox Marxism itself. Before examining the novel, I will describe how the 40-year-old manuscript was retrieved.

An explanatory note appended to the novel when it was finally published in 1974 describes the reclamation process. In 1972, while looking through other old papers, Jack Olsen discovered some tattered pages of *Yonnondio*, long believed lost or destroyed. A thorough search turned up more pages, scraps, and scrawls in yellowed notebooks. Other parts, evidently once in existence, seemed irrevocably lost. In 1972–73, working in the "solitude and protection" of the MacDowell Colony, Tillie completed *Yonnondio* in "arduous partnership" with "that long ago young writer." Olsen tells us that "the first four chapters, in final or near-final form when fitted together, presented only minor problems. The succeeding pages [which became four more chapters] were increasingly difficult to reclaim." In some sections Olsen had to choose from many versions. She had to decipher scrawls, piece together fragments, decide what to include or omit, and guess where several scenes belonged. "But it is all the old manuscripts—no rewriting, no new writing," Olsen's note explains. She felt she "didn't have any right" to revise what "that long ago young writer" had intended for print ("A Note" 157–158; Rosenfelt interview). The novel's title, taken from the title of a Whitman poem, is an Iroquois word meaning "lament for the lost." The dirge concludes: "A muffled sonorous sound, a wailing word is borne / through the air for a moment, / Then blank and gone still, and utterly lost." Olsen never finished the novel, and the title serves as an elegy for people like the Holbrooks, the main characters; for the incompleteness of the novel itself; and for Olsen's interrupted, nearly "lost" writing career.

The remainder of this chapter has two major components. The first summarizes and comments on *Yonnondio* as a whole; the second analyzes in detail its four provocative narrative intrusions.

Yonnondio traces the Holbrook family's futile search for a decent living over a two-and-a-half-year period. Their desperate odyssey takes them from a Wyoming mining community to an unproductive farm in the Dakotas and finally to a suffocating slaughterhouse neighborhood in Omaha. We recall that Olsen's parents struggled unsuccessfully to farm in Nebraska, while her father moonlighted at various jobs, including one in a packinghouse; *Yonnondio*'s packinghouse scenes were also drawn from Olsen's firsthand knowledge of the industry in Kansas City, where she worked as a trimmer and was jailed for organizing workers. To show the family's response to their poverty and transience, which is often in incomplete thoughts and unspoken fears and dreams, Olsen "becomes," in turn, the consciousness of the six-year-old Mazie, her mother Anna, and briefly, her father Jim. (Interpolations of acerbic editorial comment, which I will subsequently discuss, compose a fourth narrative thread.) While her characters' memories, fears, and unspoken ambitions flit backward and forward in time, the "story" begins at a relatively specific time, the early '20s, and progresses in a traditional chronological manner.

The novel opens with the piercing, early-morning blast of the mine whistle, which announces the beginning of another day's labor for the mining community. While Jim Holbrook descends into "the iron throat," Anna Holbrook, lacking the barest essentials, struggles to care for their growing family—all the while dreading the whistle's blast, which during the day signals an accident at the mine. The Holbrooks seek a better life on a tenant farm, which after the mining town, initially seems like paradise. Although the work is grueling, the family flourishes and even enjoys some festivity, a midsummer barn dance, for which Anna "recklessly" buys bright hair ribbons (41). Mazie responds well to "the drama of things growing," the opportunity to attend school, and the encouragement of their educated, humanitarian neighbor, old Mr. Caldwell.

When drought and depression prices force them off the farm, the Holbrooks move to Omaha, where Jim takes a job underground again—in a sewer, this time—and later in a packinghouse. In the novel's penultimate scene, the workers try desperately to slow down the literally killing pace of the "Beedo" speed-up system, which becomes especially oppressive during a summer heat wave.[1] As the days grows hotter, they all suffer, but the stronger ones try to spell those "near their limit of endurance" (144). When the convey gets jammed, the foreman fines the workers for carelessness and becomes suspicious of Kryckszi, who has been organizing them to slow the pace. One man faints with heat prostration; another, a victim of a heart attack, is docked pay and charged for the company ambulance that carts him away. After a bursting steam pipe badly scalds a number of women, the boss yells, "Stay where you are. . . . You'll be docked for every second you aint workin. And fined for carelessness" (146).

Jim and Anna turn on one another and the children out of anger, anxiety, and exhaustion. She blames him for not adequately supporting the family, and, like the miner-father in Lawrence's *Sons and Lovers*, he blames her for the burden of "your damn brats" (15). When Jim drinks, he beats Anna and the children. One night, while the rest of the children sleep, Mazie overhears her drunken father rape her mother, who is weak and ill from a miscarriage that occurred in his absence ("Can't screw my own wife. . . . Hold still" [91]). Anna hemorrhages. After his drinking bouts, however, a remorseful Jim feels tenderness for his family and makes "vows that life will never let him keep" (107).

Along with this dark picture of "human wreckage" Olsen conveys her passionate belief in human potential (148). One balmy spring day Anna takes the children to the outskirts of Omaha in search of dandelion greens to eat. A spell comes over Anna ("Mazie felt the strangeness rising in her mother, not like sickness strange, something else"), who suddenly grabs a dandelion with a seedy white head and, in one great breath, fills the air with white fluff. Next she impulsively blows one of their paper bags full of air, pops it loudly, and laughs. In her playful mood she braids the stems of dandelions, boasting, "We'll make a chain a block long," and then wraps young Jimmie in it. They come upon an empty lot on a river bluff lush with grass, dandelions, flowers, and blossoms that have fallen from a catalpa tree. Declaring their fragrance "that best smell," Anna scoops up a handful of the catalpa blossoms, shows the children how to suck honey out of one end, and points out the vivid markings inside. "Yes, Benjy, they do feel velvet inside. Rub it on your cheek" (117). Momentarily, Anna is even further transformed: "A remote, shining look was on her face, as if she had forgotten them, as if she had become someone else, was not their mother any more." Anna

> smiled so radiantly, Mazie's heart leapt. Arm in arm, they sat under the catalpa. That look was on her mother's face again, her eyes so shining and remote. She began stroking Mazie's hair in a kind of languor, a swoon. Gently and absently she stroked. . . .
>
> > I saw a ship a sailing
>
> her mother sang.
>
> > A sailing on the sea. . . .
> > I saw a ship a sailing
> > And on that ship was me.
>
> The fingers stroked, spun a web, cocooned Mazie into happiness. . . .

But the spell is soon broken:

> "I'm hungry," Ben said.
> "Watch me jump," Jimmie called. . . . Momma, Mazie, watch. You're not watching!"
> The wind shifted, blew packing house. A tremble of complicity ran through Mazie's body; with both hands she tethered her mother's hand to keep it stroking, stroking. Too late. Something whirred, severed, sank. *Between a breath, between a heartbeat, the weight settled, the bounds reclaimed.*
> "I'm watching," Anna called. The mother look was back on her face, the mother alertness, attunement, in her bounded body. . . .
> Never again, but once, did Mazie see that look—the other look—on her mother's face. (117–120)

Only for a moment Anna tasted that "happiness and farness and selfness" so long buried, and so nearly extinguished, under the imperatives of motherhood (119).

Another moment of relief comes in the novel's ambiguous conclusion, which follows the description of the packinghouse's hellish conditions. Jim returns from work so depleted he cannot even speak; he lies by the stoop in an evening shadow. Despite the extreme heat, Anna has been canning jars of jelly and fruit all day, but when her knees begin to tremble, she forces herself to keep standing (*"You know if you set down you'll never make yourself get up again"* [149]). "It is all heat delirium and near suffocation," when suddenly

> *Bang!*
> Bess who has been fingering a fruit-jar lid—absently, heedlessly drops it— aimlessly groping across the table, reclaims it again. Lightning in her brain. She

releases, grabs, releases, grabs. I can do. Bang! I did that. I can do. I! A look of neanderthal concentration is on her face. That noise! In triumphant, astounded joy she clashes the lid down. Bang, slam, whack. Release, grab, slam, bang, bang. Centuries of human drive work in her; human ecstasy of achievement; satisfaction deep and fundamental as sex: *I can do, I use my powers; I! I!* Wilder, madder, happier the bangs. The fetid fevered air rings with Anna's, Mazie's, Ben's laughter; Bess's toothless, triumphant crow. Heat misery, rash misery transcended. (153)

In *Mother to Daughter Daughter to Mother* Olsen recounts a dream her mother had, while dying, of the universal human baby, "holy with possibility," that Bess so apparently represents. In the dream, Ida Lerner felt a baby in her arms, "the human baby, before we are misshapen; crucified into a sex, a color, a walk of life, a nationality" (263). With the banging of baby Bess's fruit-jar lid, Olsen announces with a crescendo her belief in the innate drive to assert and create.

While mother and children laugh with delight at baby Bess, brother Will arrives with a borrowed radio, and they listen in wonder: "From where, from where, thinks Mazie, floating on her pain; like the spectrum in the ray, the magic concealed; *and hears in her ear the veering transparent meshes of sound, far sound, human and stellar, pulsing, pulsing. . . .* (153). With "meshes of sound, far sound . . . pulsing," the text hints that Mazie not only hears the radio but also presciently senses a future, distant rebellion "against what will not let life be" (49). Her spirits lifted, Anna calls gently to Jim, "Come in, get freshened up. Here, I'll help you. The air's changin, Jim. I see for it to end tomorrow, at least get tolerable" (154). There is a significant difference between the masses making for the barricades and the fleeting relief of this final passage. This tentatively upbeat ending—a nine-year-old's vague intuition, a slight improvement in temperature, and an infant's triumphant discovery of her powers—is at odds with the measure of revolutionary elan typical of '30s proletarian novels.

This was not the conclusion Olsen herself originally intended. *Yonnondio* was set in the '20s because Olsen envisioned the novel as a variant of the *kunstlerroman*—that is, a portrait of a radical artist as a young woman—with a time frame extending into the '30s as Mazie Holbrook matured. Olsen's conception of the novel in 1932 differed considerably from its form when it was published over 40 years later. Her original outline went as follows: Jim Holbrook gets involved in a packinghouse strike that politicizes Anna and the older Holbrook children (Mazie and Will) and involves some of the women in the packinghouse as strike leaders; embittered by the length of the strike and humiliated by his inability to support his family, Jim deserts them; Anna dies trying to give herself an abortion; one of the younger Holbrook children dies, too, and the remaining children are dispersed; Mazie and Will join the homeless youth migrating to California and in the Imperial Valley become organizers and join the CP; young Jimmie Holbrook becomes a jazz musician, but it is in Mazie, who becomes a writer, that political consciousness and personal creativity coalesce (Rosenfelt, "Thirties" 390; Rosenfelt interview; Duncan 219). Had Olsen completed the novel she intended to write, the "far sound" Mazie heard in the lines quoted above would have become foreshadowing for the packinghouse strike, for Mazie's becoming a CP organizer, and for her development into a revolutionary writer. Moreover, Olsen planned for the novel to have the closure lacking in *Yonnondio*'s ambiguous conclusion, where the future is an open question.

Olsen herself now considers the "political correctness" of her projected plan for *Yonnondio* amusing, pointing out that it would have included elements of both a "strike" and a "conversion" novel, two common types of proletarian novels. Even in its incomplete form, however, *Yonnondio* contains elements of these often formulaic novels. As in many proletarian novels, demarcations in *Yonnondio* between the exploited workers ("hard, bitter, strong") and the exploiting mine or factory owners ("fat bellies") are clearly drawn, and revolution is inevitable ("Someday the bowels will grow monstrous and swollen with these old tired dreams, swell and break, and strong fists batter the fat bellies") (49, 14).

Yonnondio also depicts the working class as the subject of history, reflecting a standard assumption by '30s leftists. In the 60 years since then, however, Marxists have begun to question the historic role Marxism has assigned the working class, and some argue that ours is an age in which no single, identifiable subject of history exists.[2] Art critic Hal Foster usefully defines class as "a construct of specific social praxis, not a historical datum always 'there' to be represented," as it appears in *Yonnondio* and other proletarian novels (143). Multiple differences—as exemplified by the revolt of Third World peoples, feminism, racial "minorities," sexual groups, the problem of the role of intellectuals in revolutionary struggle, the antinuclear and environmental movements, etc.—cannot be reduced to a common identity or a simple logic of class. Confronted with increasing social complexity, we can either deny differences, or we can accept them as constitutive of the social field and recognize political struggle as practices that articulate those differences (Laclau 117).

Yonnondio confronts one of the differences within the working class that the '30s CP minimized—the divisive effects of sexism. At a time when Avram Landy, representing the CP leadership, minimized tensions between working-class women and men, asserting, "it is because the husband is exploited [by capitalism] that the housewife's position is wretched and miserable" (64), the novel implicitly emphasizes the way in which the sexual division of labor militates against working-class unity. The novel depicts Jim and Anna's taunting one another and his abandoning the family for days at a time; Jim "struck Anna too often to remember," and, at one point (as noted above), rapes her (15). Their visions of the future also clash, with a psychic division of labor accompanying the material one. Anna frets that her children will go uneducated, is thoughtful about her friend Marie's wish that their daughters enter convents rather than live in poverty and bear more children "to get their heads blowed off in the mine" (10). Jim, on the other hand, wonders what "earthly use can a woman have" except childbearing. As a man he must never reveal his fear of the mine, and when Anna pushes him to consider the dangers of his job, he tells her, "Quit your woman's blabbin" (10).

In *The Origin of the Family, Private Property, and the State,* Engels argued that the husband is the bourgeois while the wife represents the proletariat (744). This relationship of domination/subjection provides a structural basis for animosity rather than mutual understanding and solidarity within the working class. Although Jim is not politicized (except in the envisioned version of the novel), his perception of "wife" would not readily expand to incorporate "political comrade." In fact, Jim vents his rage at Anna rather than at his capitalist boss. As the other side of this perverse equation, Anna occasionally reduces Jim to a mere breadwinner, blaming him for not adequately supporting the family, a responsibility both of them assume is primarily, if not exclusively, his. Such opposition makes class camaraderie problematic at best, and the Party minimized the consequences of the sexual division of labor at some cost.

Since tensions between Anna and Jim ease considerably during the brief period of relative prosperity on the farm, *Yonnondio* implies that gender-based antagonisms are related in a simple cause-and-effect way to economic oppression. According to the prevailing view of '30s Party members, a socialist revolution would sweep away sexual oppression in its wake (as noted in Chapter 2, one *Daily Worker* headline proclaimed about the Soviet Union: "All [Sex] Inequality Abolished by the October Revolution"), and Party women tended to defer their hopes for a feminist future. Nevertheless, whatever Olsen's intention at the time, *Yonnondio* also provides evidence that the social construction of gender is an entrenched, unconsciously reproduced phenomenon that will not overturn itself simply by "tailing" a transformation in economic relations.

Yonnondio is marked by stylistic shifts from reportive to consciously stylized prose. The packinghouse scenes, for example, are written in the sharply focused naturalistic detail of muckraking, whereas the Holbrooks' sensations, dreams, potent silences, and hunger-induced hallucinations are described in lyrical, surrealistic, and stream-of-consciousness narrative forms. Olsen strains away from traditional narrative to suggest the Holbrooks' longing to move beyond their historical constraints. Denied rational, sequential thought and speech, however, the Holbrooks can formulate only truncated questions. Thus, in the following representative passage, after Mazie half wakes from a feverish sleep, content expresses itself in form:

> The sun is slanting its long last rays through the window. An iridescence floats on her hand, rainbows the wall, shifts in scales of hue here and there in the room. What is it, what is it? The hanging prism? One of the rays, touching it, has cracked open; burst; unfolded the radiance. The other rays still slant unbroken — straight shafts of light, clear threads of glass. Are the rainbows, the floating pools, the radiance folded into each one of them too? Where kept? How hidden? The wonder dazes her head and she turns her hand to hold the stammering light, unlock its magic, but she grasps shadows. . . . (151)

The sunlight's elusive iridescence casts the Holbrooks' lives into stark, colorless relief. What they are forbidden dwarfs their meager possibilities. At various times Mazie, Anna, and Jim are supraconscious and semiconscious (sometimes they are both at once), but they are "inarticulate," to employ Olsen's word for Andy Kva-ternick (a character who will be discussed below) (14). While their wishes and dreams transcend the grim empirical present, their silences—it is all "a voiceless dream to be endured"—suggest the limits of that empirical present for the working class (73, 89). What is absent and what is present are in constant tension, one informing the reader of the other.

The narrator of the interpolations (which I will subsequently discuss in detail) is joined by three other narrators—Mazie, Anna, and Jim. Together these four con-stitute a collective protagonist, which DuPlessis defines as a way of organizing the text "so that neither the development of an individual against a backdrop of supporting characters nor the formation of a heterosexual couple is central to the novel" (163). One of the progressive effects of the collective protagonist is a merging of the public and private spheres that a patriarchal and capitalist system would have us keep separate. The use of a collective protagonist also implies that problems bourgeois culture would have us view "as individually based are in fact social in cause and cure" (DuPlessis 179).

Because form is profoundly dependent on historical change, the best that working-class writing can do is to prefigure post-individual forms in some pro-visional sense; so long as "monadic isolation" exists "as a social fact," the indi-vidual point of view will predominate (Jameson, *Marxism* 357). Nevertheless, *Yonnondio*'s reliance on heteroglossia and the novel's four narrators represent an attempt to move beyond an individual point of view toward more collective forms—in structures of narrative suggesting the structures of social change.

The presence of a feminist voice in the novel also pluralizes the text. Written over 30 years before the existence of the women's movement that would welcome *Yonnondio*'s publication in 1974, the novel emphasized many of the physiological events that shape women's lives—pregnancy, childbirth, miscarriage, battery, and rape. This is remarkable at a time when these topics seldom appeared in litera-ture, including proletarian writing. And Olsen's unsentimental presentation of institutionalized motherhood has forced on the American literary canon a subject hitherto forbidden except in idealized form. Ambiguous phrases from "Tell Me a Riddle"—"lovely mouths devoured," "the long drunkenness," "the drowning into needing and being needed" (93)—could just as well describe the experience of Anna Holbrook, who is so depleted by her children's dependency that she sinks into a "dream paralysis" (52).

What Jim derisively calls "woman's blabbin," like Butch's complaint to the narrator in Le Sueur's *The Girl* ("you got words for everybody"), approximates a labeling of *Yonnondio*'s heteroglossic impulses. Mazie, with her special sensitivity to language, lists the words she knows, tells her brother stories, recites poetry. Moreover, she vocally opposes the sexual division of labor, even though neither of her parents does: "Why is it always me that has to help? How come Will gets to play?" (142). In the penultimate, packinghouse scene, it is a woman "who [has] a need to put things into words," who chants the workers' plight in kitchen imagery (144). And when Mis' Kryckszi takes care of the children after Anna's miscarriage, she sings them "not lullabies, but songs of her own country in which her fierce anger flashed" (90). As noted earlier, the novel concludes with baby Bess "banging out her emerging identity" with a fruit-jar lid (Cora Kaplan 7). Although the novel was not published in the '30s, *Yonnondio's* foregrounding of its female characters helped to balance the emphasis in proletarian writing on the male industrial worker. But it is important to note that the novel also shows sympathy for the frustration and degradation of working-class men.

During the '30s Olsen "felt a certain kinship with Henry Roth" because of his working-class origin and because *Call It Sleep* (1935), which she read and admired during the later stages of her work on *Yonnondio*, was considered unusually subjective, personal, and "too psychological" (Rosenfelt interview). Printed 26 times, *Call It Sleep* is an imaginative, complex, and critically acclaimed proletarian novel that records two years (from age six to eight) in the childhood of a Jewish working-class immigrant, David Schearl. The conditions of poverty, repressive Hebrew school, adolescent sex, parental conflicts, and fears—real and imagined—are refracted through the mind of this precocious, vulnerable child. Because the novel, like parts of *Yonnondio,* is narrated through the consciousness of a child trying to understand a shattered and oppressive world, both human potential and its tragic waste seem more pronounced.

However, since the more dogmatic Marxist critics skeptically viewed literature concerned primarily with domestic and psychological subjects, *Call It Sleep* stirred controversy in *New Masses.* The first reviewer dismissed it in a paragraph, concluding, "It is a pity that so many young writers drawn from the proletariat can make no better use of their working class experience than as material for introspective and febrile novels" (cited in Rideout 189). In the following issue *New Masses* published a letter protesting the review, and Edwin Seaver calmed the waters by siding with the protest against the original review (Rideout 189).

As a parent Olsen became intrigued by "the shaping of human beings" and the gradual development of class consciousness—not in "the usual conversion sense" but in the "everyday sense . . . in an earned, in a bone way"; in the intended version of *Yonnondio* it would have been "things like memories of Anna" that would have affected Mazie's becoming a revolutionary (Rosenfelt interview). By making the subtleties of psychological and emotional development the stuff of proletarian writing, Olsen hoped to make a "major contribution to revolutionary literature" (Rosenfelt interview). The tenets of proletarian realism, however, imply that mental and emotional states are a "Bohemian," bourgeois concern, not a suitable subject for working-class literature.

The novel includes four narrative intrusions or interpolations, separated typographically from the rest of the text (apparently for emphasis), by an omniscient narrator. Like "I Want the Women Up North to Know," these interjections attack formalism, which elevates aesthetic concerns over sociopolitical ones. Olsen views her art as pedagogical: "I was writing the reason why we have to have a revolution," she has said about *Yonnondio.* She did not trust the novel, if stripped of these didactic passages, fully to affect her readers, to make them "get the impact," and to indicate the causes and remedies for the Holbrooks' misery, which they themselves perceive and articulate only in a limited way (Rosenfelt interview). Olsen quite deliberately adhered to the principles of socialist realism, which, as defined by Edwin Seaver in _New Masses_ (22 October 1935), demanded that the writer "take a conscious part in leading the reader through the maze of history toward Socialism and the classless society" (23–24).

These four indented passages interrupt _Yonnondio_'s narrative much as Brecht's _Verfremdung_ ("estrangement effect") disrupts his plays (although, since Brecht's literary work had not yet been translated into English and circulated in the United States, Olsen could not have known that she was employing a device similar to Brecht's). Such intrusions counter traditional realism, in which the present social order appears as natural, static, and immutable rather than contradictory, discontinuous, and, potentially, the object of revolutionary change. The interpolations also announce the gulf between art and reality, which realism effaces but Brecht's epic theater foregrounds. Conventional realism assumes the reader to be a passive recipient of a representation, whereas Brecht and Olsen attempt to jolt the audience/reader into an active spectatorship that may lead to their opposing the status quo. _Yonnondio_ deliberately dispels what James Kavanagh terms the "fiction-effect," refusing the posture of a unified coherence that traditional realist novels assume (30).

The novel's four narrative intrusions, which concern a failure of understanding or communication, challenge readers in several ways. In each of the interpolations the changeling narrator assumes different stances and voices. Because the multiple-voiced narrator and the subject with which she is concerned display the novel's impulse toward heteroglossic structures, the four narrative intrusions require close examination.

The first begins as a dark reverie on Andy Kvaternick, to whom we have been indirectly introduced at the beginning of the novel. Andy is the thirteen-, maybe "nearer to fourteen"-year-old son of Marie and Chris, a miner who died "buried under slaty roof that the company hadn't bothered to timber." Jim Holbrook must leave early one day because, as he explains to Anna, "I gotta stop by Kvaternicks and get the kid. He's starting work today" (9). That work, of course, is the work of Jim and of Andy's dead father: work in the coal mine. Anna reports to Jim, "'Marie was tellin me, it would break Chris's heart if he only knew. He wanted the kid to be different, get an edjication'" (10). This is all we know of Andy before the narrative intrusion.

The interpolation begins, "Andy Kvaternick stumbles through the night" which is filled with "lost and crying voices." Andy's mind is a "black sea," "wild and stormy," in which "shipwrecked thoughts plunge and whirl." Andy, a lost soul in a world of lost souls, "breathes frantic, like an almost drowned man" (13). We do not know how many years into the life of Andy the narrator has plunged us, and the information is of no importance. The abrupt beginning of this narrative intrusion indicates the bleakness of the world to which we have been introduced at the novel's beginning and the inability of those caught in it to understand it. We realize that, despite his father's dreams for his son, Andy's fate was sealed at the moment of his birth.

Through the interpolation's first paragraph the narrator has described Andy and his circumstances, but at the beginning of the second paragraph the stance of the narrator changes, and she begins to address Andy. "But it [breathing] is useless, Andy. The coal dust lies too far inside; it will lie there forever, like a hand squeezing your heart, choking at your throat. The bowels of the earth have claimed you" (13). The narrator understands Andy's state as the boy does not and informs him of it rather matter-of-factly. The tone of this paragraph suggests that Andy is just one more case of many such cases the narrator has seen. However, as the narrative intrusion continues, the narrator is not dispassionate about Andy, the individual representative of an oppressed and benighted group of people.

In the next two paragraphs the narrator's mode of address to Andy changes from informing to commanding: "Breathe and breathe, Andy, turn your eyes to the stars." Having informed him of the futility of his breathing, the narrator urgently charges him to continue it. The narrator knows the inevitability of Andy's fate, and she continues to inform him of it ("Trying so vainly in some inarticulate way to purge your bosom of the coal dust"), but her knowledge cannot keep her from urging this human being to struggle in his own ignorant way (14). Her commands sound much like pleas to Andy to continue to fight for life.

The commands work in yet another manner, as basic directions for living ("breathe," "walk"). Andy, ignorant and lost, is the product of a world of such commands. Like his father, the boy exists in a world fully controlled by the mining company. Andy's existence, like that of his father, depends completely on his responding to his bosses' commands (the narrator refers to the roof-support pillar "the super ordered you to rob" [14]). The command is a form of address Andy understands, or at least to which he responds. What is different about the narrator's commands is not that they will lead to a different outcome for Andy, but that they come from someone who recognizes him as a human being like other human beings.

Although the command is a form of address to which Andy can respond, the narrator recognizes that Andy will not comprehend what she has enfolded in the command structure. Almost as though she knows that any explanation of his position in life is wasted on Andy, she confines direct social analysis to two brief sentences. "Earth sucks you in, to spew out the coal, to make a few fat bellies fatter. Earth takes your dreams that a few may languidly lie on couches and trill 'How exquisite' to paid dreamers" (14). This quick explanation, lost on Andy, is not lost on us as readers—and to ensure that it is not, the narrator returns to a version of it in a later interpolation. At this moment in this narrative intrusion we are, among other things, alerted how *not* to read this work. We are not reading "Sailing to Byzantium"; Olsen does not care "to keep a drowsy Emperor awake." As for Andy, whose "thoughts lie shipwrecked and very still far beneath the black sea of your mind," the narrator departs from him by reasserting his life as it is.

"You have taken your man's burden, and you have the miner's only friend the earth gives, strong drink, Andy Kvaternick" (15).

In the first interpolation we overhear a narrator who is familiar with the plight of the worker speaking frankly, but sympathetically, to an individual worker; however, in the second intrusion the narrator's primary audience and forms of address are quite different. The second intrusion occurs just after the siren has sounded, signaling an accident in the mine. The women, with "tearless faces, watching," gather at the mine to await news (30). As readers, we too await news, but, instead of providing that news immediately, the narrator pointedly asks us: "And could you not make a cameo of this and pin it onto your aesthetic hearts?" Suddenly, the narrator has broken off the story and turned on us. She has picked up the "how exquisite" point developed so briefly in the previous intrusion and is aiming it at us.

Unlike the commands of the previous interpolation, the first two paragraphs of this intrusion are structured around two carefully phrased questions—the opening question and the later, "You will have the cameo?" We seem to have powers Andy does not have. We have powers to make choices. Thus Olsen creates momentary potential for dialogue between us and the narrator. We do not need the basic life-giving commands addressed to Andy. But what are these powers we seem to have?: Those that allow us to choose to anesthetize ourselves by aestheticizing capitalism's harsh consequences, turning them into decorative objects of art; those that allow us to misread this novel, shrinking from its social commentary by turning it into a piece of literary art. But with the question structure (". . . could you not make . . .?"), it is clear that if this work is read as a decorative cameo of art, it is not Olsen's doing. We have the powers. How will we exercise them?

After the initial question we are given a litany of assertions about how the elements of the scene qualify for inclusion in an aesthetic object: "Surely it is classical enough for you—the Greek marble of the women, the simple, flowing lines of sorrow, carved so rigid and eternal. Surely it is original enough—these grotesques, this thing with the foot missing, this gargoyle with half the face gone and the arm" (30). This is a checklist, and insofar as we find the scene's elements commensurate with these criteria, we become the objects of the narrator's biting irony. Here she sorts the redeemable from the damned among her readers. To the damned she directs the question: "You will have the cameo?" It seems we have made a choice—clearly the wrong choice—and in so doing have thwarted potential for dialogue. But in this intrusion Olsen has yet an elaborate course for us as readers to run.

If we will have the cameo, we are relocated in the narrator's discourse. Because of the wrong choice we have made, we are no longer readers of whom she asks questions; we are now readers to whom she issues orders: "Call it Rascoe, Wyoming, any of a thousand mine towns in America, the night of a mine blowup. And inside carve the statement the company already is issuing— 'Unavoidable catastrophe'" (31). In the abrupt shift from the question to the command structure, those of us who have accepted the cameo have become, like Andy in the first intrusion, pitifully ignorant—dependent on, but not understanding, capitalism's greater power, manifest in the mining company. But the narrator, while sympathetic to Andy's dependence on her, refuses the dependence of those who have adorned themselves with the cameo. Rather, as she relocates us, she commands us to acknowledge the greater power on which we are dependent by carving the company's words in our cameo. Presumably we are to wear this cameo like a well-decorated scarlet letter, but unlike Hester Prynne, we deserve our designation.

The interpolation's concluding paragraph begins: "A cameo of this, then." But whom is the narrator addressing? Since she seems to create a version of the cameo in the remainder of the narrative interruption, she seems to be addressing herself. She seems to be saying, "if this is what they want, I'll give it to them now, and send them on their way." But has the narrator become complicitous with the powers of the status quo by creating a cameo for us? Not in the case of this particular cameo. What she gives us is a parody of an aesthetic cameo, and if we choose to accept and wear it, considering it a decorative work of art, we demonstrate our ignorance and complicity.

Silence and stillness predominate among the elements of Olsen's cameo, reflecting on the most classic of "cameos," Keats's "Ode on a Grecian Urn," to which the subjects of silence and stillness are central: "Thou still unravished bride of quietness." Keats's narrator is driven by the urn to a frenzy of questions addressed to the urn. He is driven by the urn's silence and stillness to imagine worlds of mad pursuit, of struggles to escape, of pipes and timbrels, of wild ecstasy. This power to stir his imagination prompts him to conclude that the urn will remain in the future and "in midst of other woe / Than ours, a friend to man." In his frenzy of imagination the narrator, at the poem's conclusion, hears the urn's assertion (an assertion much like an inscription in a cameo) "'Beauty is truth, truth beauty,'" and the narrator concludes "—that is all / Ye know on earth, and all ye need to know." Olsen's cameo is a world apart, reflecting on Keats's world apart.

Olsen's narrator also finds her subjects in silence and stillness, but she leaves them there. Calmly, she asks no questions, asserting: "No sobs, no word spoken." She has no need to question because she knows and will tell the causes of their silence: "Sorrow is tongueless. Apprehension tore it out long ago." These subjects have been silenced, not because an urn-artist has frozen them in time, but because their tongues have been torn out. Of her subjects Olsen says, "And in the smothered light, carved hard, distinct, against the tipple, they all wait." But they wait in stillness not because an urn-artist has frozen them in space. Rather, as we hear earlier in this narrative intrusion, "In the War to Live, the artist, Coal, sculptured them. It was his Master hand that wrought the intricate mosaic on this face—splintered coal inlaid with patches of skin and threads of rock." Truth does not lie in the beauty referred to in this cameo: "No sound, only the whimpering of children, blending so beautifully with the far cry of blown birds" (30, 31). Truth lies in the people's stillness and silence and in the causes of their stillness and silence.

Is there any room for imagination in this cameo? Almost. In this cameo it is not the narrator's imagination that is stirred. This is a narrator of harsh reality. But there is a stirring of imagination. This is the final element in the cameo: "The wind, pitying, flings coal dust into their eyes, so almost they could imagine releasing tears are stinging." In this ironic moment in which the master hand that sculpted them into stillness cannot control the wind that "flings coal dust into their eyes," the people can "almost" imagine their own stinging tears (31). In this cameo these people can almost imagine being fully alive.

In this cameo, as it parodies Keats's "Ode," Olsen has stripped the narrator of the controlling power of imagination and has severed truth and beauty. In so doing she has torn the aesthetic heart out of her own cameo. Once again we see Olsen writing, as Trotsky believed necessary, in strategic relation to bourgeois texts, usurping their forms for a discourse of resistance.

If we as readers can accept this dismembered cameo, perhaps we are not damned after all. Perhaps we are qualified to continue reading—and to maneuver against the dominant culture "outside" the text. Referring elliptically to Jim's surviving the accident in the mine shaft, the paragraph that breaks out of the narrative intrusion begins: "'He'll be back.' Brought up quiet and shaken five days later" (31). This seems not far removed from the condition of the potentially redeemed reader who, recognizing that "sorrow is tongueless," meets Olsen's challenge to forge conditions in which all people can speak.

The third narrative intrusion, which occurs as Elias Caldwell is about to die, is related to the second. It too deals with the silencing of a classical voice of knowledge. We have been carefully introduced to "Old Man Caldwell," an honored oddity among his neighboring South Dakota farmers. An early settler in the region, he was college educated and has long been something of a patriarch for the people in the area.

Caldwell takes a strong interest in Mazie, sharing his knowledge with her: "Then told her why the stars seemed dancing, how old stars were, how they lived and died, and of a people living long ago, the Greeks, who had named these stars and had found in their shapes images of what was on earth below" (44). He teaches Mazie and the other Holbrook children playful, imaginative poems:

> O Were I a Lum Ti Tum Tum
> In the land of the alivoo fig
> I'd play on the strum ti tum tum
> To the tune of the thinguma jig. (47)

He has conversations with Anna:

> "Vultures running it now. It doesn't make any difference whether it's republican or democrat; the same hand pulls the strings." She [Mazie] was going to ask him what he meant, but Anna answered into the kettle of steaming tomatoes, "The bellwether leads the flock all right, but who is it sees they're led how he wants? The one that trains the bellwether." (45)

He says to Anna, "'Mrs. Holbrook, children have marvelous minds. I hate to see what life does to 'em'" (45).

Old Man Caldwell is a complicated force in the story. If we look simply at what he has taught Mazie, some understanding of the stars and the Greeks, some nonsense verse, he seems to have given her nothing that will help her deal with the hard reality of her life. If we look at his conversations with Anna, they seem nothing more than exchanges of platitudes. However, just before the narrative interruption, Caldwell, dying, says to Mazie, "'Keep that wondering, Mazie, but try to *know*. Build on the knowing with the wondering.'" He continues, "'Mazie. Live, don't exist. Learn from your mother, who has had everything to grind out life and yet has kept life. Alive, felt what's real, known what's real. People can live their whole life not knowing.'" But he does not stop with "'learn from your mother.'" He recognizes that "'there is more—to rebel against what will not let life be'" (49).

Almost immediately after Caldwell's urging Mazie to see the need for rebellion, the narrative intrusion begins: "An old man, Elias Caldwell, death already smothering his breast, tries to tell a child something of all he has learned, something of what he would have her live by—and hears only incoherent words come out" (49). Here is Caldwell with vital knowledge for Mazie, trying to get it out before he dies, hearing himself babble. The narrator says, "Yet the thoughts revolve, revolve and whirl, a scorching nebula in his breast, sending forth flaming suns that only shatter against the walls and return to chaos. How can it be said?" (49). It is important to note that Caldwell, with his thoughts sending forth flaming suns, lies in antithesis to Andy Kvaternick (of the first narrative intrusion) whose "thoughts lie shipwrecked and very still far underneath the black sea of your mind" (15). Caldwell has an essential perspective Andy will never have. But it is equally important to note that neither thought process results in communication and neither escapes chaos. How can this be? Caldwell seems to have made some of the right choices that few others in the story have made. The interpolation continues with the narrator inside Caldwell's mind: "Once I lived in softness and ease and sickened. Once I chose a stern life, turning to people hard, bitter and strong—obscure people, the smell of soil and sweat about them—the smell of life . . . But I failed. I brought them nothing" (49–50). Caldwell's thoughts at the end of his life, then, are nearly as chaotic as Andy's thoughts have always been.

Caldwell is probably as close as we come in the novel to a classic liberal. He has moved from a life of comfort to a life with "the people" (we know his large farm house has modern "conveniences" that make it a world apart from the Holbrooks' house). He has appreciated the "obscure people, the smell of soil and sweat about them—the smell of life." Never has he realized how close such a perspective is to the aesthetic perspective dealt with briefly in the first and largely in the second narrative intrusions. Even his realization of failure is couched in paternalistic terms: "I brought them nothing." Far too late has Caldwell realized what could have saved him from liberalism: the necessity "to rebel against what will not let life be."

The narrative intrusion ends: "To die, how bitter when nothing was done with my life. And the nebula whirls and revolves, sending its scorching suns that break in a chaos of inarticulateness about this child with a sound of fear. Nothing of it said" (50). The narrator realizes where the "tragedy" of this scene lies. It is not in Caldwell's recognizing that he has done nothing with his life, but in the fact that his unrealized potential fragments into inarticulate chaos around young Mazie—the child to whom Caldwell so much wanted to communicate knowledge, the child who so much wanted Caldwell to communicate with her—and all the future workers she represents.

The fourth narrative intrusion draws on elements of the first three and occurs soon after Jim and his already overburdened co-workers in the sewer have been told they must increase their productivity. Tracy, one of the workers, responds by quitting his job. Jim, astounded by Tracy's action, says to himself, "'Alright for Tracy to talk, he doesnt have a wife and brats. But no man has any business having 'em that wants to stay a man. Having to take all that goddamn crap . . . Not that they aren't worth it though,' thinking of Jimmie. 'What else you got?'" (75–76). The narrative intrusion is in a voice quite different from the voices of the first three. It is very close to the voice of Jim. In fact, the intrusion begins with Jim's words: "'Alright for Tracy to talk, alright, he didn't have a wife and kids hangin round his neck like an anchor'" (76). At first it seems that the narrator has taken on Jim's perspective. The interpolation describes Jim's experience, but signals that something more is happening. In the second paragraph a Dos Passos-like running together of words mixes with Jim's voice: "And Tracy was young, just twenty, still wet behind the ears, and the old blinders were on him so he couldn't really see what was around and he believed the bull about freedomofopportunity and a chancetorise and ifyoureallywanttoworkyoucanalwaysfindajob and ruggedindividualism and something about pursuitofhappiness" (76–77). But this displacement of style is not the only clue that this passage represents more than Jim's voice. Early in the passage, the narrator has a perspective that seems close to Jim's, yet is somewhat greater than Jim has yet had. This voice seems to be Jim's, yet more than Jim's.

The larger perspective appears in the third paragraph: "So he [Tracy] threw it up, not yet knowing a job was God, and praying wasn't enough, you had to live for It, produce for It, prostrate yourself, take anything from It, for was it not God and what came was it not by Its Divine Providence, and nothing to do but bow to It and thank It for Its mercifulness to you, a poor sinner who has nothing to sell but your labor power" (77). Jim has quit one job, and life has continued to be enormously difficult as he has tried his hand at two other jobs. Maybe Jim has gained the perspective to comment on what it means for someone to quit a job. But Jim has never yet had the degree of perspective that would generate allegory. The allegory continues: "So he threw it up, the big sap (not knowing), he renounced God, he became an atheist and suffered the tortures of the damned, and God Job (being full up that generation) never took him back into the fold only a few days at a time, and he learned all right what it meant to be an infidel, he learned" (77). No, this is not Jim, but it is not so far removed from Jim.

With the allegorical structure and the uncertainty about whether the narrator has assumed Jim's voice, we, as readers, realize that we are in a complicated situation similar to that of the second narrative intrusion. This is a classical cameo view of the usually veiled collusion between traditional religion and capitalism in their efforts to maintain order. For the moment it seems clear that this narrator, sensitive to years of grinding oppression of workers, is speaking from the point of view of a worker who has managed to rise to the bitter perspective of irony.

If this is what the narrator has done, we may have a solution to a problem running through all the narrative intrusions. Who will speak for the oppressed workers? Drowning Andy is incapable. The Keatsean aesthete is intolerably incapable. The classical liberal, Old Man Caldwell, is incapable. So maybe it must be a worker who has lived through oppression and has gained perspective. That seems a viable solution. But something still seems wrong. We have an individual worker gaining perspective through two classical aesthetic structures: allegory and irony. By now we should know that something is out of place.

The intrusion's final paragraph grants us clarity:

> And there's nothing to say, Jim Tracy, I'm sorry, Jim Tracy, sorry as hell we weren't stronger and could get to you in time and show you that kind of individual revolt was no good, kid, no good at all, you had to bide your time and take it till there were enough of you to fight it all together on the job, and bide your time, and take it till the day millions of fists clamped in yours, and you could wipe out the whole thing, the whole goddamn thing, and a human could be a human for the first time on earth. (79)

This is not the voice of Jim, and it is not the voice of a single enlightened worker. Instead, it is the voice of a group of workers like Jim—but an enlightened group. Further, we now recognize that the apparently ironic, allegorical passage was far more complicated than it looked when it seemed to be in the voice of a single worker much like Jim.

We now know that the passage must be viewed from a double perspective: that of the individual worker who has not yet realized the necessity of collective action, and that of collectivized workers who can see the possibility of being "a human for the first time on earth." In the first perspective the allegory must be taken as true, lived as reality. The individual worker, in the attempt to survive, must know that a job is God, must "live for It, produce for It." Hence, the narrator in the first narrative interruption commands Andy to continue what he does despite her recognition that Andy lives ignorantly within the structure that oppresses him. And with that knowledge of the God Job, the individual worker is denied ironic and allegorical perspective. In the second, collectivized point of view, there is ironic and allegorical perspective on individual subjugation and revolt. Such individualism is part of the "whole goddamn thing" that collective action could "wipe out" (79). And so we find Olsen, at the end of the last narrative interruption, apparently sanctioning two classical aesthetic structures. But these are no longer merely aesthetic structures—they have been "reborn" as tools of collective action. They are now lenses through which collectivized workers can see the twin oppressive structures of capitalism and traditional religion.

This "rebirth" of structures often associated with the aesthetic is symptomatic of Olsen's view of how writing can work. Not succumbing to the reductive simplicities of Gold's view of proletarian literature, Olsen has held a view much closer to that of Trotsky in *Literature and Revolution*. The structures of bourgeois literature do not belong to bourgeois literature alone. What makes those structures bourgeois is not their nature, but their use.

The four narrative intrusions constitute an exploration of the conditions necessary to maximize the possibility of heteroglossia. The tongues of the workers have been torn out. They have been silenced. Their multiple voices must be restored. How can that be done? Why not let a new generation of workers speak for themselves? Andy exemplifies one problem here. He has been born into the same world of oppression his parents inhabited and does not understand how it oppresses him. Tracy exemplifies another problem here. He has seen his own oppression, and he has rejected it by walking away from it. But in his individual action he simply abandons his fellow workers. Why not have someone else speak for the workers? Who has done that? Aesthetes of the Romantic stripe who have created cameos out of workers' lives? Classic liberals who have patronizingly construed the workers' lives? No, the workers must speak for themselves, but they can do so only if they learn to speak collectively—stealing the structures of communication from the oppressors and putting them to their own uses. The interpolations also provide guidelines for readers, directing us as we proceed through the novel how to read—and how not to read—structures we are accustomed to finding in aesthetic works and exemplifying how those structures can be used to subvert the dominant culture from which they have been appropriated.

History precedes form, and *Yonnondio*, as any other text of working-class writing, remains subsumed by bourgeois form. However, this novel (a cultural product of the '30s, when it was written, not of the '70s, when it was published) subverts elements not only of bourgeois culture but also of the '30s CP and orthodox Marxism. While *Yonnondio*'s critique of capitalism is foregrounded and full-blown, the novel also presciently resists some tendencies of Party politics and orthodox Marxism—such as productivism and its concomitant privileging of the industrial worker; the separation of public and private spheres; the subordination of gender issues to those of class; and the teleological notion that revolutionary struggles will achieve an ideal, static "state."

In *Yonnondio* Olsen strains away from her early '30s proletarian writing, her evolving lyrical style lending itself readily to the novel's two major themes— working-class familial relations and the complexity, susceptibility, and potential of human consciousness. Despite the Party's minimizing of consciousness as a site for ideological struggle, *Yonnondio* suggests, as DuPlessis argues in another context, that "one of the major powers of the muted is to think against the current" (196). "Reader, it was not to have ended here," Olsen laments in a note appended to the unfinished novel. On the contrary, in *Yonnondio* Olsen has written "beyond the ending."[3]

SEVEN

Literature as
"No One's Private Ground"[1]: Olsen's
Tell Me a Riddle and *Silences*

. . . a good novelist can do without everything but the remnant of his balls.

Norman Mailer, quoted in *Silences*

Tea on a tray for his "elevenses"; absolute silence in his working hours, and good meals at appropriate intervals.

What Edmund Wilson's second wife, Elena, provided him (as described in a letter from Louise Bogan to May Sarton, quoted in *Silences*)

. . . I, like many other women who work, especially as writers, was terrified of having children. . . . I had bought the prevailing sexist directive: you have to have balls (be a man) to write. In my opinion, having a child is easily the equivalent of having balls. In truth, it is more than equivalent: ballsdom is surpassed.

Alice Walker, from "One Child of One's Own," *In Search of Our Mothers' Gardens.*

"Commitment" is more than just a matter of presenting correct political opinions in one's art; it reveals itself in how far the artist reconstructs the artistic forms at his [/her] disposal, turning authors, readers and spectators into collaborators.

Terry Eagleton, referring to Walter Benjamin's "The Author as Producer"[2]

The areas on which *Yonnondio* focused—domestic labor, familial relations, thwarted creativity, and the complex realm of consciousness—hindsight finds noticeably absent not only from Olsen's other '30s writing but also from most proletarian literature and from discussions of its "proper" settings and subjects. From the '50s on, however, these areas constitute Olsen's central concerns. While

Olsen's "message" continues to be agitational in her "second period," the rhetorical model is more heteroglossic than that of her '30s publications. Moreover, like *Yonnondio*, *Tell Me a Riddle* and *Silences* foreground institutionalized motherhood, exposing what Olsen has rightly termed a "taboo area; the last refuge of sexism . . . [the] least and last explored, tormentingly complex *core* of women's oppression."[3] As it has been socially constructed, motherhood is an Achilles heel of the women's movement: Even the women whom the movement has most benefited, the educated professionals, learn that in our social system the pretense of equal opportunity collapses around the issue of responsibility for children. *Tell Me a Riddle*'s title story and *Silences* are virtually unique in American writing for their uncompromising look at the anguish of women who must choose between having children and the need to carry on other serious work. That more women than men have valued Olsen's fiction reminds us that textual meaning, rather than being fixed, is a consequence of a reader's particular situation in the world.

When Olsen resumed writing in the '50s, she continued writing working-class discourse in a period when, unlike the '30s, there was little support for doing so.

> When I began to write again . . . I was writing absolutely against the grain. That was the time of "the affluent society." That was the time of Holden Caulfield's "everything's phony". . . . the time when despair was fashionable. . . . the time when you didn't have books about people who had to work for a living [or] . . . old people who were having a hard time . . . let alone [books about] what it is to be a mother having to raise a child alone in a world that is not nurturing to human life.[4]

"I Stand Here Ironing," a story published in 1956 about "a mother having to raise a child alone," broke Olsen's 20-year literary silence. Olsen has said that the story "is somewhat close to my own life" (Martin 23). "I Stand Here Ironing" became the first of four stories collected in *Tell Me a Riddle* (1961).

These stories examine the marginalization and potential empowering of various groups of oppressed people, particularly women, by experimenting with potentially democratizing modes of discourse. Deborah Rosenfelt has rightly placed Olsen in

> a line of women writers, associated with the American Left, who unite a class consciousness and a feminist consciousness in their lives and creative work, who are concerned with the material circumstances of people's lives, who articulate the experiences and grievances of women and of other oppressed groups—workers, national minorities, the colonized and the exploited—and who speak out of a defining commitment to social change. ("Thirties" 374)

Although *Tell Me a Riddle* shows a range of marginalized lives, Olsen is far from content with merely portraying this multiplicity in American society. As Rosenfelt observes, Olsen writes out of a "commitment to social change," and this chapter will discuss some of Olsen's narrative/political strategies that exemplify that commitment.

The modes of discourse with which Olsen experiments in developing her narrative strategies, many of which I have discussed in the chapter on *Yonnondio*, are those she has derived and recreated from long and careful listening to the voices of marginalized people. The cacophony of their voices, Olsen recognizes, embodies a potentially democratizing force. Noting some of Olsen's uses of empowering discursive forms in *Silences*, Elizabeth Meese writes that "by means of a polyvocal chorus she [Olsen] questions silence and allows others to participate in the same process. . . . She then calls upon the reader to write the text—no longer her text, but occasioned by it and by the voices speaking through it" (110). The experiments noted by Meese as well as several other experiments pervade *Tell Me a Riddle*.

As I observed when discussing *Yonnondio*, some of Olsen's specific uses of discursive modes and the political/social changes they work to bring about are prefigured in Bakhtin's general concept of "heteroglossia." For Bakhtin, again, there are two competing forces in language use: "Every concrete utterance of a speaking subject serves as a point where centrifugal as well as centripetal forces are brought to bear" (*Dialogic* 272). The "centripetal" or "monologic" force presses toward unity, singularity of meaning; it attempts to assert its dominance by silencing uses of language that deviate from it. On the other hand, the "centrifugal" or "heteroglossic" force resists the dominance of monologism by fragmenting and disrupting it. The myriad heteroglossic voices of the marginalized constitute a social and political force against the tyranny of dominant discursive modes in any language community. Those such as Olsen who observe, record, and honor the multiple heteroglossic voices engage in the democratizing enterprise of amplifying dominated and marginalized voices.

Bakhtin's metaphor of "carnival" displays the nexus of heteroglossia and political/social power. Carnival, with its various simultaneous activities, is a site in which many of the usual societal impositions of class and order are suspended while the populace participates in multiple ways of parodying or mimicking the dominant culture's behavior. Terry Eagleton has described Bakhtin's notion of carnival in these terms: "The 'gay relativity' of popular carnival, 'opposed to all that [is] ready-made and completed, to all pretence at immutability', is the political materialization of Bakhtin's poetics, as the blasphemous, 'familiarizing' language of plebeian laughter destroys monologic authoritarianism with its satirical estrangements" (*Against* 117). As Dale Bauer develops her project "to determine a viable intersection between feminism . . . and modern/postmodern criticism, particularly through Bakhtin," she finds that "women 'on the threshold' of a social or cultural crisis" (such as Edith Wharton's Lily Bart and Kate Chopin's Edna Pontellier, who are among the characters Bauer discusses) "become powerful in the marginal realm which constitutes the carnival world" (2, 13). For Olsen women are among the marginalized groups "on the threshold." In *Tell Me a Riddle*, in several instances of carnival-like atmosphere, heteroglossia is unleashed to engage in a powerful, playful satirizing of the dominant culture.

The nurturing and recording of heteroglossia has democratizing potential, but heteroglossia itself and the recording of it also contain hazards both for the multiplicity of speakers and for those who listen to their voices. The collection of stories in *Tell Me a Riddle* presents a wide range of individual, marginalized voices competing for our attention. Unless readers/listeners make connections among a variety of voices, many of which are foreign to their own, the potential for genuine democracy latent within the cacophony of heteroglossia is lost. If they remain unconnected from each other, the competing voices lapse into a white-noise excess of sound that becomes unintelligible. Rejecting many traditional modes of authorial control, Olsen refuses opportunities to make connections for us and presses us to make connections among those voices ourselves. The social/political act of connecting otherwise isolated and marginalized voices realizes the democratizing potential of heteroglossia, and Olsen demands that we participate in such action.

To participate properly, we must be permeable to multiple voices, and in some characters in *Tell Me a Riddle*, Olsen shows us both the benefits and risks of receptivity to heteroglossia. Multiple voices often compete within a single character, displaying that character's complex web of ties to others and to the past. Heteroglossia on this level often operates in *Tell Me a Riddle* and other works by Olsen to undermine and offer alternatives to bourgeois individualism. But Olsen does not idealize the individual permeable to heteroglossia; she shows us hazards that exist in individual manifestations of heteroglossia (e.g., Whitey's isolation in "Hey Sailor, What Ship?" and the multiple voices that threaten to overwhelm the narrator of "I Stand Here Ironing"). *Tell Me a Riddle* asks us to be cognizant of the dangers we face as we assume the role Olsen insists we assume—that of active readers alert to the connections among a multiplicity of marginalized voices.

Throughout the stories in *Tell Me a Riddle* Olsen pits heteroglossic modes of discourse she associates with the oppressed against oppressors' monolingual/ monological modes of discourse. In the title story, Jeannie's sketch of Eva "coiled, convoluted like an ear" suggests Olsen's narrative/political strategies. Olsen's writing, like an ear "intense in listening," is permeable to the heteroglossic differences constitutive of a complex social field. The stories collected in *Tell Me a Riddle* strain away from the prevailing narrative and social order by "hearing" and incorporating the suppressed voices of mothers, those of the working class, and the dialects of immigrants and African-Americans; by deconstructing the opposition between personal and political; and, in the title story, by honoring the communal polyphony of a dying visionary.

A second and related narrative/political strategy is a reworking of traditional relationships among writer, text, and reader. The stories collected in *Tell Me a Riddle* subvert the concept of textual ownership, affirming the reader not as an object but, reciprocally, as another subject. Many dominant discursive practices still take for granted that the act of reading will be a subjection to a fixed meaning, a passive receiving of what Bakhtin terms "monologue." In Bakhtin's view of monological discourse, the writer directly addresses the readers, attempting to anticipate their responses and deflect their objections; meanings are seen as delivered, unchanged, from source to recipient. In Bakhtin's terms, monologue is "deaf to the other's response; it does not await it and does not grant it any *decisive force*" (cited in Todorov 107).

Heteroglossic discourse, on the other hand, acknowledges "that there exists outside of it another consciousness, with the same rights, and capable of responding on an equal footing, another and equal *I*" (cited in Todorov 107). *Tell Me a Riddle*'s heteroglossia acknowledges the other consciousnesses that exist outside the text. As Meese indicates about similar strategies in *Silences*, *Tell Me a Riddle* activates its reader-subjects while subverting authorial domination; in the tradition of Bertolt Brecht's theater and Jean-Luc Godard's cinematic montage, it turns writer and readers into collaborators.

The two categories of Olsen's narrative/political strategy I have identified— her recording of heteroglossia and her reworking of relationships among writer, text, and reader—constitute the two major divisions of this chapter's discussion of *Tell Me a Riddle*.

In *Tell Me a Riddle*'s first story, "I Stand Here Ironing," Olsen begins her recording of heteroglossia by exploring problems that fragment lives and discourse and by experimenting with narrative forms that display that fragmentation. Emily, the daughter of the unnamed narrator, had been born into "the pre-relief, pre-WPA world of the depression," and her father, no longer able to "endure . . . sharing want" with the 19-year-old mother and child, had left them when Emily was eight months old (10). The infant "was a miracle to me," the narrator recalls, but when she had to work, she had no choice but to leave Emily with "the woman downstairs to whom she was no miracle at all" (10). This arrangement grieved both mother and child: "I would start running as soon as I got off the streetcar, running up the stairs," the narrator remembers, and "when she saw me she would break into a clogged weeping that could not be comforted, a weeping I can hear yet" (10–11). Then came months of complete separation, while the child lived with relatives. The price for reunion was Emily's spending days at "the kinds of nurseries that [were] only parking places for children. . . . It was the only place there was. It was the only way we could be together, the only way I could hold a job" (11). Their situation improved with the presence of "a new daddy" (12). Although the narrator still worked at wage-earning jobs, she was more relaxed with her younger children than she had been with Emily: "it was the face of joy, and not of care or tightness or worry I turned to them." But, the narrator adds, by then it was "too late for Emily" (12).

The narrative is laced with references to the pressure of circumstance, the limits on choice: "when is there time?"; "what cannot be helped" (9); "it was the only way" (11); "We were poor and could not afford for her the soil of easy growth" (20); "She is the child of her age, of depression, of war, of fear" (20). Both mother and daughter have been damaged: While Emily expresses fear and despair casually ("we'll all be atom-dead"), her mother suffers because "all that is in her [daughter] will not bloom" (20). All the narrator asks for Emily is "enough left to live by" and the consciousness that "she is more than this dress on the ironing board, helpless before the iron" (21).

The story includes two major discursive forms. The form that appears through most of the story is indirect, circling, uncertain; it is heteroglossic. The other form, which Olsen points out and discards in one paragraph near the story's end, is direct, clipped, and assertive.[5] It is a version of the reductive dominant discourse contributing to the pressure of the circumstances in which Emily and her mother struggle to survive. With these two forms of discourse Olsen introduces issues that concern her in all the stories in *Tell Me a Riddle*: language as power; dominant versus subversive modes of discourse; heteroglossia.

The second major discursive form, the direct, is introduced by the narrator of "I Stand Here Ironing" in this way: "I will never total it all. I will never come in to say: She was a child seldom smiled at. Her father left me before she was a year old. I had to work her first six years when there was work, or I sent her home and to his relatives. There were years she had care she hated" (20). What the narrator offers here is what she will not say and what she will not do. She will not "total"—sum up—Emily's life in a direct, linear, cause-and-effect way. The instances of emphatic certainty in Olsen's 1934 publications have given way to a pensive, speculative tone in "I Stand Here Ironing" and *Tell Me a Riddle*'s other stories, which at points raise the "kind of question for which there is no answer" (16). The mother's refusal to "total" Emily's life is Olsen's refusal of answers couched in '30s economic determinism. *Tell Me a Riddle* probes—but does not attempt to resolve—the complex relation between individual lives and social forces.

The other major discursive form—with its many modes of indirectness, false starts, and uncertainties—is signaled in the form of address at the beginning of the story. The narrator says, "I stand here ironing, and what you asked me moves tormented back and forth with the iron" (9). This "you" (never clearly identified, but likely one of Emily's high school teachers, a guidance counselor, or a social worker) is the ostensible audience to whom the narrator's discourse is directed. However, in this most indirect form of address, the entire story takes place in the mind of the narrator, who is speaking to herself as though rehearsing her discourse for the "you." We do not know whether this discourse ever passes from the silence of the mother's mind to the hearing of the audience (the teacher or counselor) for whom it is being rehearsed.

The narrator must rely on indirect discursive forms as she looks back over her life with Emily: "Why do I put that first? I do not even know if it matters, or if it explains anything" (10); "In this and other ways she leaves her seal, I say aloud. And startle at my saying it. What do I mean? What did I start to gather together, to try and make coherent?" (18). These fitful "digressions" typify the movement of the story's first major discursive form. The user of that form, far from reducing her subjects to linear, cause-and-effect patterns, displays in multifaceted discourse her own complicated and ultimately irreducible forms of interdependence with

her subjects. The form is heteroglossic; it is a "voice" made of many voices:
Caught in the memory of conflicts between Emily and her sister, Susan, "each
one human, needing, demanding, hurting, taking," the mother says, "Susan
telling jokes and riddles to company for applause while Emily sat silent (to say to
me later: that was *my* riddle, Mother, I told it to Susan)" (16–17). As employed
in this and other stories in the collection, heteroglossia is not solely a matter of
multiple voices within or among cultures or subcultures; it is often the multiple
and conflicting voices that make up one person. Olsen's displays of individual
heteroglossia, the fragmenting of voices constituting a self and that self's interdependence with others, become one means by which her work offers alternatives to bourgeois individualism.

At the beginning of the story, the words of the unidentified teacher or counselor and the mother's reaction to those words create a complex intermingling of
voices. The mother has been asked to assist in helping Emily: "'I wish you would
manage the time to come in and talk with me about your daughter. I'm sure you
can help me understand her. She's a youngster who needs help and whom I'm
deeply interested in helping.'" The next line of the story is "'Who needs help.'. . ."
(9; ellipsis Olsen's). Who indeed? This entangling of the helpers and the helped,
including the suggestion that the mother is being asked for the very aid she herself
may need in order to assist Emily, is indicative of the ways in which the narrator's
thinking and discourse proceed. She cannot, in language, fully demarcate herself
from Emily or from those whose lives became entangled with Emily's in the past,
such as an unsympathetic nursery school teacher: "And even without knowing, I
knew. I knew the teacher that was evil because all these years it has curdled into
my memory, the little boy hunched in the corner, her rasp, 'why aren't you
outside, because Alvin hits you? that's no reason, go out, scaredy'" (11). Facing the
incessant pressure of time and circumstance—"when is there time to remember,
to sift, to weigh, to estimate, to total?"—the narrator recognizes that multiple
voices and memories constantly threaten to engulf her (9).

The nonlinear mode of discourse is so often replete with complexity of
meaning that it risks falling into meaninglessness and the equivalent of silence. In
this story that risk is most acute at moments when the mother cannot find the
language to respond to Emily. While looking back over her life with Emily, the
mother returns to times when she could respond to her daughter with nothing
more than silence.

> There was a boy she loved painfully through two school semesters. Months later she
> told me how she had taken pennies from my purse to buy him candy. "Licorice was
> his favorite and I brought him some every day, but he still liked Jennifer better'n
> me. Why, Mommy?" The kind of question for which there is no answer. (15–16)

On the night in which this story takes place, the mother is remembering such details of Emily's life and instances of failed communication between mother and
daughter. The cumulative details from the various stages of Emily's life and the
crowding of voices force the narrator to say near the story's end: "because I have

been dredging the past, and all that compounds a human being is so heavy and meaningful in me, I cannot endure it tonight" (20). A richness of meaning approximating meaninglessness and the equivalent of silence weighs on the mother when she says of Emily, "This is one of her communicative nights and she tells me everything and nothing as she fixes herself a plate of food" (19). Yet for the narrator a reliance on nonlinear discourse with its attendant hazards is not only a matter of what her circumstances have forced upon her. It is also a matter of choice.

The narrator must use nonlinear heteroglossic modes if her goal in telling Emily's story is, as she says it is, to "Let her [Emily] be." The complicated, conflicting stuff of which human beings are made can be discussed only nonreductively in nonlinear discourse, in a manner that has some chance of "letting them be." To adopt the dominant, linear, reductive mode of discourse is to usurp and control Emily, as Le Sueur would argue, and it is to abandon the hope with which the story ends: the narrator's hope that Emily will know "that she is more than this dress on the ironing board, helpless before the iron" (20–21).

The two major discursive forms in "I Stand Here Ironing"—the indirect, uncertain, circling form, and the direct, clipped, assertive form—appear again in "Tell Me a Riddle," and, again, Olsen uses them to explore language as power; dominant versus subversive modes of discourse; and heteroglossia. The story begins with a battle between Eva and David, who have been married for 47 years, most of them spent in poverty. In the dialect of Russian-Jewish immigrants, they bitterly dispute whether to sell their home and move to a retirement cooperative operated by David's union. He craves company while Eva, after raising seven children, will not "exchange her solitude for anything. *Never again to be forced to move to the rhythms of others*" (76). David and Eva use a not-always-direct, but relentlessly assertive and minimal form of discourse in their perpetual quarreling. We find that mode of discourse in their opening fray:

> "What do we need all this for?" he would ask loudly, for her hearing aid was turned down and the vacuum was shrilling. "Five rooms" (pushing the sofa so she could get into the corner) "furniture" (smoothing down the rug) "floors and surfaces to make work. Tell me why do we need it?" And he was glad he could ask in a scream.
> "Because I'm use't."
> "Because you're use't. This is a reason, Mrs. Word Miser? Used to can get unused!" (73)

They poke at each other with as few words as possible, using words not as instruments of communication but as weapons of combat and control. Further, each uses any available means to suppress the other's minimal discourse. She turns down her hearing aid and turns on the vacuum cleaner. He turns on the television "loud so he need not hear" (75).

The text only gradually reveals Eva's long-ago status as a revolutionary orator; only through fragments of dialogue and interior monologue do we learn that this obdurate, rancorous woman, who now wields power only by turning off her hearing aid, was once an orator in the 1905 Russian revolution. Models for Eva included Olsen's own mother. Another was Seevya Dinkin, who shares "Riddle"'s dedication with Genya Gorelick.[6] Gorelick had been a factory organizer in Mozyr, a famous orator, and the leading woman of the Jewish Workers' Alliance, the Bund of pre-revolutionary Russia. Her son, Al Richmond, has written about the role Gorelick played in the 1905 revolution, when she was just nineteen:

> . . . the 1905 revolution burst forth like the splendid realization of a dream, shaking the Czarist regime enough to loosen its most repressive restrictions, so that revolutionaries at last could address the public, not any more through the whispered word and the surreptitious leaflet but openly and directly in large assemblies. She discovered her gifts as a public orator. She was good, and in her best moments she was truly great. (8; cited in Rosenfelt, "Divided" 19)

"Tell Me a Riddle" illuminates, as no polemic could, the terrible cost of a sexual division of labor. David, who has worked outside the home, has sustained a vitality and sociability. But he has lost the "holiest dreams" he and Eva shared in their radical youth, seems to accept American "progress," and would rather consume TV's version of "This Is Your Life" than reflect on his own (119; 83). Insulated at home, Eva has felt less pressure to assimilate, to compromise her values, and has preserved those dreams. But the many years of 18-hour days, of performing domestic tasks "with the desperate ingenuity of poverty" (years in which David "never scraped a carrot") have transformed her youthful capacity for engagement into a terrible need for solitude (Rosenfelt "Divided" 19; *TMR* 74). In "Divided Against Herself: The Life Lived and the Life Suppressed," Rosenfelt explores the theme of the "buried life" as it appears in "Tell Me a Riddle" and Agnes Smedley's *Daughter of Earth*. In "Tell Me a Riddle" the buried life is Eva's engaged, articulate, political self, whereas in *Daughter of Earth* it is the intimate, maternal, domestic self. Both texts protest a division of labor that prevents women from being whole.

When David learns that Eva is dying of cancer and has at best a year to live, he sees the pointlessness of debating the sale of the house and takes her on a cross-country visit to children and grandchildren, despite her continued desire to be alone. At the home of Vivi, a daughter with five children, including a newborn, Eva witnesses a reenactment of her own years of exhausting motherhood with a painful ambivalence: "*How was it that soft reaching tendrils also became blows that knocked?*" (95). When the new baby is put in her lap, "she holds him stiffly, *away* from her," and for the remainder of the visit refuses to touch him. Eva, who had deeply loved her own "seductive" babies, knows only too well "*what the feel of a baby evokes*," that "warm flesh like this . . . had claims and nuzzled away all else" (91, 93).

A staunch atheist, Eva is offended when another daughter lights Friday evening candles in the Jewish ritual of benediction. David explains that Hannah does it for "heritage," for "tradition," while Eva insists that she does it "for emptiness" (90).

"Does she look back on the dark centuries? Candles bought instead of bread and stuck into a potato for a candlestick? Religion that stifled and said: in Paradise, woman, you will be the footstool of your husband, and in life—poor chosen Jew—ground under, despised, trembling in cellars. And cremated. And cremated." (90)

Hannah has only emptiness for tradition, partly because Eva asked of her "only hands to help" as she was growing up (91). One of the costs of Eva's denying her political and intellectual passions in those years of mothering is the loss of heritage she might have transmitted to her children. She did not share with them the things that had given her own life meaning.

As Eva is dying she slips into the indirect discursive mode. After years of bitter silence, she begins to speak, sing, and recite incessantly. Fragments of memories and voices, suppressed during her years of marriage and motherhood, emerge as the old woman nears death. Eva, like the mother in "I Stand Here Ironing," becomes an individual embodiment of heteroglossia. Eva had announced her desire for solitude, but ironically she returns in her reverie to the time when she was engaged with others in a revolutionary movement. She sings revolutionary songs from her youth and in a "gossamer" voice whispers fragments of speeches she had delivered in "a girl's voice of eloquence" half a century before (119). Her babble is a communal one; she becomes a vehicle for many voices.

Eva's experiences while dying may have been partly modeled on those of Ida Lerner. "In the winter of 1955," Olsen reports in *Mother to Daughter Daughter to Mother*, "in her last weeks of life, my mother—so much of whose waking life had been a nightmare, that common everyday nightmare of hardship, limitation, longing; of baffling struggle to raise six children in a world hostile to human unfolding—my mother, dying of cancer, had beautiful dream-visions—in color." She dreamed/envisioned three wise men, "magnificent in jewelled robes" of crimson, gold, and royal blue. The wise men ask to talk to her "of whys, of wisdom": "*But as they began to talk, she saw that they were not men, but women: That they were not dressed in jewelled robes, but in the coarse everyday shifts and shawls of the old country women of her childhood, their feet wrapped round and round with rags for lack of boots. . . .* And now it was many women, a babble" (261, 262). Together, the women sing a lullaby.

Like Ida Lerner, on her deathbed Eva becomes the human equivalent of a heteroglossic carnival site.

> *One by one they [the thousand various faces of age] streamed by and imprinted on her—and though the savage zest of their singing came voicelessly soft and distant, the faces still roared—the faces densened the air—chorded into*
>
> children-chants, mother-croons, singing of the chained love serenades, Beethoven storms, mad Lucia's scream drunken joy-songs, keens for the dead, work-singing. . . . (106)

Olsen blurs the distinction between high and popular culture in the diversity of cultural forms that sustain Eva: her beloved Chekhov, Balzac, Victor Hugo; Russian love songs; revolutionary songs; a "community sing" for elderly immigrants; and *Pan del Muerto*, a folk-art cookie for a dead child.

The barrage of voices and references that constitute Eva at her death return us to the danger I referred to in discussing "I Stand Here Ironing"— that multivocal, heteroglossic discourse may result in the equivalent of silence. Despite the danger, heteroglossia's cacophony is preferable to the dominant discourse's reductive forms. As for Emily in "I Stand Here Ironing," what will "let Eva be" is heteroglossia. After years of living in silence and near silence, Eva emerges in heteroglossia. Yet in both stories the richness of meaning released in Emily's and Eva's heteroglossic utterances threaten to result in the equivalent of silence.

In *Tell Me a Riddle* mimicry provides examples of subversive, indirect modes of discourse jousting with dominant monolithic modes; however, in mimicry Olsen finds the occasion to examine hazards in marginalized discourse's competing with the dominant discourse. Like other forms of parody, mimicry constitutes a powerful form of heteroglossia. Aimed against an official or monologic language, mimicry divides that system against itself. However, mimicry's ability to oppress the oppressor may be a snare for the mimic. To make her mother laugh, or out of the despair she felt about her isolation in the world, Emily, in "I Stand Here Ironing," imitates people and incidents from her school day. Eventually her gift for mimicry, pantomime, and comedy lead to first prize in her high school amateur show and requests to perform at other schools, colleges, and city- and state-wide competitions. However, her talent and achievement do not remedy her isolation: "Now suddenly she was Somebody, and as imprisoned in her difference as she had been in anonymity" (19). By exercising her parodic talent, Emily unwittingly exchanges one form of marginalization for another.

Like Emily, Whitey in "Hey Sailor, What Ship?" has a knack for mimicry, which he exhibits, for example, when telling Lennie about the union official who fined him: "(His [Whitey's] old fine talent for mimicry jutting through the blurred-together words)" (44). Whitey, a seaman being destroyed by alcoholism, is no less isolated than Emily in "I Stand Here Ironing," a point to which I will return in a moment. Lennie and Helen, who have been Whitey's friends and political comrades for years (Whitey saved Lennie's life during the 1934 Maritime Strike), and their three daughters are his only friends—indeed, the only people he can "be around . . . without having to pay" (43).[7]

Whitey's seaman's argot, slurred by alcohol, competes for our attention with an authorial voice (both are presented in standard type). In addition, an italicized narrative shifts between a third person or authorial point of view and Whitey's consciousness; often the point of view is not readily identifiable as that of one or the other—or it changes mid-sentence. Olsen does not use quotation marks to delineate Whitey's words from the third-person narrative or to separate any of the other voices. Thus dialogized, the text belies androcentric notions of textual ownership and authorial control.

Indeed, Olsen grants Whitey's marginalized voice textual dominance, and family members at times adopt or request his discourse. Lennie greets Whitey with an affectionate "you S.O.B." (26); Jeannie welcomes him by "using his long ago greeting," the salutation of seamen, "Hey Sailor, what ship?"; and the younger children parrot him and beg him to repeat favorite stories and rhymes (31). Even Lennie and Helen expect tales of travel and adventure. Helen, the one family member who does not slip into Whitey's dialect, nevertheless defends it as harmless against Jeannie's disapprobation. Even the narrator borrows his slang ("And he swizzles it down, pronto" [23]) and, at other points, slides into Whitey's voice, the two becoming indistinguishable.

However, an irony of "Hey Sailor, What Ship?" is that it is mimicry of the mimic, Whitey, that contributes to Whitey's fate, a fate similar to Emily's. The family engages in an affectionate mimicking of the salty language that sets Whitey apart from their other acquaintances:

> Watch the language, Whitey, there's a gentleman present, says Helen. Finish your plate, Allie.
>
> [Whitey:] Thass right. Know who the gen'lmun is? I'm the gen'lmun. The world, says Marx, is divided into two classes. . . . [ellipsis Olsen's]
>
> Seafaring gen'lmun and shoreside bastards, choruses Lennie with him.
>
> Why, Daddy! says Jeannie.
>
> You're a mean ole bassard father, says Allie.
>
> Thass right, tell him off, urges Whitey. Hell with waitin' for glasses. Down the ol' hatch.
>
> *My* class is divided by marks, says Carol, giggling helplessly at her own joke, and anyway what about ladies? Where's *my* drink? Down the hatch. (35)

Thus, mimicry functions in "Hey Sailor, What Ship?" as one form that entices Whitey out of isolation and into the family, while simultaneously diminishing the importance of Whitey as "other." The behavior of the family in relation to Whitey, despite what seems to be their shared political beliefs and practice, becomes a microcosm for the dominant culture's behavior in relation to much marginalized discourse. Charmed by difference (the history of music in American popular culture exemplifies the point), the mainstream culture co-opts the marginalized discourse, stripping it of its power as "difference," and diminishes its force in a process of homogenization. Olsen's references to mimicry in these stories constitute part of her running commentary on the power of dominant and subversive modes of discourse and the complications of identity marginalized people and their discourses face.

In addition to mimicry, "Hey Sailor, What Ship?," like other stories collected in *Tell Me a Riddle*, manifests heteroglossia by incorporating genres that "further intensify its speech diversity in fresh ways" (Bakhtin, *Dialogic* 321). Although this strategy is not uncommon among fiction writers, Olsen employs it more than many. In "Hey Sailor, What Ship?" Olsen has inserted a valediction (because the story is a farewell to Whitey, this insertion becomes a valediction within a valediction). Whitey learned it as a boy from his first shipmate, and one of the children asks him to recite it. Originally delivered in 1896 by the Phillipine hero Jose Rizal before he was executed, it concludes:

Little will matter, my country,
That thou shouldst forget me.
I shall be speech in thy ears, fragrance and color,
Light and shout and loved song. . . .

Where I go are no tyrants. . . . (42) (ellipses Olsen's)

Jose Rizal would have been an insurgent against both Spanish and American domination of the Philippines, and the recitation implicitly condemns American imperialism and the Cold War, at its height when Olsen wrote "Hey Sailor, What Ship?"

Whitey's recitation also eulogizes his (and Olsen's) youthful hopes for a socialist America, which have been snuffed out by Cold War strategists:

Land I adore, farewell. . . . (ellipsis Olsen's)
Our forfeited garden of Eden. . . .

Vision I followed from afar,
Desire that spurred on and consumed me,
Beautiful it is to fall,
That the vision may rise to fulfillment. (41)

Moreover, the valediction associates Whitey, who has been destroyed as much by *"the death of the brotherhood"* as by alcoholism, with political martyrdom. Whitey, who has attempted to keep '30s militancy alive in a period of political reaction, feels estranged from the complacent younger seamen. "These kids," he complains to Lennie, "don't realize how we got what we got. Beginnin' to lose it, too." One "kid," who had overtime coming to him, "didn't even wanta beef about it" (44). As the ship's delegate, Whitey nevertheless took the grievance to the union, which had become a conservative, alien bureaucracy, and was fined for "not taking it [the grievance] up through proper channels" (44). The younger seamen also lack the sense of solidarity Whitey and Lennie experienced during the '30s: "Think anybody backed me up, Len?" . . . *Once, once an injury to one is an injury to all. Once, once they had to live for each other. And whoever came off the ship fat shared, because that was the only way of survival for all of them. . . . Now it was a dwindling few"* (45). And, finally, because Whitey's efforts to stay sober have consistently failed and his health is rapidly deteriorating, Jose Rizal's valediction also functions as his own farewell address.

Yet there is a dimension to Whitey that cannot be explained in political or economic terms, adding a complexity to Olsen's "second period" work that is largely absent from her '30s published writing. Even in his youth, when both he and the Left were robust, Whitey was tormented by an emotional disorder that manifested itself in an inability to have sexual relations except when *"high with drink."* Many years later, at "the drunken end of his eight-months-sober try," Lennie and Helen hear a "torn-out-of-him confession" that the psychosexual problem persists, and likely, it will remain a riddle (44, 46). The story ends with its plaintive refrain— "Hey Sailor, what ship?"—which mourns the tragic waste of Whitey's life as well as suggests the disorientation, diminished options, and uncertainty of radicals in a period of right-wing ascendancy. Far from presenting a version of Gold's unified, robust, proletarian hero[/ine], *Tell Me a Riddle* suggests—in its characterization of Whitey; of Emily and her mother; of David, Eva and Jeannie; and of the mothers and daughters in "O Yes," discussed below—that it is (to underscore a point made in my Introduction) the *cleavages* within individuals and social movements that constitute the starting points and terrain for political struggle.

Both Whitey and Emily exemplify dangers in heteroglossic, subversive modes of discourse. Emily's and Whitey's individual talent allows each of them to joust with the dominant discourse. However, those individual talents, unlinked to other heteroglossic voices also intent upon jabbing at the dominant discourse, leave both Emily and Whitey without the supporting network of similar subversive voices. Without that support, they experience the dominant discourse's subsuming power and are returned to marginalized positions and forms of silence.

Mimicry and the two major forms of discourse—the direct and the indirect, and the risk that the cacophony of multivocal discourse may result in the equivalent of silence—play major roles in "O Yes." Helen, Lennie, and their daughters appear again in this story about the difficulty of sustaining a friendship across racial lines. Lennie and Helen's 12-year-old, Carol, is Euro-American; Parialee, her neighbor and closest friend from their earliest years, is African-American. "O Yes," which begins with Helen and Carol's attending Parialee's baptismal service, is permeable to the speech of "others"—songs by three church choirs; parishioners' shouts; Parialee's newly learned jivetalk; and the African-American dialect of Parialee's mother, Alva. Carol, who has never before experienced the intense emotionalism that erupts during the service (chanting, shrieking, fainting), is a stranger in the world of an all-African-American congregation. Trapped in heteroglossia's cacophony, Carol falls into the silence of a near faint, and once again, an abundance of meaning approaches silence.

Yet, in the first of the story's two parts, a far more reductive and controlling mode of discourse—an assertion/affirmation form of "dialogue"—presents itself as a counter to heteroglossia. In the dialogue's highly structured environment, the preacher takes the lead by making assertions that the congregation affirms. The dialogue includes the preacher's words, such as "And God is Powerful," and the congregation's response, "O Yes" and "I am so glad" (52, 54). The reductive and controlling mode of discourse in which the assertions are assigned to the figure of power, the preacher, and the affirmations to his followers, the congregation, replicates the structure of society outside the church. Exercising their role in the dialogue, the parishioners seem to be playing out the subservient parts African-Americans have so often been assigned within the society. Yet, within the church, heteroglossia persistently strains against the constraining mode of discourse. In "O Yes," as throughout *Tell Me a Riddle*, two major discursive forms—heteroglossia and, in this case, the countering assertion/affirmation dialogue—vie for power.

A complicated version of mimicry is prominent in "O Yes." What I identified earlier as a conventional assertion/affirmation structure placed in the midst of a swirling heteroglossia contains complex elements of a form of mimicry in which the preacher and congregation wittingly or unwittingly dramatize the roles of dominant and marginalized people, oppressor and oppressed. As the drama of the dialogue intensifies, it threatens to overpower heteroglossia by reducing it to the near monological assertion/affirmation exchanges between a leader and followers. Much of that drama takes place in the sermon delivered at Parialee's baptismal service. The narrator tells us that the subject of the sermon is "the Nature of God. How God is long-suffering. Oh, how long he has suffered" (51). The narrator has shown us a version of the classic Christian mystery of incarnation: God as the maker of human beings who suffer and God as the human victim of suffering. This dual role of perpetrator and victim becomes central to the sermon/response's dialogic structure. Early in the sermon the preacher chants, "And God is Powerful," to which the congregation responds "*O Yes*" (52). Here, again, we find an assertion/affirmation structure in which the preacher assumes the lead in the dialogue by making assertions that the congregation, in its role as follower, responds to by affirming.

Other dimensions of the dialogue quickly emerge. The preacher, working the theme of the great judgment day, blows an imaginary trumpet and announces: "And the horn wakes up Adam and, Adam runs to wake up Eve, and Eve moans; Just one more minute, let me sleep, and Adam yells, Great Day, woman, don't you know it's the Great Day?" (53). The basic assertion/affirmation structure is still operating, but within that structure the preacher in godlike fashion now creates characters who in turn engage in their own dialogues. The scene becomes increasingly heteroglossic. Immediately after the created Adam's rousing call to a sleeping Eve ("Great Day, woman, don't you know it's the Great Day?"), one of the choirs responds, "*Great Day, Great Day*" (53). Is the choir responding to the voice of the created Adam or to the preacher? The answer is of little consequence. What is important here is that the structure of the assertion/affirmation dialogue has dictated conditions that the congregation follows. Whichever "leader," real or imaginary, they respond to in the course of the sermon, they persistently replicate their role as affirmers of the leader's assertion. Thus, what emerges from this heteroglossic scene is a powerful counter to heteroglossia, a discursive structure that imposes unity and control by locking participants into predetermined traditional roles.

The force for unity within heteroglossia intensifies as the imaginary dimension of the dialogue escalates. The preacher moves from assertions about God and the creation of characters such as Adam and Eve to assuming the role of God, and with that move the form of his discourse shifts from assertion/affirmation to promise/affirmation. Having just asserted the multiple roles of God in relation to human beings (friend, father, way maker, door opener), the preacher proclaims: "I will put my Word in you and it is power. I will put my Truth in you and it is power." The response is "*O Yes*" (55). Soon after, the narrator says, "Powerful throbbing voices. Calling and answering to each other" (56). The narrator captures the vibrant force of the unity within heteroglossia when she says, "A single exultant lunge of shriek" (56).

What are we to make of this univocalizing of heteroglossia? The sexual implications that have been accumulating in this scene and that culminate in the orgasmic "single exultant lunge of shriek" invite an instructive digression into Mae Gwendolyn Henderson's discussion of an orgasmic "howl" in Toni Morrison's *Sula*. Henderson, who skillfully employs Bakhtinian analysis, observes of Sula's orgasmic cry: "The howl, signifying a prediscursive mode, thus becomes an act of self-reconstitution as well as an act of subversion or resistance to the 'network of signification' represented by the symbolic order. The 'high silence of orgasm' and the howl allow temporary retreats from or breaks in the dominant discourse" (33). The "single exultant lunge of shriek" has similar functions in the church scene in "O Yes." The parishioners have repeatedly experienced the intense repetition of the constraining assertion/affirmation and promise/affirmation structures that mimic the dominant discourse of power to which the congregation members are subjected outside the church. The shriek becomes an act of "self-reconstitution" and, at the same time, a "subversion or resistance to the 'network of signification'" that constrains the parishioners.

Henderson argues persuasively that Sula's orgasmic howl occurs at the moment at which she is located "outside of the dominant discursive order," but also when she is poised to re-enter and disrupt the discursive order. For Henderson, Sula's howl becomes a primary metaphor for African-American women writers whose objective is not "to move from margin to center, but to remain on the borders of discourse, speaking from the vantage point of the insider/outsider" (33, 36). This point of difficult balance is, I suggest, where Olsen places the African-American congregation at the moment of the "single exultant lunge of shriek."

But what more is there in the story to justify such a reading of this univocalizing of heteroglossia? Alva, Parialee's mother, will give us some indications. After Carol's near faint, Alva blames herself for not having been more attentive to Carol's being brought into a situation she had no basis for understanding. Attempting to explain the situation to Carol after the fact, Alva says, "'You not used to people letting go that way. . . . You not used to hearing what people keeps inside, Carol. You know how music can make you feel things? Glad or sad or like you can't sit still? That was religion music, Carol.'" Speaking of the congregation Alva says, "'And they're home, Carol, church is home. Maybe the only place they can feel how they feel and maybe let it come out. So they can go on. And it's all right'" (59–60). So we seem to have our answer. The univocalizing of heteroglossia is a shared singular escape of people who are trapped in multiple ways. They seem to choose to surrender the heteroglossia of their suffering to the univocal escape of the church/home. But is it "all right"?

The story's first section ends with an italicized rendering of what Alva did not say to Carol. This reverie—which remains silent, unspoken to Carol—stands as a response (like the earlier italicized responses of the congregation and the choirs) to an earlier series of the preacher's assertions. Earlier in the sermon the preacher proclaims: "He was your mother's rock. Your father's mighty tower. And he gave us a little baby. A little baby to love." The congregation responds: "*I am so glad*" (54). Alva's silent reverie begins:

> *When I was carrying Parry and her father left me, and I fifteen years old, one thousand miles away from home, sin-sick and never really believing, as still I don't believe all, scorning, for what have it done to help, waiting there in the clinic and maybe sleeping, a voice called: Alva, Alva. So mournful and so sweet: Alva. Fear not, I have loved you from the foundation of the universe.* (61)

Alva follows the voice "*into a world of light, multitudes singing,*" and the reverie ends: "*Free, free, I am so glad*" (61). The reverie's mixture of dream and reality parallels the mixture of the imaginary and the real in the sermon situation and seems to stand as Alva's singular response (not an affirmation) to the preacher's assertions in the sermon. But this is not a completely singular response, and it is not totally devoid of affirmation. When Alva acknowledges, "still I don't believe all," she locates herself, like Henderson's African-American female writer, both within and outside the church, inside yet resisting the univocality, outside yet resisting the conflation of the imaginary and the real. But we must remember that this is what Alva does *not* say to Carol, or to Helen, or as far as we know to anyone other than us. What is the force that creates this silence? Is it the circumstances of Alva's daily life? Is it the church?

We cannot begin to answer these questions without looking at the structure of the second part of the story. Just as Alva's reverie functions as a response to the sermon, the second part of the story stands as a response to the first part. In the second part, which takes place in the world of Helen and Len (or Lennie) and their daughters, Carol and Jeannie, a univocalizing force parallels that of the church in part one. In the second part the force against heteroglossia is the junior high school, which officially and unofficially attempts to separate Carol and Parialee, univocalizing Carol and other Euro-American students while shutting out Parialee and other African-American students. Because she is African-American, Parialee will not be tracked into Carol's accelerated classes; and even if she were initially admitted to them, the necessity to care for younger siblings while her mother works the 4-to-12:30 night shift would quickly put her behind in her studies. Carol is "college prep," whereas Parialee will likely not finish junior high, predicts Jeannie, a 17-year-old veteran of the public school system. According to Jeannie, "you have to watch everything, what you wear and how you wear it and who you eat lunch with and how much homework you do and how you act to the teacher and what you laugh at. . . . [ellipsis Olsen's] And run with your crowd" (63). Peer pressure is tremendous, and Carol and Parialee would be ostracized for attempting to be friends. Jeannie contrasts their "for real" working-class school with one in a nearby affluent neighborhood where it is fashionable for whites and blacks to be "buddies": " three coloured kids and their father's a doctor or judge or something big wheel and one always gets elected President or head song girl or something to prove oh how we're democratic" (65).

The junior high school has its parallel to the preacher—the teacher, Miss Campbell (nicknamed "Rockface")—and in this parallel Olsen further suggests dangers in the monologic impulses within the church's heteroglossia. Godlike in the junior high school kingdom, the bigoted teacher has the power to decide whether Parialee can be trusted to take Carol's homework assignments to her when Carol has the mumps: "Does your mother work for Carol's mother?" Rockface asks Parialee. "Oh, you're neighbors! Very well, I'll send along a monitor to open Carol's locker but you're only to take these things I'm writing down, nothing else" (67). Like the preacher, Rockface has the power to make Parialee respond. In drill-master fashion, Rockface insists: "Now say after me: Miss Campbell is trusting me to be a good responsible girl. And go right to Carol's house. . . . Not stop anywhere on the way. Not lose anything. And only take. What's written on the list" (67). However, we know of this not because Parialee told Carol. The account of Rockface appears in a passage that parallels Alva's reverie—what she did not say to Carol. The passage in which Parialee accounts for Rockface appears in a section in which she has been talking to Carol, but the Rockface passage begins: "*But did not tell.*" The knowledge we have of Rockface from Parialee is, like the knowledge we have of Alva's inner world, one more silence in Carol's world.

What are we to make of this chilling structural parallel between the worlds of the dominant and the marginalized, the oppressor and the oppressed? Certainly we must hear Olsen's warning that the marginalized imperil their identities by replicating, even through mimicry, structures of the dominant discourse. The African-American congregation risks imposing on itself the dominant culture's reductive and oppressive structures. But has the congregation yet succumbed? Perhaps not. Perhaps they as a collective, unlike the individuals Emily and Whitey, keep their identities apart from what they mimic (or in Whitey's case, what mimics him). Perhaps insofar as the assertion/affirmation structure (so dangerously reminiscent of the dominant discourse's reductive structures) remains embedded in a cacophonous atmosphere of heteroglossia, it remains a viable form of mimicry; and the African-American church maintains a delicate ecology of inside/outside with alternative structures and voices constantly checking and offsetting the structures of an oppressive discourse. Certainly the scene within the church approximates what Bakhtin identifies as heteroglossia in its fullest play—carnival—in which people's multiple voices play in, around, and against the dominant culture's hierarchical structures. Perhaps insofar as the African-American church remains a world about which Alva can say, "still I don't believe all," a world where she can be simultaneously inside and outside, it remains a dynamic social unit capable of resisting its own oppressive impulses.

Those readers who are strangers to the powerful culture of the African-American church cannot be sure how to assess that world and, like Carol, experience an abundance of meaning that approaches silence. In fact, Carol is a very useful point of reference for Olsen's readers. The story is a tangled web of explanations Carol never hears about historical circumstances that have enmeshed her. Carol hears neither Alva's reverie, which partly explains the phenomenon in the church, nor Parialee's account of Rockface. Further, as the story nears its end, Carol in desperation asks Helen a basic question, openly pleading for a response: "'Mother, why did they sing and scream like that? At Parry's church?'" But in place of a response we find:

> *Emotion,* Helen thought of explaining, *a characteristic of the religion of all oppressed peoples, yes your very own great-grandparents*—thought of saying. And discarded.
>
> *Aren't you now, haven't you had feelings in yourself so strong they had to come out some way?* ("what howls restrained by decorum") — thought of saying. And discarded.
>
> Repeat Alva: *hope . . . every word out of their own life. A place to let go. And church is home.* And discarded.
>
> *The special history of the Negro people—history?—just you try living what must be lived every day*—thought of saying. And discarded.
>
> And said nothing. (70)

Once more, Carol is met with silence.

We as readers may, like Carol, expect answers to our many questions about the disjunctures and potential connections among the lives and worlds of the story's characters. But Olsen, like Helen, does not supply definitive answers. We are privileged to hear more than Carol hears, but Olsen does not answer our questions about how the lives and worlds might be connected. Is Helen's silence at the end of "O Yes" a failure in relation to her daughter? Is Olsen's silence in relation to us a failure of authorial responsibility?

To address these questions I turn to my discussion's second major division, Olsen's reworking of relationships among writer, text, and reader. Helen's silence provides insight into Olsen's designs on us as readers and our relationships to issues of dominant and marginalized people and their discourses. To return to Meese's previously cited observation, Olsen repeatedly "calls upon the reader to write the text—no longer her text, but occasioned by it and by the voices speaking through it" (110). Helen thinks, but does not say: *"Better immersion than to live untouched"* (71). Structured immersion is what Olsen plans for us. Olsen demands that we not be passive receptors, but that we, in Bakhtinian terms, join in the heteroglossia. Olsen has skillfully structured textual gaps and developed strategies for readers' identifying with characters—structures and strategies that require readers to contribute to the emergence of heteroglossic meaning. In those gaps and moments of identification we are not given free rein as readers, but we are asked to act responsibly as members of a complex human community.

To observe Olsen's craft in teasing out our active participation, I return first to "Tell Me a Riddle." Eva craves solitude: *"Never again to be forced to move to the rhythms of others"* (76). And she is tired of the talk: "'All my life around babblers.

Enough!'" (82). Eva exercises her greatest control and feels triumphant when she manages to gain and maintain periods of silence. Olsen has given us a difficult kind of central character, one whose fierce desire for the silence she believes she has earned resists the telling of her story. We as audience are caught in the uncomfortable position of hearing the story of someone who wants her story left in silence. We are interlopers. We, like David, violate Eva's solitude and silence, and the narrator, seemingly torn between telling the story and honoring Eva's longing for silence, contributes to our discomfort.

The story's title and the presence of the phrase "tell me a riddle" in the story itself indicate sources of our uneasiness. In the story, the phrase "tell me a riddle" appears in the context of the "command performance." On the visit to daughter Vivi's, a visit Eva felt forced to make when she really wanted to go home, the narrator tells us very nearly from Eva's own perspective: "Attentive with the older children; sat through their performances (command performance; we command you to be the audience)" (94). Here the traditional notion of "command performance" is reversed. It is not the performer who enacts her role by command; it is the audience who performs its role by command. Eva is trapped. She is once again at the mercy of others' needs and desires.

In her role as command audience, Eva "watched the children whoop after their grandfather who knew how to tickle, chuck, lift, toss, do tricks, tell secrets, make jokes, match riddle for riddle" (94). She watched David interact with the grandchildren in the expected ways, in all the ways in which she would not: "(Tell me a riddle, Grammy. I know no riddles, child)" (94). Eva, the command audience, plays her attentive role up to a point, but she does not fully meet expectations. To the command "Tell me a riddle," she responds with a form of her prized silence, thwarting conventional expectations about grandparent-grandchild interactions.

Conventional expectations about interactions between us as audience and Eva and her story are also thwarted. We cannot be merely passive listeners to Eva's story. Whereas monologic discourse is, again, as Bakhtin asserts, "deaf to the other's response," even the title "Tell Me a Riddle" signals the necessity of our response. From the moment we read the title, we are told to act: "Tell Me a Riddle." We expect to hear a story, but we are told to tell a riddle. We, like Eva, are a command audience, and we, like Eva, find ourselves responding with our own versions of silence. We, the command audience, have been identified with Eva, the command audience, and with her desire for silence. Again, we are put in the uncomfortable situation of wanting to be silent listeners to the story of someone who wants her story left in silence.

Why should we be subjected to this discomfort? On one level we are put in this position because of the narrator's sympathy with Eva's desires. Eva's is a story that needs to be told, yet the narrator sympathizes with Eva's hunger for silence. The compromise for the narrator is to disrupt our complacency as audience. We will hear the story, but not on our terms: We will hear the story as a command audience. What better way to force us to realize the complexity of Eva's situation than to force us into a position resembling Eva's experience as command audience? But there is another reason for our discomfort. As in *Yonnondio* and *Silences*, Olsen disrupts our passivity, demanding that we as readers share responsibility for completing Eva's story.

But how do we exercise our responsibility? We have some clues in David's response to Eva. To David it seemed that for 70 years she had hidden an "infinitely microscopic" tape recorder within her, "trapping every song, every melody, every word read, heard, and spoken" (118). She had caught and was now releasing all the discourse around her: "'you who called others babbler and cunningly saved your words'" (119). But the harsh realization for David was that "she was playing back only what said nothing of him, of the children, of their intimate life together" (118). For David, the air is now filled with sound; yet that sound is the equivalent of silence. To him the danger referred to in my discussion of "I Stand Here Ironing"—that multivocal, heteroglossic discourse may result in the equivalent of silence—has become reality.

However, here we have a new perspective on the danger. The danger lies not in the discourse but in the audience. Because David hears nothing of Eva's life with him, the sounds become meaningless. His is an individualistic, self-centered response. But, crucially, what are these sounds to us as command audience? We have experienced the discomfort of being listeners to the story of one who does not want her story told, but now, at the end of her life, she speaks. If we identify with David's individualistic perspective, we will not understand Eva; her sounds will be the equivalent of silence. However, if we value Eva's identification with all humankind, we are an audience for whom Eva's last words have meaning.

Olsen aids us in valuing Eva's links to all humankind. One of those aids is a resuscitated David with whom we are invited to identify once he has remembered what he had long forgotten. Finally, David comes to a partial understanding of Eva's last words. When she brokenly repeats part of a favorite quotation from Victor Hugo, David remembers it, too, reciting scornfully: "'in the twentieth century ignorance will be dead, dogma will be dead, war will be dead, and for all humankind one country—of fulfillment'? Hah!" (120). But Eva's feverish cantata finally awakens in the old man memories of his own youthful visions:

> Without warning, the bereavement and betrayal he had sheltered—compounded through the years—hidden even from himself—revealed itself,
> > uncoiled,
> > released,
> > *sprung*
> and with it the monstrous shapes of what had actually happened in the century. (120)

David realizes with sudden clarity the full price of his assimilation into America's "apolitical" mainstream: "'Lost, how much I lost'" (121). He and Eva "had believed so beautifully, so . . . falsely?" (122; ellipsis Olsen's):

> "Aaah, children," he said out loud, "how we believed, how we belonged." And he yearned to package for each of the children, the grandchildren, for everyone, *that*

joyous certainty, that sense of mattering, of moving and being moved, of being one and indivisible with the great of the past, with all that freed, ennobled. Package it, stand on corners, in front of stadiums and on crowded beaches, knock on doors, give it as a fabled gift. (122)

David also realizes that Eva's revolutionary faith did not die with his: "*Still she believed?* 'Eva!' he whispered. 'Still you believed? You lived by it? These Things Shall Be?'" (123). This story's epigraph, "These Things Shall Be," is the title of an old socialist hymn expressing hope for a future just society. Another riddle, then, is the puzzle of revolutionary consciousness: Under what circumstances does it develop, dissipate? How does it sustain itself when confronted by "monstrous shapes"—the rise of fascism, two world wars, the extermination of six million Jews, the threat of global extinction?

The second aid Olsen provides us in valuing Eva's ties to all humankind is Eva's granddaughter, Jeannie (the same Jeannie of "Hey Sailor, What Ship?" and "O Yes," now in her twenties) to whom the legacy of resistance is passed on. Jeannie, who works as a visiting nurse and has a special political and artistic sensibility, cares for Eva in the last weeks of her life. As Rachel Blau DuPlessis notes, the old young/woman dyad provides an alternative to prevailing textual and societal emphases on successful or failed heterosexual romance.[8] "'Like Lisa she is, your Jeannie,'" Eva whispers to Lennie and Helen, referring to the revolutionary who taught Eva to read more than 50 years before. It is at the end of the passage in which Eva compares Jeannie to Lisa that Eva says, "'All that happens, one must try to understand'" (112, 113).

Those words constitute Eva's hope for Jeannie and Olsen's most basic demand on us as active readers. Recognizing the persistent threat of being so flooded with meaning that we may be faced with meaninglessness and the equivalent of silence, we must persist in the attempt to understand. In that attempt we must recognize the dangers of the bourgeois individualism into which we, like David, are constantly tempted to retreat. Olsen provides structures, such as the command audience structure I have discussed, to force us out of our passive individualistic roles as readers and to invite us into a web of interconnected, heteroglossic roles.[9] If we accept the invitation, we must do more than value Eva's identification with all humankind: We must remember if we have forgotten (the model of David) or learn if we have never known (the model of Jeannie) the complicated histories of worlds like those in which Eva lived and struggled. At the least, we are required to do our part in keeping alive the historical circumstances of oppressive Czarist Russia and the connections among all oppressed groups. Eva and Olsen require us to learn the very histories to which America's "apolitical" mainstream would have us remain oblivious. With Jeannie, we are challenged to carry on Eva's legacy of resistance.

Olsen provides one further aid in valuing Eva's links to all humankind, an aid not limited to the collection's final story. The subject of motherhood so prominent in "I Stand Here Ironing," "O Yes," and "Tell Me a Riddle" provides a crucial reference point for our accepting a heteroglossia linking all humankind. Olsen has rightly referred to motherhood as a "taboo area; the last refuge of sexism . . . [the] least and last explored, tormentingly complex *core* of women's oppression." At the same time, Olsen believes that motherhood is, potentially, a source of "transport" for women, moving them beyond some of the constraints of individualism.[10] Responsible for what Olsen terms "the maintenance of life," mothers are often exposed to forms of heteroglossia, with their attendant benefits and hazards (*Silences* 34). In exploring the complexity of motherhood, Olsen renders versions of it that are "coiled, convoluted like an ear"—versions that may serve as models for the necessary hearing of heteroglossia.

I return to Helen's silence at the end of "O Yes." We can read Helen's silence as one of several textual comments on the limits of authority; indeed, it may have been through the experience of parenting that Olsen learned the limits of authorial control, which her texts so willingly concede. As an involved parent, one is forced to live intensely "in relation to," as the boundary between self and other is constantly negotiated. Such negotiating provides a model in which the ability to listen to constantly changing, heteroglossic voices is prized. When Carol asks, "why do I have to care?", the narrator tells us the following about Helen:

> Caressing, quieting.
>
> Thinking: *caring asks doing. It is a long baptism into the seas of humankind, my daughter. Better immersion than to live untouched.* . . . [ellipsis Olsen's] *Yet how will you sustain?*
>
> *Why is it like it is?*
>
> Sheltering her daughter close, mourning the illusion of the embrace.
>
> *And why do I have to care?*
>
> While in her, her own need leapt and plunged for the place of strength that was not—where one could scream or sorrow while all knew and accepted, and gloved and loving hands waited to support and understand. (71)

Although we risk being flooded by a multiplicity of meaning that approaches meaninglessness and the equivalent of silence, we as readers must submit to the "immersion," the "long baptism" that allows us to be the proper "ear" for the complexity of heteroglossia.

We have similar models at the end of "I Stand Here Ironing" and "Tell Me a Riddle." The mother listens to Emily on "one of her communicative nights . . . [when] she tells me everything and nothing" (19). The mother does not respond to Emily, but says to herself, to the teacher or counselor, and to us, "Let her be. So all that is in her will not bloom—but in how many does it? There is still enough left to live by" (20–21). In "Tell Me a Riddle" Jeannie, who has listened carefully to Eva's dying heteroglossia, is not actually a mother; but, like a mother, she is a caretaker, a nurturer, a listener.

However, Olsen asks more of us than listening. As Helen says to herself, "*caring asks doing.*" In none of these models in *Tell Me a Riddle* is the mother figure a passive listener; rather, she is a listener responsive to heteroglossia. Even when multiple voices so overwhelm her that she is caught in silence (Emily's

mother, Helen, Eva), she can sometimes caress or embrace, knowing the communicative power of such actions. As active readers, then, we are provided
models of careful listening, leading to action. Olsen does not proscribe the field
of political/social action that we as active readers might enter. However, she does
demand that we work to understand the many voices of the oppressed. In "I
Stand Here Ironing," the mother says of Emily, "Only help her to know," a command the dying Eva echoes: "All that happens, one must try to understand."
These words embody imperatives for us. And these mother figures, who live compassionately and interdependently in a multicultural and heteroglossic dynamic,
become models for us as readers.

Olsen demands another, related form of action from her readers. In the collection, *Tell Me a Riddle*, we have been exposed to many moments in which
characters sensitive to heteroglossia have been so inundated with complexity of
meaning they have lapsed into silence. We have heard what the unnamed mother
in "I Stand Here Ironing," Alva, Helen, and Eva have *not* been able to say to
those most immediately connected to them. If the silence is perpetuated, these
characters risk, as do Emily and Whitey, being subsumed by the dominant discourse. Olsen requires us, as readers of the complete collection, to hear the
various oppressed voices and to make and articulate connections among them,
connections the separate characters may not be able to see, or may only partially
see. With such actions we become collaborators with Olsen in the democratizing
enterprise of amplifying dominated and marginalized voices. We join her in a
commitment to social change.

Silences (1978), a nonfiction book that catalogues impediments to a writer's productivity, is Olsen's most unconventional and heteroglossic text. The first half is
composed of three essays by Olsen; the second half is a montage including excerpts from writers' diaries and letters spliced together with Olsen's headings and
commentary. Crossing gender, race, and class boundaries, Olsen quotes male and
female, Euro- and African-American, known and unknown writers. By extensive
use of citation (what Bakhtin's colleague Volosinov termed "reported speech"), *Silences* undercuts the conventional rhetorical model of speaker/message/listener
by adding not only a third voice but dozens of voices. Both writer and reader must
address themselves not simply to each other, but to the extra, complicating party
or parties. Because these additional voices in the language act alter the discourse
from a dualistic exchange to a complex social one, *Silences* strains away from
bourgeois individualism, from "monadic isolation as a social fact," to return to
Jameson's phrase.

Silences began as a talk titled "Silences in Literature," which Olsen delivered
in 1962 at the Radcliffe Institute's weekly colloquium (*Harper's Magazine* published a version in 1965). These dates are significant. This polemical essay is an
even greater achievement because Olsen produced it, like most of her fiction,
before the most recent women's movement provided an audience favorable to

such expression. Drawing on an older feminist tradition, Olsen was a forerunner—like Le Sueur, Smedley, Virginia Woolf, Doris Lessing, and others—of the movement that would eventually claim her.

"What *are* creation's needs for full functioning?" Olsen asks at the beginning of "Silences in Literature." "I have had special need to learn all I could of this over the years, myself so nearly remaining mute and having to let writing die over and over again in me" (6). "Silences" refers not to natural pauses, the time necessary for renewal and gestation, but to "the unnatural thwarting of what struggles to come into being, but cannot" (6). Olsen explores first the silences of some prominent male writers—Hardy, Melville, Rimbaud, Gerard Manley Hopkins, Kafka. While sympathetic to all these writers, she identifies most closely with Melville. Her 20-year silence is surpassed by his "thirty-year night" (8); and her desire for solitude, conflicting with the need to earn money, is paralleled by Melville's confession to Hawthorne: "I am so pulled hither and thither by circumstances. The calm . . . the silent grass-growing mood in which a man ought always to compose,—that, I fear, can seldom be mine. Dollars damn me" (7–8). A wage-earner most of her life, Olsen reminds us that Melville was nearly 70 before he could quit his customs house job and again have time for writing. By that time, his journal reveals, "age, dull tranquilizer," had measurably slowed him (8).

"Silences in Literature" then looks briefly at nineteenth-century women writers, implicitly commenting on the role of the sexual division of labor in silencing women: Nearly all nineteenth-century women writers were unmarried or married late in their thirties; few had children; all had servants. Until recently the Twentieth Century had a similar record. Most women writers did not marry, or, if they married, remained childless; all had household help "or other special circumstances" (16). Even women who have enjoyed the luxury of servants, however, have been "trained to place others' needs first, to feel these needs as their own . . . their satisfaction to be in making it possible for others to use their abilities" (17). Quoting Virginia Woolf's diary, Olsen makes clear the effect of such training: "Father's birthday. He would have been 96, 96, yes, today; and could have been 96, like other people one has known; but mercifully was not. His life would have entirely ended mine. What would have happened? No writing, no books;—inconceivable" (17). Olsen concludes the essay by describing her own 20-year silence. This essay's lesson is implicit but clear: economic freedom, usually the result of class privilege, is most vital to creativity.

The book's second essay, "One Out of Twelve Writers Who Are Women in Our Century," derived from a talk given at the 1971 Modern Language Association Forum on Women Writers in the Twentieth Century and appeared in *College English* in 1972. Olsen acknowledges that men actually publish only four to five books for every one published by a woman; she arrived at her twelve-to-one ratio by using critical, not commercial, acclaim as her criterion. She gauges that acclaim by "what supposedly designates it: appearance in twentieth-century literature courses, required reading lists, textbooks, quality anthologies, the year's best, the decade's best, the fifty years' best, consideration by critics or in current reviews" (24). Even if one argues that her tabulating has not been sufficiently systematic, she insists that "*any figure but one to one would insist on query: Why? What, not true for men but* only for women, *makes this enormous difference?*" (24).

Olsen begins to answer this question by noting "how much conviction" it takes to become a writer. It requires a belief in "the importance of what one has to say, one's right to say it," which is "difficult for any male not born into a class that breeds such confidence [and] almost impossible for a girl, a woman" (27). Moreover, would-be women writers consciously or unconsciously sense that "women writers, women's experience, and literature written by women are by definition minor" (29). (Olsen adds that "Mailer will not grant even the minor: 'the one thing a writer has to have is balls'" [29].)

Although in this century most women writers have had access to the higher education previously denied women, the education these women receive may not foster their becoming writers as much as it encourages their male counterparts. Olsen refers to Elaine Showalter's pioneering study, "Women and the Literary Curriculum," published in *College English* (May 1971), that discussed university textbooks in which women, until recently, have had little place. Jean Mullens, who furthered Showalter's work with a study published in *College English* (October 1972), reported that in the 112 most-used freshman English textbooks, 92 percent of the selections were by men. Mullens also addressed the more subtly undermining effect of the textbooks' content and language.

Under the prevailing sexual division of labor, a wife/mother's domestic, familial duties far outstrip those of husband/father. Another reason *Silences* gives for the one-to-twelve ratio, then, is that generally women, and not men, have had to sacrifice marriage and children in order to write, a price only a few have been willing to pay. Quotations from other writers make Olsen's point. "Them lady poets must not marry, pal" is how poet John Berryman (who married several times) puts it. "A woman has to sacrifice all claims to femininity and family to be a writer," Sylvia Plath believed. "Perfection is terrible. It cannot have children. It tamps the womb" (30–31). *Silences* also includes an incident from the life of Thomas Mann's daughter. When she revealed to her analyst an ambition to become a great musician, he advised her to choose between her art and "fulfillment as a woman, between music and family life" (31). "Why must I choose?" she asked. "No one said to Toscanini or to Bach or my father that they must choose between their art and personal, family life" (31).

Most women, even ones with class privilege, have been bred to "spare" their men, to give them the uninterrupted quiet and creature-comfort conducive to productivity. In order to write, Virginia Woolf had to exorcise this demon, this tendency to be "the angel in the house": "It was she who used to come between me and my paper . . . who bothered me and wasted my time and so tormented me that at last I killed her . . . or she would have plucked out my heart as a writer" (34). Olsen quickly adds that "*there is another angel, so lowly as to be invisible,* . . . with whom Virginia Woolf (and most women writers, still in the privileged class) did not have to contend" (34). Olsen's term for her is "the essential angel," the one responsible "for daily living, for the maintenance of life": "Almost always in one form or another (usually in the wife, two-angel form) she has dwelt in the house of men. . . . Men (even part-time writers who must carry on work other than writing) have had and have this inestimable advantage toward productivity" (34). This angel, "essential" to Rilke's "great task," was "like a sister who would run the house like a friendly climate, there or not there as one wished . . . and would ask for nothing except just to be there working and warding at the frontiers of the invisible" (34).

Olsen observes "how curiously absent" both of these angels are from the content of most men's books, "except perhaps on the dedication page: *To my wife, without whom* . . ." (34–35). More twentieth- than nineteenth-century women writers have had children, and Olsen predicts that as a result a "new richness will come into literature." But she also fears that their work will be "lessened, partial," because the

> fundamental situation remains unchanged. Unlike men writers who marry, most will not have the societal equivalent of a wife. . . . [and may] suffer what seventy years ago W.E.B. Du Bois called "The Damnation of Women": "that only at the sacrifice of the chance to do their best work can women bear and rear children." (32–33)

The third essay in *Silences* originally appeared as the afterword for the Feminist Press's 1972 reprint of Rebecca Harding Davis's *Life in the Iron Mills*.[11] Olsen discovered *Life in the Iron Mills* at 15 when she bought a water-stained bound volume of the *Atlantic Monthly* for ten cents in an Omaha junkshop. The volume included the novella in serialized form, although it was published anonymously, as contributions to the *Atlantic* standardly were in 1861. *Life in the Iron Mills* seemed to say to young, impressionable Tillie Lerner: "Literature can be made out of the lives of despised people," and "You, too, must write" (117). Olsen recalls that she was "ignorant of any process whereby [she] might find the name of the author" of the novella, but 30 years later, reading on her lunch hour in the San Francisco Public Library, she stumbled upon a reference to *Life in the Iron Mills* and its author in the collected *Letters of Emily Dickinson*. Olsen was not surprised to learn that the author was a woman (117).

When it was published, *Life in the Iron Mills* "was an instant sensation" and "recognized as a literary landmark. A wide and distinguished audience . . . spoke of it as a work of genius" (*Silences* 66). But when Rebecca married Clarke Davis, an ambitious attorney, journalist, and abolitionist, she put his career first, bore three children, and within a decade had lost her place in the literary world. (Since they met only after she had written the novella, only a mischievous female muse could have prompted Rebecca to give the contemptible overseer of the iron mills her future husband's Christian name.)

Olsen's powerful afterword (or "biographical interpretation," as it is termed) is 40 percent longer than and nearly as provocative as the novella, itself. It tells the haunting story of Davis's personal odyssey from a writer and a latent feminist to her advocacy, after marriage and children, of woman-as-household-angel. Discussing much of Davis's biography and oeuvre—which have been buried, forgotten—Olsen persuades us of its value to nineteenth-century American history, writing, and women's studies. She also argues that Davis's own oppression as a woman sensitized her to some of the constrictions of working-class life.

We are indebted to Olsen for bringing *Iron Mills* to the attention of the Feminist Press and for her rich, lively commentary on the historically resonant contradictions within Davis's biography and canon. However, I differ somewhat with Olsen's assessment of the novella's place in literature and Davis's relation to the work. Olsen's biographical interpretation, written with 100 years of hindsight, indicates the now transparent link between Davis's thwarted desire for a literary career and her sympathy for the Wheeling mill workers—but history may not have provided such insight, as Olsen claims, to Davis, herself. Despite their intentions, both the novella and Olsen's afterword suggest that in addition to feeling a genuine concern about industrialism's effects on workers, Davis unconsciously used the mill workers as a "safe" mechanism with which to protest her own circumscription, partly repressing and partly displacing a latent feminist voice. *Iron Mills*, then, is "two" texts, one about foundry workers and one about Rebecca Harding Davis; one is spoken, the other strains to keep silent.

Olsen claims that Davis must have used "trespass vision" (62) in order to understand the Wheeling working class, but Davis's conceptions were not uncanny; they were those of one who had little if any substantive contact with the working class.[12] The following passage suggests that Davis did, indeed, observe Wheeling residents as they passed her house and during her habitual walks: "You may pick the Welsh emigrants, Cornish miners, out of the throng passing the windows, any day. They are a trifle more filthy; their muscles are not so brawny; they stoop more. When they are drunk, they neither yell, nor shout, nor stagger, but skulk along like beaten hounds" (*Iron Mills* 15). But this passage's diction—"a trifle more filthy," "stoop," "skulk," "beaten hounds"—makes me uneasy; and elsewhere, the narrator describes the workers as having lived "massed, vile, slimy lives, like those of the torpid lizards" (*Iron Mills* 13). These descriptions of the working class resemble those found, for example, in Stephen Crane's *Maggie: A Girl of the Streets* (1892), Jack London's *The Iron Heel* (1907), and John Steinbeck's *In Dubious Battle* (1939). *Iron Mills* predates by 30 years even the earliest of these novels, but Davis shares with these later writers not an unqualified identification with the working class but a profound, complex ambivalence toward it—a mixture of identification, sympathy, paternalism, and fear. She paints the workers as mere victims, in need, perhaps, of a kindly benefactor such as the Quaker she provides Deborah at the novella's conclusion.

We sense from the novella and the afterword that Davis, who had the variegated consciousness of a middle-class reformer, could more comfortably conceive of a working class with potential for creative expression than imagine its capacity for rebellion. In the character of the Quaker she suggests that for all its artistic promise, the working class must depend for its betterment on the enlightened, charitable elements of the middle class. Neither the bond between Hugh and Deborah nor the liaison between Deborah and the Quaker approach equality. In both cases, the misshapen woman/worker—for all her courage and tenacity—remains dependent. Deborah commits a crime to enable a man to pursue his craft, just as Davis would later write for pulp magazines to fund her husband's professional and political projects. Presumably Hugh's creativity "justifies" Deborah's crime, but could Deborah's creativity—or Davis's—have provided grounds for such action? I am not advocating an orthodox proletarian realism here, as if Davis failed to assign her heroine a properly progressive role. Rather, I am suggesting that history may have precluded Davis's even conceiving of human relations undefined by gender and class hierarchies.

Davis's vision of the working class is not "trespass," as Olsen claims; it is that of a middle-class woman faced with foregoing intimacy, affection, marriage, and children if she chooses fully to develop her faculties. James Kavanagh's wedge into texts, achieved by looking "not at that [to] which the text points, but at that *away from which it points*," informs our reading of *Iron Mills* (36): it should be examined as women's, not working-class, writing and, secondarily, as a middle-class reformer's view of the working class. As such, it can inform us about the complexities of a historical period. A desire to counter the assumption that writing by and about women and the working class is inferior to canonical literature must be accompanied by a recognition that its contradictions, as those of any texts, may be historically revealing. We gloss over these contradictions at some cost.

Part Two of *Silences*, with the title, "Acerbs, Asides, Amulets, Exhumations, Sources, Deepenings, Roundings, Expansions," extends the thought of Part One's three essays by quoting from dozens of writers' letters and diaries. Olsen allows others to elaborate on those essays in their own voices. Part Two, one reviewer has noted, "contains all the paraphernalia of private notetaking: quotation without comment, or with comment abbreviated and jerky; . . . soliloquy; italics; parentheses; cryptic remarks . . . sighs and exclamations." This reviewer is not suggesting that *Silences* was published prematurely, before it had been properly edited; indeed, she describes the book as having a language of "sweeping, insistent, repetitive movement" (Trueblood 18–19). A description of a much earlier form of radical discourse applies to *Tell me a Riddle* and *Silences*, where Olsen employs

> typography to press words themselves toward an almost extralinguistic force straining at the very limit of written language. Partly an attempt to reproduce in print the emphatic gesture and timbre of voice, this energy is also a means to render the opaque sources of power and powerlessness legible. (Klancher 116)

The peculiar form of *Silences'* second part, like Lessing's various notebooks in *The Golden Notebook*, interrupts narrative—and hence social—order at the level of sentence as well as genre.

The multiple relationships between Parts One and Two are key to Olsen's formal experiments in *Silences*. "The organization" of Part Two, Olsen tells us, "follows the order of thought in the original essays [Part One], page by page" (119). Thus, Part Two echoes Part One, with Olsen giving voices that have been exhumed from silence in Part One further opportunity to speak in Part Two. Often voices in Part Two expand upon what they had begun to say and/or what Olsen had begun to say about them in Part One. Hardy provides an example. After Olsen's, Hardy's is the first voice we hear in Part One:

> "Less and less shrink the visions then vast in me," writes Thomas Hardy in his thirty-year ceasing from novels after the Victorian vileness to his *Jude the Obscure*. ("So ended his prose contributions to literature, his experiences having killed all his interest in this form"—the official explanation.) (6)

In this passage, we hear Hardy's voice, then Olsen's voice, then the voice of "the official explanation." In the parallel section of Part Two, Hardy's own words fill nearly three of the section's five pages, and those words expand upon Hardy's words in Part One. Thus, one function of Part Two is to resist silence by amplifying the voices shown to be silenced or nearly silenced in Part One.

The Hardy example displays another relationship between Parts One and Two. Part Two not only expands the voices of Part One but also catalogues the genres and subgenres of the silences imposed on the voices of Part One. As if completing an exposé, Olsen identifies in Part Two genres or "varieties" of silence: "Censorship Silences," "Political Silences," "Political Silences. A woman form," "Absences That Are a Kind of Silence." These "genres" of silence will no longer be allowed to stand in silence; they are being called out and named.

This process begins in the Hardy example. In Part One we hear a cryptic and tantalizing account of Hardy's silence and its cause. To repeat, Olsen describes Hardy as "ceasing from novels after the Victorian vileness to his *Jude the Obscure*." Then we hear "the official explanation." By labeling it "official" Olsen suggests that it is itself a silencing of the truth, but in Part One neither she nor Hardy elaborates. However, in Part Two we are given more information about the kind of silence to which Hardy fell prey. "Later, even with *Tess*, even with *Jude*, the great mature novels written when he was financially less at the mercy of publishers, there yet remained the massive class and sexual (i.e., sexist) censorship of his time; the rigidly circumscribed form of the novel as then practiced, to continue to defeat him" (122). According to Olsen here, it was a "form," a genre, that defeated him. Yet, clearly, as Olsen recognizes, it is not only the genre, "novel," that imposes silence but also a genre of human behavior in relation to the form "novel."

In Part Two Olsen exposes the adherence to established literary, social, and political forms or genres that impose silences. Thus, Olsen labels the genre of silence imposed on Hardy "Censorship Silences" and subdivides that genre into "Immoral! Immoral!," "Having to Censor Self," "Work Withheld," and "Publishers' Censorship" (142–143). Having given us a glimpse of the silence in Part One, in Part Two she and the other authorial voices name the imposed silences and provide a more complete hearing of what these silences are and what it is to live in them. They are brought out into the open, "amulets" demystified. Again, in Part

One the silence Hardy suffered was "the Victorian vileness to his *Jude the Obscure*." In Part Two, Hardy has far more words to describe that "Victorian vileness," including, "Perhaps I can express more fully in verse, ideas and emotions which run counter to the inert crystallized opinion—hard as a rock—which the vast body of men have vested interests in supporting" (125). Later in Part Two, after its extensive exposure, Olsen labels that pernicious genre of silence "Censorship Silence."

There is, then, within the entire book's heteroglossia, a fundamental dialogic relationship between Parts One and Two. In that dialogic relationship the multiple voices of silenced authors emerge to name and describe oppressing silences and in so doing resist them. One episode in Part Two provides a surprising dramatizing of imposed silence. In that episode Olsen identifies "a profit making economy" as the source of a "literary atmosphere that sets writers against one another, breeds the feeling that writers are in competition with each other." Olsen notes as example, "(In its extremest sense, Hemingway's feeling that the measure of success would be 'to knock Tolstoy out of the prize ring': literature as prize ring!)" (170, 171). What is surprising here is not the analysis, but the frame in which Olsen places it. The episode begins, "What follows is the blues," and then an abrupt command: "Writer, don't read it." At the end of the episode, Olsen says, "(Writers, you can start reading again here.)" (169, 172). This episode about writers' being set against one another—about writers' "isolation, loneliness"— begins with the writer Olsen's commanding the exclusion of other writers from her reading audience. Yet this is no simple matter of Olsen's setting herself against other writers.

As we have seen her do before in *Yonnondio*, for example, she uses this episode to sort out her reading audience. Any writer-reader who obeys the command has allowed herself to be knocked out of the prize ring and deserves her fate. The writer-reader Olsen is cultivating is the one who disobeys such commands. Indeed, we find within the episode remarks addressed to "the writer" who has disobeyed the command and has read on: "The attitude [of which she is critical]: nobody owes you (the writer) anything; the world never asked you to write" (172). To obey the command is to engage in one more form of adherence to authority, and Olsen disavows such an audience. To disobey the command is to remain among the heteroglossia of voices speaking out against imposed silences.

A major theme extended from Part One to Part Two is that women—as wives, mothers, sisters, daughters, lovers, secretaries, and housekeepers—have provided services that have enabled men to write. Olsen quotes Katia Mann: "My portion was to see to it that he [Thomas Mann] had the best circumstances for his work." And Jorge Borges has said,

> My mother has always had a hospitable mind. She translated Saroyan, Hawthorne, [Herbert] Read, Melville, Woolf, Faulkner. She has always been a companion to me and an understanding and forgiving friend. For years she handled all my secretarial work, answering letters, reading to me, taking down my dictation and also traveling with me. . . . It was she who quietly and effectively fostered my literary career. (220)

In a letter to May Sarton, poet Louise Bogan described, approvingly, what Edmund Wilson's second wife, Elena, provided him: "Now all moves smoothly: tea on a tray for his 'elevenses'; absolute silence in his working hours, and good meals at appropriate intervals" (221). Olsen points out that Bogan had no such support—and a daughter to raise, alone. When an interviewer asked Mrs. William Carlos Williams if her husband was writing very much when they became engaged, she replied: "No; once in a while he would send me a poem. But he was busy building up his [medical] practice. After we were married he wrote more. I saw to it that he had time" (221). Katherine Anne Porter was asked a related question in a *Paris Review* interview:

> But haven't you found that being a woman presented to you, as an artist, certain special problems? It seems to me that a great deal of the upbringing of women encourages the dispersion of the self in many small bits, and that the practice of any kind of art demands a corralling and concentrating of that self and its always insufficient energies.

She replied,

> I think that's very true and very right. You're brought up with the . . . curious idea of feminine availability in all spiritual ways, and in giving service to anyone who demands it. And I suppose that's why it has taken me twenty years to write this novel; it's been interrupted by just anyone who could jimmy his way into my life. (216)

Some quotations, such as the following from Norman Mailer, require no comment by Olsen:

> I have a terrible confession to make—I have nothing to say about any of the talented women who write today. Out of what is no doubt a fault in me, I do not seem able to read them. Indeed I doubt if there will be a really exciting woman writer until the first whore becomes a call girl and tells her tale. At the risk of making a dozen devoted enemies for life [Mailer's estimate is far too conservative—CC], I can only say that the sniffs I get from the ink of the women are always fey, old-hat, Quaintsy Goysy, tiny, too dykily psychotic, crippled, creepish, fashionable, frigid, outer-Baroque, *maquille* in mannequin's whimsy, or else bright and still-born. Since I've never been able to read Virginia Woolf, and am sometimes willing to believe it can conceivably be my fault, this verdict may be taken fairly as the twisted tongue of a soured taste, at least by those readers who do not share with me the ground of departure—that a good novelist can do without everything but the remnant of his balls. (238)

Simply by quoting Mailer in the context of *Silences* Olsen parodies his remarks, seizing language originally used against women for her own purpose. What Jane Marcus claims for Woolf in *A Room of One's Own* and *Three Guineas* also describes what Olsen achieves in *Silences*: "By quotation she sought to rob history of its power over women," acting as "raider on received history" (cited in Meese 92).

Critics' descriptions of *Silences* vary because its form resists a generic label. Deborah Rosenfelt, for example, terms it "a sustained prose poem"—and, indeed,

American Poetry Review glowingly reviewed it; Margaret Atwood uses the terms "grab bag," "scrapbook," and "patchwork quilt" to describe the book in her favorable *New York Times* review (1); Erika Duncan perhaps most accurately describes it as "a collaging of words of other writers on the subject with her own" (221). A polyvocal text, *Silences* does not provide the unicentered voice one has been taught to expect in a book, especially one of nonfiction.

Silences—to borrow Lessing's terms for *The Golden Notebook*—"talk[s] through the way it was shaped" (Lessing 33), its form subverting notions of textual ownership and a monological, unicentered discourse. Elizabeth Meese points out that *Silences* uses quotation so extensively that the words of others outnumber those of Olsen, "the perfect ventriloquist" (112). Olsen further resists authorial control by refusing to conclude; instead she allows Rebecca Harding Davis to speak her book's conclusion. *Silences* also demystifies book-as-final-product by recalling its own, often precarious progression from silence, to speech (the unwritten talks that become the essays), to writing. Moreover, its grab-bag quality allows readers to select the quotations that speak to their own experience, in a sense writing the text themselves, and the pages' blank spaces openly invite readers "to participate in the text's creation, to break the silences by inscribing themselves" (Meese 110, 112). *Silences* places subjectivity in process, making the moment of reading one in which meanings are set in motion rather than solidified.

Olsen's writing offers its readers something traditional modern art does not. While modern art strives to renew our perception of the world, it seldom accounts for the causes of our perception's "initial numbness" (Jameson, *Marxism* 374). Olsen unmasks the fact of work and production, one of the keys to historical thinking and "a secret as carefully concealed as anything else in our culture" (Jameson, *Marxism* 407). Although Olsen portrays work in diverse forms (with scenes from a coal mine, a farm, a packinghouse, etc.), she foregrounds domestic labor, and especially child care, which may be the most "naturalized," invisible labor of all, the secret *most* carefully concealed. Moreover, in a commodity culture, one that by definition effaces the signs of work on its products, *Silences* focuses on writing "at the point of production," forcing readers to confront the class and patriarchal character of the structures in which it is produced. It exposes, for example, the hidden labor that often supports literary production and, in some cases, may even make it possible. In emphasizing domestic labor, Olsen, by implication, treads on the sacred ground of Marxism's primacy-of-production theory. Similarly, by highlighting the issue of child care, she enters a "taboo area" that the women's movement, including its socialist-feminists, has yet fully to confront.

Olsen, like a handful of others—Le Sueur, Agnes Smedley, Josephine Herbst, Marge Piercy, Doris Lessing, Denise Giardina, and Alice Walker come most readily to mind—works toward a synthesis that fuses feminism to other forms of radical analysis. From her earliest published writing, Olsen has been concerned with issues of class and race as well as gender. Her story "O Yes" (1957), for example, is about both the socialization of children, a feminist concern, and the way issues of class and race converge in public schools. Although bourgeois women play only a minor role in Olsen's fiction, they appear as victimizers. *Silences*, however, treats all women as victims of male hegemony, granting bourgeois women the latitude Olsen's fiction grants working-class men.

Olsen's 1934 publications and *Tell Me a Riddle* and *Silences* represent two different forms of cultural practice. The first draws on dominant forms of signification, taking them for granted but using them to convey an oppositional message. The second considers the production of meaning itself a site of cultural and political struggle. In Olsen's oeuvre we see a shift from an emphasis on the first to an emphasis on the second form of cultural resistance. This was not a deliberate, conscious shift. "I never *thought* in terms of form," Olsen insists, her voice resonating. "I thought in terms of *content*. When people ask me about form, I'm still that way . . . I don't *think* in terms of form" (Rosenfelt interview).

Form is not, however, the initial mold from which a writer starts but the final articulation of content (Jameson, *Marxism* 328–329). Olsen's genuinely democratic content articulates itself in dialogic, multivocal texts that prefigure post-individual cultural forms. In a sense, Olsen's sociopolitical vision has enabled her to write what under our prevailing social order cannot yet be written. Olsen may not be conscious of a relationship between her own anti-authoritarian and post-individual impulses and the way she constructs a text; and when she has "completed" a work, like any writer, she may not be aware of all its implications, especially its formal ones. A writer's intention, after all, does not circumscribe the range of meanings evoked by a text. That Olsen may not be fully aware of her own achievement does not lessen it, however. With Virginia Woolf in "The Leaning Tower," Olsen's texts proclaim: "Literature is no one's private ground; literature is common ground" (125).

Conclusion

Well, I agree that the Communists are rats. But, on the other hand, remember this. When you go out to shoot rats, you've got to shoot straight.

Richard Nixon

The most massive and brutal attempts to deny the existence of an analytic category occur with respect to class.

Lillian Robinson

Women?
Yes.

A (short) poem by Lillian Robinson, titled "The Question,"
from *Robinson on the Woman Question*

Perhaps the most haunting memory from my preschool days in the '50s is my fear of going to the bathroom alone. I remember insisting that my mother accompany me because I believed—with a child's stubbornness and with the sort of transposing that goes on in a child's mind—that an evil, threatening Bolshevik was lurking behind our shower curtain. We could not yet afford a television; my parents considered themselves "apolitical," concerned largely about their (non-fundamentalist) church, their children, and "making ends meet"; and from all reports I was a bold and independent child, especially for "a girl." That I nevertheless feared Communists behind the iron/shower curtain—having watched only Kate Smith's warbling "God Bless America" and "When the Moon Comes over the Mountain" and the western *Red Ryder* on other people's TVs—suggests the pervasiveness of anticommunism during the Red Scare. Meridel Le Sueur and Tillie Olsen had to endure, with others of their generation, the blighting of their radical past.

226

The documentary *Seeing Red: Stories of American Communists* provides the following reminders of the McCarthy Period:

REAGAN: Hello. In the traditional motion picture story the villains are usually defeated. The ending is a happy one. I can make no such promise for the picture you are about to watch. The story isn't over. You in the audience are part of the conflict. How we meet the Communist challenge depends on you. What has happened so far, what is happening now, is far from encouraging. (BACKGROUND RIOT NOISE) And what do you think this is? The face of Communism in America. (1)

HOOVER: It is a way of life—an evil and malignant way of life. It reveals a condition akin to disease that spreads like an epidemic. And like an epidemic a quarantine is necessary to keep it from infecting this nation. (1)

NIXON: A lot of people may raise the question, "Why all this hullabaloo about being fair, particularly when the people you're investigating are a bunch of traitors?" In fact, I've even heard some people say, "After all, they're a bunch of rats, why don't we go out and shoot them?" Well, I agree that the Communists are rats. But, on the other hand, remember this. When you go out to shoot rats, you've got to shoot straight. (14)

PHILBRICK: As I travel around I still hear people say, "But why are you so hard on Communists? They're just another political party like any other—and a poor minority at that—and so misunderstood." We don't want them misunderstood, and that's why we're making this film. And that's why I say they are liars, dirty, shrewd, (MUSIC) godless, determined, and it is *not* an American political party like any other. It's an outlaw organization taking its orders and instructions from another government to do everything possible to destroy our government. It's an international (MUSIC) criminal conspiracy. (1)

I Led Three Lives, a television program produced from May 1953 to mid-1956, translated this perspective on Communism into a medium for popular consumption. As described in *The Complete Directory to Prime Time Network TV Shows*, this program was based on the actual story of Herbert A. Philbrick, who claimed to have led three lives—that of average American, CP member, and counterspy for the FBI. In *I Led Three Lives*, Communists "really were behind every bush, and anyone with liberal views was indeed suspect. . . . Dark alleyways and secret cell meetings in basements were part of every episode" (Brooks and Marsh 364).

Philbrick himself served as the show's technical consultant, and the program enjoyed the approval and cooperation of J. Edgar Hoover and the FBI, which reviewed all the scripts. "The Communist schemes included sabotage of vital industries, stealing government secrets, [and] dope-smuggling (to poison the nation's youth). . . . One episode even had the Commies plotting to undermine the U.S. guided-missile program by converting vacuum cleaners into bomb launchers" (364). "'We're not trying to deliver a message,'" the production company maintained, while Richard Carlson, who played Philbrick (and got a cut of the profits), insisted, "'I'm just an actor,'" although he did see his role as a "public service" (364, 365).

Virginia Stefan, the actress who played Eva Philbrick, "expressed amazement at the seriousness with which some viewers took the show. 'It's hard to believe, but people actually write us and ask us to investigate Communists in their neighborhood'" (365). (As Brooks and Marsh report, these letters were turned over to the FBI.) Perhaps Stefan should not have been surprised by the audience's response. The program—which opened with an announcer ominously intoning, "This is the fantastically true story of Herbert A. Philbrick, who for nine frightening years did lead three lives"—had the appearance of a documentary (364). Breweries most frequently sponsored I Led Three Lives, but oil and steel companies, banks, and utilities continued to sponsor reruns well into the '60s. Brooks and Marsh conclude their summary (published in 1988) of the program: "Today, however, I Led Three Lives is simply an especially interesting reflection of a very different time" (365).

Not so fast. Not so very different. In 1983 Reagan delivered his "Evil Empire" speech in which he identifies "the struggle between right and wrong and good and evil," referring to those who live in "totalitarian darkness" as "the focus of evil in the modern world." In that speech, as starkly antithetical as the comments above by Hoover, Nixon, and Philbrick, Reagan approvingly cites the white-bucked entertainer Pat Boone's version of better dead than Red: "'I would rather see my little girls die now, still believing in God, than have them grow up under communism and one day die no longer believing in God'" (140, 139). And, just before I wrote these words, Reagan declared from the stage of the 1992 Republican Convention: "But we stood tall and proclaimed that Communism was destined for the ash heap of history. We never heard so much ridicule from our liberal friends. The only thing that got them more upset was two simple words: "'evil empire'" ("Excerpts" A8).

To return to my Preface, with the collapse in 1989 of the Soviet Union and the Eastern Bloc, the American media has embraced capitalism's global ascendancy and gleefully consigned Communism to history's dustbin. Historians of the American Left may have to work harder than ever to insist that the American Communist Party represented something far more complicated than the brutal authoritarianism of Stalin and post-Stalin regimes. On the other hand, because Cold War mythologies of Communist monolithism will now lose some of their currency in American culture, we may now find less resistance to the complicated legacy of the American Communist Party. Le Sueur and Olsen hold a special place in that complicated legacy.

Le Sueur's and Olsen's texts not only strain away from capitalism's acquisitive individualism but also provide a wedge into problems that have internally plagued the Left. They foreshadow, if only in a muted, provisional sense, questions about Marxism and Leninism that theorists, including feminists, have much more recently and explicitly raised. A social analysis based largely on a mode of production is inherently limited. Perhaps the familiar "crisis of Marxism" can be partly understood as the failure of singular models to explain social reality or generate compelling alternatives. Le Sueur's and Olsen's texts presciently resisted the primacy-of-production theory and the CP's reduction of the social terrain's heterogeneity to centers (males in the industrial workplace, for example) and margins (women in the domestic sphere, for example). *Yonnondio*, for example, focused largely on working-class familial relations and concluded with a baby realizing her power by gleefully banging a fruit-jar lid. And, like Clara Zetkin's women comrades (referred to in Chapter 2) about whom Lenin "could scarcely believe [his] ears," the women in *The Girl* show a keen interest in sexuality.

The Left has failed to attract numbers to its ranks partly because it has historically both feared and trivialized people's "nonmaterial" needs. As noted in Chapter 2, Sheila Rowbotham refers to this tendency as the Left's "horror of cosiness." Le Sueur criticized this dread of intimacy in *The Girl*, "Our Fathers," and "Corn Village." She was first exposed to a strain of Protestant asceticism through her stern, indomitable grandmother, whom she described as emotionally and sexually "mute." And the inhabitants of the rural community ("Corn Village") in which Le Sueur grew up were similarly closed, wary, emotionally deformed. But to a degree this asceticism also marked the Communist Party, which did not resist the legacy from Western metaphysics that falsely separates the emotional "realm" from rational intelligence. The Party generally considered psychological and emotional categories unmaterialist, unrelated to "real" politics (Rebecca Pitts's "Women and Communism," discussed in Chapter Two, is one notable exception). And yet Le Sueur's and Olsen's heterodox texts treat these categories, as did Pitts, as fundamentally political, dissolving the artificial distinction between public and private, between Party line and personal experience, between political consciousness and emotional need.

Democratic centralism, the hierarchical Bolshevik form of organization adopted by the CP and some other leftist groups, has been attacked as more centralist than democratic since the 1956 revelations of Stalin's crimes. Socialist-feminists have been among its most vocal critics. Sheila Rowbotham argues that "the form in which you choose to organize is not 'neutral,' it implies certain consequences. . . . If you accept a high degree of centralization . . . you necessarily diminish the development of the self-activity and self-confidence of most of the people involved" (*Fragments* 75). For the women's movement, self-activity and self-confidence have been high priorities and so have become "part of the very act of making a movement" (75). We are reminded of the comment of Ruth Maguire, a former CP member interviewed in *Seeing Red*: "there is a great connection between ends and means. . . . I think there's a direct relationship between how we might have built a party that was democratic and the kind of society that might have come out of *that*."[1] Many feminists similarly require that a group's organizational form be *itself* radically democratic, rejecting the centralist model in favor of more diffuse, smaller groups, in which everyone is encouraged to participate. While ostensibly approving of democratic centralism, Le Sueur unselfconsciously wrote *The Girl*, in which several women organize, independently of men, an enclave of half-realized participatory democracy (albeit not so identified), prefiguring what feminists would now call a self-help group. And the radically democratic content of Olsen's "second period" writing articulates itself in a pluralistic, diffuse, anti-authoritarian form.

Against the transcendent Party, Le Sueur and Olsen, like many of today's socialist-feminists, asserted the importance of their own concrete experiences, experiences of domination and exploitation that Leninist theory marginalizes. They implied that "the personal is political" long before that phrase became a household slogan among socialist-feminists. By now old news, this slogan is nevertheless still timely. Although it has become "rather an embarrassment as if everyone had heard it all before . . . hearing and doing are different matters. The questions remain" (Rowbotham, *Fragments* 141).

One of the remaining questions may be the crucible of the women's movement: responsibility for children. This issue has not been a priority for the movement because during the '60s and '70s many feminists forewent or delayed childbearing. With the '80s and '90s baby boom, however, even the women whom the movement has most helped to advance, its educated professionals, have with a sense of deja vu felt that old shock of sudden recognition, that familiar "click": equal professional opportunity vanishes around the issue of who will take care of the kids. As one veteran feminist and new mother remarked in a 1983 issue of *Mother Jones*, "the truth begins to dawn: mothers are the women the world most wants to keep in their place" (Swartley 34). And in a 1986 issue of *The Village Voice*, columnist Ellen Willis calls for a radical child-rearing movement that confronts the reality of our post-housewife era. Moreover, Nancy Chodorow, Dorothy Dinnerstein, and Isaac Balbus, among others, have argued persuasively that an end to mother-monopolized child-rearing is requisite for building an egalitarian society.

Olsen has pioneered in this area as has no other American writer. "Tell Me a Riddle" illuminates, as no polemic could, the anguish of women who must choose between having children and the need to carry on other serious work. Her unsentimental treatment of the overwhelming burden and satisfaction of motherhood has helped a younger generation of women writers to treat that subject with an unprecedented honesty.[2] Olsen's and Le Sueur's '30s writing illuminates the cracks in the CP's idealized, good-housekeeping Comrade/Mom, a creature not unrelated to today's mythic Superwoman, who, politically mainstream or Left, can presumably "do it all." That more women than men have valued Olsen's and Le Sueur's iconoclasm reminds us that textual meaning, rather than being absolute, is a consequence of a reader-subject's being in a particular situation in the world.

New constituencies have emerged in the advanced industrial world during the past two decades—feminists, national minorities, peace and anti-intervention activists, environmentalists, lesbians/gays/bisexuals, AIDS activists, tenants and other neighborhood groups, and so on—that have kept radical tendencies alive after the eclipse of the New Left. Whereas '30s Marxists considered the working class to be the decisive revolutionary protagonist, many leftists now believe we must confront multiple and overlapping forms of domination (class, patriarchal, racial, bureaucratic, consumer and media related) without reducing that reality to any one of its elements. The new social movements must build ties to working-class and labor struggles, but the class dimension of domination must be taken into account without minimizing other dimensions of domination.

With that said, however, I want to return to a point raised in my Introduction: If many '30s intellectuals mistakenly subordinated all social issues to those of class, at the present historical juncture class is not a fashionable category of analysis among literary scholars, including feminists. It is as if we have actually or conveniently imbibed the middle-class myth—a myth that has been useful historically in the United States for social control. In a recent *Nation* editorial, Vicente Navarro comments on the way that middle-class myth was deployed during the 1992 election year. The Democratic Party can revive itself, so the political pundits say, only by focusing on the needs of middle Americans—needs that are portrayed as different from those of people of color and the poor. "In this political discourse," Navarro observes, "the pundits' concern for the middle class has an antiminority flavor." It is an all-too familiar move, this playing on and promoting racism as a way to divide ordinary Americans, keeping them from uniting to improve their lives. The editorial also points out that the majority of Americans actually belong to the working class, not to the middle class.[3] Members of our working population, both the poor and the nonpoor, have *common* problems, Navarro rightly claims, identifying the need for health insurance as an example. But "the middle-class discourse" veils this reality, aiming "to divide rather than unite the working class—the actual majority of this country. By referring to a mythical middle-class majority as an entity separate from 'the others,' the divisive message is clear. The 'others' are presented as minorities, and racism is called on to do the rest" (361, 381).

This obfuscation of class as a category of analysis has consequences within the academy, forestalling alliances across identities of race, culture, gender, and sexuality among scholars and among our students. I am reminded of classroom experiences in which students who are active in campus groups (the Asian-American Student Union, the African-American Student Alliance, the Gay and Lesbian Task Force, etc.) react with surprise and confusion at their identification with the "wrong" text—the Chinese-American who wonders why "Tell Me a Riddle"'s Eva "is my grandmother"; the *puertorriqueña* who says she never expected to find her "mother's story" in *Yonnondio*; the Euro-American, virulently opposed to multicultural education, who finds her miner-grandfather's struggle in *Storming Heaven* and announces that "if including texts like *Storming Heaven* in the curriculum is part of what multiculturalism is all about," she must begin to examine her prejudices. These students do not recognize their shared working-class interests.

Far too often, students who have rejected what Richard Ohmann terms "the fatuous universalism of the right" do so by taking up a politics of identity that, as Ohmann observes, "makes any sort of embracing social movement against capitalist patriarchy hard indeed to imagine." We see on college campuses, Ohmann continues, "a politics of separate issues" with little "perception that these issues are knit together in a whole system of domination," which might be collectively opposed (33). However, analyzing working-class writing helps in developing such perception and in students' beginning to understand that "the core curriculum is neither Shakespeare nor Alice Walker. It is accounting, computer programming, training for service jobs or for Wall Street high flying, acceptance of such divisions of labor as natural and unchangeable, the quiet reproduction of inequality, and political hopelessness" (34).

Working-class writing has potentially far broader categorical parameters—with significant implications for progressive social and political change in the United States—than many people recognize. As I have said, working-class writing often coincides with other literary categories; frequently, writings by Euro-American women, people of color, and ethnic minorities also qualify as "working-class," even though readers and critics usually identify the texts only in terms of gender, race, or ethnicity. For example, anthologies such as *This Bridge Called My Back: Writings by Radical Women of Color* (1983), edited by Cherríe Moraga and Gloria Anzaldúa, and *Making Face, Making Soul/Haciendo Caras* (1990), edited by Anzaldúa, illuminate ways in which race, ethnicity, and sexual orientation intersect with class to produce distinctive narratives of working-class women's lives. And writing by immigrants such as the Jewish writer Anzia Yezierska is often "working-class" as well as "ethnic" or "immigrant" writing. Moreover, Janet Zandy's groundbreaking *Calling Home: Working-Class Women's Writings* (1990) could be as accurately termed a "multicultural" anthology as a "working-class" anthology. Its contributors include many women of color as well as Euro-American working-class women, lesbians as well as heterosexuals. One way to subvert the "core curriculum" that Ohmann identifies is to discuss these intersections—and potential alliances—with our students and colleagues. If working-class literature emerges as a literary category, we can begin to imagine courses in (multicultural) working-class literature in which students do not get the sense that they have identified with the "wrong" text, in which identity politics is scrapped in favor of a political consciousness capable of decoding the middle-class myth discussed by Navarro.

David Simpson asks a generation of literary critics "for whom hermeneutic anxiety was a basic condition of self-consciousness" to ponder "the relation of first-world hermeneutic skepticism to the fates of those outside the professoriat, both near and far" (726). In "A View from the Garden" Alexander Saxton—a labor historian, working-class novelist, and victim of McCarthy Period harassment—speaks as if responding to Simpon's challenge: "The danger," Saxton observes, "is that the potential successes of the left in intellectual and moral discourse may tend, in isolation, to generate a left scholasticism, an academy within the academy, desperately vulnerable to the controlling careerism of the academy." According to Saxton, "the road to survival that corresponds to the perilous opportunities now opening for the American left is to bring to life organic linkages between left intellectuals in the still rather privileged gardens available to them, and those who labor in the limbs and stomach of the monster outside"

(39). Is it too much to hope, then, as Ohmann does, that our intellectual endeavors might extend beyond "canon reform or a dissident reading of *Paradise Lost*" to "something that will allow human beings to flourish in their common weal" (32, 34)?

Fredric Jameson rightly argues that "only the emergence of a post-individualistic social world, only the reinvention of the collective and the associative, can concretely achieve the 'decentering' of the individual subject . . . only a new and original form of collective social life can overcome the isolation and monadic autonomy of the older bourgeois subjects" (*Political* 125). However, when Jameson looks at the '30s (specifically, its Marxist literary criticism), he mistakenly concludes that it "generated polemics which we may think back on with nostalgia but which no longer correspond to the conditions of the world today" (*Marxism* ix). He dismisses, then, a rich legacy of *Kulturkampf* that, as James D. Bloom points out, anticipated many of Left critics' current concerns, such as "the scruple against presuming Olympian distance from culture"; the complexities of coordinating professional and political practice; "the dialectics of literary representation and historical change"; the "tension between aestheticism and social consciousness"; and "the very criteria of literariness" (9, 10, 81). Thirties' Marxists also anticipated the contemporary canon wars, insisting, as Henry Hart put it in his introduction to *American Writers' Congress* (1935), that American literature "depict the aspirations, struggles and sufferings of *the mass* of Americans" (9). And when Alan Wald calls for "redirecting the study of U.S. cultural formation away from myths, themes, symbols, and elitist networks" to "focusing more . . . on conquest and invasion, capital accumulation, urbanization, colonial and imperial expansion, and late capitalism, as the framework that nurtures and limits the context in which active agents create culture," he implicitly acknowledges a debt to his '30s precursors in materialist criticism ("Theorizing" 30).

A few "second wave" feminists have also acknowledged a debt to their '30s precursors. Rosalyn Baxandall, for example, observes that "a number of the women's liberation movement activists of the late 1960s were red diaper babies, grew up with such terms as 'male chauvinism' and the 'woman question,' and heard frequent gossip about which Party families were backward about women." Baxandall reminds us that "the 'woman question' was a radical nineteenth-century term, and only the Communist party continued its use" (271).[4] Betty Friedan's identifying in *The Feminine Mystique* (1963) a "problem that has no name" may for many signal the beginning of feminism's "second wave," but during the postwar period and the '50s there were voices countering those of the advertisers, mainstream women's magazines, and Freudian psychologists so effectively portrayed in the documentary *The Life and Times of Rosie the Riveter*. Betty Millard, a member of the *New Masses* editorial board, for example, published a two-part article, "Woman Against Myth" (30 December 1947, 6 January 1948), echoing Rebecca Pitts's prescient "Women and Communism" (*New Masses*, 1935) and anticipating many "second wave" concerns. Millard reports that despite misgivings about "Woman Against Myth" among some *New Masses* editors (with the exception of Millard, all of them were male), it received substantial support from some Party members, and *New Masses* printed letters responding favorably to it. That the Party issued Millard's two-part article as a pamphlet (International Publishers, 1948) indicates its willingness to draw attention to her views.[5]

What Sara Evans observes about the New Left also applies to the Old: "the new left did more than simply perpetuate the oppression of women. Even more importantly, it created new arenas—social space—within which women could develop a new sense of self-worth and independence . . . and having heightened women's self-respect, it also allowed them to claim the movement's ideology for themselves" (244). As I said near the conclusion of Chapter 2, the CP's work among women in the '30s should be carefully evaluated as part of the struggle for women's liberation in the United States. Many women developed an awareness of their own potential, a sense of collectivity, and an understanding of America's social system through Party-related activities. As I have said, that Party leadership was overwhelmingly male and that its bureaucracy functioned undemocratically "from the top down" is a matter of record. But the creative maneuvering within that patriarchal hierarchy—by Party women, its "loyal opposition," and its rank-and-file members—has yet to be thoroughly explored.

We now have in print a discrete body of work that can be identified as writing by or about U.S. working-class women. The Feminist Press, cofounded in 1970 by Florence Howe and Paul Lauter, has a distinguished history of publishing and reprinting working-class women's writing. West End Press, largely through the efforts of John Crawford, has since 1976 published and reprinted working-class women's writing, including Meridel Le Sueur's, and Arno Press has reprinted some working-class women's writing, including two of Josephine Herbst's novels, *Money for Love* (1977; 1929) and *Nothing Is Sacred* (1977; 1928). And in the '80s the press of the School of Industrial and Labor Relations at Cornell University (known as the ILR Press) began a Literature of American Labor Series that includes Theresa Serber Malkiel's *The Diary of a Shirtwaist Striker* (1910; 1990). A note included in texts published in the series explains its purpose: to "bring back into print some of the best literature that has emerged from the labor movement" in the United States and Canada. "We are defining literature broadly," the note continues, to include "novels, biographies, autobiographies, and journalism."

The Politics of Literature: Dissenting Essays on the Teaching of English (1970), edited by Louis Kampf and Lauter, raises issues still relevant for scholars of working-class writing, who are "up against the great tradition," to borrow the title of one of the collection's essays. And since its inception in 1975, the journal *Radical Teacher* has consistently supported working-class studies, as has the Radical Caucus of the Modern Language Association. Since 1968, Caucus members have organized MLA sessions addressing working-class concerns, including working-class women's writing.

Tillie Olsen has also worked to restore forgotten, out-of-print women's writing, especially working-class women's writing. Shelley Fisher Fishkin gives us Florence Howe's account of Olsen's role in the Feminist Press:

. . . in 1970, when Tillie Olsen "gave *Life in the Iron Mills* to the Feminist Press and said she had written a biographical and literary afterword that we could have as well, that changed the whole course of publishing for the Feminist Press." Up to that point the Feminist Press had planned to bring out "short biographical pamphlets about writers and women of distinction in all kinds of work, and . . . feminist children's books," observes Howe, "but we had not thought of doing works from the past until [Tillie] handed [us] *Life in the Iron Mills*, and followed that up the following year with *Daughter of Earth*." A key chapter of publishing history was in the making. At first "the Feminist Press had the reprint field to itself." Then other publishers jumped in—Virago and the Women's Press in the mid '70s, and Beacon, Rutgers, Pandora, Illinois, ILR Press, Oxford, and scores of others in the '80s. (5)

Moreover, Olsen has tirelessly encouraged and promoted the work of living women writers, especially working-class women writers—with Linda McCarriston, an Irish-American working-class poet (*Eva-Mary*, 1991), and Fae Myenne Ng, a Chinese-American working-class fiction writer (*Bone*, 1993), providing only two recent examples.

The pioneering work of the Feminist Press, *Radical Teacher*, the Radical Caucus, and others has been furthered by publications such as Nicholas Coles's "Democratizing Literature: Issues in Teaching Working-Class Literature" (*College English*, November 1986); *Working Classics: Poems of Industrial Life*, edited by Peter Oresick and Coles (1990); Zandy's *Calling Home: Working-Class Women's Writings* (1990); Rabinowitz's *Labor and Desire: Women's Revolutionary Fiction in Depression America* (1991); Laura Hapke's *Tales of a Working Girl: Wage-Earning Women in American Literature, 1890–1925* (1992); Jon Christian Suggs's edited volume, *American Proletarian Culture: The Twenties and Thirties* (1993); Karyn L. Hollis's work on the writings by women who attended the Bryn Mawr Summer School for Women Workers; and Pam Annas's "Pass the Cake: The Politics of Gender, Class, and Text in the Academic Workplace," which appears in *Working-Class Women in the Academy: Laborers in the Knowledge Factory* (1993), edited by Michelle M. Tokarczyk and Elizabeth A. Fay. Moreover, biographies of Josephine Herbst (by Elinor Langer, 1984), Agnes Smedley (by Janice R. MacKinnon and Stephen R. MacKinnon, 1988), and Mary Heaton Vorse (by Dee Garrison, 1989) have appeared. Such publications signal that working-class writing may be emerging as a visible, if not yet "legitimate," category of literary studies (I agree with the assertion by Lillian Robinson that appears as an epigraph to this Conclusion, especially when it is applied to English Departments: "the most massive and brutal attempts to deny the existence of an analytic category occur with respect to class" [*Sex* 66]).

"To approach working-class culture," Lauter argues,

> we must lay aside many of our presuppositions about what literature *is* and is *not*. We must begin by asking in what forms, on what themes, in what circumstances, and to what ends working people spoke and sang to one another. How did they gather, examine, transmit, and renew their experiences? First, we need a broader definition of what we can call 'literature.'" ("Working-Class" 111)

In her introduction to her study of working-class British literature, *The Industrial Muse* (1974), Martha Vicinus similarly calls for a broader definition of literature: "What we call literature, and what we teach, is what the middle class—and not the working class—produced. Our definition of literature and our canons of taste are class bound; we currently exclude street literature, songs, hymns, dialect and oral story telling, but they were the most popular forms used by the working class" (1).

Robinson's *Sex, Class, and Culture* (1978; reissued in 1986) also unmasks the class-bound nature of what universities consider "literature" and calls for "a radical redefinition" of the term (224). "Working/Women/Writing," one of the dozen essays (all by Robinson) examines the personal histories—collected in the scrapbook *I Am a Woman Worker*[6]—of rank-and-file women factory workers who studied at the Associated Schools for Workers in the 1920s and '30s. (Perhaps the best known among these schools was the Bryn Mawr summer institute, the subject of a memorable documentary, *The Women of Summer*[1985]). About *I Am a Woman Worker* Robinson concludes:

> I wish to suggest that, whatever we have been taught, cliches or sentimentality need not be signals of meretricious prose, and that ultimately it is honest writing for which criticism should be looking. It is essential to recognize literature that can enhance our understanding of the conditions that define women's lives, and, in order to gain insight into what women experience, I do not feel that we have to "relax our standards." Instead, writing like this can force a reevaluation and a re-ordering of those standards and turn them on their heads. And this sort of process, this sort of reading, tells us something we urgently need to know about both women and literature. (252–253)

Robinson reminds us that working-class women's writing "gives form to the experiences of the *majority* of women" (225; my emphasis). She offers an alternative standard for literature, startling for its simplicity and for its revolutionary implications: It "should help us learn about the way things are, in as much depth and fullness as possible and by any means necessary" (230).

Lauter notes the importance of comparing African-American and Euro-American working-class cultural materials. "Almost all writing produced by African-Americans is, by any definition, working-class literature," Lauter rightly asserts, observing that "most of the authors have working-class origins, and their subjects and audiences are generally working-class people like themselves" ("Working-Class" 119). Although African-American and Euro-American working-class cultural forms derive from different traditions, if we examine how these forms were produced and how they functioned within working-class communities, some important similarities emerge. In *Black Culture and Black Consciousness: Afro-American Folk Thought from Slavery to Freedom*, for example, which Lauter considers "required reading" for those interested in working-class cultural forms, Lawrence Levine has collected firsthand descriptions of the creation of spirituals mainly in postbellum African-American churches. Levine found that originality and innovative form, both prized by the bourgeois aesthetic, were not primary considerations in creating spirituals. New songs, which varied tunes and lyrics familiar to people's communities, were deliberately constructed from old ones. Moreover, like oral storytelling, the spirituals were often created communally, with an individual's creation considered less significant than that of a group.

Indeed, as Lauter observes,

> much working-class art is created and experienced in group situations—not in the privacy of a study, but in the church . . . the work site, the meeting hall, the quilting bee, or the picket line. It is thus rooted in the experiences of a particular group of people facing particular problems at a particular time. It is not conceived as timeless and transcendent. . . . ("Working-Class" 113–114)

Similarly, the contributors to I Am a Woman Worker violated "a fundamental precept of bourgeois aesthetics that good art . . . celebrates what is unique and even eccentric in human experience or human personality. Individual achievement and subjective isolation are the norm, whether the achievement and the isolation be that of the artist or the character" (Robinson, Sex 226). The contributors to I Am a Woman Worker, in contrast, "wrote about their lives in order to develop their potential as part of their class and its struggle—a commitment that they did not separate from self-actualization." Although Robinson does not dismiss the importance of oppressed people's writing as a means of establishing identity, she is "even more impressed by the notion that doing so may be understood as a process that integrates one into one's community and helps to create and unite the community itself, instead of underscoring the purportedly inherent conflict between the individual and the group" (232).

While there are differences among the relatively few scholars attempting to theorize working-class writing, they all share the recognition that canonical views of the nature and status of "literature" have seriously impeded attempts to understand and value working-class discourse. These scholars have variously argued that we must look through something other than "aesthetic" lenses when evaluating working-class writing. I suggest that all these scholars are looking through various pragmatic lenses: that is, not unlike their '30s predecessors, they are looking at connections between discourse and society, asking, among other questions, how society shapes discourse and how discourse shapes society. Those employing pragmatic lenses are less preoccupied with the undecidability of meaning than with language uses. They think of language, as Eagleton has put it, "as something we do" (Literary 147).

If extended to working-class writing, an argument Annette Kolodny made in 1980 about women writers partly explains working-class writing's current marginal status in the literary canon. Discussing women writers such as Charlotte Perkins Gilman, whose work dropped out of sight until the Feminist Press reissued The Yellow Wallpaper in 1973, Kolodny argued that the reason for Gilman's disappearance

> may not be due to any intrinsic lack of merit in the work but, instead, to an incapacity of predominantly male readers—those readers who have traditionally been

invested with the authority to record literary history—to interpret competently and appreciate fully women's texts. Such readers may have been as unacquainted with the texts' real-world contexts as with their informing literary contexts. The result was that these readers did not read the texts well; and, blaming the difficulty on *what* was read rather than on *how* it was read, they accorded the text—and not themselves—diminished status. (590)

Change "male readers" to "readers from the professional-managerial class"—the class in which most literary agents, editors, reviewers, taste-making intellectuals, critics, and professors reside—and we begin to see that canon-making aesthetic values arise partly out of class conflict.

My study resides, then, at the nexus of two related fronts in the culture wars neglected even by many progressive academics: the effort to expand the literary canon by legitimating working-class writing and the struggle to preserve and revision the history of the American Left. One result of anticommunist, pro-capitalist ideology in literary studies has been, as Wald points out,

the disempowerment of the population of ordinary people who are denied a genuine history of their own cultural activities through access to authors who wrote about strikes, rebellions, mass movements, the work experience, famous political trials, the tribulations of political commitment, as well as about love, sex, the family, nature, and war from a class-conscious, internationalist, socialist-feminist, and antiracist point of view. Instead, the population [of ordinary people] is often exclusively presented with literary role models that inculcate notions of culture that distort visions of possibilities for social transformation. ("Culture" 284–285)

Wald's remarks about the disempowerment of ordinary people remind me, again, of my disempowered "ordinary" students, who can neither hope for nor envision forms of coalition building in an increasingly multicultural United States partly because they lack knowledge of labor history and progressive movements for social change prior to the Civil Rights Movement and feminism's "second wave." My students are astonished—and even incredulous—when I tell them, for example, that in 1912 in Lawrence, Massachusetts, textile workers representing about 45 language groups united in a successful strike against long hours, pay cuts, and speed-up. And professors who in their scholarship and pedagogy are moving away from narrow conceptions of English and American literature to broader notions of "Cultural Studies" rarely think, despite their interdisciplinary inclinations, about the place of labor and working-class studies under that rubric. Roger Kimball's tenured (and untenured) radicals in literature and cultural studies departments have much to learn from U.S. historians such as those who composed the American Social History Project, founded by Herbert G. Gutman, and produced the groundbreaking two-volume *Who Built America? Working People and the Nation's Economy, Politics, Culture, and Society* (1989; 1992).

The texts included in my study represent two distinct forms of agitational cultural practice that refract in narrative form the conflicting political tendencies within Le Sueur and Olsen. Much of Le Sueur's reportage and to a lesser extent

Olsen's 1934 publications draw on dominant forms of signification to convey a subversive message. In these works both writers display their impulses to sanction elements of a Michael Gold kind of proletarian realism. Their discourse is some-times significantly marked by dominant discursive modes: the '30s reportage of Le Sueur and Olsen remained largely, in Bakhtinian terms, "monological." Re-strained by monologism, the reportage of neither Le Sueur nor Olsen (although the latter made some significant attempts) broke free from a model in which readers are conceived more as passive receivers than as active, collaborative con-structors of meaning. Thus much of their '30s reportage exists within the very mode of production they opposed, at odds with the very collectivity they espoused.

Le Sueur's *The Girl* and several of her stories and Olsen's "second period" texts, on the other hand, experiment with ways to challenge the ideological char-acter of the signification process itself. While the challenge is more forceful in the works of Olsen (partly because it is more systematically developed) than in those of Le Sueur, it must not be overlooked in either writer. In this second group of texts both writers resist Gold's dicta and mine the bourgeois literary traditions (Le Sueur's boast that she could not be forced out of her lyric style) for devices that can be effectively turned against bourgeois culture itself. I have identified several of those devices as they contributed to Le Sueur's and Olsen's experiments with heteroglossia. It is in the movement toward embodying heteroglossia that both writers were most revolutionary. In that movement they challenged bour-geois conceptions of the individual; they challenged the reductionism and monologism of the dominant culture's modes of communication as well as the monologism of the CP's proletarian realism; further, they disrupted traditional notions of audience as passive receivers. Dominant discursive practices take for granted that the act of reading will be a *subjection to* a fixed meaning, whereas *Tell Me a Riddle* and *Silences*, for example, offer an alternative way of conceiving the writer's and reader's roles. Both works foreground the processes by which they generate meaning, disrupting and activating their reader-subjects while subverting authorial control.

When the authorial voice is granted exceptional status, writers appear to need no complement, as Bakhtin has noted; the natural state of being appears to be solitary, independent of others. The definition of Bakhtin's "monologism" bears repeating here: It "denies that there exists outside of it another consciousness, with the same rights, and capable of responding on an equal footing, another and equal I (*thou*). . . . the *other* remains entirely and only an *object* of conscious-ness." Olsen's dialogized texts, however, subvert unicentered discourse and the concept of textual ownership, affirming the reader not as an object but as another subject, a reciprocal "thou." These texts implicitly acknowledge that in the act of reading, reader-subjects engage in an active, complex, and creative process not unlike that of writing. Whereas monologism is "deaf to the other's response," even the title *Tell Me a Riddle* demands that an "other" speak. As I have shown, both Le Sueur and Olsen experimented with forms that invite us to be engaged in counter-hegemonic efforts. *Silences*, formally the most heterodox of the texts considered here, suggests one form that a counter-hegemonic writing might take. An anti-conjurer, Olsen refuses to lull her readers with the illusion of mimetic representation. The reader is no longer simply a consumer. In the tradition of Brecht's theater and Jean-Luc Godard's cinematic montage, *Silences* invites readers to collaborate in a discourse of resistance.

"Men make their own history," says Marx, "but not of their own free will; not under circumstances they themselves have chosen but under the given and inherited circumstances with which they are directly confronted." And so it is with women. Le Sueur and Olsen exemplified the "audacity within confinement"—to repeat a phrase from Thomas Mann that Olsen is fond of quoting—that this well-known passage from Marx implicitly advocates. As Le Sueur's and Olsen's lives and discourse of resistance suggest, such "inherited circumstances" include not only economic conditions and political traditions but also other—although not separable—categories of human experience. These two writers suture the split between public and private—a split, as Jane Gallop has put it, "which keeps our lives out of our knowledge" (4). The "riddle" that Le Sueur's and Olsen's work challenges us to engage—though never, finally, to resolve—requires that we consider political activity not as something confined to a single class, party, gender, ethnic group, or cause but as something undertaken within a kaleidoscopic social terrain and, simultaneously, within "the fibres of the self and in the hard practical substance of effective and continuing relationships" (Williams, *Marxism* 212). Creating a counter-hegemony by connecting many different forms of struggle, including those not primarily "public" and "economic," leads to a more profound and compelling sense of revolutionary activity. Le Sueur's and Olsen's most subversive, heteroglossic writing—in necessarily "partial, scrappy, subsidiary, and preparatory" form (Trotsky 163)—strains toward the post-individual, collective, associative cultural forms of a different social order.

NOTES

EPIGRAPH

1. Kenin's song by this title was a spinoff of "Ballad for UnAmericans," written and composed in 1947 by Lee Hays and Walter Lowenfels and first published in 1948 in *People's Songs Bulletin,* the predecessor to *Sing Out!* "Ballad for UnAmericans," in turn, was a takeoff on "Ballad for Americans," written by John Latouche and composed by Earl Robinson in 1938. The "Ballad for Americans" was recorded and sung widely in the 1940s by artists as diverse as Paul Robeson and Bing Crosby (it was even sung at the 1940 Republican Convention). Kenin first published his song in the July–August 1983 issue of *Folknik,* the Newsletter of the San Francisco Music Club.

INTRODUCTION

1. Christina L. Baker, James D. Bloom, Barbara Foley, Laura Hapke, Walter Kalaidjian, Barbara Melosh, Charlotte Nekola, Cary Nelson, David Peck, Paula Rabinowitz, Deborah Rosenfelt, Suzanne Sowinska, Jon Christian Suggs, Harvey Teres, Alan Wald, and Douglas Wixson are among the literary scholars reexamining the '30s. *Revisioning Thirties' Culture,* for example, edited by Sherry Lee Linkon and Bill V. Mullen, will be published in 1995 by the University of Illinois Press. But it is important to underscore what Alan Wald tirelessly points out to scholars reexamining the '30s: Too often radical literature has been viewed within the narrow confines of the 1930s as if that decade were an aberration in U.S. history rather than part of a sustained resistance to capitalism. As Wald argued persuasively in a presentation at the 1993 American Studies Association Convention, the Left cultural practices of the 1930s, '40s, '50s, and '60s are all linked to the same tradition. Thus Wald is editing a series, "The Radical Novel in the United States Reconsidered," of paperback reprints, with new introductions, of leftist novels originally published between the 1920s and the early '60s.

2. For a useful discussion of the distinctions between the working class and the bour-geoisie, see the conclusion to Raymond Williams' *Culture and Society: 1780–1950*. For an overview of work promoting working-class writing, see my Conclusion.

3. The phrase is Susan Sontag's, from *Styles of Radical Will*, cited in Rich 281.

4. Lauter's essay was originally published by *Radical Teacher*. My references to this essay are to the version appearing in Hartman and Messer-Davidow. See two other relevant essays by Lauter — "American Proletarianism" and "Race and Gender" — as well as his *Canons and Contexts*.

5. It is a promising sign that some academics of working-class origin have identified themselves as such. See Tokarczyk and Fay; Zandy, *Liberating Memory*; and Dews and Law.

6. See Rabinowitz, *Labor*; and Rosenfelt, "Thirties."

7. For a valuable, extensive characterization of materialist-feminism, to which I am indebted, see Newton and Rosenfelt's introduction to *Feminist Criticism and Social Change*.

8. Letter to Constance Coiner, 19 July 1992.

9. I conducted interviews of Le Sueur, Olsen, Reeva Olson, Angela Ward, Dorothy Healey, Ruth Maguire, and Edna Whitehouse. I also interviewed Lucy Kendall, although I do not cite the interview, and (by telephone) Jessica Mitford, although she did not come to the United States until 1939 and joined the Party in 1943. I interviewed Bill Bailey to get a male's perspective on the Party's handling of "the woman question" during the '30s. I interviewed Genora Johnson Dollinger (by telephone); she was a member of the Socialist Party and later of the Socialist Workers Party, but her involvement in the 1937 Flint Strike and other activities brought her into contact with the CP. I have listened to interviews of Le Sueur, Olsen, Annette Rubinstein, and Myra Page conducted by other scholars. And I was informed by the comments Harriet Magil made about women in the Party during Paul Buhle's interview of her husband, A. B. Magil.

10. It is by now a well-known question whether works signed by Volosinov were actu-ally written by Bakhtin. For an explanation of the origin of the controversy, see the translators' preface to Volosinov, *Marxism* (ix).

11. See also Bakhtin, *Speech* 60–102.

12. By this term I mean the work any text does, implicitly or explicitly, to support or subvert the dominant culture; of course, both supporting and subverting elements are often present in any single given text. In *Repression and Recovery* Cary Nelson uses "cultural work" in his discussion of marginalized poets (1910–45) — particularly women, African-Americans, and Leftists. James D. Bloom uses a related term, *Kulturkampf* ("cul-ture-struggle"), to identify the effort that Michael Gold and Joseph Freeman devoted themselves to.

13. See Hunter 361, n1.

14. See, for example, Kelley; Painter; Steve Nelson, Barrett, and Ruck; Naison; Keeran; Prickett; and the Tamiment Library's Oral History of the American Left Col-lection.

15. For a discussion of the complex and alternative senses of "experience," see Williams, *Keywords* 126–129.

16. Although Le Sueur, Olsen, and other interviewees were generally welcoming and patient, I laughed and winced — recognizing shared experience and anxiety — when I read Stuart Timmons's introduction to his biography of Harry Hay. Timmons acknowledges that his "was an intense project, which created a deep and sometimes explosive relation-ship" with Hay and provides the following example: "After more than a year of intimate

interviews . . . we got into a scrap about homophobia in the Communist Party. He [Hay] got upset seemingly because, though he had suffered prejudice at the hands of his former CP comrades, his loyalty to their shared ideals survived. With great emotion and conviction, he declared that 'homophobia' was not a word, or even a concept, at the time of his troubles. When I failed to appreciate this, he stood up from his kitchen table, shot me a withering glance, and growled, 'I'm not sure we are able to communicate at all!' . . . We quickly made up—and resolved the problem—but I learned the contradictions of a committed life" (xiii–xiv). Because the Party's views toward feminism were central to my project, I needed to raise feminist issues repeatedly in interviews, and Le Sueur, Olsen, and others underscored Annette Rubinstein's caution, cited above, note 8.

17. This appears as an epigraph in Daniel Aaron's *Writers on the Left*, vii.

18. See, for example, Baxandall; Dennis; Dixler; Foley; Gosse; Healey and Isserman; Langer; Loader; Mitford; Nekola and Rabinowitz; Rosenfelt; Rubens; Shaffer. For oral histories see, for example, Twentieth-Century Trade Union Women; Women in California.

CHAPTER 1

1. Irene Paull, writer, CP member, and close friend of Le Sueur, described Le Sueur as producing "the agit-prop work that was needed. . . . but at the same time . . . maintain[ing] her literary integrity with what she wrote in her notebooks" in a letter to Le Sueur's biographer, Neala Schleuning, 1976. This and other excerpts from the letter appear in Schleuning, *America* 119.

2. According to a telephone conversation with A. B. Magil (17 August 1992), Ellis, Gropper, Kunitz, Magil, and Potamkin were delegates from the New York City John Reed Club; Gold attended as an individual delegate, not as a representative of the John Reed Club; John Dos Passos had been invited but was unable to attend; and Herbst and Herrmann attended as "observers," invited by Gold. Information about the delegation provided by Fred Ellis and others in *New Masses* (February 1931) differs slightly: "The American delegates . . . representing the John Reed Club and the *New Masses*, were Fred Ellis, Michael Gold, William Gropper, Joshua Kunitz, A. B. Magil and Harry Alan Potamkin. . . . There were, in addition, two guest delegates from America, John Herrmann and Josephine Herbst, representing the sympathetic writers. Many regrets were expressed that John Dos Passos, who had been invited was unable to attend" (6).

3. Bedacht's name was not included in the taped interview; Magil supplied the name during a telephone conversation, 8 July 1992.

4. There are interesting similarities, as well as differences, between Gold's nine tenets of proletarian realism and the "Instructions for Contributors," written by George S. Schuyler, that Henry Louis Gates, Jr., tells us had been widely circulated by 1929 among black writers and in the journals in which black authors could most readily publish. Gates reprints these instructions, which he terms "ironclad," in a chapter on Zora Neale Hurston in *The Signifying Monkey: A Theory of Afro-American Literary Criticism* (1988). One of several similarities between Schuyler's and Gold's dicta lies in their shared call for a simple and direct style. "Short, simple words," Schuyler intones. "No attempt to parade erudition to the bewilderment of the reader." At several points, Schuyler's and Gold's directives unselfconsciously reflect assumptions of the dominant culture that has marginalized them and the people to whom they are writing. Schuyler, for example, makes the following points: "The

heroine should always be beautiful and desirable, sincere and virtuous. The hero should always be of the he-man type, but not stiff, stereotyped, or vulgar" (179). Gates's point about these "Instructions for Contributors" is similar to mine about Gold's tenets. The "Instructions" "enable us to begin to understand the black milieu against which Hurston would define herself as a writer" just as the tenets of proletarian realism enable us to begin to understand the context in which Olsen and Le Sueur defined themselves as writers.

5. According to Marcus Klein, Itzok Granich became Michael Gold in 1920; before that he had published under the name Irwin Granich (234; 319, n6). In a memoir, Gold explains that Corporal "Michael Gold," a veteran of the Union Army and "an upright, fiery old man," was the father of a boyhood friend on the Lower East Side ("The Writer" 183).

6. This revealing passage merits quoting at length:

> At the age of twelve I carried in my mind a morbid load of responsibility.
>
> I had been a precocious pupil in the public school, winning honors not by study, but by a kind of intuition. I graduated a year sooner than most boys. At the exercises I was valedictory orator.
>
> My parents were proud, of course. They wanted me to go on to high school, like other "smart" boys. They still believed I would be a doctor.
>
> But I was morbid enough to be wiser than my parents. Even then I could sense that education is a luxury reserved for the well-to-do [although Gold did not sense that it was a luxury reserved for "boys," the word he consistently uses in referring to students]. I refused to go to high school. More than half the boys in my graduating class were going to work; I chose to be one of them.
>
> It was where I belonged. I figured it out on paper for my parents. Four years of high school, then six years of college before one could be a doctor. Ten years of study in all, with thousands of dollars needed for books, tuition, and the rest.
>
> There were four of us in the family. My mother seemed unable to work [she was immobilized by grief; Gold's sister had recently been killed in an accident]. Would my father's banana peddling keep us alive during those ten years while I was studying?
>
> Of course not. I was obstinate and bitter; my parents wept, and tried to persuade me, but I refused to go to high school. . . .
>
> I was trying to be hard. For years my ego had been fed by every one's praise of my precocity. I had always loved books; I was mad about books; I wanted passionately to go to high school and college. Since I couldn't, I meant to despise all that nonsense. . . .
>
> [My English teacher] presented me with a parting gift. It was a volume of Emerson's Essays, with her name and my name and the date written on the flyleaf.
>
> I thanked her for the book, and threw it under the bed when I got home. I never read a page in it, or in any book for the next five years. I hated books; they were lies, they had nothing to do with life and work. (*Jews Without Money* 220–221)

As a young man, Gold managed to acquire some more schooling, which he later denied. He took a high school cram course at night at the City College in New York. But he was working 12 hours a day at the time, fell asleep in class despite his struggle to stay alert, and quit in "humiliation." In 1914 he wangled admission to Harvard as a provisional student. He left after the first semester, but only because he could not simultaneously support himself and attend college. He had been "delighted with Harvard—with the atmosphere, his classes, and himself. He found the work easy enough, studied assiduously, and, as he re-members it, did well in his courses" (Folsom 225). Gold's response to his thwarted efforts is captured in "Love on a Garbage Dump" (*New Masses*, 1928). The story begins: "Certain enemies have spread the slander that I once attended Harvard college. This is a lie. I worked on the garbage dump in Boston, city of Harvard. But that's all" (cited in Folsom 226). As Folsom notes, "Gold's critics like to cite this passage to expose his 'anti-intellectual-ism,' especially since it seems so patently disingenuous. They fail, however, to note that 'Love on a Garbage Dump' is a fiction, specifically labelled '32nd Attempt at a Short Story' on its first publication. They ignore, or are ignorant of, the reasons for Gold's hostility" (226).

7. One of reportage's predecessors was naturalism. Naturalism's legacy gave writers of reportage permission to record social conditions with brutal frankness. "Tell your yarn and let your style go to the devil," Frank Norris had written in 1899. "We don't want litera-ture, we want life" (cited in Kazin 75).

Muckraking journalism, another predecessor of reportage, was most vigorous from about 1902 to 1912, when a group of editors and publishers made common cause with novelists, journalists, historians, economists, and others to expose the underside of Ameri-can capitalism. The muckrakers appropriated one of the earliest forms of mass culture for its revelations, the cheap popular magazine.

Muckrakers did not pose as objective reporters of balanced journalism. *McClure's Magazine* published, for example, Ida Tarbell's account of the shady business practices of the Standard Oil Company; Lincoln Steffens's exposés of the role of reputable citizens as well as ward bosses in corrupt city and state governments; and Ray Stannard Baker's indict-ments of racial discrimination. Upton Sinclair's *The Jungle* is the classic example of muckraking in novel form. The social journalism of such writers as John Reed, Mary Heaton Vorse, and John Spivak also prefigured reportage. Although muckrakers and social journalists were sometimes charged with peddling sensationalism, they had no more need to distort the facts than would writers of reportage during the Depression.

8. Aaron adds, however, that Jerome "never commanded the complete admiration or respect of his subordinates and had very little influence on the intellectuals" (446, n8).

9. Curtius wrote *European Literature and the Latin Middle Ages* (1948), among other works, and translated *The Waste Land* into German. Peter Godman reports that in 1948 Curtius wrote to Eliot, "I dream of a secret directorate for western cultural politics, . . . just 3, 4, 5, who were of the same opinion." According to Godman, "Eliot approved of this idea, which finds parallels in his own reflections on 'The Class and the Elite' in *Notes Towards a Definition of Culture*." Godman notes that "little ingenuity is required to guess who two of its [the directorate's] members were to be" (7).

10. For some of the factors contributing to the retreat, see Wald, "Intellectuals" (178–179) and *The New York Intellectuals*.

11. Rabinowitz provides a useful list of now-obscured Left journals from the period (186–187). In my study of Le Sueur and Olsen, I have found *The Working Woman* and *Woman Today* to be of particular interest.

12. For a list of the other signatories, see Hart 11–12.

13. As a result of Gold's attack, the *New Republic* received an unprecedented amount of mail, most of it protesting Gold's positions, and for two months the correspondence section ran responses to Gold—and then replies to the responses. The furor would likely have continued had it not been terminated by the editors. In the December 17, 1930, issue, they affixed the title "The Final Round" to letters related to the controversy and in a note

announced that "the Gold-Wilder controversy is hereby called on account of darkness. No further letters on this subject will be published" (141). Commenting in 1932 on the controversy's significance, Edmund Wilson observed that "there is no question that the Gold-Wilder row marked definitely the eruption of the Marxist issues out of the literary circles of the radicals into the field of general criticism. After that, it became very plain that the economic crisis was to be accompanied by a literary one" ("Literary" 320). The Gold-Wilder controversy and its implications have been discussed in detail elsewhere—see Aaron (239, 241–243); Bloom (55–56); Klein (243–248); Peck (129–132, 169–178); and Rideout (153–154).

14. Written by H. H. Lewis and titled "Liberal," this piece, according to Jack Conroy and Curt Johnson, originally appeared in *The Rebel Poet* Oct.–Nov. 1931. (Conroy and Johnson included "Liberal" in *Writers in Revolt: The Anvil Anthology* [219]; it appears in a slightly different version in Mangione 32.) However, when I looked at the New York Public Library's microfilm of *The Rebel Poet*, I found an Oct.–Nov.–Dec. issue but not an Oct.–Nov. issue in 1931. In fact, I could not find "Liberal" in any 1931 issue. The microfilm included a note at the beginning of the reel indicating that some pages were "lacking, missing, [or] mutilated," although no pages were missing from the Oct.–Nov.–Dec. issue. From my informal and sometimes frustrating sampling, '30s Left periodicals—particularly the more obscure ones, such as the "little" literary magazines and *The Working Woman* and *Woman Today*—seem to be in poorer condition than many mainstream publications from the period.

15. This predominance of masculinity has been noted in the literature of other protest movements. For example, Barbara Christian notes that while protest novels such as Richard Wright's *Native Son*, James Baldwin's *The Fire Next Time*, and Ralph Ellison's *Invisible Man* have received sustained attention, Petry's *The Street* (1946), a proletarian protest novel that has much in common with *Native Son* and was the first novel by an African-American woman to focus on the struggles of a working-class black mother in an urban ghetto, has been largely ignored. Christian believes that this discrepancy can be partly explained by the emphasis in the civil rights and Black Power movements on "the muscular path of black manhood" (18). Christian continues, "Though they valued literature as protest, the Black Power movements of the 1960s portrayed women as adjuncts to men, a perspective that Alice Walker, June Jordan and Audre Lorde would later come to criticize" (19). Christian also comments on the pressure to subordinate black women's concerns to the push for "Black Unity," a situation that parallels the CP's willingness during the '30s to subordinate women's issues in favor of working-class solidarity: "At a time when Black Unity meant that women should not protest their conditions as women, Petry's analyses of the ways in which black men vented their frustrations on black women must have seemed (at best) strategically incorrect" (19).

CHAPTER 2

1. *The Working Woman* and *Woman Today* have been obscured. My research indicates that only four libraries around the country hold hard copies of *The Working Woman*, so most readers can get access to it only on microfilm and only through interlibrary loan. Moreover, no one library has a complete series of this publication, even on microfilm. The Tamiment Library at New York University and the Hoover Institution at Stanford own hard

copies of *The Working Woman* (the Tamiment has only one issue; the Hoover Institution has issues from 1929–35). The New York Public Library owns hard copies of some issues from 1933–35, and the American Communist Party Headquarters owns hard copies of some issues from 1929–31. Only the Tamiment Library houses *Woman Today* (on microfilm).

2. This headline appears in an article credited only to "Irene."

3. Harriet Magil's remarks were part of an interview Paul Buhle conducted of her husband, A. B. Magil. Readers interested in her comments should note that her name does not appear in the Tamiment Library's Oral History of the American Left catalog. The detailed index accompanying the A. B. Magil tapes when I received them through inter-library loan included Harriet Magil's name but erroneously described her remarks as having to do with women in the *Socialist* Party. My point here is not to besmirch the in-valuable Oral History of the American Left Collection but to underscore what I said in the Introduction, that much of the history of Party women is in need of excavation.

4. "Women and Communism," as well as essays by Inman and Hutchins, have been reprinted in Nekola and Rabinowitz.

5. Circulation was also estimated at 12,000. Anna Damon's name appears as editor in the January 1930 issue. In issues from February 1930 through October 1934 no editor is listed in the masthead, although in the November 1933 issue, in a fine-print "Statement of the ownership, management, circulation . . . required by the Act of Congress of March 3, 1933," Anna Damon is named as editor (15). Margaret Cowl is named as editor in the masthead of the November 1934 issue. In the March 1934 issue, Working Woman Pub-lishing Company was listed as the publisher of *The Working Woman*. Before that, the Central Committee of the CPUSA is listed as publisher.

6. We need to exhume the powerful visual as well as written record of the American Left. Cary Nelson's *Repression and Recovery*, which includes a large number of illustra-tions, represents one important attempt to retrieve not only poetry but also visual images from cultural oblivion. As Nelson reports in his preface, many of these illustrations have not been reproduced since they were first published and now exist only in private collec-tions or in rare book rooms in a few libraries.

7. Flynn's relationship to this column on the "women's page" was likely a compli-cated one. As Baxandall reports, Flynn "herself wanted to be taken seriously as a revolutionary and resented being appointed to stereotypical female positions, like heading the Women's Commission or giving fund-raising talks." Flynn "believed she could not excel if she identified with women, so she had no choice but to try and make herself one of the men. . . . Her life shows both the possibilities and inherent limitations of trying to make it in a man's world without the backup of a feminist movement that could stress accountability and collective strength" (271, 272). Dorothy Healey corroborated Baxandall's assessment of Flynn's feeling that stereotypically female tasks were a "comedown" (interview).

8. The reply abruptly ends: "What must the women do to make the men folk" with-out punctuation.

9. So as not to wrench Mitford's passage from its humorous context, I should add that the passage was preceded by Mitford's describing herself as a lousy housekeeper and followed by: "Not so Bob [Treuhaft, her husband], who, declaring himself in fervent agreement with Lenin, positively drove me from the nest. He implored me to seek some outside employment and put the running of the household in more competent hands" (104).

10. Zetkin 49. Olsen said the proverb was usually paraphrased in ways such as, "If you drink water, you want to drink clear water, not from a muddy pool" (Rosenfelt interview).

11. Communist Archie Brown, however, made at least one notable exception, as Dorothy Healey recalls with apparent delight. She remembers a conversation she had with Brown while riding on a streetcar with him to a YCL meeting: "I was fourteen and he must have been sixteen. I had just read Krupskaya's *Memories of Lenin*, and the thing that impressed me was on the question of sex, how Lenin had decried promiscuity, using the example of the glass of water—that just as you wouldn't want your lips to be on a glass that was muddied by other people's lips, the same was true in a sexual relationship. Archie was having a lot of interesting sexual relationships at the time, and I told him this story very self-righteously. After all Lenin had said it, and anything Lenin said was supposed to be the final word on any question you wanted answered. I was absolutely appalled when Archie turned to me and said, 'Look, I will follow anything that Lenin says on politics, but I understand that in Lenin's apartment there were two very narrow beds at opposite ends of the bedroom, one for Krupskaya and one for Lenin, and they didn't even sleep together. *That guy knew nuttin' about sex!* That's for sure! And I'm not taking my leadership from him!'" (30).

12. Dorothy Healey, who read a draft of this manuscript, disagreed somewhat with my assessment of the Party's approach to the child-care issue. "I could give you a whole bunch of pamphlets," she said, that "repeated [child care] as a big demand." She commented that historians have largely ignored these pamphlets. "We sold them by the tens of thousands. And sometimes by the millions. . . . that was our communication, that was our link, our lifeline, to the masses." She pointed out that child care for women workers was a demand, for example, of the Communist-led United Cannery, Agricultural, Packing, and Allied Workers of America, about which Vicki L. Ruiz has written in *Cannery Women, Cannery Lives: Mexican Women, Unionization, and the California Food Processing Industry, 1930–1950*. But Healey added that child care was not a "top issue" of the Party. "I can't think of women's issues that *were* at the top of the agenda." In fact, "women leaders did not want to be assigned 'women's work.' Elizabeth Gurley Flynn fought like hell against having to be on the Women's Commission because that was a comedown" (interview).

13. See Sklar.

14. Telephone conversation with Genora (Johnson) Dollinger, 6 and 7 October 1986, Los Angeles.

15. Quotations in this paragraph and the next are from the documentary. According to Genora (Johnson) Dollinger, one of the eight women attending the reunion had actually been a member of the Detroit Auxiliary; a ninth woman was added to the film after the reunion (telephone conversation, 6 and 7 October 1986). In this and subsequent discussions of other documentaries, I cite (without page numbers) transcriptions in my possession of *Union Maids* and *Seeing Red* and notes taken verbatim while viewing *With Babies and Banners* and *The Life and Times of Rosie the Riveter*.

16. Wyndham Mortimer, assigned by the UAW to direct the fight against General Motors, and his replacement, Bob Travis, were CP members. "The strike committee chairman, Bud Simons, was a Communist, as were 'nearly all of the seven members of the strike committee.' Henry Kraus, a Communist, edited *The Flint Auto Worker*. Maurice Sugar, the UAW's attorney, was very close to the Party" (Klehr 232-233). Some Socialist Party members were important in the strike: Victor, Walter, and Roy Reuther, Merlin Bishop, and Kermit Johnson, chairman of Chevrolet Plant 4. Ted La Duke was, or became after the strike, a Lovestoneite (Cochran 110–112, 366). Dorothy Kraus, head of food supplies and distribution, and hence influential in the Auxiliary, was very close to the CP, if not a member. According to Genora (Johnson) Dollinger, however, political diversity rather than

uniformity characterized the Auxiliary and Brigade, and most of the women were politically unaffiliated.

17. Kate quickly added that the police were typically vicious, not generous. Soon thereafter police shot three black men for resisting an eviction on Chicago's South Side. They were shot in the back while carrying furniture.

18. See my review of *Dorothy Healey Remembers.*

CHAPTER 3

1. Hedges 2. Hedges refers to Le Sueur's grandmother as Antoinette Lucy. Le Sueur's daughter, Rachel Tilsen, gave me her great-grandmother's complete name, adding that her nickname was "Netty."

2. In this citation, I have altered Le Sueur's punctuation in "The Ancient People," p. 22, because the punctuation in "The Ancient People" creates some ambiguity about whether this is one or two slogans. That ambiguity is resolved by my punctuation and by that in *Crusaders*, p. 40, where it is clear that these were two separate slogans of the temperance movement.

3. Recorded interviews with Meridel Le Sueur, 26 March 1985, in Los Angeles, and 24 August 1989, in Hudson, Wisconsin. Subsequent references to these interviews will be made parenthetically in the text with the word "interview."

4. Rachel Tilsen, one of Le Sueur's daughters, told me that, to her knowledge, she owns the only existing copy of *Plain English*, which was published in Fort Scott, Kansas. Rachel has asked book finders to search for the book, but they have not been successful. I took notes from *Plain English* in Tilsen's home in August 1989 and have not yet tried to locate a copy.

5. "Fire and ax" appears in the preface, xxiii, of a more recent edition of *Crusaders* (St. Paul: Minnesota Historical Society Press, 1984) than the 1955 edition otherwise cited.

6. Most sources give this date. Linda Ray Pratt adds that information in FBI files obtained via the Freedom of Information Act suggests that Le Sueur joined the Party in the mid-'30s. According to the files, an informant told the FBI "of a rift in the family when Arthur Le Sueur heard that Meridel had joined the Party," dating the episode in 1936 ("Woman writer" 249; 263, n1).

7. Telephone conversation with Rachel Tilsen, 1 April 1992.

8. Where I cite Le Sueur's journals in this book, I have in most cases used the language and punctuation exactly as they appear in the journals. However, with Le Sueur's permission, I have occasionally made slight changes in order to enhance readability.

9. "Red-diaper" baby was an expression popularly used by leftists for the children of Communist Party members.

10. Interview of Myra Page conducted by Nora Ruth Roberts, 15 January 1991; interview of Annette Rubinstein conducted by Nora Ruth Roberts, 8 January 1991. I am grateful to Nora Roberts for sharing these tapes with me.

11. Accounts of Peggy Dennis's abortions appear in her autobiography. Dennis commented on abortions imposed by Party decision in "A Response" 456.

12. Afterword 231. And yet, in her late forties Gale adopted a homeless two-year-old girl. And, despite her radical politics—feminism, pacifism, prominent support for La Fol-

lette's Progressive Party, and opposition to conventional Christianity—at age 50 Gale para-
doxically married William Breese, a wealthy manufacturer and banker, conservative
Republican, and Presbyterian elder (Loughridge 222).

13. Telephone conversation, 1 April 1992.

14. Mitford adds: "Only much later, in a very different political climate, did the Committee find itself once more the object of derision, when it was virtually laughed to death by
the Merrie Men of the New Left who were called to testify in the sixties. For example, on
one occasion Jerry Rubin appeared in response to his subpoena dressed as a soldier of the
Revolutionary War; another time he came before the Committee wearing a Santa Claus
costume. This was good theatre, hugely enjoyed by the press. In thus mocking the Committee, the radicals of the sixties doubtless helped to hasten its eventual downfall in 1968"
(195–196).

15. The term "pink-tinged" appears in Schleuning, *America* 25. Since the cant of this
review, headlined "Red Party Line Is Catch Line in New Abe Lincoln Book," suggests
what Le Sueur was up against during the McCarthy Period, I quote from it at length:
"Frankly we think an old hand like Meridel Le Sueur is an unfair match for a youngster at
least until they [sic] have had a few workouts in the manly art of intellectual self-defense.
After that we can trust them to go the distance with Meridel any day. Now we don't
particularly favor burning Meridel's book . . . but we think it should be restricted for use in
some way, perhaps through the schools, so that it will be read only in context with other
books about Abe Lincoln . . . which approach the problem from a traditional American
viewpoint" (Milwaukee *Sentinel*, 28 November 1954, cited in Schleuning, *America* 109).

16. In a telephone conversation, 1 April 1992, Rachel Tilsen described the creative
writing classes as the main source of income from 1935 to 1950 and disputed Elaine
Hedges's report that the children's books "sold well enough to provide Le Sueur with a
small but steady income for many years" (16).

17. Telephone conversation, 1 April 1992.

18. Khrushchev delivered his speech in February to a closed session of the Twentieth
Congress in Moscow. American CP leaders did not receive a full report on Khrushchev's
charges against Stalin until the end of April, when a copy of his secret speech was read at
a meeting of the national committee in New York City. "The effect was devastating, as
people who had devoted two or three decades of their lives for a cause they believed the
Soviet Union embodied listened to Khrushchev's authoritative account of the tortures,
frame-ups, unjust imprisonments, and executions that Stalin had ordered in the name of
defending socialism" (Isserman, *Which Side* 249–250).

19. Telephone conversation with Rachel Tilsen, 1 April 1992; Hedges 17.

20. That this collection had a limited circulation may be the reason I have not seen it
mentioned in discussions of Le Sueur's work. It is available at the Minnesota State Historical Society.

21. The journals from the last 30 years remain in Le Sueur's possession. The others
are housed under restriction at the Minnesota Historical Society.

22. When Pete Seeger and Woody Guthrie "were riding the rails" they stopped in Minneapolis to sleep on Le Sueur's floor. More than forty years ago, on Le Sueur's fiftieth
birthday, Seeger gave Le Sueur her first tape recorder, urging her to tape interviews with
people. Referring to Seeger and Guthrie, Le Sueur says, "I had people's speech, they had
people's song," and she adds, "for the people you've grown with in militant struggle, there's
an affection you can't express" (Grossman 1D, 3D). Some of the 30 sponsors of the
community festival included the Central America Resource Center, the Minnesota Com-

munist Party, the Minneapolis Arts Commission, the Minnesota Peace and Justice Coalition, the Minnesota and the Twin Cities National Organization for Women chapters, the Twin Cities National Lawyers Guild chapter, the Women's International League for Peace and Freedom, and several women's studies programs, bookstores, and small presses.

23. At times Le Sueur's resistance was explicit. For example, after she told me that she had daily, memorable conversations with Alexander Berkman when he and her mother were lovers, I asked her how old she had been at the time. I assumed that the sophistication of the conversations with Berkman and hence their consequence to Le Sueur's political and social development would have differed according to her age. "What does it matter how old I was?" she asked.

24. See Frederick Manfred's "An Unforgettable Beer with the 'Mother Bard,'" *Minneapolis Sunday Tribune* 12 Sept. 1971; McAnally 5, 33, 43, 64, 68 (the book is unpaginated, but to aid readers who might look at McAnally, I paginated the book, beginning with the introduction); Schleuning, *America* 16; Grossmann 3D.

25. To assist readers in finding this citation, I paginated McAnally, beginning with the introduction. This appears on p. 71.

26. Brown probably also figures prominently in the journals beyond the '30s, but I limited my reading of the journals to that decade.

27. Hedges 32; "antagonistic and controlling" from Pratt, Afterword 227; Le Sueur said in our interview that she and Arthur "didn't get along" and that her mother was "awfully domineering."

28. One cannot expect disclosure of family discord in what amounts to a public eulogy. Moreover, as already noted in the text, *Crusaders* sought to reaffirm Meridel's faith in the Midwest populist tradition during the "dark time" of McCarthyism. However, Le Sueur added a 19-page preface to the 1984 reprint of *Crusaders* that does not attempt to explain the 1955 biography's personal and historical contexts and is as honorific as the biography itself.

29. Le Sueur also indicates in this passage from her journal that her own "suffering also wrenched me out of it further. . . . I was wrenched out completely" (vol. 7, 235).

30. Among the exceptions: Hedges, Clausen, and Gelfant.

31. Wright's contribution to *The God That Failed* also appears, in expanded form, in Chapters 4–6 of his *American Hunger*.

32. As Robert Shaffer notes, "during the Popular Front period 'the people' came to have an almost mystical connotation" in Party discourse, "similar to its use by some sectors of the left in the late 1960s. In the 1930s it meant 'the working class and its allies,' or more often just progressive people" (Shaffer 84). Although Le Sueur frequently uses "people's culture," to my knowledge she has not defined it. "People's culture" has been used historically to suggest the inter-class nature of anti-fascist cultural work, which draws not only on the cultural production of the working class but also on the efforts of progressive individuals of other classes.

33. The 1984 West End Press reprint of "Women on the Breadlines" includes a slightly different version of the editorial chiding than that appearing in *New Masses*.

34. In ensuing discussions, I will provide readings of multiple antithetical structures. Bartine has argued that antithetical structures are among several rhetorical figures and speech acts that could be identified and analyzed early in children's reading instruction and that such analysis could be systematically built upon throughout their education. See *Reading, Criticism*, chapters three and seven.

35. In conversation with the author, 24 September 1984.

CHAPTER 4

1. When I questioned Le Sueur about the strain of biological determinism I see in her work, she said, without elaborating, that she does not believe men are inherently violent (interview).

2. Parts of the novel appeared separately as short stories: "They Follow Us Girls" in *Anvil*, July–Aug., 1935; "Salvation Home" in *New Masses*, Jan. 10, 1939; "Sure Honey!" in *New Anvil*, June–July, 1939; "I'm Going I Said" in *New Masses*, Jan. 9, 1940; "Father of the Earth" in *The Fountain*, March 1942; "O Prairie Girl Be Lonely" in *New Caravan*, 1945 — reprinted in *Cross Section 1947: A Collection of New American Writing*, ed. Edwin Seaver, New York, 1947. This information is included in the publication information in *The Girl*.

3. Remark made by John Crawford (Le Sueur's editor and publisher, West End Press) to author, 16 July 1985, Los Angeles.

4. The following analyses of a few speech acts as they contribute to heteroglossia stand as one example of types of reading activity I advocated in my Introduction.

5. See Jones.

6. The year 1939 was pivotal, even catastrophic, for the Party, as it made a clumsy transition from the Popular Front against fascism to the new united front against the war, which lasted until the German invasion of the Soviet Union in 1941. From August 22, when the Stalin-Hitler non-aggression pact was signed, until the end of the year, the Party moved from its pro-Roosevelt, to its "Second Imperialist War" position, trying to justify along the way not only the pact but the Red Army's invasion of Poland and Finland. The CP's shift in domestic political strategy lagged behind its shift in international strategy, and Roosevelt, genuinely popular among the Party rank-and-file, did not come under personal attack until early November. It has been established that Le Sueur wrote the first draft of *The Girl* in 1939; one could argue that just *when* during that year it was written would have to be determined in order to measure precisely how far the novel departed from the official Party line on domestic issues.

7. In *Sociology of Religion* Max Weber defines ascetic Protestantism as an "ethic of vocation in the world" which demanded "not celibacy . . . but the avoidance of all erotic pleasure. . . . not the ascetic death-in-life of the cloister, but an alert, rationally controlled patterning of life, and the avoidance of all surrender to the beauty of the world, to art, or to one's own moods and emotions. . . . its unique result was the rational organization and institutionalization of social relationships" (183).

8. Some readers might charge Le Sueur with sexual stereotyping in her characterizations of Karl and the unnamed narrator, whose responses to the pregnancy are polarized. He is completely insensitive, whereas she is overwhelmed with feeling. Karl neither wants the child nor responds to the narrator's needs. He comes home drunk and noisy, if he comes home at all; he gets embarrassed and angry when the narrator vomits in an alley as a result of her pregnancy and walks ahead of her on the street, so as not to be seen with her; he urges her to try abortion remedies ("Get rid of it. That's what everybody does nowadays. . . . It's nothing, then it's all over" [80]) and shouts at her when she greets this command with silence. In this stalemate over the unborn child, Karl and the narrator stop communicating almost altogether. Karl is neither likable nor admirable, although he tries to find work, does not abandon the narrator, and is not physically abusive. Karl is not as oppressive as Butch in *The Girl* because Karl does not seem to affect the narrator very much; his behavior does not spoil — or even penetrate — her "trance of wonder" (82).

9. The journal entry's date clarifies that Le Sueur was not referring to "Corn Village," which she had already published. However, the themes referred to here are extensions of those in "Corn Village."

10. In the first note to "Childbirth in Literature," Carol H. Poston points out that exceptions to this would be instances of women writing in journals, diaries, and letters—places where a great repository of birth literature exists. For examples of early "close" birth literature, Poston recommends the selections by Margery Kempe and Alice Thornton in *by a woman writt*, ed. Joan Goulianos (Baltimore: Penguin Books, 1973).

11. See Kolodny. I return to her argument in my Conclusion.

12. Quoted by Schleuning, "Regionalism" 30.

13. I have again borrowed DuPlessis's phrase, "between complicity and critique," because it applies so well to Le Sueur.

CHAPTER 5

1. Tillie Olsen sent me a copy of this letter.

2. Years later, as an international visiting scholar to Norway, Olsen was quite moved when she unexpectedly came upon the original of that statue in a Bergen museum (interview).

3. Elinore Randall's letters, written from the Wyoming prairies, were published in book form as *Letters of a Woman Homesteader*. Directed by Richard Pearce, *Heartland* was released in 1980.

4. Rosenfelt interview; Duncan 212. This pregnancy was neither planned nor desired. Why Olsen, who underwent several abortions in her lifetime, did not have an abortion in this case is not known. When asked about this chapter in her life, she quotes Rosa Bonhuer: "What I paint belongs to everybody. My personal life belongs to me" (Rosenfelt interview).

5. Cantwell went on to say that her metaphors were "startling in their brilliance," and he compared her writing to that of Elizabeth Madox Roberts, whom Olsen greatly admired ("Little" 295, 297). "The Iron Throat" was changed very little for the publication of *Yonnondio* (1974). It became the first ten pages of the novel's 16-page opening chapter.

6. Julie Olsen Edwards's autobiographical essay, "Class Notes from the Lecture Hall," discusses how growing up as a working-class "Red-diaper baby" has shaped Edwards's work as a community college teacher. The essay appears in Zandy, *Liberating Memory*.

7. Jack Olsen and Reeva's former husband, Leon Olson, differently anglicized the surname of their father, Abraham Olshansky, an active Party member.

8. Under the auspices of the Works Project Administration, the Federal Writers' Project (1935–43) gave work to unemployed writers. Richard Wright, Ralph Ellison, Studs Terkel, Saul Bellow, Nelson Algren, Meridel Le Sueur, and Mary Heaton Vorse were variously supported by the project.

9. Telephone conversation, 16 July 1989.

10. Jack Olsen's Statement to the House UnAmerican Activities Committee in 1952 is worthy of citing in its entirety (Julie Olsen Edwards sent me a copy of this statement at the time of Jack's death):

All of my adult life I have tried to be a good citizen, a good neighbor, a good shop-mate, a good union man and a good father to my children. I have tried to exercise my duties and my rights as a loyal American citizen—by interesting myself in and speaking out on public issues, by voting for candidates who seemed to me to be right, by serving on public committees and in organizations working for the common welfare, and by serving in the Armed Forces of my country.

I have tried to be a good union man by joining and actively helping to build my unions—aiding in what ways I could in trying to improve the wages, hours and working conditions of myself and my fellow working man.

I have tried to be a good father by instilling in my children a love for decency and respect for the opinions of their fellow men; by teaching them to love their country—its magnificent history—its constitution and its bill of rights and by teaching them that love of country demands of Americans that they fight to keep it free and democratic.

These things I have tried to do within the limits of my understanding.

I believe that I would be less than a good citizen if I did not resist with all of my power efforts of this committee to curtail our freedoms, to smear, intimidate and punish citizens without due course of law; to attack and vilify legitimate trade unions and their leaders, and to make meaningless our constitution and our bill of rights.

I believe that your committee in spite of protestations to the contrary comes here as prosecutor, judge and jury—with preconceived notions about me—and with a gavel to silence when I chose to object.

I have always been outspoken in my opinions and beliefs and in any demo-cratic atmosphere still am. Those people who know me will know how to assess the attempts of this committee to picture me otherwise.

I am now and always have been opposed to force and violence. I am now and I always have been devoted to peace and democracy for my country. I am now and I always have been an opponent of this type of legislative inquisition. I can do no less than try to maintain my honest views.

I cannot with good conscience testify before this committee in such a manner as to open me, my friends or my acquaintances to further attacks which inevitably follow from this committee. I cannot with good conscience place in jeopardy or-ganizations to which I may [be] or may have been affiliated. I cannot with good conscience allow my testimony to endanger the jobs and livelihoods of others.

That is why I chose to stand on the Bill of Rights and particularly its First and Fifth Amendments in my appearance before this wholly un-American committee.

11. She was also named by Addy's wife, Juana, who, as an FBI agent, informed the PTA leadership about Communists in their organization. And novelist/screenwriter Budd Schulberg named her as Tillie Lerner.

12. She was Radcliffe Institute Fellow from 1962–64 and awarded a grant by the National Endowment for the Arts in 1967. She taught at Amherst in 1969–70 and at Stanford in 1972, where she conducted a graduate writing seminar and the University's first course on women and literature. The 1971 volume of *Best American Short Stories* was dedicated to Olsen, and she was a grantee at the MacDowell Colony, a New England retreat for art-ists, in 1972–73. She was Writer-in-Residence at MIT in 1973 and a Distinguished Visiting Professor at the University of Massachusetts, Boston, in 1974. In 1975 Olsen won

the American Academy and National Institute of Arts and Letters Award for a distinguished contribution to American Literature, and she won a 1975–76 Guggenheim Fellowship. In 1978 she was a Board of Regents Visiting Lecturer at the University of California, San Diego. In 1979 the University of Nebraska awarded her an honorary doctorate. In 1980, in conjunction with England's issuing of stamps commemorating Charlotte and Emily Brontë, George Eliot, and Elizabeth Gaskell, Olsen was selected by a committee of British scholars "as the woman writer best exemplifying in our time the ideals and literary excellence" of these four writers. According to one article written about the commemoration, all of these writers, including Olsen, "forged significant changes in social attitudes toward women and workers" (Martin 45). In 1980 Olsen traveled as an International Visiting Scholar to four Norwegian universities; served as a Radcliffe Centennial Visitor and Lecturer; and received the Unitarian Women's Federation annual "Ministry to Women" award. The mayor and board of supervisors of San Francisco, where she has lived most of her life, declared May 18, 1981, "Tillie Olsen Day" in that city. In 1982 she received an honorary doctorate in literature from Knox College, and the 20th Ozarks Arts Interpretation Festival featured a three-act dramatization of *Yonnondio: From the Thirties.* In 1983 the "five quad cities colleges" of Iowa and Illinois held a "Tillie Olsen Week and Symposium." Olsen received honorary degrees from Hobart and William Smith College in 1984 and from Clarke University in 1985. From 1985–86 she was a Bunting Institute resident and for a quarter in 1986 was a visiting professor at the University of Minnesota. She was a Board of Regents Visiting Lecturer at the University of California, Los Angeles, in 1987. Olsen has read at the New York, San Francisco, and Cleveland Poetry Centers and at the Walker Art Center in Minneapolis. She has been a keynote or featured speaker at a wide variety of symposia, forums, and conferences, and has read and/or spoken at a number of college campuses—Johns Hopkins, Smith, Yale, Stanford, Harvard, Dartmouth, Reed, Carleton, Columbia, MIT, Sarah Lawrence, and the University of California, Los Angeles, among others. I gleaned much of this information from Olsen's 1987 vita, the most recent one available.

13. The Fort Point Gang originated in 1978 with seven men—Joe Passen, Bill Bailey, Al Richmond, Lou Goldblatt, Frank Jones, Jack Olsen, and Jim Kendall—all lifelong labor activists, union leaders, and former members of the American Communist Party whose lasting friendships had taken root many years before in San Francisco, a union stronghold. The group, which walks four miles along the shore of the San Francisco Bay to Fort Point, has grown to 20 or 30, depending on the turnout on a given day, and now includes women and a few younger people (some credit Tillie with first crashing the gender gate). The weekly ritual includes touching the chain-link fence bordering Fort Point. As Bill Bailey explained to me when I walked with the group, touching the fence is like clasping a talisman, a gesture of hope that they will return at least one more time.

The ritual walk is followed by an equally ritualistic gathering at Eppler's Bakery on Chesnut Street, where the group pushes together formica tables and settles in with coffee, pastries, memories of the Old Left, and lively discussions of current political events. The Fort Point Gang's camaraderie sparks the curiosity of Eppler's other patrons and has captured the loyalty of the women who work behind the counter. When Jack Olsen died, these women bought several dozen long-stemmed carnations as a tribute to Jack, which the Gangers threaded into their talisman, the chain-link fence.

Bailey, former ILWU Local 10 Vice President and a former leader in the Marine Workers Industrial Union, spoke about the Fort Point Gang when two benches at Fort Point were dedicated to the memory of Lou Goldblatt, one of the original Gangers and for

34 years secretary-treasurer of the ILWU: "While we tell everyone that it was the exercise that got us started, I can assure you that it was more than that. . . .The past was too precious to forget and the future too threatening and dangerous for us to sit idly by. . . . We needed each other way back when, as we need each other today. We have developed a concern for each other. If somebody doesn't show up for our weekly walk, we become agitated. . . . We've sent more get-well cards and made more trips to hospitals than ever before. . . . The need for this kinship, this human love, this special warmth that we give each other. . . . It gives meaning to our lives, where we came from, the battles we fought" (from a videotape of the dedication, 16 August 1986, borrowed from Bailey).

14. Julie Olsen Edwards sent me a copy of this letter, dated February 27, 1989.

15. Olsen's "The Iron Throat" was included in the anthology, which was edited by Granville Hicks, Michael Gold, and four other men; Joseph Freeman wrote the preface. The other women included were Meridel Le Sueur, Josephine Herbst, Agnes Smedley, Muriel Rukeyser, Grace Lumpkin, and Genevieve Taggard.

16. In a telephone conversation, 2 December 1985. Olsen was speaking loosely here. Of course there were terrible penalties for sexual freedom even after Sanger had taken up the cause of birth control, as Olsen knows. As Linda Gordon notes, even as late as 1936, after Sanger and others had been advocating contraception for 25 years, nearly half the nation's 75 top medical schools gave their students no instruction in birth control methods. Although "a 1937 poll showed that 79% of U.S. women believed in birth control," and social workers consistently reported high interest in contraception among working-class women, "those who did not have access to private doctors regularly were effectively deprived of contraceptive information [because] clinics served only a negligible fraction of the population" (320).

17. However, Olsen believes that Dennis "never intended that her autobiography would be taken as it has been taken, to speak for the situation of most Party women . . . but it has been interpreted as such." Olsen emphasizes that Dennis's experience was that of the wife of a prominent Party leader; her experience varied from that of the rank-and-file (interview).

18. Not all the people imprisoned under the Smith Act were "husbands." One former female Party leader I interviewed, who asked to remain anonymous, was incarcerated under the Smith Act. One of her complaints about the Party was that it made no arrangements for the care of her two small children during her eight months in jail.

19. See Gornick 248. Gornick, born into the Jewish working class in 1936, was a "Red-diaper" baby, the daughter of passionate Communists. At 15 she joined the Labor Youth League, the Party's last incarnation of the Young Communist League, but at 20, the Khrushchev Report "snapped the last thread in a fabric of belief that was already worn to near disintegration" (10). Her book is the result of a year's interviewing some 40 former CP members about their experiences in the Party. Her criterion for selecting her subjects was that they considered the years in the Party to have been the shaping force in their lives, and her questions turned on the emotional meaning of the political experience ("What did you feel then? . . . What did it mean to leave?") (24). *The Romance* is critically sympathetic to the Party experience.

20. Telephone conversation, 18 June 1989.

21. In view of the Party's position on homosexuality, it is ironic that Elizabeth Gurley Flynn, who became the first woman selected as national chairman of the CP, was likely involved in a lesbian relationship with Dr. Marie Equi, an open lesbian with whom Flynn lived from 1926–36 (see Baxandall 31).

22. I have documented some of these costs in "Silent Parenting in the Academy." Among other objectives, the essay pays tribute to Olsen's pioneering work on the issue of "silent parenting."

23. Le Sueur used that phrase in "Annunciation" to describe how she hoped her as yet unborn child would be in the future.

24. Cary Nelson notes: "On August 22, 1934, *The Daily Worker* published 'Merchant Marine' by Harry Alan Potamkin (1900–33), identifying it as based on correspondence to *The Daily Worker* and the *Marine Workers' Voice*, and reminding us that Potamkin was the first to use workers' correspondence as a theme for poetry. Potamkin had published 'Mecklenburg County,' identifying it as 'a poem based on worker correspondence to the *Daily Worker*,' in the June 24, 1933, issue of the newspaper, p. 5" (283, n112).

25. For a definition of reportage, see Chapter 1. Longshoremen in Bellingham, Seattle, Tacoma, Aberdeen, Portland, Astoria, San Francisco, Oakland, Stockton, San Pedro, and San Diego went on strike. For accounts of the strike see Green, Brecher, Bruce Nelson, and Quin.

26. For a review of a rock-opera based on the Seattle strike, see Bartine and Coiner.

27. On a very basic level, Olsen may have felt "the near impossibility" of her project partly because her young daughter, Karla, would not go to sleep and let her mother write. At the time she wrote "The Strike," Olsen was working at San Francisco's Palace Hotel as a linen checker. She came home from work, intending to write "The Strike," but "Karla wanted her momma's attention" (telephone conversation with Olsen, 10 September 1988).

28. See Stott 182–183. Although Stott briefly discusses "The Strike," he applies his claim that "a writer, by the fact of writing, has moved from the immediacy of his experience" generally to print reportage.

CHAPTER 6

1. According to Carolyn Rhodes, this system was devised by Charles E. Bedaux, who sold it to many American and European companies during the '20s and '30s: "Bedaux measured work in units which he called (in his own honor) B's, and he defined the normal rate of work as one B per minute, or sixty B's per hour. The system was adaptable . . . to any steps within an industrial process. Bedaux-trained experts, when employed by a company, were supposed to base the acceptable 60-B rate on a good worker, yet one whose speed of work represented what an average person could do. Such a worker's output became the standard. After the standard was set, all workers who produced from 45 to 60 B's per hour would receive standard wages. Any faster worker earned a proportional bonus, not only for himself or herself, but also for the foreperson and higher officials, in progressively smaller percentages for people higher up the managerial line, with the sharp decrease in share of benefits counterbalanced by the larger number of underlings who contributed to the pool for higher personnel." Bedaux's method of payment was advantageous for management, including the lowest level of bosses, but disadvantageous for workers: "it meant that the bosses at every level, even those who directly supervised the workers, had a vested interest in speeding up production" (24). Chapter 8 of *Yonnondio* dramatizes the horror of the Beedo system as experienced by Jim Holbrook and the other packinghouse workers. Jim, who had predicted that the summer would "Be hell," punning on the B's of work measurement, speaks of the foreman who enforces the speed-up system as "That prick . . . that pusher.

Beedo hisself, in person" (133). Born in France in 1887, Bedaux came to the U.S. at 20 and became a citizen in 1917. He made a fortune out of his efficiency system but died in disgrace as a collaborator with the Nazis during World War II (Rhodes 25).

2. For example, see Balbus, Laclau, Ryan.

3. I have borrowed this phrase and concept from DuPlessis. She defines "writing beyond the ending" as "the invention of strategies that sever the narrative from formerly conventional structures of fiction and consciousness about women" (x). However, I believe "strain away from" is often more accurate than "sever."

CHAPTER 7

1. Woolf 125.

2. Eagleton, *Marxism* 62.

3. *Silences* 202. I did not quote the rest of the sentence ("and, I believe, transport as woman") because it is not relevant to my immediate point. However, it is important to clarify that Olsen believes motherhood to be the "core" of "transport" as well as "oppression" for women.

4. Pacifica radio broadcast, 8 March 1985.

5. For discussions of history of reading strategies and earlier defenses of indirect and figurational structures against schemes for linguistic reductionism, see Bartine, *Early English Reading*.

6. In the edition of *Tell Me a Riddle* I have used for this book, the title story is "for two of that generation, Seevya and Genya." In a more recent edition, Olsen also dedicates the story to her parents.

7. Olsen modeled Whitey partly on Filipino men she knew who hungered for contact with families at a time when U.S. immigration law kept Filipino women and children from entering the United States (interview).

8. DuPlessis also notes the several other alternative plots proposed by Charlotte Perkins Gilman in *The Man-Made World; Or, Our Androcentric Culture* (1911): "The objection of a woman asked to give up her career ('her humanness') for marriage, the discontent of the middle-aged woman who wants not more love but more business in life, the ties between women, and the interaction between mother and child, including painful and disappointing aspects" (243, n8).

9. Patrocinio P. Schweickart outlines a promising model for reading based on a joining of reader-response theory and feminist theory. Her model contains some of the characteristics Olsen's writing demands of readers. Schweickart finds that feminist theory can move "beyond the individualistic models of [Wolfgang] Iser and of most reader-response critics" toward a "collective" model of reading. Describing the goal of that model, Schweickart observes that "the feminist reader hopes that other women will recognize themselves in her story, and join her in her struggle to transform the culture" (50, 51). It must be added that Olsen, like Schweickart, would have women and men "join her in her struggle to transform the culture."

10. *Silences* 202. For an enlightening discussion of *Tell Me a Riddle* in relation to other works dealing with motherhood, see Gardiner. Gardiner also suggests Jeannie's function as a model for readers when she notes that "at the end of the story, Jeannie has absorbed her grandmother's consciousness," allowing Eva to be "the agent of a revolution-

ary and transcendent ideal that can be passed from woman to woman, of a commitment to fully human values" (163).

11. The press's first big seller, *Iron Mills* has sold at least 45,000 copies and gone through at least nine editions.

12. Harding was unmarried and living in her upper-middle-class home when she wrote *Iron Mills*. Olsen herself acknowledges that Davis would have had no access to the iron mills: "She was house-bound, class-bound, sex-bound . . . . She would not have been permitted to go unescorted, or to linger, or to initiate or participate too actively in any conversation" (*Silences* 62).

CONCLUSION

1. The connection between ends and means to which Maguire refers divided the CPUSA as recently as its Twenty-fifth National Convention, held in Cleveland in December 1991. According to Max Elbaum's report in *The Nation*, "the convention was polarized to an extent not seen in U.S. Communism since the traumatic upheavals of the mid-1950s." The "sanctity" of democratic centralism was reaffirmed, as were other elements of '30s doctrine: "The salvation of the working class rests in a vanguard that, by definition, embodies the correct ideology. Defense of that vanguard, especially its leadership, 'by any means necessary' . . . is not just legitimate, it is a revolutionary duty." Those "who questioned these positions were excluded from the incoming leadership slate elected by the convention," and "some 200 seated and excluded delegates" held separate meetings to establish an alternate structure, called Committees of Correspondence. "The committees are designed to work toward 'renewing the struggle for social progress and socialism, and putting an end to undemocratic practices which have caused so much damage to the Marxist and Communist movement,' according to spokesman John Case, one of the dozens of just-ousted National Committee members involved in the new formation." Some founders of the committees intend to leave the Party, while "others hope to stay and continue the struggle for reform, though many of these expect to be expelled." The "base of the committees consists of the more than 900 CPUSA members"—approximately one-third of the Party's current membership—"who signed a reform manifesto" that had circulated in the Party since October 1991 (158–162).

2. For unsentimental portrayals of motherhood in literature, see, for example, Leslie Marmon Silko, "Lullaby"; Jane Lazerre, *The Mother Knot* and *The Powers of Charlotte*; Kim Chernin, *In My Mother's House*; Sue Miller, *The Good Mother*; Alice Walker, *In Search of Our Mothers' Gardens*; Toni Morrison, *Beloved*; Carolyn Chute, *The Beans of Egypt, Mine*; Alix Kates Shulman, *Memoirs of an Ex-Prom Queen*; Amy Tan, *The Kitchen God's Wife*; and many of Grace Paley's short stories. Most of these writers acknowledge an enormous debt to Olsen.

3. Navarro apparently defines "working class" as those whose "financial identity is defined by hourly wages." He cites Erik Olin Wright of the University of Wisconsin, whom he identifies as "one of the most respected scholars in the analysis of social class structure." According to Wright, "manual, supervised, unskilled and semiskilled workers represent more than 50 percent of the adult working population. They are the core of the working class, and they and their dependents represent the majority of the population" (361).

4. In tracing the influence of the Old Left on the New, Maurice Isserman comments that "Red-diaper babies" were well represented among the founders of SDS (*Hammer* 206).

Isserman notes: "The role of 'red diaper babies' in the New Left has often been commented on, perhaps most perceptively by one of them, Dick Flacks: see, for example, his article entitled 'Making History vs. Making Life: Dilemmas of an American Left,' *Sociological Inquiry* 46 (1976): 263–280. The most colorful comment on the topic comes from Norman Podhoretz: 'As one read about the student radical leaders in the press . . . one kept coming upon scions of what could be called the First Families of American Stalinism. . . . [The New Left] was in the end turning out to be a movement by the children of McCarthy's victims to avenge their parents on the flesh of the country which had produced him.' Podhoretz, *Breaking Ranks: A Political Memoir* (New York: Harper and Row, 1979), p. 253" (*Hammer* 242–243, n65). Links exist, too, between the Old Left and the Gay Liberation Movement, despite the Party's failure to take a stand on homosexuality as an issue and its retrograde policy on gay and lesbian members (beginning in 1948, they were dropped from membership because, in the Party's view, their vulnerability to FBI blackmail made them too great a security risk). A biographer of Harry Hay, Stuart Timmons, argues that "the skills for organizing and belief in revolutionary change" that Hay acquired during his years in the CP fostered his "founding in 1950 of the Mattachine Society, the underground organization acknowledged by historians as the starting point of the modern gay movement" (xiv). According to Timmons, all five Mattachine founders had been Party members or fellow travelers. Timmons credits Hay's Party experience with his conceptualizing gays as an oppressed cultural minority and homosexuality as a civil right.

5. Telephone conversation with Millard, 5 September 1992.

6. This scrapbook, like the other collections from the Associated Schools, was a mimeographed volume. *I Am a Woman Worker* has been reissued from Arno Press (1974) in its Women in America series; the reprint is a reduced photocopy of the original.

WORKS CITED

Aaron, Daniel. *Writers on the Left.* 1961, 1992. New York: Oxford UP, 1977.

Althusser, Louis. "Ideology and Ideological State Apparatuses (Notes towards an Investigation)." *Lenin and Philosophy and Other Essays.* New York: New Left, 1971. 123–173.

American Social History Project. Herbert Gutman, Founding Dir. *Who Built America?: Working People and the Nation's Economy, Politics, Culture, and Society.* 2 vols. New York: Pantheon, 1989, 1992.

Anderson, Sherwood. "A Writer's Notes." *New Masses* Aug. 1932: 10.

———. "At Amsterdam." *New Masses* Nov. 1932: 11.

"Are Artists People?" *New Masses* Jan. 1927: 5–9.

Armstrong, Nancy. "Introduction: Literature as Women's History." *Genre* 19 (Winter 1986): 347–369.

Atwood, Margaret. "Obstacle Course." *New York Times Book Review* 30 July 1978: 1.

Bailey, Bill. Interview conducted by Constance Coiner, 23 July 1989, San Francisco.

Baker, Christina L., with Myra Page. *In a Generous Spirit: The Life of Myra Page.* Urbana: U of Illinois P, 1995.

Bakhtin, M. M. *The Dialogic Imagination.* Ed. Michael Holquist. Trans. Caryl Emerson and Michael Holquist. Austin: U of Texas P, 1981.

———. *Speech Genres and Other Late Essays.* Trans. Vern W. McGee. Ed. Caryl Emerson and Michael Holquist. Austin: U of Texas P, 1986.

Balbus, Isaac. *Marxism and Domination: A Neo-Hegelian, Feminist, Psychoanalytic Theory of Sexual, Political, and Technological Liberation.* Princeton: Princeton UP, 1982.

Bartine, David. *Early English Reading Theory: Origins of Current Debates.* Columbia: U of South Carolina P, 1989.

———. *Reading, Criticism, and Culture: Theory and Teaching in the United States and England, 1820–1950.* Columbia: U of South Carolina P, 1992.

Bartine, David, and Constance Coiner. Rev. of *Seattle 1919,* by Rob Rosenthal. *Labor's Heritage* Fall 1992: 28–31.

Bauer, Dale M. *Feminist Dialogics: A Theory of Failed Community.* Albany: State University of New York P, 1988.

Baxandall, Rosalyn Fraad. *Words on Fire: The Life and Writing of Elizabeth Gurley Flynn.* New Brunswick: Rutgers UP, 1987.

Bell, Anna Vera. Letter. *The Working Woman* Mar. 1935: 13.

Bernstein, Carl. *Loyalties: A Son's Memoir.* New York: Simon, 1988.

Blake, William. "Holy Thursday (II)." *Introduction to Literature: Poems.* Ed. Lynn Altenbernd and Leslie L. Lewis. 3rd ed. New York: Macmillan, 1975. 324.

Bloom, James D. *Left Letters: The Culture Wars of Mike Gold and Joseph Freeman.* New York: Columbia UP, 1992.

Bloor, Ella Reeve. *We Are Many.* New York: International, 1940.

Blosser, Beatrice. Letter. *Woman Today* Jan. 1937: 26.

Booth, Wayne. "Freedom of Interpretation: Bakhtin and the Challenge of Feminist Criticism." *Critical Inquiry* Sept. 1982: 45–76.

"Bread, Butter, and Beyond." *Proc. of the Second Annual Jack Olsen Memorial Meeting and Scholarship Awards Program.* 3 May 1991. San Francisco.

Brecher, Jeremy. *Strike!* San Francisco: Straight Arrow, 1972.

Brenner, Johanna, and Nancy Holmstrom. "Women's Self-Organization: Theory and Strategy." *Monthly Review* Apr. 1983: 34–51.

"Broad Is the Path." *The Working Woman* Apr. 1935: 11.

Brooks, Tim, and Earle Marsh. *The Complete Directory to Prime Time Network TV Shows 1946–Present.* 4th ed. New York: Ballantine, 1988.

Browder, Earl. *The People's Front.* New York: International, 1938.

Buhle, Mari Jo. *Women and the American Left: A Guide to Sources.* Boston: G. K. Hall, 1983.

———. *Women and American Socialism 1870–1920.* Urbana: U of Illinois P, 1983.

Burkom, Selma, and Margaret Williams. "De-Riddling Tillie Olsen's Writings." *San Jose Studies* 2 (1976): 65–83.

C. D. Letter. "Work Among Women: Attitudes Which Hinder the Work." *Party Organizer.* Sept.–Oct. 1931: 30.

Cantwell, Robert. Letter. *The New Republic* 22 Aug. 1934: 49.

———. "The Little Magazines." *The New Republic* 25 July 1934: 295–297.

Chodorow, Nancy. *The Reproduction of Mothering: Psychoanalysis and the Sociology of Gender.* Berkeley: U of California P, 1978.

Christian, Barbara. "A Checkered Career." Rev. of *The Street,* by Ann Petry. *The Women's Review of Books* July 1992: 18–19.

Clausen, Jan. Rev. of *The Girl,* by Meridel Le Sueur. *Motheroot Journal* Spring 1980: 3.

Cochran, Bert. *Labor and Communism: The Conflict that Shaped American Unions.* Princeton: Princeton UP, 1977.

Coiner, Constance. Rev. of *Dorothy Healey Remembers: A Life in the American Communist Party,* by Dorothy Healey and Maurice Isserman. *The Women's Review of Books* March 1991: 10–11.

———. "Literature of Resistance: The Intersection of Feminism and the Communist Left in Meridel Le Sueur and Tillie Olsen." *Left Politics and the Literary Profession.* Ed. Lennard J. Davis and M. Bella Mirabella. New York: Columbia UP, 1990. 162–185. Rpt. in Linkon and Mullen.

———. "'No One's Private Ground': A Bakhtinian Reading of Tillie Olsen's *Tell Me a Riddle.*" *Feminist Studies* 18.2 (Summer 1992): 257–281. Rpt. in Hedges and Fishkin, 71–93; in Nelson and Huse, 169–195; and in Rosenfelt, *Casebook* (forthcoming 1995).

————. "Silent Parenting in the Academy." *Listening to Silences: New Essays in Feminist Criticism*. Ed. Elaine Hedges and Shelley Fisher Fishkin. New York: Oxford UP, 1994. 197–224.

Coles, Nicholas. "Democratizing Literature: Issues in Teaching Working-Class Literature." *College English* 48.7 (1986): 664–680.

Conroy, Jack, and Curt Johnson, eds. *Writers in Revolt: The Anvil Anthology*. New York: Lawrence Hill, 1973.

Coward, Rosalind, and John Ellis. *Language and Materialism: Developments in Semiology and the Theory of the Subject*. Boston: Routledge, 1977.

Crossman, Richard, ed. *The God That Failed*. New York: Harper and Brothers, 1949.

Culler, Jonathan. *On Deconstruction*. London: Routledge, 1983.

Davis, Rebecca Harding. *Life in the Iron Mills*. 1861. Old Westbury, NY: The Feminist P, 1972.

Dennis, Peggy. "A Response to Ellen Kay Trimberger's Essay, 'Women in the Old and New Left.'" *Feminist Studies* 3 (Fall 1979): 451–461.

————. *Autobiography of an American Communist: A Personal View of a Political Life 1925–1975*. Berkeley: Lawrence Hill, 1977.

Dews, C.L. Barney, and Carolyn Leste Law, eds. *This Fine Place So Far From Home: Voices of Academics from the Working Class*. Philadelphia: Temple UP, 1995.

Dinnerstein, Dorothy. *The Mermaid and the Minotaur: Sexual Arrangements and Human Malaise*. New York: Harper and Row, 1977.

Dixler, Elsa Jane. "The Woman Question: Women and the American Communist Party, 1929–1941." Diss. Yale U, 1974.

Dos Passos, John. "The New Masses I'd Like." *New Masses* June 1926: 20.

Draper, Theodore. "The Popular Front Revisited." *The New York Review of Books* 30 May 1985: 44–50.

Duncan, Erika. "Coming of Age in the Thirties: A Portrait of Tillie Olsen." *Book Forum* 6 (1982): 207–222.

DuPlessis, Rachel Blau. *Writing Beyond the Ending*. Bloomington: Indiana UP, 1985.

Eagleton, Terry. *Against the Grain: Essays 1975–1985*. London: Verso, 1986.

————. *Literary Theory: An Introduction*. Minneapolis: U of Minnesota P, 1983.

————. *Marxism and Literary Criticism*. Berkeley: U California P, 1976.

"Editor's Reply." *The Working Woman* July 1933: 13.

Edwards, Julie Olsen. "Class Notes from the Lecture Hall." *Liberating Memory: Our Work and Our Working-Class Consciousness*. Ed. Janet Zandy. New Brunswick: Rutgers UP, 1995.

Elbaum, Max. "De-Stalinizing the Old Guard." *The Nation* 10 Feb. 1992: 158–160, 162.

Ellis, Fred, et al. "The Charkov Conference of Revolutionary Writers." *New Masses* Feb. 1931: 6–8.

Engels, Friedrich. *The Origin of Family, Private Property, and State*. Excerpted in *The Marx–Engels Reader*. Ed. Robert C. Tucker. New York: Norton, 1978. 734–759.

"Equal Rights Amendment." *Woman Today* Mar. 1936: 11.

Evans, Sara. "The Rebirth of the Women's Movement in the 1960s." (Excerpted from Chapters 1 and 9 of *Personal Politics: The Roots of Women's Liberation in the Civil Rights Movement and the New Left*, by Sara Evans [New York: Knopf, 1979].) *Women and Power in American History: A Reader, Vol. II, from 1870*. Ed. Kathryn Kish Sklar and Thomas Dublin. Englewood Cliffs: Prentice Hall, 1991. 239–247.

Falk, Candace. *Love, Anarchy and Emma Goldman*. New York: Holt, 1984.

Farrell, James. *A Note on Literary Criticism.* New York: Vanguard, 1936.

"The Final Round." *The New Republic* 17 Dec. 1930: 141.

Fine, Sidney. *Sit-Down.* Ann Arbor: U of Michigan P, 1969.

Fishkin, Shelley Fisher. "Reading, Writing, and Arithmetic: The Lessons *Silences* Has Taught Us." MLA Convention 27–30 December 1988. Version in Hedges and Fishkin.

Flynn, Elizabeth Gurley. "The Feminine Ferment." Weekly column. *Sunday Worker Magazine* 3 Oct. 1937: 10.

———. "Slave of a Slave." Weekly column. *Sunday Worker Magazine* 23 Jan. 1938: 10.

———. "Taking Toll." Weekly column. *Sunday Worker Magazine* 19 Dec. 1937: 10.

Foley, Barbara. *Radical Representations: Politics and Form in U.S. Proletarian Fiction, 1929–1941.* Durham: Duke UP, 1993.

———. "Women and the Left in the 1930s." *American Literary History* 2 (Spring 1990): 150–169.

Folsom, Michael Brewster. "The Education of Michael Gold." *Proletarian Literature of the Thirties.* Ed. David Madden. Carbondale: Southern Illinois UP, 1968. 222–251.

Foner, Philip S. *Women and the American Labor Movement: From the First Trade Unions to the Present.* New York: Free P, 1979.

Foster, Hal. *Recodings: Art, Spectacle, Cultural Politics.* Port Townsend, WA: Bay P, 1985.

Freeman, Joseph. *An American Testament.* New York: Farrar Rinehart, 1936.

Gage, Amy. "The Insistent Voice." *Minnesota Monthly* March 1988: 24–32.

Gallop, Jane. *Thinking Through the Body.* New York: Columbia UP, 1988.

Gardiner, Judith Kegan. "A Wake for Mother: The Maternal Deathbed in Women's Fiction." *Feminist Studies* 4 (June 1978): 146–165.

Garrison, Dee. *Mary Heaton Vorse: The Life of an American Insurgent.* Philadelphia: Temple UP, 1989.

Gates, Henry Louis, Jr. *The Signifying Monkey: A Theory of Afro-American Literary Criticism.* New York: Oxford UP, 1988.

Gelfant, Blanche. "Meridel Le Sueur's 'Indian' Poetry and the Quest/ion of Feminine Form." *Women Writing in America: Voices in Collage.* Hanover: UP of New England, 1984. 71–91.

Gilbert, James Burkhart. *Writers and Partisans: A History of Literary Radicalism in America.* New York: John Wiley, 1968.

Godman, Peter. "T. S. Eliot and E. R. Curtius: A European Dialogue." *Liber* Oct. 1989: 5, 7.

Gold, Michael. "America Needs a Critic." *New Masses* Oct. 1926: 7–9.

———. "Change the World." *Daily Worker* 31 July 1937: 7.

———. *Jews Without Money.* 1930. Afterword by Michael Harrington. New York: Avon, 1965.

———. "John Reed and the Real Thing." *New Masses* Nov. 1927: 7–8.

———. "Let It Be Really New." *New Masses* June 1926: 20, 26.

———. "Notes of the Month." *New Masses* Apr. 1930: 3–5.

———. "Notes of the Month." *New Masses* Sept. 1930: 3–5.

———. "Toward an American Revolutionary Culture." *New Masses* July 1931: 12–13.

———. "Towards Proletarian Art." *Mike Gold: A Literary Anthology.* Ed. Michael Folsom. New York: International, 1972. 62–70.

———. "Wilder: Prophet of the Genteel Christ." *The New Republic* 22 Oct. 1930: 266–267.

———. "The Writer in America." *The Mike Gold Reader.* Intro. by Samuel Sillen. New York: International 1954. 181–188.

Gordon, Eugene. "The Lenin Heritage." *New Masses* 23 Jan. 1934: 26.

Gordon, Linda. *Woman's Body, Woman's Right: A Social History of Birth Control in America.* New York: Penguin, 1976.

Gornick, Vivian. *The Romance of American Communism.* New York: Basic, 1977.

Gosse, Van. "'To Organize in Every Neighborhood, In Every Home': The Gender Politics of American Communists Between the Wars." *Radical History Review* (Spring, 1991): 109–141.

Gottlieb, Annie. "Feminists Look at Motherhood." *Mother Jones* Nov. 1976: 51–53.

Gramsci, Antonio. *Selections From the Prison Notebooks.* Ed. and Trans. Quintin Hoare and Geoffrey Nowell Smith. New York: International, 1971.

Green, James R. *The World of the Worker: Labor in Twentieth-Century America.* New York: Hill and Wang, 1980.

Grossmann, Mary Ann. *St. Paul Pioneer Press Dispatch.* 11 Feb. 1990: 1D, 3D.

Guilbaut, Serge. *How New York Stole the Idea of Modern Art: Abstract Expressionism, Freedom, and the Cold War.* Trans. Arthur Goldhammer. Chicago: U of Chicago P, 1983.

H. M. "Prize Letter." *Sunday Worker Magazine* 23 Aug. 1936: 13.

Hapke, Laura. *Tales of the Working Girl: Wage-Earning Women in American Literature, 1890–1925.* Literature and Society Series. New York: Twayne P, 1992.

Hart, Henry, ed. *American Writers' Congress.* New York: International, 1935.

Healey, Dorothy. Interview conducted by Constance Coiner, 27–28 December 1989, Washington D.C.

Healey, Dorothy, and Maurice Isserman. *Dorothy Healey Remembers: A Life in the American Communist Party.* New York: Oxford UP, 1990.

Hedges, Elaine, ed. *Ripening: Selected Work, 1927–1980.* By Meridel Le Sueur. Old Westbury, NY: The Feminist P, 1982.

Hedges, Elaine, and Shelley Fisher Fishkin, eds. *Listening to Silences,* New York: Oxford UP, 1994.

Henderson, Mae Gwendolyn. "Speaking in Tongues: Dialogics, Dialectics, and the Black Woman Writer's Literary Tradition." *Changing Our Own Words: Essays on Criticism, Theory, and Writing by Black Women.* Ed. Cheryl A. Wall. New Brunswick: Rutgers UP, 1989. 16–37.

Hicks, Granville, "The Literary Caravan." Rev. of *The Gods Arrive,* by Edith Wharton; *Obscure Destinies,* by Willa Cather; and *The Sheltered Life,* by Ellen Glasgow. *The Modern Quarterly* 6.3 (Autumn 1932): 98–100.

Hicks, Granville, et al., eds. *Proletarian Literature in the United States.* New York: International, 1935.

Hollis, Karyn L. "Liberating Voices: Autobiographical Writing at the Bryn Mawr Summer School for Women Workers, 1921–1938." *College Composition and Communication* 45.1 (1994): 31–60.

———. *Resisting Voices: Writing at the Bryn Mawr Summer School for Women Workers, 1921–1938.* Englewood Cliffs: Prentice Hall (forthcoming).

Holt, Alix. *Alexandra Kollontai: Selected Writings.* Trans. Alix Holt. New York: Norton, 1977.

Holtman, Rachel. "International Women's Day." *The Communist* Mar. 1930: 204–209.

Hunter, J. Paul. *Before Novels: The Cultural Contexts of Eighteenth-Century English Fiction.* New York: Norton, 1990.

Hutchins, Grace. *Women Who Work*. New York: International, 1934.

Ibarro, Felipe. "Where the Sun Spends the Winter." Letter. *New Masses* 9 Jan. 1934: 22.

Inman, Mary. *In Woman's Defense*. Los Angeles: The Committee to Organize the Advancement of Women, 1940.

Irish, Margaret H. "Childbirth—A Woman's Problem." *The Working Woman* May 1933: 17.

Isserman, Maurice. *If I Had a Hammer . . . The Death of the Old Left and the Birth of the New Left*. New York: Basic, 1987.

———. *Which Side Were You On?: The American Communist Party During the Second World War*. Middletown, CT: Wesleyan UP, 1982.

"Jack Olsen, longtime S.F. labor leader, dies at 77." *Oakland Tribune* 2 Mar. 1989: B6.

Jacobus, Mary. "The Difference of View." *Women Writing and Writing about Women*. Ed. Mary Jacobus. London: Croom Helm, 1979.

———. "The Question of Language: Men of Maxims and *The Mill on the Floss*." *Writing and Sexual Difference*. Ed. Elizabeth Abel. Chicago: U of Chicago P, 1982. 37–52.

Jameson, Fredric. *Marxism and Form*. Princeton: Princeton UP, 1971.

———. *The Political Unconscious: Narrative as a Socially Symbolic Act*. Ithaca: Cornell UP, 1981.

Jehlen, Myra. "Archimedes and the Paradox of Feminist Criticism." *Signs* 6 (Summer 1981): 575–601.

Jerome, V. J. "No Quarter to Trotzkyists—Literary or Otherwise." *Daily Worker* 20 Oct. 1937: 6.

Jones, Ann Rosalind. "Writing the Body: Toward an Understanding of *l'Ecriture feminine*." *The New Feminist Criticism: Essays on Women, Literature and Theory*. Ed. Elaine Showalter. New York: Pantheon, 1985. 361–377.

Kalaidjian, Walter. *American Culture Between the Wars: Revisionary Moderism and Post-Modern Critique*. New York: Columbia UP, 1993.

Kampf, Louis, and Paul Lauter, eds. *The Politics of Literature: Dissenting Essays on the Teaching of English*. New York: Vintage, 1970.

Kaplan, Cora. Introduction to *Yonnondio: From the Thirties*. By Tillie Olsen. London: Virago, 1980.

Kaplan, Justin. *Lincoln Steffens: A Biography*. New York: Simon, 1974.

Kavanagh, James H. "'Marks of Weakness': Ideology, Science and Textual Criticism." *Praxis* 5 (1981): 23–38.

Kazin, Alfred. *On Native Grounds: An Interpretation of Modern American Prose Literature*. 1942. Garden City: Doubleday, 1956.

Keeran, Roger. *The Communist Party and the Auto Workers Unions*. Bloomington: Indiana UP, 1980.

Kelley, Robin D. G. *Hammer and Hoe: Alabama Communists during the Great Depression*. Chapel Hill: U of North Carolina P, 1990.

Kessler-Harris, Alice. *Out to Work: A History of Wage-Earning Women in the United States*. New York: Oxford UP, 1982.

Kessler-Harris, Alice, and Paul Lauter. Introduction. *The Unpossessed*. By Tess Slesinger. 1934. Old Westbury, NY: The Feminist P, 1984.

Klancher, Jon. *The Making of English Reading Audiences 1790–1832*. Madison: U of Wisconsin P, 1986.

Klehr, Harvey. *The Heyday of American Communism: The Depression Decade*. New York: Basic, 1984.

Klein, Marcus. *Foreigners: The Making of American Literature 1900–1940.* Chicago: U of Chicago P, 1981.

Kolodny, Annette. "Reply to Commentaries: Women Writers, Literary Historians, and Martian Readers." *New Literary History* 11 (Spring 1980): 587–592.

Kostelanetz, Richard. *The End of Intelligent Writing: Literary Politics in America.* New York: Sheed, 1974.

Krupskaya, Nadezhda. "Sane Birth Control." *Sunday Worker Magazine* 19 July 1936: 2.

Kunitz, Joshua. See Neets, J. Q.

Laclau, Ernesto. "'Socialism,' the 'People,' 'Democracy': The Transformation of Hegemonic Logic." *Social Text* (Spring/Summer 1983): 115–119.

Landy, A[vram]. *Marxism and the Woman Question.* Toronto: Progress, 1943.

Langer, Elinor. *Josephine Herbst: The Story She Could Never Tell.* Boston: Little, 1984.

Lauter Paul. "American Proletarianism." *The Columbia History of the American Novel.* Ed. Emory Elliot, et al. New York: Columbia UP, 1991. 331–356.

———.*Canons and Contexts.* New York: Oxford UP, 1991.

———."Race and Gender in the Shaping of the Literary Canon: A Case Study From the Twenties." *Feminist Studies* 9.3 (Fall, 1983): 435–463. Rpt. in Newton and Rosenfelt, 19–44.

———."Working-Class Women's Literature—an Introduction to Study." *Radical Teacher* 15 (Dec. 1979): 16–26. Rpt. in *Women in Print I.* Ed. Joan E. Hartman and Ellen Messer-Davidow. New York: Modern Language Association, 1982. 109–125. Rpt. in *Feminisms: An Anthology of Literary Theory and Criticism.* Ed. Robyn R. Warhol and Diane Price Herndl. New Brunswick: Rutgers UP, 1991. 837–850.

"Legend of the 'Weaker Sex' Effectively Smashed by the Position of Women in the Soviet Union: All Inequality Abolished by the October Revolution." *Daily Worker* 2 Sept. 1935: 5.

Lenin, V. I. From *Women and Society,* in *The Woman Question: Selections from the Writings of Karl Marx, Frederick Engels, V. I. Lenin, Joseph Stalin.* New York: International, 1951.

Leslie, Irene. "Lenin on the Woman Question." *The Communist* March 1936: 245–252.

Lessing, Doris. *A Small Personal Voice: Essays, Reviews, Interviews.* Ed. and intro. Paul Schlueter. New York: Vintage, 1975.

Le Sueur, Marian. *Plain English.* Fort Scott, Kansas: The People's College, 1916.

Le Sueur, Meridel. "Afterword: A Memoir." *Guardian Angel and Other Stories.* By Margery Latimer. Old Westbury, NY: Feminist P, 1984. 230–235.

———. "The Ancient People and Newly Come." *Growing Up in Minnesota: Ten Writers Remember Their Childhoods.* Ed. Chester G. Anderson. Minneapolis: U of Minnesota P, 1976. 17–46.

———. "Annunciation." *Ripening: Selected Work, 1927–1980.* Ed. Elaine Hedges. Old Westbury, NY: Feminist P, 1982. 124–132.

———. "Corn Village." *Salute to Spring.* 1940. New York: International, 1977. 9–25.

———. *Crusaders.* New York: Blue Heron, 1955.

———. *The Dread Road.* With editorial assistance from Rachel Tilsen, John Crawford, Michael Reed, and Patricia Clark Smith. Albuquerque: West End, 1991.

———. "Evening in a Lumber Town." *New Masses* July 1926: 22–23.

———. "The Fetish of Being Outside." *New Masses* 26 Feb. 1935: 22–23.

———. Foreword. *The Pavement Trail: A Collection of Poetry and Prose from the Allis-Chalmers Picket Lines.* [No city or publisher provided.] June 1946.

———. "Formal Education." *Harvest Song: Collected Essays and Stories.* Albuquerque: West End, 1990.

———. *The Girl.* Minneapolis: West End, 1978.

———. *The Girl.* Unpublished manuscript, 1939. In Le Sueur's possession.

———. *I Hear Men Talking: Stories of the Early Decades.* Ed. and afterword by Linda Ray Pratt. Albuquerque: West End, 1984.

———. "I Was Marching." *Ripening: Selected Work, 1927–1980.* Ed. Elaine Hedges. Old Westbury, NY: The Feminist P, 1982. 158–165.

———. "Interview." *West End Magazine* 5:1 (Summer 1978): 8–14.

———. Interviews conducted by Constance Coiner, 26 March 1985 in Los Angeles and 24, 25, and 28 August 1989 in Hudson, Wisconsin.

———. Meridel Le Sueur Papers, 1906–1986. Restricted. Minnesota Historical Society, St. Paul.

———. *North Star Country* (excerpt). *Ripening: Selected Work, 1927–1980.* Ed. Elaine Hedges. Old Westbury, NY: Feminist P, 1982. 33–38.

———. "Our Fathers." *Ripening: Selected Work, 1927–1980.* Ed. Elaine Hedges. Old Westbury, NY: Feminist P, 1982. 114–123.

———. Preface. *Women on the Breadlines.* Minneapolis: West End, 1984.

———. "Proletarian Literature and the Middle West." *Harvest Song: Collected Essays and Stories.* Albuquerque: West End, 1990.

———. "Women on the Breadlines." *Ripening: Selected Work, 1927–1980.* Ed. Elaine Hedges. Old Westbury, NY: The Feminist P, 1982. 137–143.

Levine, Lawrence W. *Black Culture and Black Consciousness: Afro-American Folk Thought From Slavery to Freedom.* New York: Oxford UP, 1977.

The Life and Times of Rosie the Riveter. Dir. Connie Field. First Run Features, 1981.

Linkon, Sherry Lee, and Bill V. Mullen, eds. *Revisioning Thirties' Culture: New Directions in Scholarship.* Urbana: U of Illinois P, 1995.

Loader, Jayne. *Women in the Left, 1906–1941: A Bibliography of Primary Sources.* Ann Arbor: University of Michigan Women's Studies Program's Papers in Women Studies, 1974.

Losovsky, Comrade [Solomon]. "Plenum of Women Workers' Committee of the RILU." *The Communist* Mar. 1930: 224–229.

Loughridge, Nancy. "Afterword: The Life." *Guardian Angel and Other Stories.* By Margery Latimer. Old Westbury, NY: Feminist P, 1984: 215–229.

Lukacs, Georg. *Essays on Realism.* Ed. Rodney Livingstone. Trans. David Fernbach. Cambridge: MIT, 1981.

M. K. Letter. *The Working Woman* July 1933: 13.

Macherey, Pierre. *A Theory of Literary Production.* Trans. Geoffrey Wall. London: Routledge, 1966.

MacKinnon, Janice R., and Stephen R. MacKinnon. *Agnes Smedley: The Life and Times of an American Radical.* Berkeley: U of California, 1988.

Madden, David. *Proletarian Writers of the Thirties.* Carbondale: Southern Illinois UP, 1968.

Magil, A. B. Interview conducted by Paul Buhle, 31 October 1980, New York City. Oral History of the American Left Collection, Series 1. Tamiment Institute Library, New York University.

———. "Pity and Terror." *New Masses* Dec. 1932: 16–19.

Maguire, Ruth, and Edna Whitehouse. Interview conducted by Constance Coiner, 26 July 1989, Berkeley, California.

Mangione, Jerre. *The Dream and the Deal: The Federal Writers' Project 1935–1943*. New York: Avon, 1972.

Martin, Abigail. *Tillie Olsen*. Boise State U Western Writers Series 65. Ed. Wayne Chatterton and James H. Maguire. Boise: Boise State U, 1984.

Mary of Cleveland. "Prize Letter." *Sunday Worker Magazine* 16 Feb. 1936: 14.

McAnally, Mary. *We Sing Our Struggle: A Tribute to Us All for Meridel Le Sueur*. Tulsa: Cardinal, 1982.

Meese, Elizabeth A. *Crossing the Double–Cross: The Practice of Feminist Criticism*. Chapel Hill: U of North Carolina P, 1986.

Melosh, Barbara. *Engendering Culture: Manhood and Womanhood in New Deal Public Art and Theater*. Washington: Smithsonian Institution, 1991.

Millard, Betty. "Woman Against Myth (Part I)." *New Masses:* 30 Dec. 1947: 7–10.

———. "Woman Against Myth (Part II)." *New Masses:* 6 Jan. 1948: 7–10.

Mitford, Jessica. *A Fine Old Conflict*. New York: Vintage, 1978.

Montgomery, David. "To Study the People: The American Working Class." *Labor History* 21.4 (Fall 1980): 485–512.

Naison, Mark. *Communists in Harlem During the Depression*. New York: Grove P, 1983.

Navarro, Vicente. "The Middle Class—A Useful Myth." *The Nation* 23 Mar. 1992: 361, 381.

Neets, J. Q. [Kunitz, Joshua]. "Let Us Master Our Art." *New Masses* July 1930: 23.

———. "Upton Sinclair and Thornton Wilder." *New Masses* May 1930: 18.

Nekola, Charlotte, and Paula Rabinowitz, eds. *Writing Red: An Anthology of American Women Writers, 1930–1940*. Old Westbury, NY: The Feminist P, 1987.

Nelson, Bruce. *Workers on the Waterfront: Seamen, Longshoremen, and Unionism in the 1930s*. Urbana: U of Illinois P, 1990.

Nelson, Cary. *Repression and Recovery: Modern American Poetry and the Politics of Cultural Memory, 1910–1945*. Madison: U of Wisconsin P, 1989.

Nelson, Kay Hoyle, and Nancy Huse, eds. *The Critical Response to Tillie Olsen*. Westport: Greenwood P, 1994.

Nelson, Steve, James R. Barrett, and Rob Ruck. *Steve Nelson, American Radical*. Pittsburgh: U of Pittsburgh P, 1981.

Newton, Judith. "History as Usual?: Feminism and the 'New Historicism.'" *Cultural Critique* 9 (Spring 1988): 87–121.

Newton, Judith, and Deborah Rosenfelt, eds. *Feminist Criticism and Social Change: Sex, Class and Race in Literature and Culture*. New York: Methuen, 1985.

North, Joseph. "College Men and Men." *New Masses* Oct. 1929: 14.

———. Prologue. *New Masses: An Anthology of the Rebel Thirties*. Ed. Joseph North. New York: International, 1969.

Ohmann, Richard. "Political Correctness and the Obfuscation of Politics." *Radical Teacher* 42 (Fall 1992): 32–34. A longer version of this essay appeared as "On PC and Related Matters." *The Minnesota Review* 39 (Fall/Winter 1992/1993): 55–62.

Olsen, Tillie. Foreword. *Black Women Writers at Work*. Ed. Claudia Tate. England: Old Castle Books, 1989.

———. Interviews conducted by Constance Coiner, 11–12 July 1986 and 23–28 July 1989, San Francisco.

———. Interview conducted by Deborah Rosenfelt, 20 December 1980, Santa Cruz.

———. *The Life and Literary Work of Tillie Olsen*. Pacifica radio broadcast (KPFK, Los Angeles), 8 March 1985.

———, ed. *Mother to Daughter Daughter to Mother*. Old Westbury, NY: The Feminist P, 1984.

———. "A Note About This Book." *Yonnondio: From the Thirties*. New York: Dell, 1974. 157–158.

———. "Requa I." *The Best American Short Stories*. Ed. Martha Foley and David Burnett. Boston: Houghton Mifflin, 1971. 237–265.

———. *Silences*. New York: Dell, 1978.

———. "The Strike." *Partisan Review* Sept.–Oct. 1934: 3–9.

———. *Tell Me a Riddle*. 1961. New York: Dell, 1979.

———. "The '30s: A Vision of Fear and Hope." *Newsweek*: 3 Jan. 1994. 26–27.

———. "Thousand-Dollar Vagrant." *The New Republic* 29 Aug. 1934: 67–69.

———. *Yonnondio: From the Thirties*. New York: Dell, 1974.

Olsen, Tillie, with Julie Olsen Edwards. Introduction. *Mothers and Daughters: That Special Quality: An Exploration in Photographs*. New York: Aperture, 1987. 14–17.

Olson, Reeva. Interview conducted by Constance Coiner, 25 July 1989, San Francisco.

"An Open Letter to Husbands." Letter. *Woman Today* May 1936: 19.

Oral History of the American Left Collection. Tamiment Institute Library, New York University.

Oresick, Peter, and Nicholas Coles, eds. *Working Classics: Poems of Industrial Life*. Urbana: U of Illinois P, 1990.

Orr, Elaine. *Tillie Olsen and a Feminist Spiritual Vision*. Jackson: UP of Mississippi, 1987.

"Our Answer." Editorial reply. *The Working Woman* Aug. 1935: 12.

Owen, Wilfred. "Arms and the Boy." *Introduction to Literature: Poems*. Ed. Lynn Altenbernd and Leslie L. Lewis. 1963. 3rd ed. New York: Macmillan, 1975. 718.

———. "Dulce et Decorum Est." *Introduction to Literature: Poems*. Ed. Lynn Altenbernd and Leslie L. Lewis. 1963. 3rd ed. New York: Macmillan, 1975. 719.

Page, Myra. "American Women, Speak Out!" *Sunday Worker Magazine* 10 Jan. 1937: 12.

———. Interview conducted by Nora Ruth Roberts, 15 January 1991.

———. "We Want Our Children." *Sunday Worker Magazine* 28 Feb. 1937: 5.

Painter, Nell Irvin. *The Narrative of Hosea Hudson: His Life as a Negro Communist in the South*. Cambridge: Harvard UP, 1979.

Partisan Review. Contributors. 1.2 (April–May 1934): 2.

Partisan Review. Editorial statement. 1.1 (Feb.–March 1934): 2.

Peck, David Russell. "The Development of an American Marxist Literary Criticism: The Monthly 'New Masses.'" Diss. Temple U, 1968.

———. "'The Orgy of Apology': The Recent Re-evaluation of Literature of the Thirties." *Science and Society* 32.4 (Fall 1968): 371–382.

Pells, Richard. *Radical Visions and American Dreams: Culture and Social Thought in the Depression Years*. 1973. Middletown, CT: Wesleyan UP, 1984.

Phillips, William, and Philip Rahv. Letter. *New Masses* 19 Oct. 1937: 21.

———, eds. *The Partisan Reader: Ten Years of Partisan Review*. New York: Dial, 1946.

Pitts, Rebecca. "Women and Communism." *New Masses* 19 Feb. 1935: 14–18.

Poston, Carol H. "Childbirth in Literature." *Feminist Studies* 4.2 (June 1978): 19–31.

Pratt, Linda Ray. Afterword. *I Hear Men Talking*. By Meridel Le Sueur. Minneapolis: West End, 1984.

———. "Woman Writer in the CP: The Case of Meridel LeSueur." *Women's Studies* 14.3 (Feb. 1988): 247–264.

Pratt, Mary Louise. *Toward a Speech Act Theory of Literary Discourse*. Bloomington: Indiana UP, 1977.

Prickett, James R. "Communists and the Communist Issue in the American Labor Movement, 1920–1950." Diss. U of California, Los Angeles, 1975.

Quin, Mike. *The Big Strike*. New York: International, 1949.

Rabinowitz, Paula. *Labor and Desire: Women's Revolutionary Fiction in Depression America*. Chapel Hill: U of North Carolina P, 1991.

Rahv, Philip. "The Literary Class War." *New Masses* Aug. 1932: 7–10.

———. "Proletarian Literature: A Political Autopsy." *Southern Review* 4.3 (Winter 1939): 616–628.

Reagan, Ronald. "The Evil Empire." *Contemporary American Speeches: A Sourcebook of Speech Forms and Principles*. Ed. Richard L. Johannesen, et al. 1965. 6th ed. Dubuque: Kendall/Hunt, 1988.

———. "Excerpts from Talk by Reagan." *New York Times* 18 Aug. 1992: A8.

Reish, F. Letter. *The Working Woman* (Mar. 1935): 13.

Rhodes, Carolyn. "'Beedo' in Olsen's *Yonnondio*: Charles E. Bedaux." *American Notes and Queries* Oct. 1976: 24–25.

Rich, Adrienne. *Of Woman Born: Motherhood as Experience and Institution*. New York: Norton, 1976.

Richmond, Al. *A Long View from the Left: Memoirs of an American Revolutionary*. New York: Dell, 1972.

Rideout, Walter. *The Radical Novel in the United States 1900–1954*. New York: Hill and Wang, 1956.

Rivington, Ann. "Woman's Point of View." *Sunday Worker* 12 Jan. 1936: 14.

———. "Woman's Point of View." *Sunday Worker* 9 Feb. 1936: 14.

———. "Woman's Point of View." *Sunday Worker* 5 July 1936: 14.

Robinson, Lillian S. *Robinson on the Woman Question*. Buffalo: Earth's Daughters, 1975.

———. *Sex, Class, and Culture*. Bloomington: Indiana UP, 1978. Rpt. Boston: Routledge, 1986.

———. "The Vietnam Syndrome." Rev. of *The Vietnam War and American Culture*, eds. John Carlos Rowe and Rick Berg and *From Hanoi to Hollywood: The Vietnam War in American Film*, eds. Linda Dittmar and Gene Michaud. *The Nation* 20 Jan. 1992: 60–62.

Rosenfelt, Deborah. "Divided Against Herself." *Moving On* April/May 1980: 15–23.

———. "From the Thirties: Tillie Olsen and the Radical Tradition." *Feminist Studies* 7 (Fall 1981): 371–406. Rpt. in Newton and Rosenfelt.

———, ed. *Tillie Olsen's Tell Me a Riddle (A Casebook)*. New Brunswick: Rutgers UP, forthcoming 1995.

Rowbotham, Sheila. *Women, Resistance, and Revolution: A History of Women and Revolution in the Modern World*. New York: Vintage, 1974.

Rowbotham, Sheila, Lynn Segal, and Hilary Wainwright. *Beyond the Fragments: Feminism and the Making of Socialism*. 1979. Boston: Alyson, 1981.

Rubens, Lisa. "The Patrician Radical: Charlotte Anita Whitney." *California History* 65.3 (Sept. 1986): 158–171.

Rubinstein, Annette R. Interview conducted by Nora Ruth Roberts, 8 January 1991.

Ruiz, Vicki L. *Cannery Women, Cannery Lives: Mexican Women, Unionization, and the California Food-Processing Industry, 1930–1950*. Albuquerque: U of New Mexico P, 1987.

Rukeyser, Muriel. "Käthe Kollwitz." *The Norton Anthology of Literature by Women*. Ed. Sandra M. Gilbert and Susan Gubar. New York: Norton, 1985. 1783–1787.

Russ, Joanna. *The Female Man*. New York: Bantam, 1973.

Ryan, Michael. *Marxism and Deconstruction: A Critical Articulation.* Baltimore: Johns Hopkins UP, 1982.

Safire, William. *The New Language of Politics: An Anecdotal Dictionary of Catchwords, Slogans, and Political Usages.* New York: Random House, 1968.

Sanger, Margaret. "The Soviet Union's Abortion Law." *Woman Today* Dec. 1936: 8, 30.

Saxton, Alexander. "A View from the Garden." *Monthly Review* Nov. 1984: 29–39.

Scaglione, Aldo. *The Classical Theory of Composition From Its Origins to the Present: A Historical Survey.* Chapel Hill: U of North Carolina P, 1972.

Scharf, Lois. *To Work and to Wed: Female Employment, Feminism, and the Great Depression.* Westport: Greenwood, 1980.

Schleuning, Neala. *America: Song We Sang Without Knowing.* Mankato, MN: Little Red Hen, 1983.

———. "Toward a New Regionalism." *Books at Iowa* Nov. 1980: 22–41.

Schwartz, Lawrence H. *Marxism and Culture: The CPUSA and Aesthetics in the 1930s.* Port Washington: Kennikat, 1980.

Schweickart, Patrocinio P. "Reading Ourselves: Toward a Feminist Theory of Reading." *Gender and Reading: Essays on Readers, Texts, and Contexts.* Ed. Elizabeth A. Flynn and Patrocinio P. Schweickart. Baltimore: Johns Hopkins UP, 1986. 31–62.

Scott, Joan W. "Experience." *Feminists Theorize the Political.* Ed. Judith Butler and Joan W. Scott. New York: Routledge, 1992.

———. *Gender and the Politics of History.* New York: Columbia UP, 1988.

Seaver, Edwin. "Review and Comment: Socialist Realism." *New Masses* 22 Oct. 1935: 23–24.

Seeing Red: Stories of American Communists. Dir. Julia Reichert and James Klein. Heartland Productions, 1984.

Shaffer, Robert. "Women and the Communist Party, USA, 1930–1940." *Socialist Review* May–June 1979: 73–118.

Showalter, Elaine. "Feminist Criticism in the Wilderness." *Writing and Sexual Difference.* Ed. Elizabeth Abel. Chicago: U of Chicago P, 1982. 9–35.

Simpson, David. "Literary Criticism and the Return to 'History.'" *Critical Inquiry* 14 (Summer 1988): 721–747.

Sinclair, Upton. "Revolution—Not Sex." *New Masses* Mar. 1927: 11.

Sklar, Kathryn Kish. "Why Were Most Politically Active Women Opposed to the ERA in the 1920s?" *Women and Power in American History: A Reader, Vol. II, from 1870.* Ed. Kathryn Kish Sklar and Thomas Dublin. Englewood Cliffs: Prentice Hall 1991. 175–182.

Smith, Mary K. "Meridel Le Sueur: A Bio-Bibliography." M.A. Thesis. U of Minnesota, 1973.

Soule, George. "Hard-Boiled Radicalism." *New Republic* 21 Jan. 1931: 261–265.

Soviet Women Workers. "How We Live." *The Working Woman* 30 Apr. 1934: 8–9.

Sowinska, Suzanne. "American Women Writers and the Radical Agenda, 1925–1940." Diss. U of Washington, 1992.

Stott, William. *Documentary Expression and Thirties America.* London: Oxford UP, 1973.

Strom, Sharon Hartman. "Challenging 'Woman's Place': Feminism, the Left, and Industrial Unionism in the 1930s." *Feminist Studies* 9 (Summer 1983): 359–386.

Suggs, Jon Christian, ed. *American Proletarian Culture: The Twenties and Thirties.* A Bruccoli Clark Layman Book. Vol. 11 of the Documentary Series of the *Dictionary of Literary Biography.* Detroit: Gale Research, Inc, 1993.

Swartley, Ariel. "If This Were Any Other Job, I'd Shove It." *Mother Jones* May 1983: 33–37.

Taggard, Genevieve, et al. "Are Artists People?" *New Masses* Jan. 1927: 5–9.

Teres, Harvey. "Remaking Marxist Criticism: *Partisan Review*'s Eliotic Leftism, 1934–1936." *American Literature* 64.1 (March 1992): 127–153.

"Thinks Men Are to Blame." Letter. *The Working Woman* Aug. 1935: 11–12.

Timmons, Stuart. *The Trouble with Harry Hay: Founder of the Modern Gay Movement.* Boston: Alyson, 1990.

Todorov, Tzvetan. *Mikhail Bakhtin: The Dialogical Principle.* Trans. Wlad Godzich. Minneapolis: U of Minnesota P, 1984.

Tokarczyk, Michelle M., and Elizabeth A. Fay, eds. *Working-Class Women in the Academy: Laborers in the Knowledge Factory.* Amherst: U of Massachusetts P, 1993.

Trotsky, Leon. *Literature and Revolution.* 1924. Ann Arbor: U of Michigan P, 1960.

Trueblood, Valerie. Rev. of *Silences*, by Tillie Olsen. *American Poetry Review* May/June 1979: 18–19.

Turan, Kenneth. "Breaking Silence." *New West* 28 Aug. 1978: 56, 59.

Twentieth Century Trade Union Women: Vehicle for Social Change. Oral History Project, Joyce Kornbluh, dir. U of Michigan and Wayne State U.

Unger, Mildred. "Way to a Man's Heart." *Sunday Worker Magazine* 18 June 1937: 10.

Union Maids. Dir. James Klein, Miles Mogulescu, and Julia Reichert. New Day Films, 1976.

van Kleeck, Mary. "The Women's Charter." *Woman Today* Feb. 1937: 3, 26.

Vicinus, Martha. *The Industrial Muse: A Study of Nineteenth Century British Working-Class Literature.* New York: Barnes, 1974.

Volosinov, V. N. *Marxism and the Philosophy of Language.* Trans. Ladislav Matejka and I. R. Titunik. Cambridge: Harvard UP, 1986.

Vorse, Mary Heaton. *Labor's New Millions.* 1938. New York: Arno, 1969.

Wald, Alan. "Culture and Commitment: U.S. Communist Writers Reconsidered." *New Studies in the Politics and Culture of U.S. Communism.* Ed. Michael E. Brown et al. New York: Monthly Review P, 1993. 281–305.

———. *James T. Farrell: The Revolutionary Socialist Years.* New York: New York UP, 1978.

———. *The New York Intellectuals: The Rise and Decline of the Anti-Stalinist Left from the 1930s to the 1980s.* Chapel Hill: U of North Carolina P, 1987.

———. "The New York Intellectuals in Retreat." *Socialist Perspectives.* Ed. Phyllis Jacobson and Julius Jacobson. New York: Karz-Cohl, 1983.

———, ed. "The Radical Novel in the U.S. Reconsidered." [forthcoming series] Urbana: U of Illinois P.

———. "Theorizing Cultural Difference: A Critique of the 'Ethnicity School.'" *Melus* (Summer 1987): 21–33.

Walker, Alice. *In Search of Our Mothers' Gardens.* New York: Harcourt, 1983.

Ward, Angela. Interview conducted by Constance Coiner, 26 July 1989, San Francisco.

———. Oral history interview conducted by Sue Cobble. Program on Women and Work, Institute of Labor and Industrial Relations, U of Michigan/Wayne State U. U of Michigan, 1978.

Ware, Susan, *Holding Their Own: American Women in the 1930s.* Boston: Twayne, 1982.

Weatherwax, Clara. *Marching! Marching!* New York: John Day, 1935.

Weber, Max. *The Sociology of Religion.* 1922. Trans. Ephraim Fischoff. Intro. by Talcott Parsons. Boston: Beacon, 1963.

Weedon, Ann. Letter. *The Working Woman* Sept. 1935: 13. Rpt. from *New Masses* 16 July 1935.

Weinstein, James. *Ambiguous Legacy: The Left in American Politics.* New York: New Viewpoints, 1975.

Wexler, Alice. *Emma Goldman in America.* Boston: Beacon P, 1984.

"What Would You Do?" Letter-writing contest. *The Working Woman* Dec. 1934: 5.

Williams, Raymond. *Culture and Society: 1780–1950.* 1958. New York: Columbia UP, 1983.

———. *Keywords: A Vocabulary of Culture and Society.* New York: Oxford UP, 1983.

———. *Marxism and Literature.* Oxford: Oxford UP, 1977.

Willis, Ellen. "Handle With Care: We Need A Child-Rearing Movement." *Village Voice* 15 July 1986: 14–17.

Wilson, Edmund. "The Case of the Author." *The Nation* 27 Jan. 1932: 297.

———. "The Literary Class War: I." *New Republic* 4 May 1932: 319–323.

"The Winners!" *The Working Woman* Mar. 1935: 13.

With Babies and Banners. Dir. Lorraine Grey. New Day Films, 1978.

Wittig, Monique. *The Straight Mind and Other Essays.* Boston: Beacon, 1992.

Wixson, Douglas. *Worker-Writer in America: Jack Conroy and the Tradition of Midwestern Literary Radicalism, 1898–1990.* Urbana: U of Illinois P, 1994.

Woloch, Nancy. *Women and the American Experience.* New York: Knopf, 1984.

Wolf, Robert. "What There Isn't and Why Not." *New Masses* Feb. 1928: 18–21.

Women in California. Oral History Collection, California Historical Society. San Francisco, CA.

"Women's Work in the Shops." Unsigned article. *Party Organizer* Feb. 1930: 12–14.

Woolf, Virginia. "The Leaning Tower." *The Moment and Other Essays.* London: Hogarth, 1952.

Wordsworth, William. "The Solitary Reaper." *Introduction to Literature: Poems.* Ed. Lynn Altenbernd and Leslie L. Lewis. 1963. 3rd ed. New York: Macmillan, 1975. 351.

———. "The Tables Turned." Vol. 2 of *Major British Writers.* 2 vols. Ed. Walter J. Bate, et al. 1954. New York: Harcourt, 1959. 38.

Wright, Richard. *American Hunger.* 1944. New York: Harper, 1977.

Yarros, Gregory. "The Kitchen Under Socialism." *The Working Woman* Oct. 1931: 4.

Yeats, William Butler. "The Lover Tells of the Rose in His Heart." *Introduction to Literature: Poems.* Ed. Lynn Altenbernd and Leslie L. Lewis. 1963. 3rd ed. New York: Macmillan, 1975. 620.

Your Comrade in Marriage. Letter. *Sunday Worker Magazine* 23 Aug. 1936: 13.

Your Wife Betty. Letter. *Sunday Worker Magazine* 2 Aug. 1936: 15.

Zandy, Janet, ed. *Calling Home: Working-Class Women's Writings, An Anthology.* New Brunswick: Rutgers UP, 1990.

———, ed. *Liberating Memory: Our Work and Our Working-Class Consciousness.* New Brunswick: Rutgers UP, 1995.

Zetkin, Clara. *Reminiscences of Lenin.* New York: International, 1934.

Zinn, Howard. *A People's History of the United States.* New York: Harper and Row, 1980.

Zugsmith, Leane. "Statements from Leading Women on the Charter." *Women Today.* Feb. 1937: 7, 26–27.

INDEX